Empathy versus Offending, Aggression, and Bullying

Empathy versus Offending, Aggression, and Bullying advances knowledge about the measurement of empathy, using the Basic Empathy Scale (BES), and how empathy is related to offending, aggression, and bullying in community and incarcerated groups.

Empathy is widely accepted as one of the most important individual factors that are related to offending, aggression, and bullying, and it is common in many intervention projects to aim to improve empathy in order to reduce offending, aggression, and bullying. The BES was constructed by Jolliffe and Farrington (2006) and has been widely used in a number of countries. This book brings together chapters, from a broad range of contributors, which explore the application of BES in ten different countries (England, Portugal, Spain, Poland, Italy, the Netherlands, Croatia, Australia, Canada, and the USA). Each chapter reviews the use of the BES in that particular jurisdiction, its psychometric properties, and its importance in relation to offending, aggression, and bullying. The research includes samples from primary schools, secondary schools, and the community, as well as those who are justice-involved and on probation, in prisons and secure psychiatric hospitals. The book concludes with wider implications for intervention, policy, and practice.

This book will be valuable reading for students and scholars of criminology, psychology and sociology, as well as practitioners who are interested in developing their understanding of the complex link between empathy and a range of antisocial behaviours.

Darrick Jolliffe is Professor of Criminology and Head of the School of Law and Criminology at the University of Greenwich. He has published extensively in the areas of empathy, individual differences and offending, developmental life-course criminology, punishment and offending, and has conducted numerous research studies for National and International Government Agencies.

David P. Farrington, O.B.E., is Emeritus Professor of Psychological Criminology at Cambridge University. He has received the Stockholm Prize in Criminology and he has been President of the American Society of Criminology. His major research interest is in developmental criminology, and he is Director of the Cambridge Study in Delinquent Development, which is a prospective longitudinal survey of over 400 London males from age 8 to age 61. In addition to 850 published journal articles and book chapters on criminological and psychological topics, he has published 115 books, monographs, and government publications, and 161 shorter publications.

Routledge Studies in Criminal Behaviour

Pathways to Sexual Aggression
Edited by Jean Proulx, Eric Beauregard, Patrick Lussier, and Benoit Leclerc

The Psychology of Crime, Policing and Courts
Edited by Andreas Kapardis and David P. Farrington

The Sexual Murderer
Offender behaviour and implications for practice
Eric Beauregard and Melissa Martineau

Psychological Violence in the Workplace
New perspectives and shifting frameworks
Emily Schindeler, Janet Ransley and Danielle Reynald

Domestic Homicide
Patterns and Dynamics
Marieke Liem and Frans Koenraadt

Intergenerational Continuity of Criminal and Antisocial Behaviour
An International Overview of Studies
Edited by Veroni I. Eichelsheim and Steve G. A. van de Weijer

Evidence-Based Offender Profiling
Edited by Bryanna H. Fox, David P. Farrington, Andreas Kapardis and Olivia C. Hambly

Empathy versus Offending, Aggression, and Bullying
Advancing Knowledge using the Basic Empathy Scale
Edited by Darrick Jolliffe and David P. Farrington

For more information about this series, please visit: www.routledge.com/Routledge-Studies-in-Criminal-Behaviour/book-series/RSCB

Empathy versus Offending, Aggression, and Bullying

Advancing Knowledge using the Basic Empathy Scale

Edited by Darrick Jolliffe and David P. Farrington

Routledge
Taylor & Francis Group
LONDON AND NEW YORK

First published 2021
by Routledge
2 Park Square, Milton Park, Abingdon, Oxon OX14 4RN

and by Routledge
605 Third Avenue, New York, NY 10017

Routledge is an imprint of the Taylor & Francis Group, an informa business

British Library Cataloguing-in-Publication Data
A catalogue record for this book is available from the British Library

Library of Congress Cataloging-in-Publication Data
A catalog record for this book has been requested

ISBN: 978-0-367-25374-5 (hbk)
ISBN: 978-0-367-52145-5 (pbk)

Typeset in Times New Roman
by Apex CoVantage, LLC

Contents

Foreword

Empathy is a psychological concept that mainly involves the experience and understanding of other persons' emotions (e.g. Hogan, 1969). It is a very important characteristic in human life and probably contributed to the success of mankind in the process of evolution. Although great apes and other species also seem to show some kind of empathic behaviour (e.g. Campbell & de Waal, 2014), perspective taking, feeling for others, and thoughts and emotions that match other persons' thoughts and affects are issues that are as important in modern societies as in the early times of *homo sapiens*. For example, empathy or a lack of empathy is a key factor in interpersonal communication, childrearing, healthcare, education in schools, supporting vulnerable people, psychotherapy, intercultural relations, and many other fields.

Low empathy is also an important risk factor for aggression, criminal, and violent behaviour. This is the topic of the present book. Whereas research suggests a plausible basic relation between low empathy and antisocial behaviour, this is not as simple as common sense assumes. The complexity of relations between low empathy and antisocial behaviour is due to various specific features of the two constructs. The chapters in the present volume show these more nuanced relationships and provide not only up-to-date research on the topic, but also data that are helpful for policy and practice in crime prevention and offender treatment.

A key issue of research and practice is the differentiation between various aspects of empathy. Contributions to the present volume use the Basic Empathy Scale (BES; Jolliffe & Farrington, 2006). The BES is a widely used self-report questionnaire that measures affective and cognitive empathy as two core dimensions of empathy. Affective empathy indicates emotional resonance and triggers feelings that are similar to those of the other person. According to animal and some human brain research, specific mirror neurons in the ventral premotor cortex and other brain areas may play a role in imitation and empathising with other people's pain (Rizzolatti & Craighero, 2004). However, the controversial issue of mirror neurons is only a small part of the expanding brain research on empathy and theory of mind (e.g. Singer, 2006; with regard to violence, see Raine, 2013). Cognitive empathy seems to be primarily attributable to processes in the prefrontal cortex and contains perspective taking with regard to the other person's motives and intentions. For example, cognitive empathy is indicated in learned schemes of social information processing (Dodge & Pettit, 2003; Lösel, Bliesener, & Bender, 2007) and sometimes it may be strategically used as a camouflage to reach a person's own goals.

Many seriously antisocial individuals and in particular psychopathic offenders have deficits in empathy, even when confronted with scenarios where others suffer from major injuries or pain (Hare & Neumann, 2008). A callous lack of empathy and a shallow affect are 2 of the 20 items of the widely used Psychopathy Checklist-Revised (Hare, 2003). Psychopaths know the words for others' emotions and may superficially exhibit some semantic empathy, but they do not hear the underlying affective "music" (Blair, Richell, Mitchell, & Leonard, 2006). However, the topic of the relation between low empathy and antisocial behaviour goes far beyond the specific cases of psychopathic personality disorder. Accordingly, some contributions to this volume rightly address the psychopathy-empathy relation in a dimensional instead of a taxonomic approach. Although callous-unemotional dispositions may already develop in childhood (Frick, Ray, Thornton, & Kahn, 2014), there are risks of early stigmatisation. A systematic review of studies on callous-unemotional traits shows a large variety of findings (Northam & Dadds, 2020) and the group of callous-unemotional youngsters seem not yet to be as distinct as some research suggests (Lahey, 2014). Numerous prospective longitudinal studies have confirmed a pathway of early starting and relatively persistent antisocial youngsters (Jennings & Reingle, 2012), but there are other trajectories, and group-based growth curves may underestimate the flexibility in individual development (e.g. Stemmler & Lösel, 2015).

Jolliffe and Farrington (2006) have shown that the BES has clear construct validity. Although the two dimensions of cognitive and affective empathy were significantly correlated, confirmatory factor analysis supported the differentiation of both dimensions. This early research also indicated theoretically plausible relations with measures of perspective taking, various personality factors, differences between females and males, socio-economic status, and poor parental supervision. From a methodological viewpoint, it is important that the authors found no significant correlation between a social desirability scale and the BES scores. These findings and the meta-analysis of Jolliffe and Farrington (2004) suggested that the BES is a very useful and relatively easy-to-apply instrument for research on crime, violence, and other aspects of antisocial behaviour.

The present volume contains a broad range of empirical studies that provide recent evidence for both construct and criterion validity of the BES. A foreword should not repeat details of the chapters and the syntheses of the editors. Therefore, I only emphasise the immense breadth of the contents. The chapters contain empathy research from multiple countries, on various forms of crime and violence (including school bullying), different age groups, males and females, early and later phases of antisocial development (including sentenced offenders), official and self-reported delinquency, substance abuse and other health problems, offender treatment, empathy as a mediating factor, and cross-sectional and prospective longitudinal data. Together, these rich data sets underline the usefulness of the BES for assessment, theoretical conceptualisation, and practical application.

It is another strength of this volume that the contributions show both consistencies and some discrepancies between findings. This is in accordance with the recent discussions on problems of replication in psychology, medicine, and criminology (Farrington et al., 2019; Lösel, 2018). Replication does not simply mean carrying out exactly the same studies, but also involves searching for those individual, social, and ecological conditions that contribute to the variation in findings. This is highly important for basic research as well as for applications in prevention and treatment. The present volume contains various examples of both replicated and differentiating findings on the BES. This confirms previous research that, for example, has shown that low affective empathy, but not cognitive empathy, correlated with school bullying when third factors were controlled (Jolliffe & Farrington, 2011). In another study, only low affective but not cognitive empathy was related to self-reported offending (Jolliffe & Farrington, 2007). In both studies, the relation between low empathy and antisocial behaviour was only significant for males and not for females.

This book contains a clear overall validation of the BES and a solid basis for further progress, but the editors rightly emphasise that more research is necessary. In my view, future studies should include more behavioural measures of empathy in addition to questionnaire-based assessments. As we know from research on impulsivity, another important broad construct, correlations with antisocial behaviour are often lower when different data sources are used (Lösel, 2017). A second topic for more research is differentiation of the "targets" of a person's empathy. The BES is a trait-like general measure, but people may exhibit empathy only to specific individuals and not to others. For example, empathy may be a risk factor versus a protective factor, depending on whether it concerns one's own extremist group or an adverse outgroup (Lösel, King, Bender, & Jugl, 2018). Results from animal research point in the same direction (Campbell & de Waal, 2014). A meta-analysis of sex offenders revealed that victim empathy was not a significant predictor of recidivism (Hanson & Morton-Bourgon, 2009), a finding that may be due to specific defence mechanisms in this group of offenders. A third promising topic of future research is the mediating or moderating role of empathy in developmental prevention and intervention. The present volume contains various findings on these issues. Although prevention programme evaluations show significantly desirable effects on aggression, crime, and delinquency (e.g. Beelmann & Lösel, 2020; Farrington, Gaffney, Lösel, & Ttofi, 2017), even sound experimental outcome evaluations rarely investigate mediating intra-individual change processes in empathy. More knowledge on mediating and moderating effects of empathy would help to increase programme effectiveness.

In sum, the book is a comprehensive compendium of recent international research on the relation between dimensions of empathy and various forms of antisocial behaviour. It addresses numerous basic and applied issues and I strongly recommend it for practitioners, researchers, and students.

Friedrich Lösel

References

Beelmann, A., & Lösel, F. (2020). A comprehensive meta-analysis of randomized evaluations of the effect of child social skills training on antisocial development. *Journal of Developmental and Life-Course Criminology*. doi:10.1007/s40865-020-00142-8

Blair, K., Richell, R. A., Mitchell, D. G. V., & Leonard, A. (2006). They know the words, but not the music: Affective and semantic priming in individuals with psychopathy. *Biological Psychology*, *73*, 114–123.

Campbell, M. W., & de Waal, F. B. M. (2014). Chimpanzees empathize with group mates and humans, but not with baboons or unfamiliar chimpanzees. *Proceedings of the Royal Society B*, *281*. doi:10.1098/rspb.2014.0013

Dodge, K. A., & Pettit, G. S. (2003). A biopsychosocial model of the development of chronic conduct problems in adolescence. *Developmental Psychology*, *39*, 349–371.

Farrington, D. P., Gaffney, H., Lösel, F., & Ttofi, M. (2017). Systematic reviews of the effectiveness of developmental prevention programs in reducing delinquency, aggression, and bullying. *Aggression and Violent Behavior*, *33*, 91–106.

Farrington, D. P., Lösel, F., Boruch, R. F., Gottfredson, D. C., Mazerolle, L., Sherman, L. W., & Weisburd, D. (2019). Advancing knowledge about replication in criminology. *Journal of Experimental Criminology*, *15*, 373–396.

Frick, P. J., Ray, J. V., Thornton, L. C., & Kahn, R. E. (2014). Annual research review: A developmental psychopathology approach to understanding callous-unemotional traits in children and adolescents with serious conduct problems. *The Journal of Child Psychology and Psychiatry*, *55*, 532–548.

Hanson, R. K., & Morton-Bourgon, K. E. (2009). The accuracy of recidivism risk assessments for sexual offenders: A meta-analysis of 118 prediction studies. *Psychological Assessment*, *21*, 1–21.

Hare, R. D. (2003). *Manual for the revised psychopathy checklist* (2nd ed.). Toronto: Multi-Health Systems.

Hare, R. D., & Neumann, R. D. (2008). Psychopathy as a clinical and empirical construct. *Annual Review of Clinical Psychology*, *4*, 217–246.

Hogan, R. (1969). Development of an empathy scale. *Journal of Consulting and Clinical Psychology*, *33*, 307–316.

Jennings, W. G., & Reingle, J. M. (2012). On the number and shape of developmental/life-course violence, aggression, and delinquency trajectories: A state-of-the-art review. *Journal of Criminal Justice*, *40*, 472–489.

Jolliffe, D., & Farrington, D. P. (2004). Empathy and offending: A systematic review and meta-analysis. *Aggression and Violent Behavior*, *9*, 441–476.

Jolliffe, D., & Farrington, D. P. (2006). Development and validation of the basic empathy scale. *Journal of Adolescence*, *29*, 589–611.

Jolliffe, D., & Farrington, D. P. (2007). Examining the relationship between low empathy and self-reported offending. *Legal and Criminological Psychology*, *12*, 265–286.

Jolliffe, D., & Farrington, D. P. (2011). Is low empathy related to bullying after controlling for individual and social background variables? *Journal of Adolescence*, *34*, 59–71.

Lahey, B. B. (2014). What we need to know about callous-unemotional traits: Comment on Frick et al. (2013). *Psychological Bulletin*, *140*, 58–63.

Lösel, F. (2017). Self-control as a theory of crime: A brief stocktaking after 27/42 years. In C. Bijlefeld & P. van der Laan (Eds.), *Liber amoricum for Gerben Bruinsma* (pp. 232–238). The Hague: Boom.

Lösel, F. (2018). Evidence comes by replication, but needs differentiation: The reproducibility issue in science and its relevance for criminology. *Journal of Experimental Criminology*, *14*, 257–278.

Lösel, F., Bliesener, T., & Bender, D. (2007). Social information processing, experiences of aggression in social contexts, and aggressive behavior in adolescents. *Criminal Justice and Behavior*, *34*, 330–347.

Lösel, F., King, S., Bender, D., & Jugl, I. (2018). Protective factors against extremism and violent radicalization: A systematic review of research. *International Journal of Developmental Science*, *12*, 89–102.

Northam, J. C., & Dadds, M. R. (2020). Is callous always cold? A critical review of the literature on emotion and the development of callous – unemotional traits in children. *Clinical Child and Family Psychology Review*, *23*, 265–283.

Raine, A. (2013). *The anatomy of violence*. New York: Pantheon Books.

Rizzolatti, G., & Craighero, L. (2004). The mirror-neuron system. *Annual Review of Neuroscience*, *27*, 169–192.

Singer, T. (2006). The neuronal basis and ontogeny of empathy and mind reading: Review of literature and implications for future research. *Neuroscience & Biobehavioral Reviews*, *6*, 855–863.

Stemmler, M., & Lösel, F. (2015). Developmental pathways of externalizing behavior from preschool age to adolescence: An application of general growth mixture modeling. In M. Stemmler, A. von Eye, & W. Wiedermann (Eds.), *Dependent data in social sciences research: Forms, issues, and methods of analysis* (pp. 91–106). New York: Springer.

Figures

Tables

Contributors

Mark Assink is a postdoctoral researcher at the Research Institute of Child Development and Education of the University of Amsterdam, the Netherlands.

Anna Costanza Baldry† (who passed away after presenting her paper at the Greenwich conference) was a Full Professor in Forensic and Social Psychology at the Department of Psychology of the University of Campania "Luigi Vanvitelli", Italy.

Miguel Basto-Pereira is Lecturer in Psychology, Director of the Master's in Forensic Psychology at ISPA (University Institute), and researcher at the William James Center for Research, ISPA, Lisbon, Portugal.

Henriette Bergstrøm is Senior Lecturer in Criminal Psychology in the School of Law and Social Sciences at the University of Derby, UK.

Christine E.W. Bond is Associate Professor and Deputy Head of School, Learning and Teaching, in the School of Criminology and Criminal Justice and Griffith Criminology Institute, Griffith University, Australia.

Stella Compton-Dickinson is an Accredited Cognitive Analytic Therapist and Supervisor, Health Professions Registered Music Therapist, Supervisor and UKCP, BACP registered Cognitive Analytic Therapist with a central London private practice at Guy's Hospital and in Harley Street, London, UK.

Li Eriksson is Senior Lecturer in the School of Criminology and Criminal Justice and Griffith Criminology Institute, Griffith University, Australia.

David P. Farrington, O.B.E., is Emeritus Professor of Psychological Criminology at Cambridge University, UK.

Carmen González-Salinas is Associate Professor at the Faculty of Psychology, University of Murcia, Spain.

Evelyn Heynen is University Lecturer and postdoctoral researcher at the Faculty of Psychology and Educational Sciences at the Open University of the

Netherlands. She also works as postdoctoral researcher at Fier expert centre for violence in the Netherlands.

Darrick Jolliffe is Professor of Criminology and Head of the School of Law and Criminology at the University of Greenwich, London, UK.

Christopher J. Koegl is Director of Research at the Ontario Correctional Institute, and Senior Research Advisor to the Centre for Children Committing Offences at the Child Development Institute, Toronto, Ontario, Canada.

Jessie L. Krienert is Professor in the Department of Criminal Justice Sciences at Illinois State University, the United States.

Samantha McAdams is a Graduate Student in the Department of Criminal Justice Sciences at Illinois State University, the United States.

Tara Renae McGee is Associate Professor in the School of Criminology and Criminal Justice and Griffith Criminology Institute, Griffith University, Australia.

Cristina Nunes is Associate Professor with habilitation in the University of Algarve and full member of Psychology Research Centre (CIP) of University Autónoma de Lisboa, Portugal.

Pedro Pechorro is a researcher of the Psychology Research Center (CIPSI) and Assistant Professor of Justice Psychology (School of Psychology) and Criminology (School of Law) at the University of Minho, Portugal.

Noelia Sánchez-Pérez is Assistant Professor at the Faculty of Social and Human Sciences, University of Zaragoza, Spain.

Ivana Sekol is Lecturer in Criminology at the Department of Criminology and Social Sciences, University of Derby, UK.

Ellin Simon is University Lecturer at the Faculty of Psychology at the Open University of the Netherlands. She is also a psychologist at PsyQ where she offers online therapy.

Anna Sorrentino is Researcher in Social Psychology and in charge of the teaching of Forensic Psychology and Laboratory of Victimology at the Department of Psychology of the University of Campania "Luigi Vanvitelli", Italy.

Geert Jan Stams is Professor of Forensic Child and Youth Care Sciences at the University of Amsterdam, the Netherlands.

Estera Twardowska-Staszek is a psychologist and sexologist. She holds the position of Assistant Professor in the Department of Social Rehabilitation Pedagogy at Jesuit University Ignatianum in Krakow, Poland. She also runs a private practice.

Peer van der Helm is Professor at Leiden University of Applied Sciences, Researcher at Amsterdam University and Research Director of Fier (National Treatment Centre for Sexually Abused Girls) in the Netherlands.

Tihomir Vidranski is Associate Professor at the Department of Kinesiology, Faculty of Education, University of Zagreb, Croatia.

Jeffrey A. Walsh is Professor in the Department of Criminal Justice Sciences at Illinois State University, the United States.

Izabela Zych is Associate Professor in Developmental and School Psychology at the University of Cordoba, Spain.

Preface

The basic empathy scale (BES) was developed in 2006 by Darrick Jolliffe and David P. Farrington as a method of measuring the two components of empathy, namely affective empathy, or the ability to experience the emotions of others, and cognitive empathy, or the ability to accurately understand the emotions of others. Since that time, the BES has been extensively used in English-speaking countries, and it has also been translated and used to assess empathy around the world.

In October 2018, national and international scholars who had used the BES in research studies to measure empathy in relation to different forms of criminal offending, aggression, and bullying were invited to a conference at the historic Old Royal Naval College at the University of Greenwich. Each scholar presented their paper, and the relationships between empathy and these forms of antisocial behaviour were critically discussed. These papers and the subsequent discussions form the basis of the chapters of this book. The presenters are shown in the two photographs.

This book contains a comprehensive collection of empirical research studies from the UK, Canada, the United States, Italy, Australia, Italy, Spain, Poland, Portugal, and Croatia, all of which critically examine the relationship between empathy – measured using the basic empathy scale – and offending, aggression, and bullying. The research includes samples from primary schools, secondary schools, and the community, as well as those who are justice-involved and on probation, in prisons, and secure psychiatric hospitals. Wide-ranging types of antisocial behaviour are studied, ranging from the bullying behaviour of those serving sentences in Croatian prisons to aggression by Australian students attending university. Each chapter makes a unique contribution to knowledge about the potential involvement of affective and/or cognitive empathy in explaining these behaviours.

Darrick Jolliffe, University of Greenwich
David P. Farrington, Cambridge University

First photo Presenters on the first day (from left to right): Izabela Zych, Noelia Sánchez-Pérez, Jeffrey A. Walsh, David P. Farrington, Darrick Jolliffe, Miguel Basto-Pereira, Henriette Bergstrom, Anna Costanza Baldry, Tara Renae McGee, and Ivana Sekol.

Second photo Presenters on the second day (from left to right): Christopher J. Koegl, Pedro Pechorro, Darrick Jolliffe, Stella Compton-Dickinson, Peer van der Helm, Geert Jan Stams, and Evelyn Heynen.

1 Measuring empathy using the Basic Empathy Scale

Darrick Jolliffe and David P. Farrington

Introduction

The main aim of this book is to examine the relationship between empathy, as measured by the Basic Empathy Scale, and offending, aggression, and bullying. The term empathy was first introduced to the English-speaking world by Edward Titchener in his 1909 publication 'Lectures of the Experimental Psychology and Thought'. Titchener had translated the term "empathy" from the German word "einfühlung", meaning "to feel into", which was a concept that had been widely used in studying aesthetics and emotional responses to art by scholars such as Theodore Lipps (1897). Titchener's doctoral training at the University of Leipzig, with Wilhelm Wundt – a pioneering introspective psychologist – as his supervisor, surely influenced Titchener's conceptualisation of empathy as a personal introspective process about humanising objects, or of reading or "feeling oneself" into them. This interpretation maintained a close conceptual tie with empathy's origins as a trait or ability related to experiencing perspectives and emotions elicited by inanimate objects, particularly artistic ones.

One of the first to propose that it might be useful to apply empathy to living people (and the first to use the term "empathise") was the Harvard neuropsychologist Southard (1919). In Southard's seminal publication, he specifically called for research into 'the extent to which we can read ourselves into the frankly insane or psychopathic' (p. 206), while also setting out 13 questions about empathy that psychiatrists might ask themselves about their patients. These included "items" such as 'How far can you read or feel yourself into the patient?' and, in reference to the patient's behaviour, 'Is this just what a child would do?'. For the latter point Southard argued that, if the psychiatrist felt that the behaviour was 'what a child would do', then the empathic "test" was positive, because each of us readily empathises with a child. While clearly not a psychometric measure of empathy, this is the first reference in the literature attempting to "test" or measure empathy.

In addition to Southard's "Empathy Index", his 1919 work made reference to a number of important issues about empathy. For example, he suggested that differences existed between individuals in their ability to read themselves into others (i.e. empathy as an individual difference), and also noted that this difference was related to one's power of imagination. Southard also distinguished between empathy that was emotional and that which had intellectual components, while also drawing a clear distinction between empathy and sympathy. To his mind, sympathy had additional value judgements and "superiority" attached, which was not present in empathy. Empirical research over the last 100 years has subsequently provided support for many of Southard's prescient assertions.

There is no universally agreed definition of empathy, but most definitions that have been proffered make reference to either the emotional component of empathy, where one actually experiences the emotions of another person (e.g. Mehrabian & Epstein, 1972), or the intellectual or cognitive component of empathy, where one understands the emotions of another (e.g. Hogan, 1969). More recent definitions, by Davis (1983) and Cohen and Strayer (1996), explicitly define empathy as including both these affective responses and these cognitive abilities.

Empathy and antisocial behaviour

With this conceptualisation, and indeed the origins of empathy as "feeling into", it is perhaps not surprising that empathy, or more precisely a lack of empathy, is often cited as an explanation for antisocial, aggressive and criminal behaviour. Individuals who have lower levels of empathy are theorised to be more likely to act antisocially and commit offences because they are unburdened by the experience or knowledge of the emotional consequences of their actions on others. That is, the negative emotions elicited in others (or anticipated to be elicited), such as fear, distress, and sadness, as a result of one's antisocial behaviour are not factored in advance as a possible cost or consequence of the antisocial act amongst those with low empathy. Thus, people with relatively low levels of empathy are missing a key "emergency handbrake" to moderate their behaviour. A number of more detailed models of the relationship between empathy and antisocial behaviour exist (e.g. Hanson, 2003; Hoffman, 1987), but in essence these models all have the same overall formula: low empathy increases the likelihood of committing criminal offences.

The concept of empathy has also found its way into influential theories of crime, such as Gottfredson and Hirschi's General Theory of Crime (1990, pp. 89–90). A "lack of empathy" is a key, and possibly the, defining characteristic of the concept of psychopathy, which is a well-known constellation of psychological and behavioural traits associated with serious and violent offending (e.g. Blair, 2007; Hare, 1999). Arguably, of more practical importance, a lack of empathy is very often a key intervention target for psychological interventions delivered to offenders, particularly violent and sexual offenders, that are designed to reduce the likelihood of later reoffending (e.g. Mulloy, Smiley, & Mawson, 1991; Ward & Durrant, 2013).

Given the importance of empathy as a potential risk factor for offending, it is essential to have tools to measure this latent construct, and the Basic Empathy Scale (BES) developed by Jolliffe and Farrington (2006) has proven to be one of the most widely used and researched scales in the world. The items of the BES were specifically designed to address the limitations of previous measures of empathy which tended to measure sympathy (i.e. the extent to which one feels badly for another in an unfortunate situation), as opposed to affective empathy (i.e. the extent to which one shares the emotions of another), and general perspective taking (i.e. the ability to see another's point of view), as opposed to cognitive empathy (i.e. the ability to understand another's emotions).

A total of 40 items, which measured affective and cognitive empathy, were developed and these items were administered to 363 adolescents (194 males, 169 females, aged about 15). From this, exploratory factor analysis identified two cogent factors, one measuring affective empathy (11 items, e.g. 'I usually feel calm when other people are scared' – disagree), and one measuring cognitive empathy (9 items, e.g. 'It is hard for me to understand when my friends are sad' – disagree). This scale was then administered to an additional 357 adolescents along with a series of other measures to evaluate its convergent and divergent validity.

This book

The purpose of this book is to present new research on empathy, measured using the BES, and its relationship to offending, aggression, and bullying. Most of the chapters are revised and updated versions of papers given at a symposium titled 'Measuring Empathy and Behavioural Outcomes: Advancing Knowledge with the Basic Empathy Scale', held at the University of Greenwich's historic Old Royal Naval College in October 2018.

In Chapter 2, Miguel Basto-Pereira and David P. Farrington describe the importance of having a theoretically and psychometrically solid measure of empathy, and the development of the BES. These authors then chart the use of this measure across the world and assess the psychometric properties of this scale as a result of this extensive research. In their review of the literature on the BES, these authors draw attention to some key strengths of this measure, but also to some key issues that require additional research.

In Chapter 3, Evelyn Heynen and colleagues undertake a comprehensive review of the literature to identify research studies which examine the association between parental empathy and the quality of the parent-child attachment. Theoretically, parents with higher levels of empathy would be expected to be more attuned to the emotional experiences of their children, thus facilitating a stronger and more emotionally warm relationship between parents and children. Two of the five studies that were identified used versions of the BES to measure parental empathy. The results point to the potential importance of parental empathy for the strength of the relationship between parents and children.

In Chapter 4, Evelyn Heynen and colleagues use a similar systematic approach to search the literature to identify primary research studies which examined the relationship between parenting styles (i.e. authoritative, authoritarian, permissive, and neglectful parenting) and the empathy of youth. The authors were able to identify 14 studies which assessed both parenting styles and the empathy of their children (age from 10 to 20), measured in various ways including questionnaires and observations. The results of this study reveal an important relationship between certain forms of parenting and the level of empathy in youth, but also note that the estimate of the magnitude of these relationships varies depending on a number of factors.

In Chapter 5, Peer van der Helm presents a theoretical model of the potential link between low empathy and aggression and, further, discusses the importance of understanding the development of empathy in young people. van der Helm also explores the evidence which highlights the interactions between certain biological, psychological, and social risk factors and how these can negatively impact on the healthy development of empathy. This chapter concludes with an empirically informed integrated bio-psycho-social model linking adverse childhood experiences through cognitive, socio-emotional, and personality development to aggression.

Farrington and Jolliffe, in Chapter 6, examine the relationship between low empathy, measured using the BES, and both self-reported and official offending by a large sample of males and females (aged about 25) in England. This study is one of very few that have examined the relationship between empathy and offending in a community sample, as opposed to a case-control study in which the empathy level of "offenders" and a comparison group are compared. The results show that low empathy and offending are linked, but somewhat counterintuitively, that the relationship between low empathy and both self-reported and official offending was much more straightforward for females as opposed to males.

In Chapter 7, Jolliffe and Farrington use the BES to measure the cognitive and affective empathy of 299 men (aged about 32) serving a community sentence for a criminal offence in England, and compare these measures to both past offending and later reoffending. Interestingly, the results show that low empathy was associated with serious current and past offending, such as having an index offence of serious theft or having previous convictions for serious violence. The results were far less consistent when low empathy was compared to later measures of reoffending. The authors present a number of potential explanations for this unexpected finding.

The relationship between psychopathy, a constellation of psychological and behavioural traits associated with serious offending, and empathy is explored in Chapter 8 by Bergstrom, Jolliffe, and Farrington. This study uses a community sample of males and females aged about 25 years and assesses their levels of psychopathy using the PCL:SV (Hart, Cox, & Hare, 1995) and their levels of empathy using the BES. The results show that the level of psychopathy in this sample was relatively low, which would be expected in a community sample, but there is also an indication that certain dimensions of psychopathy are related to lower levels of empathy.

Chapter 9 examines the correlates of empathy amongst a sample of incarcerated young males and females in Portugal. Pedro Pechorro and colleagues use the BES and identify significant gender differences in the levels of affective and cognitive empathy in their sample. They also show that the profile of the correlates between low empathy and a number of related factors shows similarities for incarcerated young males and females, but also a range of important differences, particularly related to social anxiety. The authors reflect on how these gender differences might be usefully incorporated into gender-sensitive interventions.

The BES has also been used to assess empathy in a prison in Canada, as described by Christopher Koegl in Chapter 10. This study is one of the first to examine changes in the BES as a result of a therapeutic ethos or intervention, and the first to compare these changes in empathy to later reoffending. The results highlight the importance that empathy development may have for reducing reoffending, particularly for certain types of offenders.

In England and Wales, those who commit serious offences and are suffering from mental illness are held in secure psychiatric facilities. In Chapter 11, Compton-Dickinson and Jolliffe describe a study in which the BES was used to evaluate the impact of a unique form of music therapy delivered to adult males serving a sentence in a high-security psychiatric hospital. The results provide some evidence of empathy development over time for those who receive music therapy, and also for those for those who receive more typical therapeutic support. The benefits of music therapy for the empathy development for this challenging population are critically discussed.

Chapter 12 presents the results of a study in which a modified version of the BES, based on parental reports of a child's empathy, is compared to both parental reports of the child's negative emotionality and teacher-reported aggression in Spain. Noelia Sánchez-Pérez and colleagues' study of Spanish school children illustrates the importance that empathy may have in explaining the prevalence of school-based aggression. In addition, the results of more in-depth analyses point to the importance that certain factors may have in moderating the relationship between empathy and school-based aggression.

In Chapter 13, McGee and colleagues examine the relationship between three types of aggression (relational, online, and physical) and low affective and cognitive empathy, as well as other potentially important correlates such as low self-control and low social intelligence, in a large sample of Australian university students. The results highlight gender differences in both levels of aggression and also levels of empathy, while also indicating that the strength of association between low empathy and aggression may be different for different types of aggression and also levels of self-control.

Izabela Zych and colleagues report on a comprehensive investigation of the factor structure of the BES and its association to bullying, cyberbullying, and aggression, using a large sample of young people in Poland and an equally large sample in Spain. The results indicate that a modified version of the BES appears to fit the data much better than the original structure, and this modified version of the BES has important relationships with a number of forms of bullying and antisocial behaviour for both males and females.

School bullying, and the relatively new form of cyberbullying, are also the topic of Chapter 15, in which Anna Sorrentino and colleagues administer the BES to Italian school children, along with other relevant measures, one year apart.

The results suggest that there may be important gender differences in the level of empathy, in the most common forms of cyberbullying, and in how empathy changes over time. This chapter closes with a discussion of the implication of these findings for interventions designed to reduce cyberbullying in schoolchildren.

In Chapter 15, Jeffrey Walsh and colleagues examine the relationship between affective and cognitive empathy, and also narcissism, and compare these with US university students' retrospective experiences of bullying victimisation in high school. The findings indicate that those who report being a victim of bullying have a unique profile of both narcissism and empathy which is different from both those who report bullying others and those not involved. The implications of a lack of "healthy narcissism" and elevations in affective empathy in victims is used to frame the development of interventions designed to reduce victimisation.

Bullying and its causes and correlates have been studied not only in school settings, but also in prisons. In Chapter 17, Ivana Sekol and colleagues examine the relationship between affective and cognitive empathy using the BES and the prevalence of different types of bullying in five Croatian prisons. The results again show that females have higher cognitive and affective empathy than males. Interestingly, female and male bullies appear to differ in their most common forms of bullying, and female and male bullies also appear to have different empathy profiles. Based on more comprehensive analyses, this chapter calls into question the relative importance of empathy in explaining bullying in prison.

In the final chapter, Jolliffe and Farrington reflect on the benefits and limitations of the BES as a measure of empathy. In addition, the key findings of the previous chapters are used to highlight the current state of knowledge of the relationship between empathy, antisocial behaviour, bullying, and offending. The authors use this platform to examine the potential usefulness of interventions designed to increase empathy to reduce antisocial behaviour, bullying, and offending, and propose a research agenda which would help to clearly establish the causal relationship, and therefore likely effectiveness of interventions which aim to increase empathy.

Overall, this collection provides a comprehensive and state-of-the-art view of the study of empathy in the Western world.

References

Blair, R.J. (2007). The amygdala and ventromedial prefrontal cortex in morality and psychopathy. *Trends in Cognitive Sciences*, *11*, 387–392.

Cohen, D., & Strayer, J. (1996). Empathy in conduct-disordered and comparison youth. *Developmental Psychology*, *32*, 988–998.

Davis, M. H. (1983). Measuring individual differences in empathy: Evidence for a multidimensional approach. *Journal of Personality and Social Psychology*, *44*, 113–126.

Gottfredson, M. R., & Hirschi, T. (1990). *A general theory of crime*. Stanford, CA: Stanford University Press.

Hanson, K. R. (2003). Empathy deficits of sexual offenders: A conceptual model. *Journal of Sexual Aggression*, *9*, 13–23.

Hare, R. D. (1999). Psychopathy as a risk factor for violence. *Psychiatric Quarterly*, *70*, 181–197.

Hart, S. D., Cox, D. N., & Hare, R. D. (1995). *The Hare PCL: Screening version.* Toronto: Multi-Health Systems.

Hoffman, M. L. (1987). The contribution of empathy to justice and moral judgement. In N. Eisenberg & J. Strayer (Eds.), *Empathy and its development* (pp. 47–80). Cambridge: Cambridge University Press.

Hogan, R. (1969). Development of an empathy scale. *Journal of Consulting and Clinical Psychology, 33,* 307–316.

Jolliffe, D., & Farrington, D. P. (2006). Development and validation of the basic empathy scale. *Journal of Adolescence, 29,* 589–611.

Lipps, T. (1897). *Raumästhetik und geometrisch-optische Täuschungen.* Leipzig: JA Barth.

Mehrabian, A., & Epstein, N. (1972). A measure of emotional empathy. *Journal of Personality, 40,* 525–543.

Mulloy, R., Smiley, W. C., & Mawson, D. L. (1991). The impact of empathy training on offender treatment. *Focus on Corrections Research, 11,* 15–18.

Southard, E. E. (1919). The empathic index in the diagnosis of mental disease. *Journal of Abnormal Psychology, 13,* 199–214.

Titchener, E. B. (1909). *Lectures of the experimental psychology of thought processes.* New York: Palgrave Macmillan.

Ward, T., & Durrant, R. (2013). Altruism, empathy, and sex offender treatment. *International Journal of Behavioral Consultation and Therapy, 8,* 66–71.

Part I

The Basic Empathy Scale and parenting

2 The Basic Empathy Scale

Psychometric properties and contributions to the understanding of antisocial behaviour

Miguel Basto-Pereira and David P. Farrington

Introduction

The ability to empathise is intrinsically related to the development of human relationships and the history of civilisation. Principles of rights, equality, justice, and even the establishment of friendly relationships are promoted by the human ability to imagine ourselves in others' circumstances and to understand and feel others' emotions. Indeed, two meta-analyses have shown that empathy is positively related to prosocial behaviour (Eisenberg & Miller, 1987; Fengqin & Zhaohui, 2016) and negatively related to antisocial behaviour (Jolliffe & Farrington, 2004; van Langen, Wissink, van Vugt, van der Stouwe, & Stams, 2014). Because of its importance, empathy has been studied by researchers from various fields, including psychology (e.g. Durlak & Wells, 1997), criminology (e.g. Inzunza, 2015), and the neurosciences (e.g. Fan, Duncan, de Greck, & Northoff, 2011).

One of the biggest challenges faced by researchers is the ability to use accurate measures of empathy. In the last decades, several measures have been developed, which, it has been pointed out, have several limitations. Two major types of shortcomings have been identified: 1) measures with poor (or untested) psychometric properties and 2) conceptual challenges. Examples of poor (or untested) psychometric properties can be seen for several scales: for example, the Hogan Empathy Scale (e.g. Froman & Peloquin, 2001) and Griffith Empathy Measure (Murphy, in press) have serious construct validity problems; the number of dimensions evaluated in the Empathy Quotient is not clear (Allison, Baron-Cohen, Wheelwright, Stone, & Muncer, 2011); and the temporal stability of the Questionnaire of Cognitive and Affective Empathy is largely unknown (Neumann, Chan, Boyle, Wang, & Westbury, 2014).

Secondly, a series of limitations has been observed concerning whether and to what extent each empathy scale is in fact assessing empathy. This shortcoming is substantially more controversial because the ability of a scale to accurately evaluate a construct implies a precise definition of that specific construct. For instance, the Balanced Emotional Empathy Scale does not fully evaluate the concept of empathy (it does not include cognitive empathy), whereas the Interpersonal Reactivity Index has been criticised for evaluating more than empathy, equating empathy with sympathy (see Jolliffe & Farrington, 2006). These limitations are partially prompted by the number of different definitions of the concept of empathy that are in use, which serves to detract from its accurate assessment.

In this regard, a recent literature review summarises and broadly reflects on this problem. The review, conducted by Cuff, Brown, Taylor, and Howat (2014), identified 43 different definitions of empathy. From an analysis of all these definitions (and the similarities between them), the authors made a series of recommendations that are tremendously important for the measurement of empathy, as follows: 1) care should be taken to avoid confusion between empathy and other proximal concepts, such as sympathy or perspective-taking; 2) the concept of empathy should not be limited to the understanding and sharing of negative emotions; and 3) empathy should be assessed using two distinct but related constructs – cognitive empathy (the ability to understand others' feelings) and affective empathy (the ability to share others' emotions in responding to the perceived emotional stimulus). This latter point has been corroborated by a recent meta-analysis from the neurosciences (Fan et al., 2011), which concluded that cognitive – evaluative empathy and affective – perceptual empathy can be distinguished at the level of neural region activation. Nonetheless, the majority of scales do not distinguish those two dimensions.

These (and other) major limitations were pointed out by Jolliffe and Farrington (2004, 2006), who developed the Basic Empathy Scale (BES) to overcome them in assessing empathy.

Development of the basic empathy scale

The Basic Empathy Scale (BES), developed and first tested by Jolliffe and Farrington (2006), is a multidimensional self-report scale that measures empathy. Initially 40 items were formulated, based on the definition of cognitive empathy as the ability to understand another's emotions and the definition of affective empathy as affect congruence with another's perceived emotions. Thirty-two items based on the four basic emotions of fear, sadness, anger, and happiness, along with four items each for affective and cognitive empathy, were used to evaluate general empathy (e.g. 'I get caught up in other people's feelings easily'). The items were answered on a five-point Likert scale, from 1 = *Strongly Disagree* to 5 = *Strongly Agree*. Exploratory data analysis was conducted on a sample of 363 British adolescents in England. Using the *loadings* obtained for each item, the scale was duly reduced to 20 items (including eight reversed items): nine items measuring cognitive empathy (e.g. 'I can often understand how people are feeling even before they tell me') and 11 items measuring affective empathy (e.g. reversed: 'My friends' emotions don't affect me much').

The final version of the BES (Jolliffe & Farrington, 2006) has two dimensions (affective and cognitive empathy), allowing a total score ranging from 20 (low empathy) to 100 (high empathy) to be calculated to provide a global measure of empathy. The psychometric properties of the 20-item version of the BES were then tested on a second sample of adolescents with the same characteristics as those of the original sample. This final version showed good indicators of validity and reliability and confirmed the proposed factorial structure. The cross-cultural psychometric properties of the BES will be dealt with in the following sections.

The basic empathy scale: scientific impact

Since the BES was successfully developed by Jolliffe and Farrington (2006), many researchers in Europe and elsewhere have translated it and conducted studies to test its psychometric properties in order to adapt it for use in their own countries. These new validations created the opportunity for a new wave of studies. A simple way to analyse the uptake of the BES is to examine the number of citations/per year of the article that originally introduced it. Google Scholar is a good way to track the number of citations because it can detect and track the grey literature, such as official reports and theses, as well as articles published in peer-reviewed journals and books.

Figure 2.1 shows that the 'Development and validation of the Basic Empathy Scale' article was cited more than 850 times; moreover, since 2006, with the exception of 2015, 2017 and 2018, the number of citations has increased annually. In 2018, this work was cited more than 120 times.

Worldwide dissemination of the Basic Empathy Scale

To identify all the psychometric studies conducted using this measure of empathy, the following were performed: 1) an exhaustive analysis of all 856 citations; 2) an inquiry sent to the authors of the BES (Jolliffe & Farrington, 2006); and 3) a further search of other scientific databases (e.g. EBSCO, Scopus, PubMed, Google Scholar) using the expression "Basic Empathy Scale". Table 2.1 presents the descriptive characteristics of the 19 studies that tested the BES, including the name of the country, the BES version tested (the 20-item original version or some other reduced version), and the type of sample.

Figure 2.2 presents the countries in which studies have been conducted to test the psychometric properties of BES. Table 2.1, together with Figure 2.2, shows

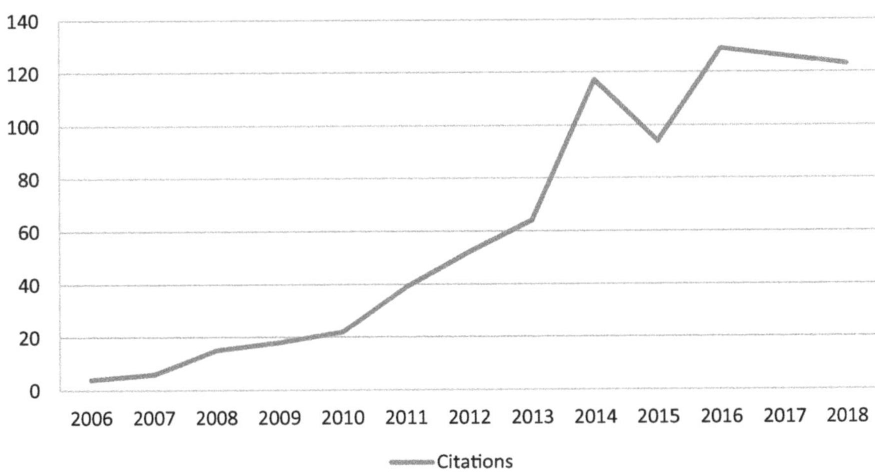

Figure 2.1 Number of citations per year of Jolliffe and Farrington (2006).

Source: Google Scholar (https://scholar.google.pt).

Table 2.1 Descriptive characteristics of the 19 studies testing psychometric properties of the BES.

Study and Country	N	*BES Version Used*	*Type of Sample*
Jolliffe and Farrington (2006); United Kingdom	720	Original Version	Youths (General Sample)
D'Ambrosio, Olivier, Didon, and Besche (2009); France	446	Original Version	Youths (General Sample)
Albiero, Matricardi, Speltri, and Toso (2009); Italy	655	Original Version	Youths (General Sample)
Delgado and colleagues (2011); Spain	2400	9 Items Reduced Version	Children
Čavojová, Sirota, and Belovičová (2012); Slovakia	429	Original Version	Youths (General Sample)
Geng, Xia, and Qin (2012); China	1524	Original Version	Youths (General Sample)
Salas-Wright, Olate, and Vaughn (2012); El Salvador	208	7 Items Reduced Version	High-Risk and Gang Involved Youths
Carré, Stefaniak, D'Ambrosio, Bensalah, and Besche-Richard (2013); France	370	Original Version	Adults
Sánchez-Pérez, Fuentes, Jolliffe, and González-Salinas (2014); Spain	290	Original & Parent Report Version	Children
Merino-Soto and Grimaldo-Muchotrigo (2015); Peru	135	9 Items Reduced Version	Youths (General Sample)
Pechorro, Ray, Salas-Wright, Maroco, and Gonçalves (2015); Portugal	221	Original Version	Youth Females (Offenders and General Samples)
Bensalah, Stefaniak, Carre, and Besche-Richard (2016); France	410	Original Version	Children
Villadangos, Errasti, Amigo, Jolliffe, and García-Cueto (2016); Spain	752	Original Version	Youths (General Sample)
Anastácio, Vagos, Nobre-Lima, Rijo, and Jolliffe (2016); Portugal	1029	Original Version	Youths (General Sample)
Heynen, van der Helm, Stams, and Korebrits (2016); Germany	94	Original Version	Youth Male Offenders
Pechorro, Kahn, Gonçalves, and Ray (2017); Portugal	377	Original Version	Youth Females (Offenders and General Samples)
You, Lee, and Lee (2018); South Korea	1524	Original Version	Youths (General Sample)
van Langen, Wissink, Stams, and van Vugt (2018); the Netherlands	2464	Original Version	Youth (Offenders and General Samples)
Zych, Farrington, Nasaescu, Jolliffe, and Twardowska-Staszek (2018); Poland	1052	Original Version	Children and Adolescents (General Sample)

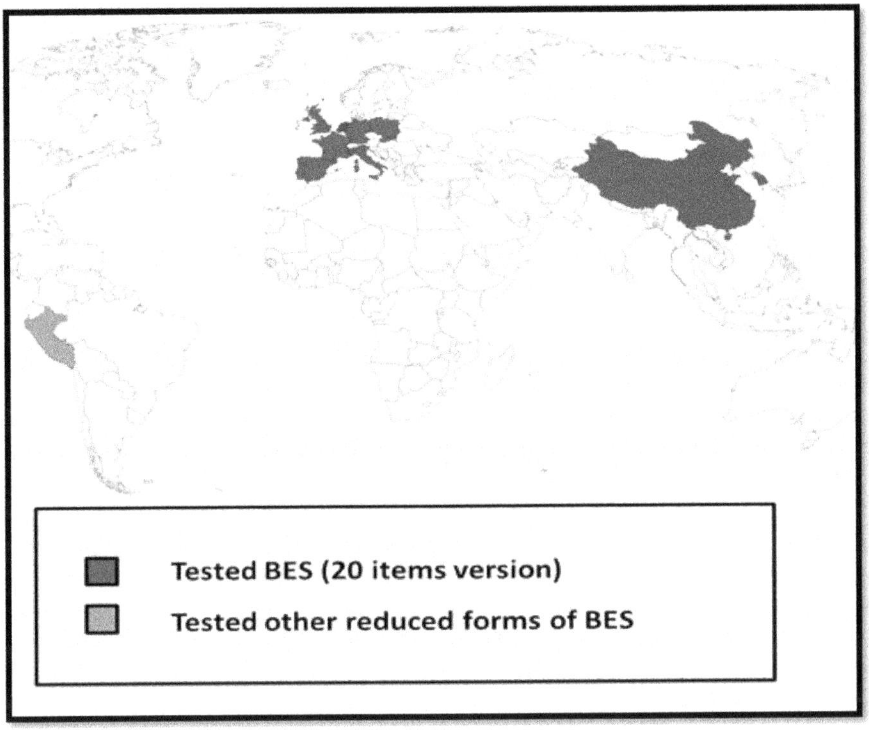

Figure 2.2 World map showing the countries where the BES (or derived forms) was tested (in separate file)

that 19 studies have been conducted in 13 countries located across three continents, namely, Europe, Asia, and South America, to validate the BES (or derived forms). The majority of them have been conducted on European populations, while two of those identified were in Asia and two were in South and Central America. Of the 19 studies, 17 are published and available online (almost all of them in peer-reviewed journals), while two studies were kindly provided by its authors (van Langen et al., 2018; Zych et al., 2018).

Cross-cultural analysis of the psychometric properties of the basic empathy scale

Our aim was to review indicators of the validity and reliability of the BES across countries. To avoid *comparing apples with oranges*, we excluded from this analysis all reduced forms and forms applied in other formats (e.g. parental self-report). Of the 19 studies presented, three had been conducted using only reduced or derived versions of the BES. Consequently, this review includes 16 psychometric studies (see Table 2.1).

Factorial validity

All 16 studies included in this analysis conducted a confirmatory factor analysis to test the relationship between each item and its corresponding dimension, affective empathy, or cognitive empathy. The nine studies conducted on mixed gender youth samples (adolescent/young adults) showed satisfactory indicators for a two-dimensional model and confirmed the theoretical structure proposed by Jolliffe and Farrington (2006). Six of these nine studies retained intact the 20-item structure; the exceptions were one study conducted in Portugal (Anastácio et al., 2016) in which four items were deleted, and the studies conducted in the Netherlands and China (Geng et al., 2012; van Langen et al., 2018), in which one item was deleted. In addition, the study conducted in Portugal by Anastácio and colleagues (2016) tested measurement invariance, the results indicating a similar factorial structure with a good fit across gender and the adolescent age range.

The confirmatory factor analysis conducted in the four studies with juvenile offender samples showed the same pattern, confirming the factorial structure proposed by Jolliffe and Farrington (2006). Nonetheless, the confirmatory analysis conducted on a sample of young female Portuguese offenders (Pechorro et al., 2017) showed a poor fit for the two-factor solution, while in the studies conducted in Germany and the Netherlands the structure was confirmed only after the deletion of some items (Heynen et al., 2016; van Langen et al., 2018). The summary table study conducted in the Netherlands also tested measurement invariance across offenders and non-offenders; while cognitive empathy appeared similar across both groups, this was not the case for affective empathy.

With regard to other age ranges the factorial structure is even less clear. All five studies that looked at other ages needed to delete items in order to confirm the original version's factorial structure. For instance, the study conducted in Poland, only after the deletion of eight items found a factorial structure suitable for children and adolescents (Zych et al., 2018). In addition, the two studies conducted in France (child and adult samples) suggested as more appropriate a new factorial structure with three dimensions – emotional contagion, cognitive empathy, and emotional disconnection – despite low emotional contagion having poor indicators of internal consistency (Bensalah et al., 2016; Carré et al., 2013).

We would expect to find significant correlations between the two subscales of BES, affective empathy and cognitive empathy, given that both constructs are theoretically correlated but not the same. The correlations found in eight general samples of young people ranged from $r = .41$, $p < .05$ in France (D'Ambrosio et al., 2009) to $r = .63$, $p < .05$ in Portugal (Anastácio et al., 2016), confirming the expected significant moderate correlations between two non-identical but theoretically related constructs. In the same way was the correlation established between affective empathy and cognitive empathy, in a mixed sample of children and adolescents ($r = .54$, $p < .05$; Zych et al., 2018). The only two studies that tested the correlations in male juvenile offenders found the same pattern, with correlations ranging from $r = .49$, $p < .05$ in Portugal (Pechorro et al., 2015) to $r = .59$, $p < .05$ in Germany (Heynen et al., 2016). Surprisingly, the only study conducted on female juvenile offenders found no significant correlation between the two BES subscales

($r = .16$, ns; Pechorro et al., 2017). Thus, the question arises: is this a limitation of the scale or a new finding regarding the relationship between affective and cognitive empathy in female offenders? Future studies should examine this question. Finally, the only study to test the relationship between cognitive and affective empathy in a sample only with children (Sánchez-Pérez et al., 2014) showed a lower correlation ($r = .32, p < .05$) than that found in studies of young people, raising questions about the true factorial structure of the BES in other age ranges.

To sum up, all the studies conducted on youth populations, including forensic populations, confirmed the factorial structure of the BES, regardless of the country. In addition, with the exception of one study conducted on female juvenile offenders, all the studies supported a moderate correlation between the two empathy subscales, as expected. In contrast, there are doubts concerning the proposed factorial structure of the BES for populations in other age ranges, for two main reasons: 1) only five studies tested the factorial structure in children and adult samples and 2) two of those suggested a three-dimensional model as the best fit for their data. Therefore, more research is needed to establish the true factorial validity of the BES.

Convergent, discriminant, and known-group validity

Almost all the studies conducted on general samples of adolescents tested for convergent validity. Many tested correlations between empathy and personality characteristics related to empathy, such as agreeableness (e.g. Villadangos et al., 2016) and social skills dimensions (e.g. Anastácio et al., 2016). Across these studies many of the correlations were confirmed and the effect size was moderate, suggesting good convergent validity (Murphy & Davidshofer, 2005). Nonetheless, there is a clear lack of studies testing convergent validity in samples other than those of young people in the general population. The only exception was that conducted by Pechorro and colleagues (2015), which tested a social anxiety measure in a sample of youth male offenders. Their results showed good convergent validity.

Regarding discriminant validity, it was also expected that the BES dimensions would have low to zero correlations with other measures evaluating theoretically unrelated constructs (Murphy & Davidshofer, 2005). Four studies tested this hypothesis: two with a general youth sample (D'Ambrosio et al., 2009; Jolliffe & Farrington, 2006); one on a sample of young male offenders (Pechorro et al., 2017); and one on a sample of children (Bensalah et al., 2016). All four studies used social desirability dimensions to test discriminant validity. The use of a social desirability scale has two major advantages: 1) it allows one to test discriminant validity, as social desirability is not theoretically expected to be related to empathy; and 2) it allows one to analyse the risk that high levels of empathy are caused by trying to create a good impression (social desirability bias). All correlations were revealed to be low ($r < .30$) and mostly non-significant, suggesting good discriminant validity and low social desirability bias of the BES across countries.

Finally, it was expected that the BES's dimensions would present significantly different scores between groups theoretically expected to have distinct levels of empathy, usually called known-group validity (Davidson, 2014). There is a great deal of literature showing that females score significantly higher than males on empathy measures (for a review, see Christov-Moore et al., 2014). The nine studies conducted on mixed gender samples of youths found, consistently and for both dimensions, higher levels of empathy in females compared with males. Nonetheless, among other age ranges not all dimensions of empathy were found to be significantly different between males and females. The only study testing known-group validity in offenders was conducted by Pechorro and colleagues (2017) on a sample of female juvenile offenders. Given that young offenders are known to have a lower level of empathy than non-offenders, the authors tested known-group validity comparing female youth offenders with female youths from the general population. They found statistically significant differences, with female offenders having the lower levels of empathy. Thus, in line with convergent and discriminant validity, the BES showed consistent known-group validity in youth populations across countries. Nonetheless, there is a clear need for further studies in this field examining other samples and age ranges.

Reliability: internal consistency and test-retest reliability

Two indicators of reliability were variously analysed in the studies, namely internal consistency and test-retest reliability. Eight of the nine general youth sample studies tested levels of internal consistency. Cronbach's alpha ranged from $\alpha = .92$ (Villadangos et al., 2016) to $\alpha = .73$ (Geng et al., 2012) for affective empathy, and from $\alpha = .96$ (Villadangos et al., 2016) to $\alpha = .66$ (D'Ambrosio et al, 2009) for cognitive empathy. The same pattern was found in the three studies conducted with youth offenders, with Cronbach's alpha ranging between $\alpha = .87$ (Pechorro et al., 2015) to $\alpha = .71$ (Heynen et al., 2016) for affective empathy and between $\alpha = .90$ (Pechorro et al., 2015) and $\alpha = .78$ (Heynen et al., 2016) for cognitive empathy. The study conducted on a sample of adults also showed satisfactory internal consistency indicators (Carré et al., 2013), reporting a Cronbach's alpha for affective empathy of $\alpha = .84$ and for cognitive empathy of $\alpha = .71$. The two studies presenting Cronbach's alpha indicators for a sample of children showed lower but nevertheless acceptable levels of internal consistency, ranging between $\alpha = .75$ (Zych et al., 2018) to $\alpha = .66$ (Sánchez-Pérez et al., 2014) for affective empathy and between $\alpha = .84$ (Zych et al., 2018) to $\alpha = .70$ (Sánchez-Pérez et al., 2014) for cognitive empathy.

Only two studies analysed test-retest reliability for affective and cognitive empathy on general samples of youths. Whereas the study conducted in China (Geng et al., 2012) suggested acceptable levels of test-retest reliability for affective empathy ($r = .71, p < .05$) and for cognitive empathy ($r = .60, p < .05$) using a four-week interval between applications, that conducted in France by D'Ambrosio and colleagues (2009) showed moderate ($r = .70$ for affective empathy) to low levels ($r = .54$ for cognitive empathy) of test-retest reliability using a three-week interval between applications. The only study conducted on a sample of adults analysing test-retest reliability also showed acceptable levels of correlations ($r = .80$ for affective empathy; $r = .61$ for cognitive empathy), using a seven-week interval between applications (Carré et al., 2013). Table 2.2 presents a detailed summary of BES validity and reliability properties across studies.

Table 2.2 Summary of Basic Empathy Scale validity and reliability properties across studies.

Study; Country; Sample	***Cognitive vs Affective Empathy***	***Reliability*** *Internal Consistency and Test-retest*	***Validity*** *Known-groups Validity with Gender Differences*	***Convergent and Discriminant Validity*** *Correlations with Personality, Social Desirability and Antisocial Measures*
Jolliffe and Farrington (2006); United Kingdom; Youths	Females ($r = .43$, $p < .05$); Males ($r = .41$; $p < .05$)	**Internal Consistency** Cronbach´s α (Affective Empathy $\alpha = .79$, Cognitive Empathy $\alpha = .85$)	Cognitive Scale – Males ($M = 32.2$; $SD = 5.1$); Females ($M = 35.0$; $SD = 3.9$); ($t = 8.3$, $p < .01$, $d = 0.63$); Affective empathy scale – Males ($M = 32.1$; $SD = 6.5$); Females $M = 40.3$ ($SD = 5.8$) ($t = 17.6$, $p < .01$, $d = 1.33$); BES Total – Males ($M = 64.3$; $SD = 9.8$); Females ($M = 75.3$; $SD = 8.3$); ($t = 16.1$; $p < .01$; $d = 1.22$);	**Personality Correlations** Agreeableness Males (Cognitive $r = .26$, $p < .05$; Affective $r = .23$, $p < .05$; Total = .30, $p < .05$) Agreeableness Females (Cognitive $r = .23$, $p < .05$; Affective $r = .18$, $p < .05$; Total $r = .24$, $p < .05$); Conscientiousness Males (Cognitive $r = .16$, $p < .05$; Affective $r = .13$, $p < .05$; Total = .17, $p < .05$); Conscientiousness Females (Cognitive = .06, n.s.; Affective = −.02, n.s.; Total = −.01, n.s.); **Social Desirability** (*Males* Cognitive $r = .03$; Affective $r = .03$; Total $r = .00$); Females (Cognitive $r = -.02$; Affective $r = .10$; Total $r = -.11$) – all *n.s.*
D'Ambrosio et al. (2009); France; Youths	General ($r = .41$, $p < .05$) Females ($r = .27$, $p < .05$); Males ($r = .42$; $p < .05$)	**Internal Consistency** Cronbach's α = .80 (Affective α = .77, Cognitive α = .66); **Test-retest Reliability** 3 Weeks Interval – BES Total $r = .66$ ($p < .05$); BES Affective $r = .70$ ($p < .05$) Cognitive $r = .54$ ($p < .05$).	BES total – Boys ($M = 70.28$; $SD = 10.27$); Girls ($M = 78.07$; $SD = 7.76$); ($F(1, 444) = 83.19$, $p < .01$, $\eta^2 = .16$) Affective Empathy ($M = 36.22$; $SD = 6.89$); Girls ($M = 41.90$; $SD = 5.71$); ($F(1, 444) = 35.72$, $p < .01$, $\eta^2 = .07$) Cognitive Empathy ($M = 34.07$; $SD = 5.22$); Girls ($M = 36.17$; $SD = 3.94$); ($F(1, 444) = 172.47$, $p < .01$, $\eta^2 = .28$)	**Social Desirability** Males (Cognitive $r = .09$; Affective $r = -.02$; Total $r = .03$); Females (Cognitive $r = .07$; Affective $r = .04$; Total $r = .06$) – all n.s.

(*Continued*)

Table 2.2 (Continued)

Study; Country; Sample	***Cognitive vs Affective Empathy***	***Reliability*** *Internal Consistency and Test-retest*	***Validity*** *Known-groups Validity with Gender Differences*	***Convergent and Discriminant Validity*** *Correlations with Personality, Social Desirability and Antisocial Measures*
Albiero et al. (2009); Italy; Youths	General ($r = .50$; $p < .05$); Boys ($r = .35, p < .01$); Girls ($r = .38$, $p < .01$).	**Internal consistency** Cronbach's $\alpha = .87$ (Affective Empathy $\alpha = .74$, Cognitive Empathy $\alpha = .86$)	BES total score – Male ($M = 3.24$; $SD = .45$); Female ($M = 3.89$; $SD = .37$); F (1, 653) = 446.95*, $\eta^2 = .406$; Affective Empathy – Male ($M = 2.92$; $SD = .57$): Female ($M = 3.81$; $SD = .49$); F (1, 653)= 105.01; $\eta^2 = .139$; BES Cognitive Empathy (CE): Male ($M = 3.64$; $SD = .49$); Female ($M = 3.99$; $SD = .38$); F (1, 653) = 406.57*; $\eta^2 = .384$	
Čavojová et al. (2012); Slovakia; Youths	Total ($r = .37$; $p < .05$); Males ($r = .21$; $p < .01$); Females ($r = .38$, $p < .01$)	**Internal Consistency** Cronbach´s α (Affective Empathy $\alpha = .85$, Cognitive Empathy $\alpha = .79$)	BES Total score – Males ($M = 64.15$; $SD = 8.41$); Females ($M = 73.18$; $SD = 8.70$); ($t = -10.862$; $p < .01$, $d = 1.05$); Cognitive Empathy – Males ($M = 33.53$; $SD = 4.95$); Females ($M = 36.08$; $SD = 4.41$); ($t = -5.584$, $p < .01$; $d = .54$); Affective Empathy – Males ($M = 30.62$; $SD = 5.85$); Females ($M = 37.10$; $SD = 6.02$); ($t = -11.247$; $p < .01$; $d = 1.09$)	
Geng et al. (2012); China; Youths	Total ($r = .32$; $p < .05$); Males ($r = .32$; $p < .01$); Females ($r = .28$, $p < .01$)	**Internal Consistency** Cronbach's $\alpha = .77$ (Affective Empathy $\alpha = .73$, Cognitive Empathy $\alpha = .72$); **Test-retest Reliability** 4 Weeks	Data by Gender and Age Group – Females with Significantly Higher Levels for BES Total Score (F (1, 1518) = 58.87, $p < .01$, $f = .20$); Affective (F (1, 1518) = 55.15, $p < .01, f = .19$) and Cognitive empathy (F (1, 1518) = 22.75, $p < .01, f = .12$).	**Antisocial Outcomes** Conduct Problems Subscale (BES Total Scale $r = -16$, n.s.; cognitive $r = -.12$, n.s.; affective $r = -.16$, n.s.)

		Interval – BES Total ($r = .70$, $p < .05$); BES Affective ($r = .71$, $p < .05$) Cognitive ($r = .60$, $p < .05$).		
Carré et al. (2013); France; Adults	–	**Internal Consistency** Cronbach's α (Affective $\alpha = .84$; Cognitive $\alpha = .71$); **Test-retest Reliability** 7 Weeks Interval Affective Empathy ($r = .80$; $p < .01$); Cognitive Empathy ($r = .61$, $p < .01$)		
Sánchez-Pérez et al. (2014); Spain; Children	Total ($r = .32$; $p < .05$)	**Internal consistency** Cronbach's α (Affective $\alpha = .66$; Cognitive $\alpha = .70$)	Females with Significantly Higher Levels for Affective Empathy Males ($M = 2.98$; $SD = .72$) Females ($M = 3.23$; $SD = .64$); $F(1,287) = 9.52$, $p = .002$, $\eta 2 = .032$), But Not for Cognitive Empathy Males ($M = 3.89$; $SD = .60$); Females ($M = 3.89$; $SD = .65$).	**Social Skills** (Cognitive Empathy $r = .16$, $p < .05$; Affective Empathy $r = .16$; $p < .05$) **Antisocial Outcomes** Aggression (Cognitive Empathy $r = -.05$, n.s.; Affective Empathy $r = -.14$; $p < .05$)
Pechorro et al. (2015); Portugal; Youth Male Offenders	Males ($r = .49$, $p < .01$)	**Internal Consistency** Cronbach's $\alpha = .91$ (Affective $\alpha = .87$; Cognitive $\alpha = .90$)	–	**Antisocial Outcomes** Antisocial Process Screening Device – Self-report (BES Total $r = -.13$; $p < .05$; Affective $r = .-17$; $p < .01$; Cognitive $r = -.02$, n.s.); ICU = Inventory of Callous-Unemotional Traits – Total (BES Total $r = -.41$; $p < .01$; Affective $r = .-43$; $p < .01$; Cognitive $r = -.28$; $p < .01$); Reactive-Proactive Aggression Questionnaire – Total (BES Total $r = .08$, n.s.; Affective $r = .00$, n.s.;

(*Continued*)

Table 2.2 (Continued)

Study; Country; Sample	***Cognitive vs Affective Empathy***	***Reliability*** *Internal Consistency and Test-retest*	***Validity*** *Known-groups Validity with Gender Differences*	***Convergent and Discriminant Validity*** *Correlations with Personality, Social Desirability and Antisocial Measures*
				Cognitive $r = .12$, n.s.); DSM-5 Conduct Disorder Symptoms (BES Total $r = .08$, n.s.; Affective $r = -.17$; $p < .05$; Cognitive $r = .05$, n.s.)
Bensalah et al. (2016); France; Children	–	**Internal Consistency** Not Tested for the 2-Factor Model; **Test-retest Reliability** Not Tested for the 2-Factor Model; Acceptable Values for the 3-Factor Model	Not tested for the 2-factor model	**Personality** – Not Tested for the 2-Factor Model; **Social Desirability** – Not Tested for the 2-Factor Model – Very Low Significant Correlations for the 3-Factor Model **Antisocial Outcomes** – Not Tested for the 2-actor Model
Villadangos et al. (2016); Spain; Youths	Total ($r = .51$; $p < .05$)	**Internal Consistency** Cronbach's α (Affective $\alpha = .92$; Cognitive $\alpha = .96$)	Females with significantly higher levels for Affective $F(1,751) = 44.12$, $p < .01$, $\eta2 = .125$ and cognitive empathy $F(1,751) = 14.16$, $p < .01$, $\eta2 = .044$ than males	**Personality Correlations** Agreeableness (Cognitive $r = .34$, $p < .01$; Affective $r = .36$, $p < .05$); Psychoticism (Cognitive $r = -.16$, $p < .01$; Affective $r = -.21$, $p < .05$); **Antisocial Outcomes** Narcissism leadership (Cognitive $r = -.04$, n.s.; Affective $r = -.26$, $p < .01$); Narcissism exhibitionism (Cognitive $r = -.01$, n.s.; Affective $r = -.01$, n.s.)

Anastácio et al. (2016); Portugal; Youths	Total ($r = .628$, $p < .001$)	**Internal Consistency** Cronbach's α (Affective $\alpha = .80$; Cognitive $\alpha = .85$)	Females scored higher than males on affective empathy (latent mean – $f = .91$, $p < .01$) and on cognitive empathy (latent mean for females = .52, $p < .01$).	**Social Skills** Importance of cooperation (Affective empathy $r = .35$, $p < .05$; Cognitive empathy $r = .34$, $p < .05$) **Antisocial Outcomes** Peer conflict Scale – Over proactive aggression (Cognitive $r = -.30$, $p < .01$; Affective $r = -.33$, $p < .01$); Relational proactive aggression (Cognitive $r = -.36$, $p < .01$.; Affective $r = -.34$, $p < .01$); Relational proactive aggression ($r = -.14$, $p < .01$.; Affective $r = -.20$, $p < .01$); Relational reactive aggression ($r = -.32$, $p < .01$.; Affective $r = -.25$, $p < .01$)
Heynen et al. (2016); Germany; Youth offenders	Males ($r = .53$, $p < .01$)	**Internal Consistency** Cronbach's α (Affective Empathy $\alpha = .71$, Cognitive Empathy $\alpha = .78$)	–	**Antisocial Outcomes** Inventory of Callous-Unemotional Traits – Total (Affective $r = .05$, n.s.; Cognitive $r = .26$, $p < .05$)
You et al. (2018); South Korea; Youths	Total ($r = .56$, $p < .05$)	**Internal Consistency** Cronbach's $\alpha = 85$ (Affective $\alpha = .78$; Cognitive $\alpha = .83$)	Females scored higher than males on affective empathy ($d = .38$, $p < .05$) and on cognitive empathy ($d = .35$, $p < .05$).	**Antisocial Outcomes** Significant correlations with bullying measures (values not reported)
Pechorro et al. (2017); Portugal; Female Youths (Offenders and non-offenders)	Forensic Sample ($r = .16$; n.s.); School Sample ($r = .36$, $p < .01$)	**Internal Consistency** Forensic sample Cronbach's α = 82 (Affective α = .81; Cognitive α = .86) School Sample Cronbach´s α = .90 (Affective α = .85; Cognitive α = .93)		**Social Desirability** (Forensic: Total $r = .13$, Cognitive $r = .03$; Affective $r = .15$); (Forensic: Total $r = .03$; Cognitive $r = .02$; Affective $r = .06$) – All non-significant **Antisocial Outcomes** Youth Psychopathy Inventory – Total (Forensic – Total $r = -.06$, n.s.; Affective empathy $r = -.17$, n.s.;

(Continued)

Table 2.2 (Continued)

Study; Country; Sample	***Cognitive vs Affective Empathy***	***Reliability*** *Internal Consistency and Test-retest*	***Validity*** *Known-groups Validity with Gender Differences*	***Convergent and Discriminant Validity*** *Correlations with Personality, Social Desirability and Antisocial Measures*
				cognitive $r = .27, p < .01$); (School – Total $r = -.20, p < .01$; Affective $r = -.23, p < .01$; Cognitive $r = -.08$; n.s.); ICU = Inventory of Callous-Unemotional Traits (Forensic – Total $r = -.02$, n.s.; Affective Empathy $r = .03$, n.s.; Cognitive $r = .01$, n.s.); (School – Total $r = -.41, p < .01$; Affective $r = -.32, p < .01$; Cognitive $r = -.35$; $p < .01$); RPQ = Reactive-Proactive Aggression Questionnaire – Total (Forensic – Total $r = .21, p < .05$.; Affective Empathy $r = .15$, n.s.; Cognitive $r = .20, p < .05$); (School – Total $r = .09$, n.s.; Affective $r = -.08$, n.s.; Cognitive $r = -.08$; n.s.); Conduct Disorder symptoms Score (Forensic – Total $r = .30, p < .01$.; Affective Empathy $r = .14$, n.s.; Cognitive $r = .32, p < .01$); (School – Total $r = .04$, n.s.; Affective $r = .02$, n.s.; Cognitive $r = .04$; n.s.)

Zych et al. (2018); Poland; Children and adolescents	Boys ($r = .54$, $p < .01$); Girls ($r = .54$, $p < .01$).	**Internal Consistency** Primary school Sample – Cronbach's $\alpha = 85$ (Affective $\alpha = .75$; Cognitive $\alpha = .84$); Middle School Sample Cronbach's $\alpha = 84$ (Affective $\alpha = .76$; Cognitive $\alpha = .77$)	Primary Education – Cognitive Scale – Males ($M = 22.25$; $SD = 5.41$); Females ($M = 23.23$; $SD = 4.77$); ($t = 2.17$, $p < .05$); Affective Empathy Scale – Males ($M = 17.28$; $SD = 5.11$); Females ($M = 20.52$; $SD = 4.97$); ($t = 7.22$, $p < .01$); BES Total – Males ($M = 39.51$; $SD = 9.35$); Females ($M = 43.73$; $SD = 8.72$); ($t = 5.14$; $p < .01$); Secondary Education – Cognitive Scale – Males ($M = 20.35$; $SD = 5.04$); Females ($M = 23.20$; $SD = 3.83$); ($t = 6.75$, $p < .01$); Affective Empathy Scale – Males ($M = 16.07$; $SD = 5.19$); Females ($M = 20.13$; $SD = 4.57$); ($t = 8.62$, $p < .01$); BES Total – Males ($M = 36.65$; $SD = 8.85$); Females ($M = 43.51$; $SD = 7.15$); ($t = 8.76$; $p < .01$).	**Social Skills** (e.g. Social and Emotional Competencies – Total Females (Affective Empathy $r = .04$, n.s.; Cognitive Empathy $r = .31$, $p < .05$) Males (Affective Empathy $r = .24$, n.s.; Cognitive Empathy $r = .54$, $p < .05$).

Empathy and antisocial outcomes

Over the last 30 years, meta-analyses have highlighted the importance of understanding empathy in order to comprehend antisocial behaviour. For instance, empathy has been found to be negatively related to several indicators of antisocial behaviour, namely offending (Jolliffe & Farrington, 2004; van Langen et al., 2014), externalising behaviour (Miller & Eisenberg, 1988), sexual offending severity (Babchishin, Hanson, & VanZuylen, 2015) and bullying (Zych, Ttofi, & Farrington, 2019). At the same time, research shows that empathy is positively related to prosocial behaviour (Eisenberg & Miller, 1987; Fengqin & Zhaohui, 2016) and can be targeted through training programmes (van Berkhout & Malouff, 2016). Nonetheless, the relationship between empathy and antisocial behaviour is far from being fully understood. The meta-analysis by Vachon, Lynam, and Johnson (2014) reported a lower correlation between affective empathy and aggression ($d = .19$, $p < .05$) than between cognitive empathy and aggression ($d = .43$, $p < .05$). Similarly, the meta-analyses conducted by Jolliffe and Farrington (2004) and van Langen and colleagues (2014) suggested a much stronger correlation between cognitive empathy and offending when compared with affective empathy, $d =-0.48$ (cognitive empathy) *versus* $d = -11$ (affective empathy) and $d = -.43$ (cognitive empathy) *versus* $d =-.19$ (affective empathy), respectively.

Both Vachon et al. (2014) and Jolliffe and Farrington (2004) suggested that measurement problems, such as reliability and construct validity, might have explained these findings. In fact, a recent study conducted by van Langen and colleagues (2014) found that the type of measure used to evaluate empathy partially mediates the relation between empathy and offending. Therefore, many former empathy measures suffer from serious limitations, including poor psychometric properties, a lack of studies confirming their validity and reliability, and their ability and being able to evaluate empathy only partially (e.g. the Hogan Empathy Scale only evaluates cognitive empathy); see Neumann et al. (2014) for a full review of the limitations of current measures to evaluate empathy.

These limitations jeopardise not only existing empirical research on empathy and offending, but also meta-analytic findings that are usually used to design effective interventions for offender populations. High-quality research on the link between empathy and antisocial behaviour relies on accurate measures, and that is one of the biggest contributions made by the BES. Since 2006, the psychometric properties of the BES have been tested in forensic samples from Portugal (Pechorro et al., 2015, 2017), the Netherlands (van Langen et al., 2018), Germany (Heynen et al., 2016) and El Salvador (Salas-Wright et al., 2012). Despite many positive indicators of the BES's validity and reliability for these populations, further research is recommended, particularly regarding the Scale's measurement invariance between forensic and non-forensic samples to ensure its validity among forensic populations.

Final considerations

Empathy is a core concept for understanding human behaviour. Meta-analytic findings suggest that low empathy is related to the development of many antisocial behaviours, from bullying to sexual offending. Nonetheless, conflicting findings on empathy (e.g. Vachon et al., 2014), and the lack of instruments to appropriately evaluate it, raise doubts about the true nature and extent of this relationship.

The BES was developed to overcome the limitations identified in previous scales. Our review suggests that the BES has good psychometric properties for general populations of adolescents and young adults. Nonetheless, future studies to confirm its test-retest reliability among youth samples are needed, as is further research on the psychometric properties of BES across forensic populations, while the construct validity of BES across other age ranges remains unconfirmed. Finally, we believe that the BES is, generally, a valid and reliable alternative for advancing knowledge about empathy in youth populations.

References

Albeiro, P., Matricardi, G., Speltri, D., & Toso, D. (2009). The assessment of empathy in adolescence: A contribution to the Italian validation of "the basic empathy scale". *Journal of Adolescence*, *32*, 393–408.

Allison, C., Baron-Cohen, S., Wheelwright, S. J., Stone, M. H., & Muncer, S. J. (2011). Psychometric analysis of the empathy quotient (EQ). *Personality and Individual Differences*, *51*, 829–835.

Anastácio, S., Vagos, P., Nobre-Lima, L., Rijo, D., & Jolliffe, D. (2016). The Portuguese version of the basic empathy scale (BES): Dimensionality and measurement invariance in a community adolescent sample. *European Journal of Developmental Psychology*, *13*(5), 614–623.

Babchishin, K. M., Hanson, R. K., & VanZuylen, H. (2015). Online child pornography offenders are different: A meta-analysis of the characteristics of online and offline sex offenders against children. *Archives of Sexual Behavior*, *44*, 45–66.

Bensalah, L., Caillies, S., & Anduze, M. (2016). Links among cognitive empathy, theory of mind, and affective perspective taking by young children. *The Journal of Genetic Psychology*, *177*(1), 17–31.

Bensalah, L., Stefaniak, N., Carre, A., & Besche-Richard, C. (2016). The basic empathy scale adapted to French middle childhood: Structure and development of empathy. *Behavior Research Methods*, *48*(4), 1410–1420.

Carré, A., Stefaniak, N., D'Ambrosio, F., Bensalah, L., & Besche-Richard, C. (2013). The basic empathy scale in adults (BES-A): Factor structure of a revised form. *Psychological Assessment*, *25*, 679–691.

Čavojová, V., Sirota, M., & Belovičová, Z. (2012). Slovak validation of the Basic Empathy Scale in pre-adolescents. *Studia Psychologica*, *54*(3), 195–208.

Christov-Moore, L., Simpson, E. A., Coudé, G., Grigaityte, K., Iacoboni, M., & Ferrari, P. F. (2014). Empathy: Gender effects in brain and behavior. *Neuroscience & Biobehavioral Reviews*, *46*, 604–627.

Cuff, B. M. P., Brown, S. J., Taylor, L., & Howat, D. J. (2014). Empathy: A review of the concept. *Emotion Review*, *7*, 1–10.

D'Ambrosio, F., Olivier, M., Didon, D., & Besche, C. (2009). The basic empathy scale: A French validation of a measure of empathy in youth. *Personality and Individual Differences, 46*, 160–165.

Davidson, M. (2014). Known-groups validity. In A. C. Michalos (Ed.), *Encyclopedia of quality of life and well-being research* (pp. 3481–3482). Dordrecht: Springer Netherlands.

Delgado, A. O., Suárez, L. A., Vega, M. A. P., Bermúdez, M. R., Jiménez, A. P., Gómez, Á. H., & Flores, M. C. R. (2011). *Instrumentos para la evaluación de la salud mental y el desarrollo positivo adolescente y los activos que lo promueven*. Retrieved from www.formajoven.org/AdminFJ/doc_recursos/201241812465364.pdf

Durlak, J. A., & Wells, A. M. (1997). Primary prevention mental health programs for children and adolescents: A meta-analytic review. *American Journal of Community Psychology, 25*, 115–152.

Eisenberg, N., & Miller, P. (1987). The relation of empathy to prosocial and related behaviors. *Psychological Bulletin, 101*, 91–119.

Fan, Y., Duncan, N. W., de Greck, M., & Northoff, G. (2011). Is there a core neural network in empathy? An fMRI based quantitative meta-analysis. *Neuroscience & Biobehavioral Reviews, 35*, 903–911.

Fengqin, D., & Zhaohui, L. (2016). Association between empathy and prosocial behavior: A systematic review and meta-analysis. *Advances in Psychological Science, 24*(8), 1159–1174.

Froman, R. D., & Peloquin, S. M. (2001). Rethinking the use of the Hogan empathy scale: A critical psychometric analysis. *American Journal of Occupational Therapy, 55*, 566–572.

Geng, Y., Xia, D., & Qin, B. (2012). The basic empathy scale: A Chinese validation of a measure of empathy in adolescents. *Child Psychiatry and Human Development, 43*, 499–510.

Heynen, E. E., van der Helm, G. P., Stams, G. M., & Korebrits, A. M. (2016). Measuring empathy in a German youth prison: A validation of the German version of the basic empathy scale (BES) in a sample of incarcerated juvenile offenders. *Journal of Forensic Psychology Practice, 16*(5), 336–346.

Inzunza, M. (2015). Empathy from a police work perspective. *Journal of Scandinavian Studies in Criminology and Crime Prevention, 16*(1), 60–75.

Jolliffe, D., & Farrington, D. P. (2004). Empathy and offending: A systematic review and meta-analysis. *Aggression and Violent Behaviour, 9*, 441–476.

Jolliffe, D., & Farrington, D. P. (2006). Development and validation of the basic empathy scale. *Journal of Adolescence, 29*, 589–611.

Merino-Soto, C., & Grimaldo-Muchotrigo, M. (2015). Validación estructural de la Escala Básica de Empatía (Basic Empathy Scale) modificada en adolescentes: un estudio preliminar. [Structural Validation of the Basic Empathy Scale Modified for Adolescents: A Preliminary Study]. *Revista Colombiana de Psicología, 24*(2), 261–270.

Miller, P. A., & Eisenberg, N. (1988). The relation of empathy to aggressive and externalizing/antisocial behavior. *Psychological Bulletin, 103*(3), 324–344.

Murphy, B. A. (in press). The griffith empathy measure does not validly distinguish between cognitive and affective empathy in children. *Australian Psychologist.*

Murphy, K. R., & Davidshofer, C. O. (2005). *Psychological testing: Principles and applications* (5th ed.). Englewood Cliffs, NJ: Prentice Hall.

Neumann, D. L., Chan, R. C. K., Boyle, G. J., Wang, Y., & Westbury, H. R. (2014). Self-report, behavioral, and neuroscientific approaches to measuring empathy: A multidisciplinary perspective. In G. J. Boyle & D. H. Saklofske (Eds.), *Measures of personality and social psychological constructs*. Chennai: Elsevier.

Pechorro, P., Kahn, R., Gonçalves, R. A., & Ray, J. (2017). Psychometric properties of basic empathy scale among female juvenile delinquents and school youths. *International Journal of Law and Psychiatry*, *55*, 29–36.

Pechorro, P., Ray, J. V., Salas-Wright, C. P., Maroco, J., & Abrunhosa-Gonçalves, R. (2015). Adaptation of the basic empathy scale among a Portuguese sample of incarcerated juvenile offenders. *Psychology, Crime & Law*, *21*(7), 699–714.

Salas-Wright, C., Olate, R., & Vaughn, M. (2012). Assessing empathy in Salvadoran high-risk and gang-involved adolescents and young adults: A Spanish validation of the Basic Empathy Scale. *International Journal of Offender Therapy and Comparative Criminology*, *57*, 1393–1416.

Sánchez-Pérez, N., Fuentes, L. J., Jolliffe, D., & González-Salinas, C. (2014). Assessing children's empathy through a Spanish adaptation of the basic empathy scale: Parent's and child's report forms. *Frontiers in Psychology*, *5*, 1438.

Vachon, D. D., Lynam, D. R., & Johnson, J. A. (2014). The (non)relation between empathy and aggression: Surprising results from a meta-analysis. *Psychological Bulletin*, *140*(3), 751–773.

van Berkhout, T., & Malouff, J. M. (2016). The efficacy of empathy training: A meta-analysis of randomized controlled trials. *Journal of Counseling Psychology*, *63*(1), 32–41.

van Langen, M. A. M., Wissink, I. B., Stams, G. J. J. M., & van Vugt, E. S. (2018). *Factor structure and measurement invariance of the basic empathy scale across Dutch juvenile offenders and non-offenders*. Manuscript submitted for publication.

van Langen, M. A. M., Wissink, I. B., van Vugt, E. S., van der Stouwe, T., & Stams, G. J. J. M. (2014). The relation between empathy and offending: A meta-analysis. *Aggression and Violent Behavior*, *19*, 179–189.

Villadangos, M., Errasti, J., Amigo, I., Jolliffe, D., & Garcia-Cueto, E. (2016). Characteristics of empathy in young people measured by the Spanish validation of the basic empathy scale. *Psicothema*, *28*(3), 323–329.

You, S., Lee, J., & Lee, Y. (2018). Validation of basic empathy scale: Exploring a Korean version. *Current Psychology*, *37*, 726–730.

Zych, I., Farrington, D. P., Nasaescu, E., Jolliffe, D., & Twardowska-Staszek, E. (2018). *Psychometric properties of the basic empathy scale in Polish children and adolescents*. Submitted for publication.

Zych, I., Ttofi, M. M., & Farrington, D. P. (2019). Empathy and callous – unemotional traits in different bullying roles: A systematic review and meta-analysis. *Trauma, Violence, & Abuse*, *20*(1), 3–21.

3 Parents' empathy and child attachment security

A brief review

Evelyn Heynen, Ellin Simon, Peer van der Helm, Geert Jan Stams, and Mark Assink

Parents' empathy and child attachment security: a brief review

Empathy is the ability to understand and share another's emotional state (Cohen & Strayer, 1996), and consists of two dimensions: *affective empathy* is an automatic emotional response to another's mental state and concerns the experience of similar emotions as others. *Cognitive empathy* is the understanding of another's mental state through perspective taking (de Wied et al., 2007; Smith 2006). The capacity for empathy is fundamental to the development and maintenance of social relationships (Anderson & Keltner, 2002; Preston & De Waal, 2002; Twemlow, Fonagy, & Sacco, 2005).

Evolutionary theory assumes that empathy involves the child's attachment system (Cassidy, Jones, & Shaver, 2013; Pietromonaco & Barrett, 2000), which regulates the child's proximity to the parent or other caregivers (Ainsworth 1979; Ainsworth & Bell, 1970; Bowlby, 1969, 1973, 1980). Empathy enables caregivers to recognise and respond to the biological needs of their child for safety and support, and to act altruistically in times of threat to ensure their offspring's survival (Eibl-Eibesfeldt, 1982; MacLean, 1985; Stern, Borelli, & Smiley, 2015). Attachment theory proposes that patterns of caregiving behaviour shape a child's "internal working model" of the self and others, and finally shape the child's socio-emotional functioning (Ainsworth, Blehar, Waters, & Wall, 1978; Bowlby, 1980).

Bowlby (1969) assumed that there were four distinguishing characteristics of child-mother attachment relationships: *proximity maintenance,* which is the desire to be near the people we are attached to; *safe haven behaviour*, which can be defined as returning to the attachment figure for comfort and safety in the face of fear or threat; *secure base behaviour*, wherein the attachment figure acts as a base of security from which the child can explore the environment; and *separation distress*, which is anxiety that occurs in the absence of the attachment figure.

Ainsworth (1979) further expanded Bowlby's work through the development of the "strange situation" observational study, which gave attachment theory an empirical basis (Bretherton, 1992). Ainsworth discovered three styles of attachment: *secure attachment, insecure-avoidant attachment, and insecure-resistant* attachment (Ainsworth et al., 1978). Later, a fourth style was discovered, namely, *insecure-disorganised attachment* (Main & Solomon, 1986, 1990). Research has shown that securely attached children develop a positive balance between searching contact with their caregiver and exploration of the environment (Ainsworth et al., 1978). They become visibly upset when their caregivers leave and are happy when they return, seeking comfort and trust. Parents of securely attached children tend to play more with their children, react more quickly to children's attachment-related needs, and are generally more responsive compared to parents of insecurely attached children.

Studies have shown that securely attached children are more empathic than insecurely attached children during later stages of childhood (Fraley, 2002; Joireman, Needham, & Cummings, 2002; Lucassen et al., 2011; Panfile & Laible, 2012). While forming a secure attachment with caregivers is normal and expected, as Hazan and Shaver (1987) have noted, it does not always happen. Research indicates that a large number of factors may hamper the development of secure attachment, particularly unresponsiveness and inconsistent behaviour towards infant's attachment-related needs during the first year of life. Insecurely attached children cry more, show higher levels of anxious behaviour and tend to avoid contact, whereas secure attachment results in high self-esteem, increased ability to build intimate relationships, social support, and the ability to share feelings with other people (Groh, Fearon, van IJzendoorn, Bakermans-Kranenburg, & Roisman, 2017).

A vast amount of research has been conducted on parental antecedents of child attachment security, such as parenting style (e.g. Nair & Murray, 2005) and maternal anxiety (e.g. Stevenson-Hinde, Chicot, Shouldice, & Hinde, 2013). For many years, research on the antecedents of secure attachment primarily focused on parental sensitivity, which is *the ability to perceive the meaning behind an infant's behavioural signals and to respond to them promptly and appropriately* (Braungart-Reiker, Garwood, Powers, & Wang, 2001; Lamb, Easterbrooks, & Holden, 1980; de Wolff & van IJzendoorn, 1997). However, sensitivity could only explain a small percentage (25% of the variation) of differences in children's attachment security, leaving a gap in the transmission of attachment from the parent to the child (van IJzendoorn, 1995; van IJzendoorn & Wolff, 1997; Verhage et al., 2016). In recent years, studies have moved beyond parental sensitivity, trying to unravel different precursors of children's attachment security (Meins, 2013; Oppenheim & Koren-Karie, 2002; Slade, Grienenberger, Bernbach, Levy, & Locker, 2005). Researchers posit that two related, but distinct, parental capacities underlie sensitive caregiving behaviour: parental mentalisation and empathy.

Parental mentalisation is *the degree to which parents show frequent, coherent, or appropriate appreciations of their infant's internal states* (Zeegers, Colonnesi, Stams, & Meins, 2017) and is often simplistically understood as synonymous with the capacity of empathy towards others (Fonagy & Luyten, 2018). It defines parents' ability to represent the mind of their child, that is, whether a parent can appropriately interpret the child's behaviour in terms of mental states, such as thoughts, emotions, and intentions (Fonagy & Luyten, 2018; Zeegers et al., 2017). In their meta-analysis, Zeegers et al. (2017) found parental mentalisation to be an independent predictor of the child's attachment security, providing evidence for the assumption that parents' ability to consider their children's internal states was important for secure child attachment, possibly supported by empathy (Fonagy, 2006; Fonagy, Gergely, Jurist, & Target, 2002; Meins, 2013; Slade et al., 2005), while the combination of parental sensitivity and mentalisation explained more variance than each predictor separately. To conclude, parents' capacity to represent their children's mind and to reflect on their children's thoughts and emotions appears to be an independent factor in children's development of attachment (Zeegers et al., 2017).

This study is a brief narrative review and preliminary meta-analysis on the relation between parents' empathy and their children's attachment security. It is hypothesised that parental affective and cognitive empathy are positively associated with child attachment security.

Method

Selection of studies

A comprehensive search of literature published until 2018 was conducted to identify relevant articles on the relation between parental empathy and the child's attachment. Computer-based and manual search methods were used to locate studies for the current meta-analysis. The computerised databases were PsycINFO, MEDLINE, and ERIC. A comprehensive search of each computerised database included the following terms and combination of terms: ("mother") OR ("father") OR ("maternal") OR ("paternal") AND ("empathy") AND ("attachment"). In addition, meta-analyses and systematic reviews were manually searched. The search process yielded 320 potentially relevant published articles.

To be considered for inclusion, studies had to meet the following inclusion criteria: (1) studies had to examine the relation between parents' empathy and child-parent attachment relationships; (2) studies had to report the Pearson's r correlation coefficient on the association between parental empathy and child attachment, or sufficient statistical information to calculate this correlation coefficient. One published article (i.e. Borelli et al., 2016) did not report a Pearson's r correlation coefficient nor information that was needed to calculate Pearson's r, therefore, this study was not included. Last (3), studies had to be written in English and published in peer-reviewed journals. When the search procedure ended, we found five studies eligible for inclusion in the present review (Black & Leszczynsk, 2013; Oppenheim, Koren-Karie, & Sagi, 2001; Quinn, 1991; Stern et al., 2015; Wieczorek-Deering, Greene, Nugent, & Graham, 1991).

Study coding procedure

Studies were coded for year of publication, the research design (cross-sectional or longitudinal), and the type of assessment procedure for empathy and attachment (questionnaire, observation, composite, or interview). Several sample characteristics were also coded: size of sample, continent in which the participants lived (Europe, North-America, or Israel), gender and average age of parents, percentage of mothers, gender and average age of children, percentage of boys, and whether a study used a general or a clinical sample. Three articles reported more than one relevant association between parental empathy and child attachment, as different attachment styles were studied (i.e. secure attachment, dismissing/avoidant attachment, preoccupied attachment, and disorganised attachment) or different dimensions of empathy (i.e. basic empathy and parental empathy). All relevant associations were extracted from each included study.

Statistical analyses

Pearson's correlation coefficient was used as a measure of effect size. In order to estimate the overall mean association between parental empathy and child attachment (i.e. the overall mean effect size), all correlations were first Fisher's *z* transformed to approximate a normal sampling distribution (Lipsey & Wilson, 2001). Next, the overall mean effect was estimated in a three-level meta-analytic model. We used this three-level approach to meta-analysis, as multiple effect sizes were extracted from three of the included studies. In this approach, the dependency in effect sizes is modelled, which is important as independency in effect sizes is an important assumption in meta-analytic research (Assink & Wibbelink, 2016). The meta-analysis was performed in the statistical program R using the syntax as presented by Assink and Wibbelink (2016).

Results

Description of the studies

A brief description of the five studies included is provided later, and the characteristics of these are summarised in Table 3.1. Two of the included studies used an adapted version of the Basic Empathy Scale (BES; Jolliffe & Farrington, 2006), assessing both cognitive and affective empathy. For their study, Black and Leszczynsk (2013) adapted the original questions to shift the emphasis from friends (e.g. 'My friends' emotions don't affect me much') to others (e.g. 'Other people's emotions don't affect me much'). Stern et al. (2015) developed the Parent Empathy Measure (PEM) based on existing measures of empathy, such as the BES (Jolliffe & Farrington, 2006), but also integrated attachment-related constructs to create an index of empathy, specific to the parent-child relationship. This measure includes subscales of cognitive and affective empathy. The remaining three studies were conducted before the development of the BES in 2006, and used observational measures, such as facial expressions, to investigate empathy (Oppenheim et al., 2001; Quinn, 1991; Wieczorek-Deering et al., 1991).

Black and Leszczynsk (2013) examined the association between children's attachment and both parental and general (or trait) empathy of the parents in a

Table 3.1 Overview of the included studies

Reference	*Year*	*Gender parent*	M *parent*	% *mother*	*Gender child*	*M child*	*Country*	*Type Empathy*	*Empathy instrument*	*Type Attachment*	*Attachment instrument*	N	*#ES*	r
Black & Leszczynsk,	2013	Mixed	–	–	B/G	4.47	USA	E/PE	E que	SA	ATTque	120	2	.28/.19
Oppenheim et al.,	2001	M	33.8	100	B/G	4.5	Israel	E	EI	PA/DiA	ATTobs	98	2	.31/.23
Quinn,	1991	M	–	100	B/G	EC	W-Europe	E	E que	SA	ATTobs	118	1	.20
Stern et al.,	2015	Mixed	36.8	90	B/G	9.90	USA	E	E que/EI	SA/DA/PA	ATTI	54/48/21	3	.43/.55/.14
Wieczorek-Deering et al.	1991	M	46.0	100	B/G	EC	W-Europe	CE	Eque	SA	Attobs	98	1	.18

Note. M = mothers; F = Fathers; *M* parents = Mean age parents; B = Boys; G = Girls; *M* Child = Mean age child, EC = Early Childhood; Country = country in which participants lived; E = Empathy general, CE = cognitive empathy; AE = Affective Empathy, PA = Parental Empathy; Empathy instrument = type of empathy assessment; E que = empathy questionnaire; E obs = Empathy observational assessment, EI = empathy interview; EM = Empathy mixed method assessment; ATTque = attachment questionnaire; ATTobs = Attachment observational assessment, ATTI = Attachment interview; ATTM = Attachment mixed method assessment; SA = Secure Attachment, DA = Dismissing Attachment, PA = Preoccupied Attachment, DiA = Disorganised Attachment; *N* = number of participants in study; #ES = number of effect sizes coded from study; *r* = Pearson's *r* correlation coefficient

North American sample ($N = 120$, $M_{age\ children} = 4.47$). They used a cross-sectional design and all constructs were measured with a questionnaire (the Kinship Center Attachment Questionnaire, the BES, and the Parenting Empathy Questionnaire, respectively). Parental empathy as well as general empathy were significantly related to child attachment: $r = .19$, and $r = .28$, respectively. There were no significant results for cognitive or affective empathy separately.

Oppenheim et al. (2001) examined the association between mothers' empathic understanding of their 4.5-year-old children's internal experience (i.e. cognitive empathy) and infant attachment in an Israeli sample ($N = 98$ dyads, $M_{age\ parents} = 33.80$). Infant attachment was assessed between the ages of 6 and 12 months using the Strange Situation Test. At the age of 4.5 years, mothers and their child were assessed again and completed the story completion task, and mothers were administered the Empathic Understanding procedure. Empathic understanding was assessed by showing 98 mothers video segments of their children and themselves and interviewing them regarding their children's and their own thoughts and feelings. Interviews were rated and classified into one empathic (Balanced) and three Non-Empathic categories. Results showed a significant correlation between empathy and ambivalent attachment ($r = .31$) and disorganised attachment ($r = .23$).

Quinn (1991) studied the association between mothers' empathy and the attachment of their infants with Down syndrome in a North American sample ($N = 118$ dyads) in a cross-sectional design. Maternal empathy was assessed using a questionnaire (the Empathy Construct Rating Scale; Monica, 1981). Infant attachment was assessed by means of observations (Attachment-Separation-Individuation-Scale). Results showed a positive and significant correlation between mother's empathy and their children's attachment ($r = .20$).

Stern et al. (2015) examined the association between the empathy of parents and their child's attachment security in a North American sample ($N = 54$ dyads, $M_{age\ children} = 9.90$, $M_{age\ parents} = 36.80$) using a cross-sectional design. Both empathy and attachment were measured using a battery of questionnaires and interview measures, including the Child Attachment Interview (CAI) and the Parent Affective and Cognitive Empathy Scale (PACES; developed by Stern et al. (2015) themselves and based on the BES). Results showed correlations between higher levels of parental empathy and secure child attachment ($r = .14$), dismissing child attachment ($r = -.43$), and preoccupied child attachment ($r = -.55$), respectively. There were no significant results for the subscales of affective or cognitive empathy.

Wieczorek-Deering et al. (1991) examined the association between general empathy (i.e. for others) of mothers and infant attachment in a Western European sample ($N = 98$, $M_{age\ parents} = 46.00$) with a cross-sectional design. The Strange Situation Procedure was used to asses infant-parent attachment, and cognitive empathy was assessed with an adaptation of the Maximally Discriminative Facial Movement Coding System (Izard, 1979) and the Facial Actions Coding System (Ekman & Friesen, 1978). The correlation between cognitive empathy and infant attachment was found to be $r = .18$.

Association between parental empathy and child attachment security

The overall mean effect size was based on 9 effect sizes derived from 5 studies, including 238 parent-child dyads. Effect sizes ranged between $r = .14$ and $r = .55$. A significant medium correlation between empathy of the parent and child attachment security was found, $r = .27$ ($t = 6.288$, $p < .001$). The small number of studies and effect sizes did not allow for further reliable heterogeneity, moderator, or publication bias analyses.

Discussion

Child-parent attachment is considered to be one of the most important bonds in human life, while a secure internal working model of attachment is a major developmental milestone for children. This chapter builds on previous meta-analyses examining the relation between parental sensitivity and mentalising capacities on the one hand and child-parent attachment security on the other hand, exploring the role of parents in the development of child attachment from a life-course perspective (Verhage et al., 2016; Zeegers et al., 2017). The present brief review integrates the extant knowledge on the relation between parents' empathy and child attachment by means of a narrative review and preliminary meta-analysis.

Our systematic search yielded five published empirical studies, including nine effect sizes, on the relation between parents' empathy and child attachment. Results indicated a moderate significant positive association between parental empathy and child attachment security. This finding supports the theoretical expectation that parental empathy is positively associated with child-parent attachment security. In evolutionary theory, for example, forming and maintaining social bonds is crucial for human development, and empathy is thought to be crucial in this respect (MacLean, 1985; Preston & De Waal, 2002). Infants who seek and accept support from their parents are assumed to be securely attached and are more likely to have received sensitive and responsive caregiving, which in turn results in a variety of socio-emotional advantages (Cassidy & Shaver, 1999; Groh et al., 2017; Johnson, Dweck, & Chen, 2007). In contrast, insecurely attached children are at increased risk for psychopathology (e.g. Colonnesi et al., 2011; Hoeve et al., 2012; Madigan, Brumariu, Villani, Atkinson, & Lyons-Ruth, 2016).

In the present review, the effect size for the association between parental empathy and child attachment ($r = .27$) was comparable to the effect sizes for the associations between parental sensitivity and attachment ($r = .25$) and parental mentalisation and attachment ($r = .30$) that were found in the meta-analyses by Verhage et al. (2016) and Zeegers et al. (2017). Whereas parental sensitivity and mentalisation constitute behavioural and cognitive dimensions of parenting (Leerkes, Crockenberg, & Burrous, 2004; Zeegers et al., 2017), parental empathy may be considered to be an affective dimension of parenting, which is the capacity to understand and share the child's emotional state (Cohen & Strayer, 1996). This empathic capacity can facilitate sensitive caregiving and foster the development of supportive interpersonal relationships (Borelli et al., 2016). Research suggests that the child's experience of its parents' empathic behaviour partly shapes the internal working model of attachment, which is a cognitive-affective scheme that provides information about the self and significant others (Bretherton & Munholland, 1999; Johnson et al., 2007). Parents' empathic caregiving may also socialise children's own empathic tendencies, orienting them towards (rather than away from) emotional engagement with others (Stern et al., 2015).

It is plausible to suggest that parental empathy will not only be associated with parental sensitivity and mentalisation, but it might also explain unique variance in the quality of child-parent attachment relationships beyond parental sensitivity and mentalisation. This is because it introduces the affective dimension of parenting as an antecedent of child-parent attachment relationships, where until now most research has focused on behavioural and cognitive dimensions of parenting as an explanation for children's attachment to their parents. As such, parental empathy could be the missing link in research on the intergenerational transmission of attachment between parent and child, which so far has focused on parents' sensitivity (Verhage et al., 2016). Both parents' metacognitive awareness of the child's mind (Zeegers et al., 2017) and parental empathy for the child (Stern et al., 2015; the present review), may prove to be unique mediators of the relation between parents' attachment representations and their children's attachment. Future studies on the transmission of attachment from parent to child should examine this possibility.

Like the intergenerational transmission of attachment, the ability to empathise might also be intergenerational. Indeed, research has shown that child and parental empathy is positively associated (Soenens, Duriez, Vansteenkiste, & Goossens, 2007). Next to a number of precursors of affective empathy that are already shown in newborn babies (Sagi & Hoffman, 1976), empathy in children develops through the exposure to empathic and sensitive behaviour of their caregivers (Robinson & Little, 1994). Therefore, especially the quality of the relationship between the child and its primary caregivers, in particular parents, is assumed to play a major role in the development of empathy in children (Laible, 2007). Results of our review and meta-analysis show that parents' empathy might contribute to child-parent relationship quality in terms of attachment security. Although the importance of studies that link parent's empathy to child attachment is apparent, we only found five studies on this subject. All five studies showed a relation between parental empathy and child attachment Two of the studies used a measurement instrument that was based on the BES (Jolliffe & Farrington, 2006). Given the small number of studies on this subject and the encouraging results, it is clear that more studies on this subject are necessary in order to be able to draw firm conclusions. Given the evolutionary importance of (cognitive and affective) empathy and the attachment bond between parent and child, further research on this association is needed to unravel the unknown variation in the transmission of both empathy and attachment from parent to child (van IJzendoorn, 1997; Verhage et al., 2016).

We therefore suggest that future researchers should investigate the relation between parents' cognitive and affective empathy, their internal working models of attachment (i.e. attachment representations), and their child's attachment security, including both mothers and fathers. Furthermore, research should focus on the mental capacities of both parents and children in order to examine to what extent reflection on each other's empathic tendencies may moderate the relation between parental empathy, mentalisation, and sensitivity on the one hand and children's internal working models of attachment and empathy on the other hand.

Limitations

The findings of this study should be interpreted in the light of several limitations. This is the first brief review and preliminary meta-analysis that integrates studies on the relation between parental empathy and attachment, and the results provide leads for future research. Notably, it is not uncommon to conduct a meta-analysis on a small sample size if the scientific field is in need of knowledge integration in a particular subject area (see Rodenburg, Benjamin, De Roos, & Meijer, 2009). For instance, Letourneau et al. (2015), recently published a brief (narrative) review and meta-analysis of only seven trials examining the effects of interventions targeting maternal sensitivity and reflective function on secure child-mother attachment relationships, showing a positive mean overall effect. Nevertheless, the limited number of studies and effect sizes implies that this meta-analysis was underpowered to test within and between study heterogeneity of effect sizes, and subsequently conduct continuous and categorical moderator analyses with sufficient statistical power (Cafri, Kromrey, & Brannick, 2010). We therefore could not compare mean effect sizes in different subgroups in a reliable way (Rubio-Aparicio, Sánchez-Meca, López-López, Botella, & Marín-Martínez, 2017), which sets limits to possibilities for generalisation of our study findings. Moreover, the number of studies and effect sizes were insufficient to conduct reliable publication bias analyses.

In addition, all five studies were cross-sectional, which might inflate the association between parental empathy and child attachment to the extent that parental empathy is assessed as a state that might be affected by the child's attachment. All samples of the included studies were Western (i.e. three North-American samples, one Western-European, and one Israeli sample), which implies that the results of this meta-analysis cannot be generalised to non-Western populations. Further, the samples of the studies consisted of 90–100% mothers. This suggests that the results cannot be generalised to (Western) fathers. Notably, research by Bögels and Phares (2008) indicates that data concerning fathers' involvement in child-rearing is often missing, and such missing data must be regarded as "systematic".

Conclusion

This brief review showed a significant positive relation between parents' empathy and the child's attachment security. Being able to get a feeling of what your child feels might be a very strong driver to respond to his or her attachment needs.

Given the limited number of studies on the relationship between parental empathy and child attachment, we stress the need for more research in this area.

References

Ainsworth, M. S. (1979). Infant–mother attachment. *American Psychologist, 34*(10), 932.

Ainsworth, M. D., & Bell, S. M. (1970). Attachment, exploration, and separation: Illustrated by the behavior of 1-year-olds in a strange situation. *Child Development, 41*, 49–67. doi:10.2307/1127388

Ainsworth, M., Blehar, M. C., Waters, E., & Wall, S. (1978). *Patterns of attachment: A psychological study of the strange situation*. Oxford: Lawrence Erlbaum.

Anderson, C., & Keltner, D. (2002). The role of empathy in the formation and maintenance of social bonds. *Behavioral and Brain Sciences, 25*, 21–22. doi:10.1017/S0140525X02230010

Assink, M., & Wibbelink, C. J. (2016). Fitting three-level meta-analytic models in R: A step-by-step tutorial. *The Quantitative Methods for Psychology, 12*(3), 154–174.

Black, K. R., & Leszczynsk, J. P. (2013). Development of child attachment in relation to parental empathy and age. *Psi Chi Journal of Psychological Research, 18*, 67–73.

Bögels, S., & Phares, V. (2008). Fathers' role in the etiology, prevention and treatment of child anxiety: A review and new model. *Clinical Psychology Review, 28*, 539–558. doi:10.1016/j.cpr.2007.07.011

Borelli, J. L., Vazquez, L., Rasmussen, H. F., Teachanarong, L., & Smiley, P. (2016). Attachment and maternal sensitivity in middle childhood. *Journal of Social and Personal Relationships, 33*, 1031–1053. doi:10.1177/0265407515616280

Bowlby, J. (1969/1982). *Attachment and loss: Vol. 1. Attachment* (2nd ed.). New York: Basic Books.

Bowlby, J. (1973). *Attachment and loss: Vol. 2. Separation: Anxiety and anger*. New York: Basic Books.

Bowlby, J. (1980). *Attachment and loss: Vol. 3. Loss, sadness and depression*. New York: Basic Books.

Braungart-Reiker, J. M., Garwood, M. M., Powers, B. P., & Wang, X. (2001). Parental sensitivity, infant affect, and affect regulation: Predictors of later attachment. *Child Development, 72*, 252–270. doi:10.1111/1467-8624.00277

Bretherton, I., & Munholland, K. A. (1999). *Internal working models in attachment relationships: A construct revisited*. New York: Guilford.

Bretherton, I. (1992). The origins of attachment theory: John Bowlby and Mary Ainsworth. *Developmental Psychology, 28*(5), 759.

Cafri, G., Kromrey, J. D., & Brannick, M. T. (2010). A meta-meta-analysis: Empirical review of statistical power, type I error rates, effect sizes, and model selection of meta-analyses. *Psychology, Multivariate Behavioral Research, 45*, 239–270. doi:10.1080/00273171003680187

Cassidy, J., & Shaver, P. R. (Eds.). (1999). Handbook of attachment: Theory, research, and clinical applications. New York: The Guilford Press.

Cassidy, J., Jones, J. D., & Shaver, P. R. (2013). Contributions of attachment theory and research: A framework for future research, translation, and policy. *Development and Psychopathology, 25*(4pt2), 1415–1434.

Cohen, D., & Strayer, J. (1996). Empathy in conduct-disordered and comparison youth. *Developmental Psychology, 32*, 988–998. doi:10.1037/0012-1649.32.6.988

Colonnesi, C., Draijer, E. M., Stams, G. J. J. M., van der Bruggen, C. O., Bögels, S. M., & Noom, M. J. (2011). The relation between insecure attachment and child anxiety: A meta-analytic review. *Journal of Clinical Child & Adolescent Psychology, 40*. doi:10.1080/15374416.2011.581623

de Wied, M., Maas, C., van Goozen, S., Vermande, M., Engels, R., Meeus, W., . . . Goudena, P. (2007). Bryant's empathy index: A closer examination of its internal structure. *European Journal of Psychological Assessment, 23*, 99–104. doi:10.1027/1015-5759.23.2.99

de Wolff, M. S., & van IJzendoorn, M. H. (1997). Sensitivity and attachment: A meta-analysis on parental antecedents of infant attachment. *Child Development, 68*, 571–591. doi:10.1111/j.1467-8624.1997.tb04218.x

Eibl-Eibesfeldt, I. (1982). Warfare, man's indoctrinability and group selection. *Zeitschrift für Tierpsychologie, 60*(3), 177–198.

Ekman, P., & Friesen, W. (1978). *Facial action coding system: A technique for the measurement of facial movement*. Palo Alto: Consulting Psychologists.

Fonagy, P. (2006). *The mentalization-focused approach to social development*. In J. G. Allen & P. Fonagy (Eds.), The Handbook of Mentalization-based Treatment (p. 53–99). New York: John Wiley & Sons Inc.

Fonagy, P., Gergely, G., Jurist, E., & Target, M. (2002). *Affect regulation, mentalization and the development of the self*. New York: Other Press.

Fonagy, P., & Luyten, P. (2018). *Attachment, mentalization, and the self*. New York: Guilford.

Fraley, C. R. (2002). Attachment stability from infancy to adulthood: Meta-analysis and dynamic modeling of developmental mechanisms. *Personality and Social Psychology Review, 6*, 123–151. doi:10.1207/S15327957PSPR0602_03

Groh, A. M., Fearon, R. M. P., van IJzendoorn, M. H., Bakermans-Kranenburg, M. J., & Roisman, G. I. (2017). Attachment in the early life course: Meta-analytic evidence for its role in socioemotional development. *Child Development Perspectives, 11*. doi:10.1111/cdep.12213

Hazan, C., & Shaver, P. (1987). Romantic love conceptualized as an attachment process. *Journal of Personality and Social Psychology, 52*, 511–524.

Hoeve, M., Stams, G. J. J., van der Put, C. E., Dubas, J. S., van der Laan, P. H., & Gerris, J. R. (2012). A meta-analysis of attachment to parents and delinquency. *Journal of Abnormal Child Psychology, 40*, 771–785. doi:10.1007/s10802-011-9608-1

Izard, C. E. (1979). *MAX: The maximally discriminative facial movement coding system*. Newark: University of Delaware Instructional Resources Center.

Johnson, S. C., Dweck, C. S., & Chen, F. S. (2007). Evidence for infants' internal working models of attachment. *Psychological Science Cambridge, 18*(6), 501.

Joireman, J. A., Needham, T. L., & Cummings, A. L. (2002). Relationships between dimensions of attachment and empathy. *North American Journal of Psychology, 4*(1), 63–80.

Jolliffe, D., & Farrington, D. P. (2006). Development and validation of the Basic Empathy Scale. *Journal of Adolescence, 29*(4), 589–611.

Laible, D. (2007). Attachment with parents and peers in late adolescence: Links with emotional competence and social behavior. *Personality and Individual Differences, 43*, 1185–1197. doi:10.1016/j.paid.2007.03.010

Lamb, M. E., Easterbrooks, M. A., & Holden, G. W. (1980). Reinforcement and punishment among preschoolers: Characteristics, effects, and correlates. *Child development*, 1230–1236.

Leerkes, E. M., Crockenberg, S. C., & Burrous, C. E. (2004). Identifying components of maternal sensitivity to infant distress: The role of maternal emotional competencies. *Parenting: Science and Practice, 4*, 1–23. doi:10.1207/s15327922par0401_1

Letourneau, N., Tryphonopoulos, P., Giesbrecht, G., Dennis, C. L., Bhogal, S., & Watson, B. (2015). Narrative and meta-analytic review of interventions aiming to improve maternal – child attachment security. *Infant Mental Health Journal*, *36*(4), 366–387.

Lipsey, M. W., & Wilson, D. B. (2001). *Practical meta-analysis*. Thousand Oaks, CA: Sage.

Lucassen, N., Tharner, A., van Ijzendoorn, M. H., Bakermans-Kranenburg, M. J., Volling, B. L., Verhulst, F. C., . . . Tiemeier, H. (2011). The association between paternal sensitivity and infant – father attachment security: A meta-analysis of three decades of research. *Journal of Family Psychology*, *25*, 986–992. doi:10.1037/a0025855

MacLean, P. D. (1985). Brain evolution relating to family, play, and the separation call. *Archives of General Psychiatry*, *42*, 405–417. doi:10.1001/archpsyc.1985.01790270095011

Madigan, S., Brumariu, L. E., Villani, V., Atkinson, L., & Lyons-Ruth, K. (2016). Representational and questionnaire measures of attachment: A meta-analysis of relations to child internalizing and externalizing problems. *Psychological Bulletin*, *142*, 367. doi:10.1037/bul0000029

Main, M., & Solomon, J. (1986). Discovery of an insecure-disorganized/disoriented attachment pattern. In T. B. Brazelton & M. W. Yogman (Eds.), *Affective development in infancy* (pp. 95–124). Westport, CT: Ablex Publishing.

Main, M., & Solomon, J. (1990). Procedures for identifying infants as disorganized/disoriented during the Ainsworth strange situation. *Attachment in the Preschool Years: Theory, Research, and Intervention*, *1*, 121–160.

Meins, E. (2013). Sensitive attunement to infants' internal states: Operationalizing the construct of mind-mindedness. *Attachment & Human Development*, *15*, 524–544. doi:10.1080/14616734.2013.830388

Monica, E. L. L. (1981). Construct validity of an empathy instrument. *Research in Nursing & Health*, *4*, 389–400. doi:10.1002/nur.4770040406

Nair, H., & Murray, A. D. (2005). Predictors of attachment security in preschool children from intact and divorced families. *The Journal of Genetic Psychology*, *166*, 245–263. doi:10.3200/GNTP.166.3.245-263

Oppenheim, D., & Koren-Karie, N. (2002). Mothers' insightfulness regarding their children's internal worlds: The capacity underlying secure child – mother relationships. *Infant Mental Health Journal*, *23*, 593–605. doi:10.1002/imhj.10035

Oppenheim, D., Koren-Karie, N., & Sagi, A. (2001). Mothers' empathic understanding of their preschoolers' internal experience: Relations with early attachment. *International Journal of Behavioral Development*, *25*, 16–26. doi:10.1080/01650250042000096

Panfile, T. M., & Laible, D. J. (2012). Attachment security and child's empathy: The mediating role of emotion regulation. *Merrill-Palmer Quarterly (1982–)*, 1–21.

Pietromonaco, P. R., & Barrett, L. F. (2000). The internal working models concept: What do we really know about the self in relation to others? *Review of General Psychology*, *4*(2), 155–175.

Preston, S. D., & De Waal, F. (2002). Empathy: Its ultimate and proximate bases. *Behavioral and Brain Sciences*, *25*, 1–20. doi:10.1017/S0140525X02000018

Quinn, M. M. (1991). Attachment between mothers and their down syndrome infants. *Western Journal of Nursing Research*, *13*, 382–396. doi:10.1177/019394599101300308

Robinson, J. L., & Little, C. (1994). Emotional availability in mother-twin dyads: Effects on the organization of relationships. *Psychiatry*, *57*, 22–31.

Rodenburg, R., Benjamin, A., De Roos, C., Meijer, A. M., & Stams, G. J. J. M. (2009). Efficacy of EMDR in children: A meta-analysis. *Clinical Psychology Review*, *29*, 599–606. doi:10.1016/j.cpr.2009.06.008

Rubio-Aparicio, M., Sánchez-Meca, J., López-López, J. A., Botella, J., & Marín-Martínez, F. (2017). Analysis of categorical moderators in mixed-effects meta-analysis: Consequences of using pooled versus separate estimates of the residual between-studies variances. *British Journal of Mathematical and Statistical Psychology*, *70*(3), 439–456.

Sagi, A., & Hoffman, M. L. (1976). Empathic distress in the newborn. *Developmental Psychology*, *12*(2), 175.

Slade, A., Grienenberger, J., Bernbach, E., Levy, D., & Locker, A. (2005). Maternal functioning, attachment and the transmission gap: A preliminary study. *Attachment & Human Development*, *7*, 283–292. doi:10.1080/14616730500245880

Smith, A. (2006). Cognitive empathy and emotional empathy in human behavior and evolution. *The Psychological Record*, *56*, 3–21. Retrieved from http://opensiuc.lib.siu.edu/tpr/vol56/iss1/1

Soenens, B., Duriez, B., Vansteenkiste, M., & Goossens, L. (2007). The intergenerational transmission of empathy-related responding in adolescence: The role of maternal support. *Personality and Social Psychology Bulletin*, *33*(3), 299–311.

Stern, J. A., Borelli, J. L., & Smiley, P. A. (2015). Assessing parental empathy: A role for empathy in child attachment. *Attachment & Human Development*, *17*, 1–22. doi:10.1080/14616734.2014.969749

Stevenson-Hinde, J., Chicot, R., Shouldice, A., & Hinde, C. A. (2013). Maternal anxiety, maternal sensitivity, and attachment. *Attachment & Human Development*, *15*, 618–636. doi:10.1080/14616734.2013.830387

Twemlow, S. W., Fonagy, P., & Sacco, F. C. (2005). A developmental approach to mentalizing communities: I. A model for social change. *Bulletin of the Menninger Clinic*, *69*, 265–281. doi:10.1521/bumc.2005.69.4.265

van IJzendoorn, M. H. (1995). Adult attachment representations, parental responsiveness, and infant attachment: A meta-analysis on the predictive validity of the adult attachment interview. *Psychological Bulletin*, *117*, 1–17. doi:10.1037/0033-2909.117.3.387

van IJzendoorn, M. H., & Bakermans-Kranenburg, M. J. (1997). *Intergenerational transmission of attachment: A move to the contextual level*. Retrieved from https://openaccess.leidenuniv.nl/handle/1887/2323

van IJzendoorn, M. H., & Wolff, M. S. (1997). In search of the absent father – meta-analyses of infant-father attachment: A rejoinder to our discussants. *Child development*, *68*, 604–609. doi:10.2307/1132112

Verhage, M. L., Schuengel, C., Madigan, S., Fearon, P., Oosterman, M., Cassibba, R., . . . van IJzendoorn, M. H. (2016). Narrowing the transmission gap: A synthesis of three decades of research on intergenerational transmission of attachment. *Psychological Bulletin*, *142*, 337–366. doi:10.1037/bul0000038

Wieczorek-Deering, D. E., Greene, S. M., Nugent, J. K., & Graham, R. (1991). Classification of attachment and its determinants in urban Irish infants. *The Irish Journal of Psychology*, *12*, 216–234. doi:10.1080/03033910.1991.10557839

Zeegers, M. A. J., Colonnesi, C., Stams, G. J. J. M., & Meins, E. (2017). Mind matters: A meta-analysis on parental mentalization and sensitivity as predictors of infant-parent attachment. *Psychological Bulletin*, *143*(12), 1245–1272.

4 Parenting style and empathy in youth

A three-level meta-analysis

Evelyn Heynen, Peer van der Helm, Ellin Simon, Geert Jan Stams, and Mark Assink

Introduction

Empathy can be defined as 'the ability to share and understand another's emotional state and context' (Eisenberg & Strayer, 1987), and this has been put forward as one of the most important instigators of human civilisation (Pinker, 2011). It is a bi-dimensional construct, with an affective and a cognitive component (Jolliffe & Farrington, 2006). *Affective empathy* refers to the capacity to experience the emotions of another (Bryant, 1982), while *cognitive empathy* is the capacity to comprehend the emotions of another (Hogan, 1969) and to respond in an adequate manner to the situation the other is experiencing (Davis, 1983; Smith, 2006).

Several studies have been conducted on empathy and its important role in social understanding and social interaction (Schwenck et al., 2014). Higher levels of empathy have been shown to be related to prosocial behaviour (Cohen & Strayer, 1987; Dadds et al., 2009; Eisenberg, Eggum, & Giunta, 2010; Jolliffe & Farrington, 2006), whereas deficits in empathy have been shown to be related to increased aggression, low fear conditioning (Popma & Raine, 2006), low impulse control, selfishness (for an overview, see Hosser & Beckurts, 2005), and callous-unemotional (CU) traits (Hare, 2013; Munoz, Qualter, & Padgett, 2011; Raine, 2013; Skeem, Polaschek, Patrick, & Lilienfeld, 2011). A vast body of research has demonstrated that lack of cognitive empathy is also related to (re)offending (see the meta-analysis by van Langen, Wissink, van Vugt, van der Stouwe, & Stams, 2014).

The development of empathy begins at birth, since precursors of affective empathy, such as affect mirroring and emotional contagion, are already present in newborn babies (Sagi & Hoffman, 1976). In addition, empathy may start to develop in children through the exposure to empathic and sensitive behaviour of their caregivers (Robinson & Little, 1994).

Therefore, especially the quality of the relationship between the child and its primary caregivers, in particular parents, is assumed to play a major role in the development of empathy (Laible, 2007).

According to attachment theory, infants need to develop a relationship with at least one primary caregiver for their successful social and emotional development, and to learn how to regulate their feelings (Holmes, 1993). Secure attachment develops when children can rely on sensitive caregivers, who attend to their needs of proximity, emotional support, and protection (Atkinson et al., 2000; de Wolff & van IJzendoorn, 1997; van IJzendoorn & de Wolff, 1997). Attachment security has been shown to be related to more empathic behaviour of young aged children (Kestenbaum, Farber, & Sroufe, 1989; Panfile & Liable, 2012; van der Mark, van IJzendoorn, & Bakermans-Kranenburg, 2002), although empathy proved to be unrelated to prosocial behaviour in a study by van IJzendoorn, Bakermans-Kranenburg, Pannebakker, and Out (2010). Notably, a recent meta-analysis has shown that insecure attachment was positively related to psychopathy, which is a personality disorder characterised by lack of empathy (van der Zouwen, Hoeve, Hendriks, Asscher, & Stams, 2018).

A vast amount of research has been conducted on the parental antecedents of child attachment security, such as parenting style (e.g. Nair & Murray, 2005). The present study aims to integrate the available literature on the development of empathy in children and adolescents from the perspective of parenting, in particular, differences in parenting styles. It is supposed that parenting styles influence the development of empathy through the particular combination of support and control that parents provide (Baumrind, 1966, 1971). Baumrind described four different parenting styles, based on the two major parenting dimensions of support and control: *authoritative parenting* (high support and high control); *authoritarian parenting* (low support and high control), *permissive parenting* (high support and low control), and *uninvolved parenting* (low support and low control).

Authoritative parenting is characterised by warmth, reasonable demands, and high sensitivity and responsiveness to the child's needs. Authoritative parenting has been shown to be related to secure attachment of children (Doinita & Maria, 2015; Millings, Walsh, Hepper, & O'Brien, 2013). Although authoritative parents have high expectations of their children, they are also able to provide their children with the resources and support they need to succeed. Authoritative parents are open and responsible, and provide their children with love and warmth in addition to limits and fair discipline, resulting in a positive development of (cognitive) empathy and perspective taking towards behaviour of others (Farrant, Devine, Maybery, & Fletcher, 2011; Soenens, Duriez, Vansteenkiste, & Goossens, 2006).

Authoritative parents tend to use inductive discipline to teach their children prosocial behaviour (moral internalisation) and empathy by modelling prosocial behaviour, expressing compassion for others, pointing out similarities among people from different backgrounds, and discussing moral beliefs and values (Dlugokinski & Firestone, 1974; Hoffman, 1970b, 1982, 1983, 1984; Hoffman & Saltzstein, 1967; Zahn-Waxler, Radke-Yarrow, & King, 1979). Hoffman (1970a) claimed that the most effective type of parenting discipline is "induction", in which parents emphasise the perspective of others, point to the distress of possible victims, and learn perspective taking and showing empathic responses towards others (Bar-Tal, Raviv, & Leiser, 1980; Holmgren, Eisenberg & Fabes, 1998; Krevans & Gibbs, 1996; Oliner & Oliner, 1988).

The *authoritarian parenting* style is characterised by exceedingly high expectations, demands, and control in contrast to low levels of warmth, guidance, and responsiveness, which has shown to be negatively associated with secure attachment (Doinita & Maria, 2015; Millings et al., 2013). Parents with an authoritarian style have very high expectations of their children, but are unable to provide sufficient (positive) feedback and nurturance. Mistakes tend to be punished harshly. Yelling and corporal punishment are also commonly seen in the authoritarian style. Authoritarian parents take decisions for their children without explanation, resulting in uncertainty and dependence of their children (Nix et al., 1999), which negatively affects personal growth, and may finally result in anxiety, loneliness, unhappiness, and aggressive behaviour (Berk, 2006). Due to their lack of warmth and unresponsive behaviour, authoritarian parents do not foster perspective taking and empathy in their children (Cornell & Frick, 2007).

Permissive parenting is characterised by low demands and high responsiveness. Permissive parents tend to be loving, but do not provide adequate control. High permissive parenting has been shown to be associated with avoidant and anxious attachment (Doinita & Maria, 2015; Millings et al., 2013), which may hamper the development of empathy (Hazan & Shaver, 1987; van IJzendoorn, 1997). These parents do not expect mature behaviour from their children and often seem more like a friend than a parent. Therefore, they may lack the authority to socialise their children, for instance, by teaching empathic responding through the provision of inductive discipline (Hoffman, 2000). Because there are few rules, expectations, and demands, children raised by permissive parents tend to have low self-control (Baumrind, 1993, 1997; Lamborn, Mounts, Steinberg, & Dornbusch, 1991). Permissive parenting results in disobedience, defiant, and impulsive behaviour of the child (Berk, 2006) as well as lack of emotional self-regulation, which may further hamper the development of empathy (Schaffer, Clark, & Jeglic, 2009).

Finally, *uninvolved* or also *called neglectful parenting* is characterised by a lack of responsiveness to a child's needs. Uninvolved parents make few to no demands and are often indifferent, dismissive, or even completely uninvolved (Lamborn et al., 1991; Steinberg, Lamborn, Darling, Mounts, & Dornbusch, 1994). Neglect negatively affects emotional development and can result in anxious or avoidant attachment of the child (Doinita & Maria, 2015; Millings et al., 2013). Uninvolved parenting is characterised as the most dysfunctional parenting style and has shown most negative impacts on the development and behaviour of the child (Todorović & Matejević, 2014). Research has shown that neglectful parenting (Barnow, Lucht, & Freyberger, 2005), authoritarian or harsh and punitive parenting (Grogan-Kaylor, 2005), and permissive parenting (Beck & Shaw, 2005; Kimonis et al., 2006) are risk factors for the development of antisocial behaviour and may hamper the development of empathy in children (Grogan-Kaylor, 2005; Nelson, Padilla-Walker, Christensen, Evans, & Carrol, 2011).

This chapter describes the results of a meta-analysis on the association between parenting style and empathy in children. It will also be investigated whether the association between parenting and children's empathy is moderated by the measurement of empathy (affective, cognitive, or empathy in general), research design (cross-sectional or longitudinal), children's gender, ethnicity, age, parents' socio-economic status (SES), measurement instruments to investigate parenting style and empathy (questionnaire or observations), and the country where the research is conducted.

Method

Study selection

A comprehensive search of the literature published until 2017 was conducted to identify research on the relation between parenting style and empathy in children and adolescents up to age 23. The included studies were found in three consecutive steps. The first step was to identify studies through keyword searches in electronic databases, including Google-Scholar, ERIC, PubMed, PiCarta, ScienceDirect, Proquest, Whiley, Narcis, and Web of Knowledge. Keywords included *parenting* and *empathy*, and several keywords related to parenting (e.g. maternal responsiveness, harsh discipline) and empathy (e.g. victim-based orientation, emotional understanding). In the second step, studies were searched by using the snowball method. This entailed inspection of the reference sections of relevant (already retrieved) articles, narrative reviews, and book chapters. In the third step, all authors of the included studies were emailed to ask whether they were working on or knew other relevant studies that were not yet found and retrieved. Finally, 14 studies examining the association between parenting style and their children's empathy were included (see Table 4.1 for an overview of included studies).

Study coding procedures

Potential moderators of the association between children's empathy and parenting were grouped into publication characteristics, sample characteristics, study characteristics, and assessment characteristics. Publication year and impact factor of the journal in which the study was published were coded as publication characteristics. As for the sample characteristics, the gender of the children in a sample (males, females, or both), the children's ethnicity (in terms of the percentage Caucasian/White children in a sample), age of the children (early childhood, middle childhood, or adolescence), and the socio-economic status of families in the sample (low, medium, or high SES) were coded. Further, as an assessment characteristic, the type of instrument that was used to assess parenting style and empathy (questionnaires or observations), and the country where the research was conducted was coded as a study characteristic. Finally, the parenting style – with the categories authoritative, authoritarian, permissive, and neglectful parenting – and the dimension of empathy – with the categories cognitive empathy, affective empathy, and empathy without further specification – were coded.

Measures of empathy in the selected studies

None of the selected studies in this meta-analysis used the Basic Empathy Scale (BES; Jolliffe & Farrington, 2006) as an empathy measure. A total of seven studies were conducted before the development of the BES in 2006. Some studies used observational measures, such as facial expressions, to investigate empathy, especially in younger children (Kiang et al., 2004; van der Mark et al., 2002; Zhou et al., 2002). Some studies (Farrant et al., 2011; McGrath & Zook, 2011;

Table 4.1 Included studies

Study	*N*	*Peer review*	*IF*	*Design*	*Country research conducted*	*Type empathy*	*Gender*	*Ethnicity*	*age*
Schaffer et al. (2009)	244	yes	1.240	CS	NA	affective	both	.20	adolescence
Farrant et al. (2011)	72	yes	1.149	CS	NA	cognitive	both	.10	Early childhood
Kiang, Moreno, and Robinson (2004)	175	yes	4.141	LT	NA	affective	both	.92	Early childhood
Soenens et al. (2006)	284	yes	2.560	CS	Europe	empathy	both d	–	adolescence
Shen, Carlo, and Knight (2013)	106	yes	1.413	CS	Europe	cognitive	both	.21	Adolescence
Cornell and Frick (2007)	87	yes	3.310	CS	NA	cognitive	both	.95	Early childhood
De Kemp, Overbeek, De Wied, Engels en Scholte (2007)	403	yes	0.690	LT	Europe	affective	both	.96	adolescence
Zhou, Eisenberg, Losoya, Fabes, Reiser, Guthrie, Murphy, Comberland and Shepard (2002)	169	yes	4.061	CS	NA	empathy	both	.78	childhood
McGrath and Zook (2011)	33	yes	1.802	CS	NA	empathy	girls	.27	childhood
Strayer and Roberts (2004)	60	yes	1.800	CS	NA	empathy	both	0.0	childhood
Miller, Johnston, and Pasalich (2014)	56	yes	1.759	CS	NA	empathy	both	.45	childhood
Antonopoulou, Alexpoulos, and Maridaki-Kassotaki (2012)	190	yes	0.0	CS	Europe	empathy	both	–	childhood
Padilla-Walker and Katherine Christensen (2011)	500	yes	2.480	LT	NA	empathy	both	.07	childhood
van der Mark et al. (2002)	125	yes	1.800	CS	Europe	empathy	girls	.95	Early childhood

Note. # Studies = number of independent studies; # ES = number of effect sizes: Intercept/Mean r = mean association between parenting and empathy; 95% CI = 95% confidence interval.

* $p < .05$; ** $p < .01$; *** $p < .001$.

Schaffer et al., 2009; Strayer & Roberts, 2004) used questionnaires distinguishing between cognitive and affective empathy, which is in line with the two-dimensional structure of the BES.

Statistical analyses

To correct for dependency in effect size caused by the extraction of multiple effect sizes from individual primary studies, a three-level random effects model was used for estimating an overall association between parenting style and empathy in youth and conducting moderator analyses. In this three-level approach to meta-analysis, three different sources of variance are modelled (van den Noortgate, López-López, Marín-Martínez, & Sánchez-Meca, 2015). The sampling variance of each effect size estimating a population effect size is modelled at the first level. At the second level, variance in effect sizes within studies is modelled (i.e. within-study variance), and at the third level, variance in effect sizes retrieved from different studies (i.e. between-study variance) is modelled. We applied the procedure and R script described by Assink and Wibbelink (2016).

Parameters were estimated using a Restricted Maximum Likelihood method. The first step was to calculate an overall estimate of the effect size. Next, whether the variance at level 2 (within studies) and the variance at level 3 (between studies) significantly deviated from zero was investigated by performing two one-sided log-likelihood ratio tests. This was done by testing whether constraining either the level 2 or level 3 variance deteriorated the model fit compared to the unconstrained model in which both variance components were estimated. In case of significant level 2 or 3 variance, univariate moderator analyses were performed to investigate which moderators significantly influenced the association between parenting style and empathy. Prior to performing analyses, a check for outliers in all Fischer z scores was performed by determining whether standardised values exceed (−)3.29, but no outliers were identified.

To test for publication bias, a trim and fill analysis was performed to investigate whether the distribution of effect sizes was asymmetrical and, if that was the case, what effect sizes should be imputed to the right or the left side of the funnel to restore the symmetry in the effect size distribution (Duval & Tweedie, 2000a, 2000b). With this procedure whether the estimated overall effect may be an underestimation or an overestimation of the true effect can be checked. If effect sizes are missing on the left side of the funnel, there is indication of publication bias in the effect sizes that are analysed.

Results

Descriptive statistics

We included 14 studies (see Table 4.1) with a total sample size of $N = 2504$ participants, and with sample sizes ranging from $N = 33$ (McGrath & Zook, 2011) to $N = 500$ (Padilla-Walker & Christensen, 2010). The mean age of participants was 10.00 years ($SD = 4.33$; range = 20.70). All included studies were published between 2002 and 2013.

Overall effect size

The overall association between parenting style and empathy was $r = .171$ ($p <$ .001), indicating a small (Cohen, 1988), but positive and significant effect. The variance at level 2 (i.e. the within-study variance) was significant, χ^2 (1) = 131.98 ($p < 0.001$), indicating heterogeneity in effect sizes that were extracted from the same studies. The level 3 between study variance was not significant, χ^2 (1) = .85 ($p = .36$). Of the total variance, 15% was distributed at level 1, 77% was distributed at level 2, and 8% was distributed at level 3. Because within-study heterogeneity was identified, moderator analyses were performed to investigate which moderators significantly influenced the strength of the association between parenting style and empathy.

Moderator analyses

The results of the moderator analyses are depicted in Table 4.2. We found significant results for type of parenting style, $F(2,62) = 10.87$ ($p < 0.001$), and empathy type, $F(2,62 = 9.40$ ($p < .001$). Only authoritative parenting was positively associated with empathy ($r = .232$; $p < .001$). There were positive effects for cognitive empathy ($r = .348$; $p < .001$) and affective empathy ($r = .240$; $p < .01$), but not for empathy in general ($r = .086$; n.s.). Also, assessment type proved to be a significant moderator, $F(2,62) = 4.09$ ($p = 0.22$), with positive effects for parent self-report questionnaires only ($r = .217$; $p < .05$) and non-significant effects for parent observations ($r = .026$; n.s.) and mixed assessments ($r = .112$; n.s.). Assessment type of empathy did not moderate the relation between parenting and empathy. Further, socio-economic status of the family significantly moderated the association between parenting and empathy: $F(2,22) = 3.88$ ($p < .05$), with positive effects for high SES ($r = .188$; $p < .001$) and middle SES ($r = .161$; $p < .01$), but not for low SES ($r = .033$; n.s.). Last, we found a moderating effect of the publication year of included studies, $F(1,63) = 6.24$ ($p < .05$), with stronger associations for more recently published studies ($b = .013$; $p < .05$).

Assessment of bias

The funnel plot (depicted in Figure 4.1) indicates that bias may be present in our results. The results of the trim and fill analysis revealed that 12 effect sizes had to be imputed on the right side of the funnel to restore the symmetry in the effect size distribution. This implies that our estimated overall association between parenting and empathy of $r = .171$ may be an underestimation of the true overall association.

Discussion

The present meta-analysis showed that authoritative parenting was positively and modestly associated with higher levels of both cognitive and affective empathy in children, which was consistent with our expectations. However, no significant associations were found between empathy and authoritarian, permissive, or

Table 4.2 Results of Bivariate Moderator Analyses.

Moderator variable	*# Studies*	*# ES*	*Intercept (95% CI) /* *Mean* r *(95% CI)*	*β (95% CI)*	F*(df1,df2)*[a]	p[b]	*Level 2 variance*	*Level 3 variance*
Parenting style	14	65			$F(2,62) = 10.872$	< .001***	.015***	.012**
Authoritative (RC)			.232 (.151; .313)***					
Permissive			.111 (−.037; .259)	−.121 (−.274; .033)				
Authoritarian			−0.038 (−.159; .083)	−.270 (−.386; −.154)***				
Type empathy	14	65			$F(2,62) = 9.402$	< .001**	.015**	.019**
Cognitive empathy (RC)			.348 (.226; 0.470)***					
Affective empathy			.240 (.065; .414)**	−.108 (−.291; .075)				
Empathy			.086 (−.016; −187)	−.262 (−.383; −.141)***				
Age-range	14	65			$F(2,62) = 1.058$	.353	.026	.002
Early childhood (RC)			.103 (−.009; .215)					
Middle childhood			.177 (.083; .271)***	.074 (−.072; .220)				
Adolescence			.204 (.120; .288)***	.101 (−.039; .241)				
Social Economic Status (SES)	7	25			$F(2,22) = 3.879$	.036*	.006	.000
Low (RC)			.033 (−.066; .131)					
Middle			.161 (.070; .251)**	.128 (.006; .262)**				
High			.188 (.126; .250)***	.155 (.039; .272)*				
Sex of the child	14	65			$F(2,62) = .839$	.437	.027	.002
girl (RC)			.096 (−.058; .251)					
boy			.084 (−.149; .317)	−.012 (−.282; .258)				
mixed gender			.186 (.125; .247)***	.090 (−.075; .254)				
Research country	13	63			$F(1,61) = .010$	.922	.027	.004
Europe (RC)			.171 (.064; .277)**					
Northern-Amerika			.164 (.088; .024)***	−.006 (−.137; .124)				
Ethnicity	12	58			$F(1,56) = 2.617$	.111	.023	.002
Caucasian			.242 (.122; .363)***	−.137 (−.306; .033)				
Impact factor	14	65			$F(1,63) = .973$	.328	.026	.002
Impact factor			.214 (.111; .317)***	−.021 (−.063; 021)				

Year of publication	14	65			$F(1,63) = 6.239$	.015*	.025	.000
Year of publication			–25.387 (–45.836; –4.938)*	.013 (.003; .023) *				
Assessment type parenting	14	65			$F(2,62) = 4.086$	.022*	.025	.000
Parent questionnaire (RC)			.217 (.163; .272)***					
Parent observation			.026 (−.129; .181)	−.192 (−.356; −027)*				
Parent mixed			.112 (.025; .199)	−.106 (−.208; −.003)*				
Assessment type empathy	14	65			$F(2,62) = 2.243$	.115	.026	.000
Questionnaire (RC)			.209 (.152; .266)***					
Observation			.099 (.009; .190)*	−.110 (−.217; −.003)*				
Composite			.137 (−.010; .284)	−.072 (−.230; −.086)				

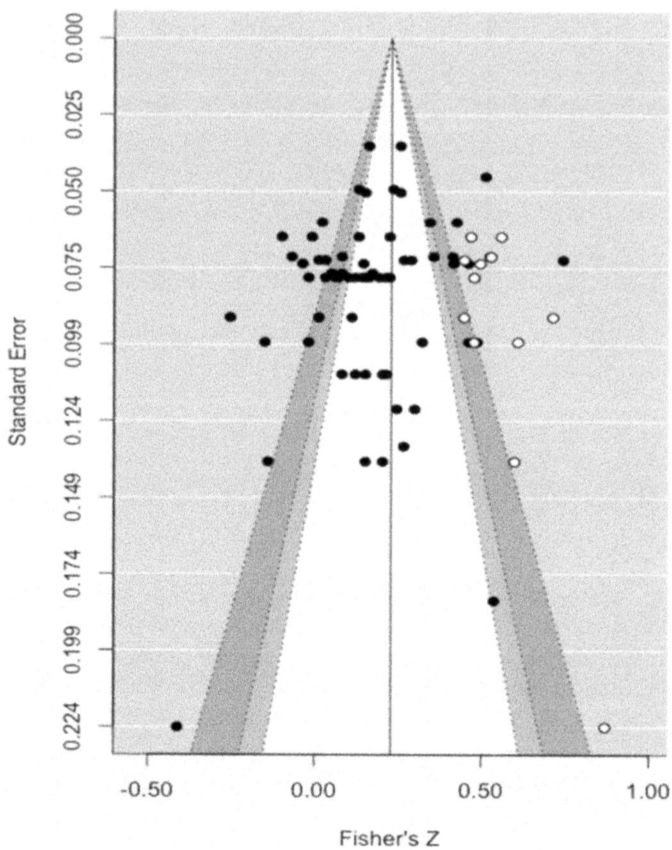

Figure 4.1 Funnel plot

neglectful parenting. The present study also tested available moderators, including children's gender, ethnicity, mean age, parents' social-economic status (SES), the type of instruments that were used to assess parenting style and empathy, and the country where the study was carried out. Results indicated that there was no moderating effect of gender, ethnicity, and age, which indicates to some degree a possible generalizability in areas across different groups of children. However, the association between parenting and child empathy was only found in samples of middle and high family SES, which suggests that the association was not present in families with a low SES. Finally, assessment type and year of publication proved to be significant moderators, with positive effects for only parent self-report questionnaires, and larger effects for more recent published studies.

Results of the present meta-analysis indicated authoritative parenting to be a positive influence on the development of empathy in children, whereas authoritarian and permissive parenting had no effect. No studies were found examining the relation between neglectful parenting and empathy. Authoritative parenting is characterised by both, reasonable parental control and high support and responsiveness (Nelson et al., 2011; Strayer & Roberts, 2004). According to Hoffman's (1970a) socialisation theory, parents who used predominantly inductive discipline (parental support and control), as opposed to power assertion, have children who are relatively prosocial and more empathic (Davis & Carlo, 2018; Hoffman, 1970a; Krevans & Gibbs, 1996). Emotions of empathy, empathy-based guilt, and the consideration of how behaviour can affect others can motivate prosocial behaviour in subsequent social situations (Krevans & Gibbs, 1996). Authoritarian parenting is defined by lack of support (warmth and responsiveness) and high parental control, whereas permissive parenting is defined by high levels of support and low parental control (Nelson et al., 2011). Given that no associations were found between authoritarian or permissive parenting and empathy in children, it is plausible to suggest that only high levels of both parental support and parental control make children more empathic. Alternatively, only low levels of both parental support and parental control may result in low levels of empathy in children. However, no studies have yet been conducted to allow this hypothesis to be tested.

Although we found no association between authoritarian parenting and lower empathy, it is possible that the more extreme cases of authoritarian parenting, designated as child abuse, may have a negative effect on the development of empathy in children. Notably, a study by Main and George (1985) showed that children who were physically abused reacted to others' distress by threatening or attacking them, suggesting empathy deficits (Main & George, 1985). A study by Straker and Jacobson (1981) found a direct link between child abuse and lower levels of empathy in children. However, Lazaro and Lopez (2010) did not find a relation between child maltreatment and low empathy. Finally, two reviews found empirical evidence for deficits in theory of mind and social understanding, which are empathy-related concepts, in children with a history of maltreatment (Benarous, Guilé, Consoli, & Cohen, 2015; Luke & Banerjee, 2013).

Moderator analyses revealed that a positive and significant association between parenting and child empathy was found in samples of middle and high SES, but not in samples of low SES, for which we found no significant association at all. This result is in line with the theory of Bronfenbrenner and Ceci (1994), who assumed that the development of specific competences in children, such as empathy, needs a stimulating environment, which is in general more often found in middle and high SES families. Another significant moderator was the assessment type of parenting style. Only when parenting styles were measured by questionnaires was a significant relation between parenting and empathy found, in contrast to observations and composite measures, for which no significant associations were found. A plausible explanation is inflation of the association through shared method variance, because in most research, parenting style and empathy were both assessed by using questionnaires. Further, somewhat larger effect sizes were found in more recent studies, which might be explained by improved assessment of empathy in recent years, and in particular the distinction between affective and cognitive empathy, given that older studies did not distinguish between affective and cognitive empathy, and thus failed to show a significant association between parenting style and empathy.

The BES (Jolliffe & Farrington, 2006) does distinguish between affective and cognitive empathy, but to date no studies exist examining the association between parenting and affective and cognitive empathy by means of the BES. However, the BES has been used as an outcome variable in studies examining child-rearing practices of professional caregivers in residential youth care. Notably, authoritative caregiving of professionals, which was reflected in a therapeutic group climate, proved to be associated with both, affective and cognitive empathy of adolescents in a study by Heynen, van der Helm, Cima, Stams, and Korebrits (2017), while van der Helm, Stams, van der Stel, van Langen, and van der Laan (2012) found a relation between authoritative caregiving of professionals and cognitive empathy, but not affective empathy.

Limitations

There are a number of limitations to this study. First, the literature search for this meta-analysis did not identify studies on neglectful parenting and empathy, perhaps because neglectful or uninvolved parenting is not viewed as a child-rearing practice by most researchers. Support and control constitute the basic dimensions of parenting, whereas neglectful "parenting" may be considered undefined as a parenting style given the absence of support and control (Nelson et al., 2011). However, it may be argued that scoring low on the defining dimensions of parenting in fact reflects neglectful parenting. Our assessment of bias showed that bias may have been present in the effect sizes we analysed. Although there was no indication of publication bias, a funnel plot showed that other forms of bias, such as selection bias, cannot be ruled out, as studies with relatively strong associations between parenting style and empathy may be underrepresented in the present meta-analysis.

A further limitation is that all studies were cross-sectional, which might inflate the association between parenting and empathy to the extent that parenting style is assessed as a state that might be affected by the child's empathy. Also, fathers were underrepresented in the studies that were included in this meta-analysis. We should therefore be cautious in generalising the findings of this meta-analysis to fathers. Notably, a narrative review by Bögels and Phares (2008) indicates that fathers show different (more child-challenging) parenting styles than mothers, while data concerning fathers' involvement in child-rearing is often missing, and such missing data must be regarded as "systematic".

Conclusions

Regarding greater empathy of children, authoritative parenting can be defined as the most successful parenting style. Authoritative parents show reasonable demands and high parental support and give their children the resources and support they need to succeed. It seems that only the combination of high support and high control fosters the healthy development of empathy in children, and that authoritative parenting, therefore, uniquely fosters empathy. A lack of either parental control or parental support had no relation to child empathy. We suggest future researchers should investigate whether a combination of a lack of parental support and parental control (i.e. uninvolved parenting) specifically puts children at risk for empathy deficits. No conclusions can be drawn in this regard, as no studies on uninvolved parenting and child empathy have been performed yet. Based on the results of this meta-analytic findings, future research should also focus on the positive association between parental support and (cognitive and affective) empathy. Intervention programs should target both parental support and parental control to foster empathy development in children, and prevent antisocial behaviour in children and adolescents (Jolliffe & Farrington, 2004, 2007; van Langen et al., 2014), raising the likelihood of a positive development.

References

Antonopoulou, K., Alexpoulos, D. A., & Maridaki-Kassotaki, K. (2012). Perceptions of father parenting style, empathy and self-esteem among Greek preadolescents. *Marriage & Familiy Review*, *48*(3), 293–310.

Assink, M., & Wibbelink, C. J. M. (2016). Fitting three-level meta-analytic models in R: A step-by-step tutorial. *The Quantitative Methods for Psychology*, *12*(3), 154–174. doi:10.20982/tqmp.12.3.p154

Atkinson, L., Niccols, A., Paglia, A., Coolbear, J., Parker, K. C. H., Poulton, L., . . . Sitarenios, G. (2000). A meta-analysis of time between maternal sensitivity and attachment assessments: Implications for internal working models in infancy/toddlerhood. *Journal of Social and Personal Relationships*, *17*, 791–810.

Barnow, S., Lucht, M., & Freyberger, H. J. (2005). Correlates of aggressive and delinquent conduct problems in adolescence. *Aggressive Behavior: Official Journal of the International Society for Research on Aggression*, *31*(1), 24–39.

Bar-Tal, D., Raviv, A., & Leiser, T. (1980). The development of altruistic behavior: Empirical evidence. *Developmental Psychology*, *16*(5), 516.

Baumrind, D. (1966). Effects of authoritative parental control on child behavior. *Child Development*, *37*, 887–907.

Baumrind, D. (1971). Current patterns of parental authority. *Developmental Psychology Monograph*, *4*, 1–103.

Baumrind, D. (1993). The average expectable environment is not good enough: A response to scarr. *Child Development*, *64*, 1299–1317.

Baumrind, D. (1997). Necessary distinctions. *Psychological Inquiry*, *8*, 176–182.

Beck, J. E., & Shaw, D. S. (2005). The influence of perinatal complications and environmental adversity on boys' antisocial behavior. *Journal of Child Psychology and Psychiatry*, *46*(1), 35–46.

Benarous, X., Guilé, J. M., Consoli, A., & Cohen, D. (2015). A systematic review of the evidence for impaired cognitive theory of mind in maltreated children. *Frontiers in Psychiatry*, *6*, 108.

Berk, L. E. (2006). Socialization within the family. In *Child development* (7th ed., pp. 563–573). New York: Pearson Education.

Bögels, S., & Phares, V. (2008). Fathers' role in the etiology, prevention and treatment of child anxiety: A review and new model. *Clinical Psychology Review*, *28*, 539–558. doi:10.1016/j.cpr.2007.07.011

Bronfenbrenner, U., & Ceci, S. J. (1994). Nature-nurture reconceptualized in developmental perspective: A bioecological model. *Psychological Review, 10*, 568–586.

Bryant, B. K. (1982). An index of empathy for children and adolescents. *Child Development, 53*, 413–425. doi:10.2307/1128984.

Cohen, J. (1988). *Statistical power analysis for the behavioral sciences*. Hillsdale, NJ: Lawrence Erlbaum.

Cornell, A. H., & Frick, P. J. (2007). The moderating effects of parenting styles in the association between behavioral inhibition and parent-reported guilt and empathy in preschool children. *Journal of Clinical Child & Adolescent Psychology, 36*(3), 305–318. doi:10.1080/15374410701444181

Dadds, M. R., Hawes, D. J., Frost, A. D. J., Vassallo, S., Bunn, P., Hunter, K., & Merz, S. (2009). Learning to "talk the talk": The relationship of psychopathic traits to deficits in empathy across childhood. *Journal of Child Psychology and Psychiatry, 50*, 599–606.

Davis, A. N., & Carlo, G. (2018). The roles of parenting practices, sociocognitive/emotive traits, and prosocial behaviors in low-income adolescents. *Journal of Adolescence, 62*, 140–150.

Davis, M. H. (1983). Measuring individual differences in empathy: Evidence for a multidimensional approach. *Journal of Personality and Social Psychology, 44*, 113–126.

de Kemp, R. A. T., Overbeek, G., de Wied, M., Engels, R. C. M. E., & Scholte, R. H. J. (2007). Early adolescent empathy, parental support, and antisocial behaviour. *The Journal of Genetic Psychology, 168*(1), 5–18. doi:10.3200/GNTP.168.1.5-18

de Wolff, M. S., & van IJzendoorn, M. H. (1997). Sensitivity and attachment: A meta-analysis on parental antecedents of infant attachment. *Child Development, 68*, 571–591.

Dlugokinski, E. L., & Firestone, I. J. (1974). Other-centeredness and susceptibility to charitable appeals: Effects of perceived discipline. *Developmental Psychology, 15*, 128–137.

Doinita, N. E., & Maria, N. D. (2015). Attachment and parenting styles. *Procedia-Social and Behavioral Sciences, 203*, 199–204.

Duval, S., & Tweedie, R. (2000a). Trim and fill: A simple funnel-plot–based method of testing and adjusting for publication bias in meta-analysis. *Biometrics, 56*(2), 455–463.

Duval, S., & Tweedie, R. (2000b). A nonparametric "trim and fill" method of accounting for publication bias in meta-analysis. *Journal of the American Statistical Association, 95*(449), 89–98.

Eisenberg, N., Eggum, N. D., & Di Giunta, L. (2010). Empathy-related responding: Associations with prosocial behaviour, aggression, and intergroup relations. *Social Issues and Policy Review, 4*(1), 143–180.

Farrant, B. M., Devine, T. A. J., Maybery, M. T., & Fletcher, J. (2011). Empathy, perspective taking and prosocial behaviour: The importance of parenting practices. *Infant and Child Development, 21*, 175–188. doi:10.1002/icd.740

Grogan-Kaylor, A. (2005). Corporal punishment and the growth trajectory of children's antisocial behaviour. *Child Maltreatment, 10*, 283–292.

Hazan, C., & Shaver, P. (1987). Romantic love conceptualized as an attachment process. *Journal of Personality and Social Psychology, 52*, 511–524.

Heynen, E. J. E., van der Helm, G. H. P., Cima, M. J., Stams, G. J. J. M., & Korebrits, A. M. (2017). The feelings of others don't impress me much – effects of living group climate on empathy in adolescent male offenders. *Psychiatry, Psychology and Law, 24*(1), 118–127.

Hoffman, M. L. (1970a). Conscience, personality, and socialization techniques. *Human Development, 13*, 90–126. doi:10.1159/000270884

Hoffman, M. L. (1970b). Moral development. In P. H. Mussen (Ed.), *Carmichael's manual of child psychology* (Vol. 2, pp. 457–557). New York: Wiley.

Hoffman, M. L. (1982). Development of prosocial motivation: Empathy and guilt. In N. Eisenberg (Ed.), *The development of prosocial behavior* (pp. 218–231). New York: Academic Press.

Hoffman, M. L. (1983). Affective and cognitive processes in moral internalization: An information processing approach. In E. T. Higgins, D. Ruble, & W. Hartup (Eds.), *Social cognition and social development: A sociocultural perspective* (pp. 236–274). New York: Cambridge University Press.

Hoffman, M. L. (1984). Empathy, its limitations and its role in a comprehensive moral theory. In W. M. Kurtines & J. L. Gerwirtz (Eds.), *Morality, moral behavior and moral development* (pp. 283–302). New York: Wiley.

Hoffman, M. L. (2000). *Empathy and moral development: Implications for caring and justice*. New York: Cambridge University Press.

Hoffman, M. L., & Saltzstein, H. D. (1967). Parent discipline and the child's moral development. *Journal of Personality and Social Psychology*, *5*, 45–57.

Hogan, R. D. (1969). Development of an empathy scale. *Journal of Consulting and Clinical Psychology*, *33*, 307–316. doi:10.1037/h0027580

Holmes, J.E (1993). *John Bowlby & attachment theory: Makers of modern psychotherapy* (p. 69). London: Routledge.

Holmgren, R. A., Eisenberg, N., & Fabes, R. A. (1998). The relations of children's situational empathy-related emotions to dispositional prosocial behaviour. *International Journal of Behavioral Development*, *22*(1), 169–193.

Hosser, D., & Beckurts, D. (2005). *Empathie und Delinquenz* [*Empathy and delinquency*]. Hannover and Niedersachsen: Forschungsbericht des Kriminologischen Forschungsinstitutes Niedersachsen e.V.

Jolliffe, D., & Farrington, D. P. (2004). Empathy and offending: A systematic review and meta-analysis. *Aggression and Violent Behavior*, *9*, 441–476.

Jolliffe, D., & Farrington, D. P. (2006). Development and validation of the basic empathy scale. *Journal of Adolescence*, *29*, 589–611. doi:10.1016/j.adolescence.2005.08.010

Jolliffe, D., & Farrington, D. P. (2007). Examining the relationship between low empathy and self-reported offending. *Legal and Criminological Psychology*, *12*, 265–286.

Kestenbaum, R., Farber, E. A., & Sroufe, L. A. (1989). Individual differences in empathy among preschoolers: Relation to attachment history. In N. Eisenberg (Ed.), *Empathy and related emotional responses* (New Directions for Child Development No. 44, pp. 51–64). San Francisco: Jossey-Bass.

Kiang, L., Moreno, A. J., & Robinson, J. L. (2004). Maternal preconceptions about parenting predict child temperament, maternal sensitivity, and children's empathy. *Developmental Psychology*, *40*(6), 1081–1092. doi:10.1002/icd.740

Kimonis, E. R., Frick, P. J., Boris, N. W., Smyke, A. T., Cornell, A. H., Farrell, J. M., & Zeanah, C. H. (2006). Callous-unemotional features, behavioral inhibition, and parenting: Independent predictors of aggression in a high-risk preschool sample. *Journal of Child and Family Studies*, *15*(6), 741–752.

Krevans, J., & Gibbs, J. C. (1996). Parents' use of inductive discipline: Relations to children's empathy and prosocial behavior. *Child Development*, *67*(6), 3263–3277.

Laible, D. (2007). Attachment with parents and peers in late adolescence: Links with emotional competence and social behavior. *Personality and Individual Differences*, *43*, 1185–1197. doi:10.1016/j.paid.2007.03.010

Lamborn, S. D., Mounts, N. S., Steinberg, L. D., & Dornbusch, S. M. (1991). Patterns of competence and adjustment among adolescents form authoritative, authoritarian, indulgent, and neglectful families. *Child Development*, *62*, 1049–1065.

Lazaro, S., & Lopez, F. (2010). Continuity of the effects of maltreatment during childhood in adolescents in residential care. *Infancia y Aprendizaje: Journal for the Study of Education and Development*, *33*, 255–268.

Luke, N., & Banerjee, R. (2013). Differentiated associations between childhood maltreatment experiences and social understanding: A meta-analysis and systematic review. *Developmental Review*, *33*(1), 1–28. ISSN:0273-2297

Main, M., & George, C. (1985). Responses of abused and disadvantaged toddlers to distress in agemates: A study in the day care setting. *Developmental Psychology*, *21*(3), 407.

McGrath, M. P., & Zook, J. M. (2011). Maternal control of girls versus boys: Relations to empathy and persuasive style with peers. *Journal of Child and Family Studies*, *20*(1), 57–65. doi:10.1007/s10826-010-9377-4

Miller, N. V., Johnston, C. J., & Pasalich, D. S. (2014). Parenting and conduct problems: Moderation by child empathy. *Journal of Psychopathology and Behavioral Assessment*, *36*, 74–83. doi:10.007/s10862-013-9366-1

Millings, A., Walsh, J., Hepper, E., & O'Brien, M. (2013). Good partner, good parent: Responsiveness mediates the link between romantic attachment and parenting style. *Personality and Social Psychology Bulletin*, *39*(2), 170–180.

Munoz, L. C., Qualter, P., & Padgett, G. (2011). Empathy and bullying: Exploring the influence of callous-unemotional traits. *Child Psychiatry & Human Development*, *45*, 183–196. doi:10.1007/s10578-010-0206-I

Nair, H., & Murray, A. D. (2005). Predictors of attachment security in preschool children from intact and divorced families. *The Journal of Genetic Psychology*, *166*(3), 245–263.

Nelson, L. J., Padilla-Walker, L. M., Christensen, K. J., Evans, C. A., & Carrol, J. S. (2011). Parenting in emerging adulthood: An examination of parenting clusters and correlates. *Journal of Youth and Adolescence*, *40*, 730–743. doi:10.1007/s10964-010-9584-8

Nix, R. L., Pinderhughes, E. E., Dodge, K. A., Bates, J. E., Pettit, G. S., & McFadyes-Ketchum, S. A. (1999). The relation between mothers' hostile attribution tendencies and children's externalizing behavior problems: The mediating role of mothers' harsh discipline practices. *Child Development*, *70*, 896–909.

Oliner, S. P., & Oliner, P. M. (1988). *The altruistic personality*. New York: Free Press.

Padilla-Walker, L. M., & Christensen, K. J. (2011). Empathy and self-regulation as mediators between parenting and adolescents' prosocial behaviour towards strangers, friends and family. *Journal of Research on Adolescence*, *21*(3), 545–551. doi:10.1111/j.1532-7795.2010.00695.x

Panfile, T. M., & Liable, D. J. (2012). Attachment security and child's empathy: The mediating role of emotion regulation. *Merrill-Palmer Quarterly*, *58*(1), 1–21.

Pinker, S. (2011). *The better angels of our nature: Why violence has declined*. New York: Penguin Books.

Popma, A., & Raine, A. (2006). Will future forensic assessment be neurobiologic? *Child and Adolescent Psychiatric Clinics of North America*, *15*(2), 429–444. doi:10.1016/j.chc.2005.11.004

Raine, A. (2013). *The anatomy of violence, the biological roots of crime*. New York: Pantheon.

Robinson, J. L., & Little, C. (1994). Emotional availability in mother-twin dyads: Effects on the organization of relationships. *Psychiatry*, *57*, 22–31.

Sagi, A., & Hoffman, M. L. (1976). Empathic distress in the newborn. *Developmental Psychology*, *12*(2), 175.

Schaffer, M., Clark, S., & Jeglic, E. L. (2009). The role of empathy and parenting style in the development of antisocial behaviours. *Crime & Delinquency*, *55*(4), 586–599. doi:101177/0011128708321359

Schwenck, C., Göhle, B., Hauf, J., Warnke, A., Freitag, C. M., & Schneider, W. (2014). Cognitive and emotional empathy in typically developing children: The influence of age, gender, and intelligence. *European Journal of Developmental Psychology*, *11*(1), 63–76.

Shen, Y. L., Carlo, G., & Knight, G. P. (2013). Relations between parental discipline, empathy related traits, and prosocial moral reasoning: A multicultural examination. *Journal of Adolescence*, *33*(7), 994–1021. doi:10.1177/0272431613479670

Skeem, J. L., Polaschek, D. L. L., Patrick, C. J., & Lilienfeld, S. O. (2011). Psychopathic personality: Bridging the gap between scientific evidence and public policy. *Psychological Science in the Public Interest*, *12*, 95–162. doi:10.1007/1529100611426706

Smith, A. (2006). Cognitive empathy and emotional empathy in human behavior and evolution. *The Psychological Record*, *56*, 3–21.

Soenens, B., Duriez, B., Vansteenkiste, M., & Goossens, L. (2006). The intergenerational transmission of empathy related responding in adolescence: The role of maternal support. *Personality and Social Psychology Bulletin*, *33*(3), 299–311. doi:10.1177/0146 167206296300

Straker, G., & Jacobson, R. S. (1981). Aggression, emotional maladjustment, and empathy in the abused child. *Developmental Psychology*, *17*(6), 762–765. doi: 10.1037/00121649.17

Strayer, J., & Roberts, W. (2004). Children's anger, emotional expressiveness and empathy: Relations with parents' empathy, emotional expressiveness and parenting practices. *Social Development*, *13*(2), 229–254.

Steinberg, L., Lamborn, S., Darling, N., Mounts, N., & Dornbusch, S. (1994). Over-time changes in adjustment and competence among adolescents from authoritative, authoritarian, indulgent, and neglectful families. *Child Development*, *65*, 754–770.

Todorović, J., & Matejević, M. (2014). Transgenerational transmission of the beliefs of competent parenting. *Procedia-Social and Behavioral Sciences*, *141*, 275–279.

van den Noortgate, W., López-López, J. A., Marín-Martínez, F., & Sánchez-Meca, J. (2015). Meta-analysis of multiple outcomes: A multilevel approach. *Behavior Research Methods*, *47*(4), 1274–1294.

van der Mark, I. L., van IJzendoorn, M. H., & Bakermans-Kranenburg, M. J. (2002). Development of empathy in girls during the second year of life: Associations with parenting, attachment, and temperament. *Social Development*, *11*(4), 451–468.

van der Helm, G. H. P., Stams, G. J. J. M., van der Stel, J. C., van Langen, M. A. M., & van der Laan, P. H. (2012). Group climate and empathy in a sample of incarcerated boys. *International Journal of Offender Therapy and Comparative Criminology*, *56*(8), 1149–1160.

van der Zouwen, M., Hoeve, M., Hendriks, A. M., Asscher, J. J., & Stams, G. J. J. M. (2018). The association between attachment and psychopathic traits. *Aggression and Violent Behavior*, *43*, 45–55.

van IJzendoorn, M. H. (1997). Attachment, emergent morality, and aggression: Toward a developmental socioemotional model of antisocial behaviour. *International Journal of Behavioral Development*, *21*(4), 703–728.

van IJzendoorn, M. H., Bakermans-Kranenburg, M. J., Pannebakker, F., & Out, D. (2010). In defence of situational morality: Genetic, dispositional and situational determinants of children's donating to charity. *Journal of Moral Education*, *39*(1), 1–20.

van IJzendoorn, M. H., & De Wolff, M. S. (1997). In search of the absent father meta-analyses of infant-father attachment: A rejoinder to our discussants. *Child Development*, *68*, 604–609.

van Langen, M. A. M., Wissink, I. B., van Vugt, E. S., van der Stouwe, T., & Stams, G. J. J. M. (2014). The relation between empathy and offending: A meta-analysis. *Aggression and Violent Behavior*, *19*(2), 179–189. doi:10.1016/j.avb.2014.02.003

Zahn-Waxler, C., Radke-Yarrow, M., & King, R. A. (1979). Child rearing and children's prosocial initiations toward victims of distress. *Child Development*, 319–330.

Zhou, Q., Eisenberg, N., Losoya, S. H., Fabes, R. A., Reiser, M., Guthrie, I. I., . . . Shepard, S. A. (2002). The relations of parental warmth and positive expressiveness to children's empathy-related responding and social functioning: A longitudinal study. *Child Development*, *73*(3), 893–915.

Part II

Empathy and offending

5 Contextual correlates of empathy

Peer van der Helm

Introduction

Empathy is considered a fundamental property to promote cooperation and therefore survival within species (De Waal, 2010). Empathy is probably hard-wired in our brain, as recent experiments with babies as young as six months show (Stavans & Baillargeon, 2019). However, humans are also able to morally disengage themselves from others and show callous and unemotional behaviour (Bandura, 2002; Zimbardo, 2003, van Baar, Chang, & Sanfey, 2019). Young People in conflict with the law sometimes display extreme callous and unemotional behaviour and seem devoid of empathy. This is causing considerable concern in our society that has become more peaceful and aversive to deviant behaviour in recent years (Pinker, 2011, 2018). Yet early life history, trauma and Adverse Childhood Experiences (ACE) resulting in negative emotionality (Wolff & Baglivio, 2017) and the pain (Anglin, 2014) by these Young People can also explain their (lack) of moral development and empathy. Empathy has contextual correlates which can teach us more about this phenomenon but can also be used to help and treat Young People in conflict with the law. In this article, we present both an integrated model combining the bio-psycho-social model and a developmental model of empathy explaining lack of empathy of Young People in conflict with the law. We then look briefly for possibilities for change in which the living group climate, by fulfilling basic psychological needs, could help treatment in youth facilities and at special education. Recent research (also elsewhere in this volume, Heynen, van der Helm, Stams, & Korebrits (2015) shows by measuring climate quality and measuring empathy development by using the Basic Empathy Scale could help identifying empathy development but also monitor treatment motivation and treatment progress.

Origins of aggression and empathy: the biopsychosocial model

The fundamental human property to either empathise or morally disengage yourself from others is called a "dual strategy" by the neurobiologist Keysers (2011), to ensure survival. After all, in good times, caring for others, even without reciprocal benefits, can benefit the whole group, but during hard times it can be advantageous to think of yourself foremost, often at the expense of others (Boehm, 2010). But this is probably not a fixed behavioural property, as Keysers (2011) himself suggested that men make better soldiers as they tend to make more effective use of the dual strategy compared to women who often adopt a more caring attitude.

The origins of moral disengagement, aggression or antisocial behaviour are probably influenced by multiple factors (Raine, 2013). George Engel (1977) proposed a bio-psycho-social model which has gained much support in recent years (de Rosa, Sampogna, Lucioano, del Vecchio, Fabrazzo, & Fiorillo, 2018; Forrester, 2018). In this model, biological causes (genetic abnormalities and hereditary problems, brain damage and the influence of poisonous substances in early development), psychological factors (temperament, vulnerabilities), and social factors (stress, trauma, Adverse Childhood Experiences; Raine, 2013; Fairchild et al., 2016; Fairchild, van Goozen, Calder, & Goodyer, 2013; Vervoort-Schel et al., 2018; van der Kolk, 2014) interact with each other to produce stress, antisocial and callous and unemotional behaviour.

Biological causes

The propensity for callous and unemotional behaviour and a lack of empathy is partly heritable but can also be caused by multifactor environmental causes and birth problems (Raine, 2013). For example, Young People with a Mild Intellectual Disability (MID) and other clinical conditions (Autism Spectrum problems, AS) often lack the metacognition needed to understand empathy fully (Cotter et al., 2018). Negative environmental and lifestyle factors like early stress may influence epigenetic mechanisms, such as DNA methylation, histone acetylation, and microRNA expression (Torres, Baccarelli, & Bolatti, 2011). Stress in parents can even alter the gene expression and stress system of a child yet to be born (Gheorghe, Goyal, Mittal, & Longo, 2010;), ultimately making the child less social and more susceptible for rewards such as substance abuse (Popma & Raine, 2006).

In his research Graeme Fairchild showed most persistent antisocial behaviour to be associated with brain damage, especially in the dorsolateral prefrontal cortex (Fairchild et al., 2013, 2016). Biological causes can also stem from Minimal Brain Dysfunction as a result of toxic substances, accidents, child battering (Traumatic Brain Injury, TBI; Raine, 2013), or a Post-Traumatic Stress Syndrome (PTSS; van der Kolk, 2014). Recent research showed also that empathy requires cognitive effort (Cameron et al., 2019), and people with impaired executive functioning who already struggle with brain damage, trauma, and the challenges of complex modern society are probably at risk of reduced empathy through this mechanism. Wu and Dunning (2018) phrased the term “hypocognition”: what you cannot understand you cannot execute, which probably refers to empathy as well. The well-known story of Phineas Gage, who, after severe frontal lobe damage, turned from a caring family man into an antisocial violent drunk can be seen as a classic example of the implication of brain damage on empathy (Raine, 2013). Also, hypocognition may explain our apparent lack of empathy in the historical past, with cruel public punishment and barbaric acts such as throwing live cats on bonfires as a Sunday-afternoon pastime in villages (Pinker, 2011).

Psychological causes

The psychological causes related to a lack of empathy and callous unemotional behaviour can stem from specific traits like impulsivity (i.e. acting without considering the consequences of one's actions) and developmental problems (Raine, 2013). However, a lack of resilience and one's psychological vulnerability to the social environment (anxiety) are also likely shape the development of the psychological properties related to callous and unemotional behaviour and lack of empathy (van der Kolk, 2014).

Social causes

Social causes refer to the impact of the social environment and often stem from Adverse Childhood Experiences and trauma in early (peri-natal) and later adolescent life (van IJzendoorn & Bakermans-Kranenburg, 2014; Vervoort-Schel et al., 2018; Spinhoven et al., 2010). Adverse Childhood Experiences can be summarised as the effects of child maltreatment, abuse, and neglect. ACEs are a relatively new topic of interest in the scientific community because of their combined and cumulative effects over time. Those that become psychologically vulnerable because of ACEs and trauma are more likely to adopt a deviant lifestyle which puts them at risk of, once again, being victimised or becoming a perpetrator. Experienced trauma generates enduring stress and often PTSS which "eats away" at the individual's resilience. Elevated stress produces stress hormones like cortisol. Stress hormones are over extended periods toxic to the brain tissue, adding to other possible causes of brain damage (Popma & Raine, 2006). Popma and Raine (2006) showed that enduring stress made children less social, more susceptible to material rewards and addiction and to have a weaker fear conditioning response. This in turn can lead to impaired socio-moral executive functioning and less empathy, particularly when compared to more normally developing peers.

A developmental perspective on empathy deficiencies

Young People who have experienced ACE's and trauma can show developmental stagnation in a number of areas including cognitive, social-emotional and personality development (Biesta, 2012; van der Kolk, 2014). These multiple developmental lags can lead to a lack of age-adequate empathy which can contribute to further problem behaviours by creating negative (transactional) reactions from both peers and society (Deakin, Fox, & Matos, 2020; Fontaine & Dodge, 2009; Wolff & Baglivio, 2017). Often these deficiencies are highly situational and contingent to social problem situations like being socially at a disadvantage (being bullied, threatened, or ridiculed), experiencing competition, having to ask for help, or having to respect authority (van der Helm et al., 2011). Problems with cognitive, socio-emotional, and personality development, all can elicit severe callous and unemotional aggressive reactions as a result of these social problem situations.

When analysing crimes, very often these crimes have a reactive character, lacking a clear cognitive rationale, often without any or little material gains. Therefore, through a lack of understanding by the professional (policeman, social worker, forensic therapist), the behaviour is often erroneously ascribed to a developing psychopathy, schizophrenia, or a personality disorder like borderline. van der Kolk (2014) argue these DSM V diagnoses are not valid and reliable enough, especially in a forensic context. A historical and developmental perspective offers probably more progress in forensic science.

Cognitive development and empathy

Generally, present-day western competitive societies favour "Brain over Brawn" (Pinker, 2011, 2018). This can be particularly difficult for some children whose brain functioning is less developed, damaged, or compromised by trauma. This is especially the case when these children witness and compare themselves to their peers' intellectual development in a society that becomes more complex (Umbach, Raine, & Leonard, 2017; Perez, Jennings, & Baglivio, 2017). Continuous failure in educational and societal domains can lead children to experience stress, and the perception that they lack competence (van Nieuwenhuijzen et al., 2006). This can alter Social Information Processing (SIP, van der Helm et al., 2011) and can produce social isolation, something which has an impact on the pain regions in the brain (Macdonald & Leary, 2005). The practical problems created for these children by our competitive over-regulated and complex society should not be underestimated as successfully navigating this often demands good executive functioning while also prescribing tolerance and empathy for others (Pinker, 2018). But also recurring trauma can lead to a developmental stagnation as traumatic experiences and consequent PTSS can cause children to be "stranded in de past". They relive their traumas almost every day by elevated fear, flash-back's, and sometime three to four frightening dreams during the night. This erodes their cognitive coherence. They develop symptoms like dissociation and violent behaviour which are often mistaken for psychosis, callous and unemotional traits, and lack of empathy (van der Kolk, 2014).

Social-emotional empathy development

Problems with social-emotional development can be equally damaging for the child. These issues with emotional regulation appear often soon after birth and are sometimes even connected to birth problems (Suarez, Morales, Metcalf, & Pérez-Edgar, 2019). Children with MID/TBI cry more often and are less easily soothed, often leading to negative transactional processes with already burdened caregivers. These caregivers often possess their own intergenerational problems (own history of ACEs, low education, unemployment, debts, poor housing, addiction problems, single parents), and as such, lack executive functioning and the resilience to handle their child's problems (Raine, 2013).

At school entry, the impulsive, aggressive, or withdrawn behaviour of these children often leads to social isolation from peers and by being bullied, as well as negative reaction by teachers, authorities, and parents (see the story of Donta Page in: Raine, 2013).

These repeated failures and misbehaviour, unrecognised disabilities, and traumata can result in truancy and being expelled, many times over. This produces feelings of being rejected, pain, and low self-worth. Similarly, failure to recognise the need for empathy in interpersonal interactions can impair their social relations with peers. These relations then often worsen, and they attract deviant peers because of a sense of belonging, but also competence in deviant activities and a sense of autonomy (doing your own thing, being tough, "code of the street" Anderson, 2000).

Imagine a 16-year-old teen with the social emotional development of a 3-year-old child. At 3 years of age, we accept disruptive and self-focused behaviour, but not with a 16-year-old child. The negative transactional reactions of others can also lead to a hostility bias (Sato, Uono, Matsuura, & Tochi, 2009). In their seminal experiment, Sato et al., 2009 found that, while antisocial children were in a brain scanner, they decoded neutral faces as hostile faces, and there was evidence that their amygdalae reacted as if decoding an angry face. Recent research also shows that antisocial children have problems with negative social comparison, competition, authorities, and also comprehending their needs so they are unaware of when to ask for help (van der Helm et al., 2011). This last SIP problem may seem superficial, but for youth care workers it presents a real problem: if you cannot comprehend your problems you cannot ask for help (hypocognition, Wu & Dunning, 2018).

Cognitive and affective empathy in personality development

A new model of personality development proposed by Wrzus and Roberts (2017) puts forward a developmental model incorporating biological- psychological and social environmental components. These influences are like "Tessera" (small pieces in a mosaic), continuously interacting with the environment in transactional processes (Fontaine & Dodge, 2009). The idea is not new as psychiatrist Carl Rogers detailed in his 1969 writing about constructive personality change in therapy:

> The following conditions are necessary for constructive personality change: there is psychological contact between two persons. The first person we call the client is vulnerable and anxious. The second person we call the therapist is predictable or at least integrated into the therapeutic relationship. The therapist always respects the client and an unconditional empathic ability to understand his/her frame of reference and goals and communicate back to

> the client. This communication to the client of his understanding and unconditional respect (not condemning the client but his actions) must at least be present to make personality change possible

Situational triggers

Reactions from others who validate the transactional processes through reciprocal influence (Fontaine & Dodge, 2009) can provide learning opportunities through positive- or negative feelings (rejection) and also form the developing personality. Rejection does have a much stronger influence compared to positive reinforcement on the formation of a person (negative emotions have "steering priority" as emotion experts Frijda, Manstead, and Bem (2000) stated. Overcompensation with grandiose (self-overriding) and callous characteristics are often seen as a mechanism when trauma is re-enacted and psychological basic needs are frustrated time and time again (van der Kolk, 2014). Callous traits and the sensitivity to deviant others increase over time. Then (re)victimisation and criminalisation are lurking (Wolff & Baglivio, 2017) because young people can fill the void with examples of hostile personality traits of deviant others in popular culture (Vansteenkiste & Soenens, 2015). Kroger and Marcia (2011) refer to lack of personal development as a "diffuse identity" that is more often hostile due to frustration of basic needs (an "alienated diffuse identity"). Eventually these hostile perceptions can "solidify" or being internalised into negative personality "schemata" (schema therapy is based on these schemata). For example, one boy interviewed stated:

> My mother was depressed and never looked at me. Occasionally she beat me up. She has never helped me with my school and never looked at me in my school reports, it was as if I did not exist. I still feel I am not worth existing and don't care anymore.

Similarly, an interviewed girl stated:

> First my grandfather sexually abused me, then my father. I was never safe, not even in my own room. At school I was bullied, I was invisible all my life. There was nobody who cared about me, except when I went to bed with other men, then I got beautiful shoes or a leather coat. When I smoked several joints, I did not care who went over my body.

When these negative expectations of the outside world are not met, and for example, someone treats the child well or positively, some children can respond with anger and aggression because such kindness does not match their negative expectations. Empathy is something which these children cannot afford in their daily lives because in their perception the outside world is too dangerous and is always taking advantage of them (External Locus of Control, see next page).

A boy who participated in a Dutch criminal group that displayed extreme callous behaviour in a personal interview: 'We all watched DVD's from The

Godfather and Scarface and then we knew: "that's how we wanted to be"'. This alienated diffuse identity can lead to unprecedented cruel acts, for example in recent Amsterdam underworld shootings and cruel torture or killing the children of adversaries in the so called "Mocro Wars".

Other features of the Tessera model in building personality and empathy

The quality of the living environment is also important in this model. The quality of the environment can be characterised by cultural aspects, the living or home climate, the climate on the street, and the learning climate at school (Stams & van der Helm, 2017). Individuals also look for an environment that matches their own psychological factors, executive skills, wishes and desires. When it comes to partners, it has been found that individuals tend to be attracted to those like themselves. This so-called "assortative mating" can end up with aggressive or traumatised partners with deviant behaviour; finding those that behave like themselves (Krueger et al., 1998).

In general, living a life governed by perceived external forces is not instrumental for empathy development as the others are always to blame for your own misfortune (negative emotionality).

According to the Tessera model, the Locus of Control (LOC) is therefore important. By having an External Locus of Control, you believe that you have little control over outcomes in your life (van der Helm et al., 2011), you surrender more quickly to outside influences and perceive little autonomy. An External Locus of Control is associated with externalising behaviour, aggression, and lack of affective empathy (measured by the Basic Empathy Scale (BES) van Strien, 2016). However, it is important to note that there are often internalising problems underlying (pain, trauma, anxiety, depression, distrust), which are regularly not seen in treatment because externalising and aggressive behaviour receives the most attention from society and from professional treatment methods (Wolff & Baglivio, 2017; van der Kolk, 2014). For instance, perpetrators that have shown severe lack of empathy and callous and unemotional behaviour a mandated treatment method called: "learning from your crime" in the Netherlands usually overlooks contextual correlates of the particular crime and only focuses on the individual. When the perpetrator introduces this contextual information, it is generally seen as a false exculpation and lack of motivation and empathy. Often, Young People acknowledge they have done something terribly wrong but ignoring their context is seen as a lack of procedural justice and diminishes treatment motivation. They often feel treatment is to have to jump through a hoop in order to get out earlier. Sometimes, our well-intentioned treatment methods can obscure a coercive character instead of stimulating self-awareness and thereby producing an External Locus of Control and low self-worth. This produces reactive aggression:

> when you think that you have no influence or autonomy, an aggressive reaction is a natural form of coping to cover up your own lack of autonomy.

> Also, with an External Locus of Control there is less treatment motivation and willingness to change (van der Helm et al., 2011): after all, if you cannot do anything about it yourself, why bother doing it? A lack of treatment motivation is often seen as callous and unemotional, a lack of empathy and a reason for prolonged sentencing.
>
> (van der Helm et al., 2011)

Another important influence of Tessera's mosaic pieces is how one thinks about oneself. Many young people with negative childhood experiences and trauma have a low self-esteem in addition to negative emotionality (Hutteman, Nestler, Wagner, Egloff, & Back, 2015). This negative self-image influences attitudes and behaviour trough negative Social Information Processing (SIP, van der Helm et al., 2011). As a result, young people often elicit negative feedback from others, something that affects their self-image and then their negative personality further. Negative childhood experiences often have specific triggers for negative emotionality that prevent positive transactional processes such as having fun with friends and the development of empathy. Subsequent criminalisation (Deakin, Fox, & Mattos, 2020) and self-ambiguity by DSM-labelling) produce a self-fulfilling prophecy (Dings, 2020). In Figure 5.1 the bespoke mechanisms are summarised graphically.

Conclusion: developing empathy for practitioners

A lack of empathy and callous and unemotional behaviour does not have to be permanent as most children strive for a positive self-image (Hennecke, Bleidorn, Denissen & Wood, 2014). We can make use of this in mandated residential treatment and education. Under the right circumstances, young people strive for being "just" (moral behaviour, Boehm, 2010). They want to grow towards greater conscientiousness and emotional stability (Hudson & Fraley, 2015). Setting positive goals in care and at school can therefore help to change the negative aspects of personality, together with contact with fellow patients and pro-social examples. That process takes time, so changes are slow and not always linear. The process of empathy development tends to be more circular: success at school leads to a better sense of self, morality, and more empathy and that in turn leads to better school performance in the future and better social acceptance that in turn leads to a higher self-image, more empathy and better school performance (Hutteman et al., 2015; van der Kolk, 2014; van der Helm et al., 2011). This mechanism probably also works in the community and for society as a whole (Pinker, 2011, 2018). This slow and arduous process, accompanied by many drawbacks can discourage policemen, judges, staff, therapists, social workers and teachers, but it is part of the recovery process. It helps to think that most young people, as their brains mature and their lives stabilise through fewer transitions, they become better able to regulate their impulses (Roberts & Mroczek, 2008). We call this the "maturity principle": social roles become more stable, their own identity develops, and they gain more self-insight (Roberts & Mroczek, 2008): the mosaic stabilises. That

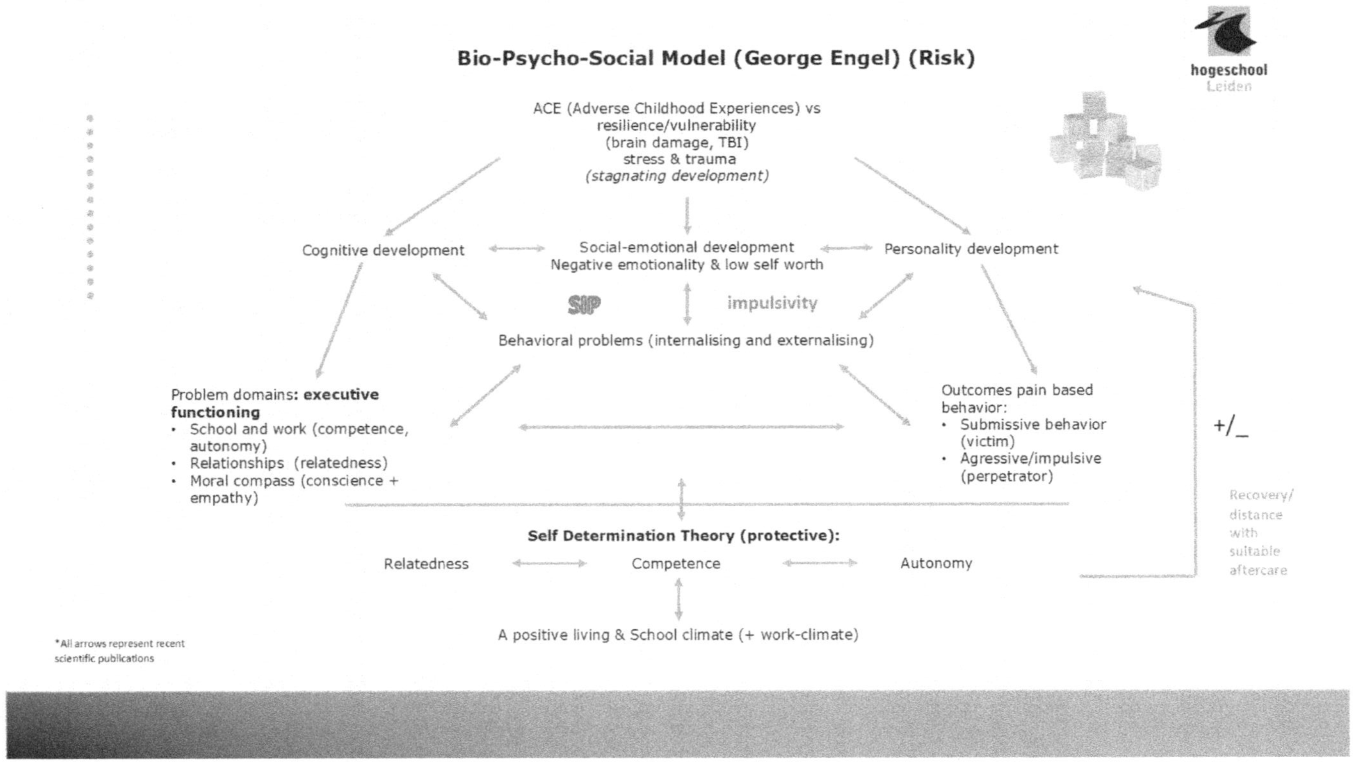

Figure 5.1 A proposed model for empathy development

is what is needed for these children in mandated forensic residential care and education.

According to a major motivational theory, Self Determination Theory (SDT, Ryan & Deci, 2017),

> the fulfillment of the basic psychological needs of relatedness, competence and autonomy play an important role in empathy development, stabilization and maturation. There is evidence that a social climate that fosters these three basic psychological needs can help to enhance treatment motivation, and cognitive, social-emotional and personality growth which in turn stimulate empathy development (Meijers, 2018; van der Helm, Kuiper, & Stams, 2018; Wolff & Baglivio, 2017; Heynen, van der Helm, Wissink, Stams, & Moonen, 2015). This is precisely what Hachtel, Vogel, and Huber (2019) found in their review on mandated treatment: a caring and authoritative treatment style (as opposed to a harsh and coercive style) was associated with Self-Determination, an Intrinsic Locus of Control and empathy development.

Also, some therapies like schema therapy and dialectical behaviour therapy have been shown to make promising progress in empathy development with adolescents (van Wijk-Herberink, 2018).

Contrary to the “nothing works” belief of the previous decades (e.g. Stams & van der Helm, 2017; Heynen, van der Helm, Cima, Stams & Korebrits, 2016), considerable progress has been made in understanding and measuring empathy development in relation to its contextual correlates (van Strien, 2016). The BES created by Jolliffe and Farrington (2006), which is typically used for empathy research, could also be used as a clinical tool to measure treatment progress together with measures of living group climate and treatment motivation (van der Helm et al., 2018). In addition, greater use of research on hypocognition (Wu & Dunning, 2018) in Young People with a MID and/or AS and those with trauma-related development (van der Kolk, 2024) could assist in the development of programs to strengthen cognitive and affective empathy.

Therefore, enhancing empathy in Young People in conflict with the law by fulfilling their basic psychological needs and creating a positive living climate could make our world safer and also stimulate recovery and hope for a “normal” living in the lives of many disadvantaged Young People in our society.

Postscript

On the brink of this chapter being finalised, we received stimulating news from Australia:

> We have opened up a unit with reduced security and higher levels of autonomy for the young people. This unit will be part of an overall operating model where there are a range of units with differentiated levels of security.

This is a significant progressive step for us and is very exciting for everyone, especially the young people in the unit. Your work in 2017 was responsible for the thinking behind the design of the model and giving us the confidence and knowledge to move to this way of accommodating young people in custody – more autonomy and less control.

References

Anderson, E. (2000). *Code of the street: Decency, violence, and the moral life of the inner city*. New York: Norton & Co.

Anglin, J. P. (2014). *Pain, normality, and the struggle for congruence: Reinterpreting residential care for children and youth*. Oxford: Routledge.

Bandura, A. (2002). Selective moral disengagement in the exercise of moral agency. *Journal of Moral Education, 31*(2). doi:10.1080/0305724022014322

Biesta, G. J. J. (2012). *The beautiful risk of education*. London: Routledge.

Boehm, C. (2010). *Moral origins: The evolution of virtue, altruism and shame*. New York: Basic Books.

Cameron, D. D., Hutcherson, C. A., Ferguson, A. M., Scheffer, J. A., Hadjiandreou, E., & Inzlicht, M. (2019). Empathy is hard work: People choose to avoid empathy because of its cognitive costs. *Journal of Experimental Psychology: General*. doi:10.1037/xge0000595

Cotter, J., Granger, K., Backx, R., Hobbs, M., Looi, C. Y., Barnett, J. H. (2018). Social cognitive dysfunction as a clinical marker: A systematic review of meta-analyses across30 clinical conditions. *Neuroscience Biobehavior Review, 84*, 92–99.

Deakin, J., Fox, C., & Matos, R. (2020, April). Labelled as "risky" in an era of control: How young people experience and respond to the stigma of criminalized identities. *European Journal of Criminology*. doi:10.1177/1477370820916728

de Rosa, C., Sampogna, G., Lucioano, M., del Vecchio, V., Fabrazzo, M., & Fiorillo, A. (2018). Social versus biological psychiatry: It's time for integration! *International Journal of Social Psychiatry*, 1–5. doi:10.1177/0020764017752969

de Waal, F. (2010). *The age of empathy: Nature's lessons for a kinder society*. New York: Random House.

Dings, R. (2020). *Not being oneself? Self-ambiguity in the context of mental disorder* (Dissertation). Radboud University, Nijmegen.

Engel, G. (1977). The need for a new medical model: A challenge for biomedicine. *Science, 196*(4286), 129–136.

Fairchild, G., Toschi, N., Sully, K., Sonuga-Barke, E. J. S., Hagan, C. C., Diciotti, S., . . . Passamonti, L. (2016). Mapping the structural organization of the brain in conduct disorder: Replication of findings in two independent samples. *Journal of Child Psychology and Psychiatry, 57*, 1018–1026.

Fairchild, G., van Goozen, S. H., Calder, A. J., & Goodyer, I. M. (2013). Research review: Evaluating and reformulating the developmental taxonomic theory of antisocial behaviour. *Journal of Child Psychology and Psychiatry, 54*(9), 924–940. doi:10.1111/jcpp.12102

Fontaine, R. G., & Dodge, K. A. (2009). The transactional development of individual social-information processing and aggressive behavior. In A. J. Sameroff (Ed.), *Transactional processes in development*. Washington, DC: American Psychological Association.

Forrester, A. (2018). Integrating social and biological psychiatry: A forensic perspective *International Journal of Social Psychiatry*, 1–2. doi:10.1177/0020764018766390

Frijda, N., H., Manstead, A. S. R., & Bem, S. (2000). *Emotions and beliefs*. Cambridge: Cambridge University Press.

Gheorghe, C. P., Goyal, R., Mittal, A., & Longo, L. D. (2010). Gene expression in the placenta: Maternal stress and epigenetic responses. *The International Journal of Developmental Biology*, *54*(2–3), 507–523.

Hachtel, H., Vogel, T., & Huber, C. (2019). Mandated treatment and its impact on therapeutic process and outcome factors. *Frontiers in Psychiatry*, *10*, 219.

Hennecke, M., Bleidorn, W., Denissen, J. J. A., & Wood, D. (2014). A three-part framework for self-regulated personality development across adulthood. *European Journal of Personality*, *28*, 289–299. doi:10.1002/per.1945

Heynen, E. J. E., van der Helm, G. H. P., Cima, M. J., Stams, G. J. J. M., & Korebrits, A. M. (2016). The feelings of others don't impress me much – effects of living group climate on empathy in adolescent male offenders. *Psychiatry, Psychology and Law*, 1–10.

Heynen, E., van der Helm, G. H. P., Stams, G. J., & Korebrits, A. (2015). Measuring empathy in German youth prison – a validation of the "basic empathy scale" (BES). In E. Heynen (Ed.), *No guts, no gains! The relation between living group climate and social development of juvenile delinquents in detention* (pp. 39–54). Amsterdam: Amsterdam University Press; Selfkant: [s.l.].

Heynen, E. J. E., van der Helm, G. H. P., Wissink, I. B., Stams, G. J. J. M., & Moonen, X. M. H. (2015). "I dont care about what you want!" The relation between juvenile delinquents responses to social problem situations and empathy in secure juvenile institutions. *Journal of Interpersonal Violence*, *33*(9), 1412–1426. doi:10.1177/0886260515618212

Hudson, N. W., & Fraley, R. C. (2015). Volitional personality trait change: Can people choose to change their personality traits? *Journal of Personality and Social Psychology*, *109*(3), 490–507. doi:10.1037/pspp0000021

Hutteman, R., Nestler, S., Wagner, J., Egloff, B., & Back, M. D. (2015). Wherever I may roam: Processes of self-esteem development from adolescence to emerging adulthood in the context of international student exchange. *Journal of Personality and Social Psychology*, *108*(5), 767–783. doi:10.1037/pspp0000015

Jolliffe, D., & Farrington, D. P. (2006). Development and validation of the basic empathy scale. *Journal of Adolescence*, *29*, 589–611.

Keysers, C. (2011). *The empathic brain*. Amsterdam: Social Brain Press.

Kroger, J., & Marcia, J. E. (2011). The identity statuses: Origins, meanings, and interpretations. In J. Schwarz & L. Vignoles (Eds.), *Handbook of identity theory and research* (pp. 31–53). New York: Springer.

Krueger, R. F., Moffit, T. E., Caspi, A., Bleske, A., & Silva, P. A. (1998). Assortative mating for antisocial behavior: Developmental and methodological implications. *Behavior Genetics*, *28*(3), 173–186. doi:10.1023/A:1021419013124

MacDonald, G., & Leary, M. R. (2005). Why does social exclusion hurt? The relationship between social and physical pain. *Psychological Bulletin*, *131*(2), 202–223. doi:10.1037/0033-2909.131.2.202

Meijers, J. (2018). *Do not restrain the prisoner's brain: Executive functions, self-regulation and the impoverished prison environment* (Dissertation). Amsterdam Free University, Amsterdam.

Perez, N. M., Jennings, W. G., & Baglivio, M. T. (2017). A path to serious, violent, chronic delinquency: The harmful aftermath of adverse childhood experiences. *Crime and Delinquency*, 3–25. doi:10.1177/0011128716684806

Pinker, S. (2011). *The better angels of our nature: The decline of violence in history and its causes*. New York: Penguin.

Pinker, S. (2018). *Enlightenment now: The case for reason, science, humanism and progress*. New York: Penguin.

Popma, A., & Raine, A. (2006). Will future forensic assessment be neurobiological? *Child and Adolescent Psychiatric Clinics of North America, 15*, 429–444. doi:10.1016/j.chc.2005.11.004

Raine, A. (2013). *The anatomy of violence: The biological roots of crime*. New York: Harper.

Roberts, B. W., & Mroczek, D. (2008). Personality trait change in adulthood. *Current Directions in Psychological Science, 17*(1), 31–35. doi:10.1111/j.1467-8721.2008.00543.x

Rodgers, A. B., Morgan, C. P., Bronson, S. L., Revello, S., & Bale, T. B. (2013). Paternal stress exposure alters sperm micro RNA content and reprograms offspring HPA stress axis regulation. *Journal of Neuroscience, 22–33*(21), 9003–9012. doi:10.1523/JNEUROSCI.0914-13.2013

Ryan, R. M., & Deci, E. L. (2017). *Self-determination theory: Basic psychological needs in motivation, development and wellness*. New York: Guilford.

Sato, W., Uono, S., Matsuura, N., & Toichi, M. (2009). Misrecognition of facial expressions in delinquents. *Child and Adolescent Psychiatry and Mental Health, 3*, 627–636.

Spinhoven, P., Elzinga, B. M., Hovens, J. G. F. M., Roelofs, K., Zitman, F. G., van Oppen, P., & Penninx, B. W. J. H. (2010). The specificity of childhood adversities and negative life events across the life span to anxiety and depressive disorders, *Journal of Affective Disorders, 126*, 103–112. doi:10.1016/j.jad.2010.02.132

Stams, G. J. J. M., & van der Helm, G. H. P. (2017). What works in residential programs for aggressive and violent youth? Treating youth at risk for aggressive and violent behavior in (secure) residential care. In P. Sturmey (Ed.), *The Wiley handbook of violence and aggression*. Chichester: Blackwell.

Stavans, M., & Baillargeon, R. (2019). Infants expect leaders to right wrongs. *Proceedings of the National Academy of Sciences of the United States of America*. doi:10.1073/pnas.1820091116

Suarez, G. L., Morales, S., Metcalf, K., & Pérez-Edgar, K. E. (2019). Perinatal complications are associated with social anxiety: Indirect effects through temperament. *Infant and Child Development*, e2130. doi:10.1002/icd.2130

Torres, J. A. A., Baccarelli, A., & Bolatti, V. (2011, June). Epigenetics and lifestyle. *Epigenomics, 3*(3), 267–277. doi:10.2217/epi.11.22

Umbach, R., Raine, A., & Leonard, N. (2017). Cognitive decline as a result of incarceration and the effects of a CBT/MT intervention: A cluster-randomized controlled trial. *Criminal Justice and Behavior*, 1–25. doi:10.1177/0093854817736345

van Baar, J. M., Chang, L. J., & Sanfey, A. G. (2019). The computational and neural substrates of moral strategies in social decision-making. *Nature Communications, 10*(1). doi:10.1038/s41467-019-09161-6

van der Helm, G. H. P., Kuiper, C. H. Z., & Stams, G. J. J. M. (2018). Group climate and treatment motivation in secure residential and forensic youth care from the perspective of self-determination theory. *Elsevier: Children and Youth Services Review, 93*, 339–344. doi:10.1016/j.childyouth.2018.07.028

van der Helm, G. H. P., Matthys, W., Moonen, X., Stams, G. J. J. M., Giesen, N., & van der Heide, E. S. (2011). Measuring inappropriate responses of adolescents to problematic social situations in secure institutional and correctional youth care: A validation study of the TOPS-A. *Journal of Interpersonal Violence, 28*, 1579–1595. doi:10.1177/0886260512468322 van der Kolk, B. (2014). *The body keeps the score: Brain, mind, and body in the healing of trauma*. New York: Penguin.

van IJzendoorn, M. H., & Bakermans-Kranenburg, M. J. (2014). Prosocial development and situational morality, neurobiological, parental and contextual factors. In *Pathways to peace: The transformative power of children and families*. Cambridge: The MIT Press. doi:10.7551/mitpress/9780262027984.003.0010

van Nieuwenhuijzen, M., Orobio de Castro, B., van der Valk, I., Wijnroks, L., Vermeer, A., & Matthys, W. (2006). Do social information processing models explain aggressive behaviour by children with mild intellectual disabilities in residential care? *Journal of Intellectual Disability Research, 50*, 801–812.

Vansteenkiste, M., & Soenens, B. (2015). *Vitamines voor groei (Du)* [*Vitamins for growth*]. Den Haag: Acco.

van Strien, D. (2016). *Veranderingen in empathie en locus of control tijdens de eerste maanden van verblijf in een residentiele instelling* [*Changes in empathy and locus of control during the first months of stay in a residential setting*] (Master's thesis). University of Amsterdam, Amsterdam.

van Wijk-Herberink, M. (2018). *Schema therapy in adolescents with externalizing behavior problems: Bridging theory and practice* (Dissertation). University of Maastricht, Maastricht.

Vervoort-Schel, J., Mercera, G., Wissink, I., Mink, E., van der Helm, P., Lindauer, R., & Moonen, X. (2018). Adverse childhood experiences in children with intellectual disabilities: An exploratory case-file study in Dutch residential care. *International Journal of Environmental Research and Public Health, 15*, 2136.

Wolff, K. T., & Baglivio, M. T. (2017). Adverse childhood experiences, negative emotionality, and pathways to juvenile recidivism. *Crime & Delinquency, 63*(12), 1495–1521. doi:10.1177/0011128715627469

Wrzus, C., & Roberts, B. W. (2017). Processes of personality development in adulthood: The TESSERA framework. *Personality and Social Psychology Review, 21*(3), 253–277. doi:10.1177/1088868316652279

Wu, K., & Dunning, D. (2018). Hypocognition: Making sense of the landscape beyond one's conceptual reach. *Review of General Psychology, 22*(1), 25–35. American Psychological Association. doi:10.1037/gpr0000126

Zimbardo, G. (2003). A situationist perspective on the psychology of evil: Understanding how good people are transformed into perpetrators. In A. Miller (Ed.), *The social psychology of good and evil: Understanding our capacity for kindness and cruelty*. New York: Guilford.

6 Empathy, convictions, and self-reported offending of males and females in the Cambridge study in delinquent development

David P. Farrington and Darrick Jolliffe

Introduction

Jolliffe and Farrington (2004) published a systematic review and meta-analysis of 35 studies comparing questionnaire measures of empathy to measures of offending. They found that low cognitive empathy ($d = -.48$) and low affective empathy ($d = -.11$) were significantly related to offending. However, there were very few studies of female offending, and the offenders in all 35 studies were all officially defined, either convicted or incarcerated. Similar conclusions were drawn in a later meta-analysis by van Langen, Wissink, van Vugt, van der Stouwe, and Stams (2014). Offending was more strongly related to low cognitive empathy ($d = -.43$) than to low affective empathy ($d = -.19$), only six out of 30 studies provided information about females, and most offender samples consisted of prisoners.

Hardly any projects have investigated the relationship between low empathy and self-reported offending in community samples. This investigation is important because low empathy may be related to the probability of getting caught, convicted, or imprisoned, rather than to the probability of offending. A review by Jolliffe and Farrington (2014) showed that self-reports were reliable and valid measures of offending. Jolliffe and Farrington (2007) studied the relationship between low empathy and self-reported offending in a school-based sample of 720 adolescents aged 14.8 on average. They found that high rate male and female offenders had lower empathy (especially affective) than low rate male and female offenders.

The main aim of this chapter is to investigate the relationship between empathy (measured by the Basic Empathy Scale or BES; Jolliffe & Farrington, 2006) and official and self-reported offending of males and females in generation 3 (G3) of the Cambridge Study in Delinquent development (CSDD). The CSDD is a prospective longitudinal study of 411 London males who were first assessed at age 8–9 in 1961–2. These males are now termed generation 2 (G2). Their parents are generation 1 (G1) and their children are G3.

Several previous papers have studied offending by the G3 children. Farrington, Ttofi, and Crago (2017) and Auty, Farrington, and Coid (2017) investigated the intergenerational transmission of convictions from G2 to G3, and mediating factors. Farrington, Ttofi, and Crago (2018) examined the intergenerational transmission of self-reported offending from G2 males to G3 males, and mediating factors. Farrington and Crago (2016) studied the concentration of convictions in families, comparing the G1-G2 families with the G2-G3 families. Farrington, Ttofi, Crago, and Coid (2015) showed that the childhood risk factors for convictions of G2 males were similar to the childhood risk factors for convictions of G3 males.

In a review of risk factors for violence, Farrington (2018) reported childhood risk factors for violence convictions of G2 males and G3 males, and Farrington and Malvaso (2019) showed that the most important childhood risk factors for both were harsh discipline/physical punishment, a convicted father and low income/poor housing. Finally, Farrington and McGee (2019) investigated childhood risk factors for convictions of G2 males and G3 males, in testing the Integrated Cognitive Antisocial Potential (ICAP) theory. However, all these previous analyses were based on searches of the criminal records of G3 children up to 2012. This chapter reports the first analyses based on searches of the criminal records of G3 children up to 2017.

Method

The CSDD

The CSDD began in 1961, and for the first 20 years it was directed by Donald West. David Farrington started working on it in 1969, and began directing the CSDD in 1982. The most recent data collections were jointly directed by David Farrington and Jeremy Coid (Farrington et al., 2006). The results of the CSDD have been described in six books (Farrington, Piquero, & Jennings, 2013; Piquero, Farrington, & Blumstein, 2007; West, 1969, 1982; West & Farrington, 1973, 1977), and in six summary articles (Farrington, 1995, 2003, 2019; Farrington & West, 1981, 1990; Farrington, Coid, & West, 2009).

At the time they were first contacted in 1961–62, the G2 boys were all living in a working-class area of South London. The vast majority of the sample was chosen by taking all the boys who were then aged 8–9 and on the registers of six state primary schools within a one-mile radius of a research office which had been established. In addition to 399 boys from these six schools, 12 boys from a local school for educationally subnormal children were included in the sample, in an attempt to make it more representative of the population of boys living in the area. Therefore, the G2 boys were not a probability sample drawn from a population, but rather a complete population of boys of that age in that area at that time. Most of the G2 boys were born in 1953.

Most of the G2 boys (357, or 87%) were White in appearance and of British origin, in the sense that they were being brought up by parents who had themselves been brought up in England, Scotland, or Wales. Of the remaining 54 boys, 12 were African-Caribbean, having at least one parent of West Indian (usually) or African origin. Of the remaining 42 boys of non-British origin, 14 had at least one parent from the North or South of Ireland, 12 had parents from Cyprus, and the other 16 boys were Caucasian and had at least one parent from another Western industrialised country.

On the basis of their fathers' occupations when they were aged 8, 94% of the G2 boys could be described as working class (categories III, IV or V on the Registrar General's scale, describing skilled, semi-skilled or unskilled manual workers), in comparison with the national figure of 78% at that time. The majority of the boys were living in conventional two-parent families with both a father and a mother figure; at age 8, only 6% of the boys had no operative father and only 1% had no operative mother. This was, therefore, overwhelmingly a traditional White, urban, working-class sample of British origin.

Interviews

The G2 males have been assessed or interviewed nine times, at ages 8, 10, 14, 16, 18, 21, 25, 32, and 48. At all ages except 21 and 25, the aim was to interview all the males who were still alive, and it was always possible to interview a high proportion: 405 (99%) at age 14, 399 (97%) at age 16, 389 (95%) at age 18, 378 (94%) at age 32, and 365 (93%) at age 48. At age 21, the aim was to interview all the convicted males and an equal number of randomly chosen unconvicted males, and 218 of the 241 target males (90%) were interviewed. At age 25, only 85 males were interviewed.

Between 2004 and 2013, efforts were made to interview the biological G3 children of the G2 males. There were 691 G3 children whose name and date of birth were known. Only children aged at least 18 (born up to 1995) were targeted. The ethical requirements of the South-East Region Medical Ethics Committee required that we contact the G2 male and/or his female partner in trying to interview the G3 children. Therefore, 20 children whose fathers refused at age 48, and 7 children who father was dead at age 48 (and where no female partner was available) were not eligible to be interviewed. An additional six G3 children who had died and three who were disabled (one Down's syndrome, one mental health problems, one severe attention deficit-hyperactivity disorder), together with two who did not know that the G2 male was their father, were considered to be not eligible.

Of the 653 eligible G3 children, 551 were interviewed (84.4%); 291 of the 343 G3 males (84.8%) and 260 of the 310 G3 females (83.9%). Of the remainder, 39 children refused, 33 parents refused, 13 children could not be traced, 14 were elusive (agreeing or not refusing but never being available to interview), and three were aggressive or problematic. This chapter focuses on the G3 children. They were interviewed at the average age of 25, and more than half were aged between 23 and 27. The mean age interviewed was similar for the 291 G3 males (25.6) and the 260 G3 females (25.4).

Criminal record searches of the G3 children

The minimum age of criminal responsibility in England and Wales is 10. Officially recorded cautions were counted as well as convictions in the Police National Computer (PNC), since cautions were routinely recorded on a national basis from 1995. In this chapter, "convictions" include cautions. Convictions were only counted if they were for "standard list" (more serious) offences, thereby excluding minor crimes such as minor traffic infractions and simple drunkenness. The most common offences that were included were thefts, burglaries and unauthorised takings of vehicles, although there were also quite a few offences of violence, vandalism, fraud and drug abuse. The definition of what is a "standard list" offence changed over time. In particular, common assault became a standard list offence in July 1995, drunk driving was added to the standard list from January 1996, and being drunk and disorderly was added in April 1997. All of these types of offences were counted.

As mentioned, there were 691 G3 children whose name and date of birth were known. Their median year of birth was 1981, and more than half were born between 1977 and 1985. They were first searched in microfiche records in 1994, and they were then searched in the PNC in 2003, 2006, 2011–12, and most recently in 2017. Because of the time intervals between an offence and a conviction, and between a conviction and its appearance in the PNC, the records only include offences committed up to the end of 2015. We have always counted the age when an offence was committed, not the age at the time of a conviction. In light of these considerations, the median age at which the G3 children were last searched was 34, and more than half were last searched between ages 30 and 37. The 31 G3 children who were abroad could not be searched, but 655 of the remaining 660 were considered to be searched. These included 342 G3 males and 313 G3 females. The other five cases had common names, and it was not clear that the correct person had been searched. Almost all G3 children (92%) were searched at least up to age 25.

Self-reported offending of the G3 children

During their interview at the average age of 25, the G3 children were asked to admit how many times they had committed specified offences in the previous five years. These offences included burglary, theft of vehicles, theft from vehicles, shoplifting, theft from slot machines, theft from work, vandalism, assault (defined according to involvement in fights), starting fights, and driving after drinking at least 10 units of alcohol, which would have caused them to fail the breathalyser test. (1 unit = 10 ml of pure alcohol. This is approximately a half-pint of beer or cider, a small glass of wine, or a single measure of spirits.) They were given a score of how many offences they admitted out of 10.

Results

Empathy versus convictions

Of the 342 G3 males, 102 (29.8%) were convicted, compared with 32 (10.2%) of the 313 G3 females, a significant difference (odds ratio or OR = 3.73, 95% confidence interval or CI = 2.42 to 5.75).

Of the 291 G3 males who were interviewed, 274 (94.2%) completed the BES and 267 of these were searched in the PNC. Of the 260 G3 females who were interviewed, 258 (99.2%) completed the BES, and 253 of these were searched in the PNC. Of these 267 G3 males, 79 (29.6%) were convicted, compared with 28 (11.1%) of the 253 G3 females, a significant difference (OR = 3.38, CI = 2.11 to 5.42).

Of the 274 G3 males who completed the BES, their average score was 35.0 on affective empathy, compared to the average score of the 258 G3 females of 41.6. These scores were significantly different: F (1,530) = 159.05, $p < .0001$. Similarly, the G3 females scored higher on cognitive empathy: mean 36.5 compared with 34.7: F (1,530) = 28.73, $p < .0001$. Affective and cognitive empathy scores were significantly correlated for males ($r = .339$) and females ($r = .384$).

Table 6.1 divides BES scores into the highest quarter, the middle half, and the lowest quarter, and shows the percentage convicted in each category. As expected,

Table 6.1 Empathy versus convictions

Empathy Score	*Not Convicted*	*Convicted*	*Total*	*% Convicted*
Males-Affective				
High (40–50)	46	15	61	24.6
Medium (31–39)	100	41	141	29.1
Low (15–30)	42	23	65	35.4
Total	188	79	267	29.6
Males – Cognitive				
High (38–45)	45	13	58	22.4
Medium (33–37)	101	40	141	28.4
Low (20–32)	42	26	68	38.2
Total	188	79	267	29.6
Females – Affective				
High (46–55)	65	3	68	4.4
Medium (39–45)	105	13	118	11.0
Low (21–38)	55	12	67	17.9
Total	225	28	253	11.1
Females – Cognitive				
High (39–45)	64	4	68	5.9
Medium (35–38)	106	11	117	9.4
Low (24–34)	55	13	68	19.1
Total	225	28	253	11.1
Juvenile Convictions				
Males – Affective				
High (40–50)	55	6	61	9.8
Medium (31–39)	124	17	141	12.1
Low (15–30)	53	12	65	18.5
Total	232	35	267	13.1
Males – Cognitive				
High (38–45)	53	5	58	8.6
Medium (33–37)	120	21	141	14.9
Low (20–32)	59	9	68	13.2
Total	232	35	267	13.1

the percentage convicted decreased as the empathy score increased. For affective empathy of G3 males, the decrease was from 35.4% of low scorers to 24.6% of high scorers, but this decrease was not significant: chi-square (2 df) = 1.80. Similarly, for cognitive empathy of G3 males, the decrease was from 38.2% of low scorers to 22.4% of high scorers, but again this decrease was not significant: chi-square (2 df) = 3.97.

The decreases for G3 females were significant. For affective empathy, the percentage convicted decreased from 17.9% of low scorers to 4.4% of high scorers: chi-square (2 df) = 6.25, *p* = .044. For cognitive empathy, the percentage convicted decreased from 19.1% of low scorers to 5.9% of high scorers: chi-square (2 df) = 6.66, *p* = .036.

Would empathy be significantly related to convictions of G3 males if a more extreme category of convictions was studied? Of the 79 convicted G3 males with BES scores, 35 were convicted as juveniles (before age 18). It is known that an early age of onset predicts a large number of convictions and a long duration of criminal careers (e.g. Farrington et al., 2013). Therefore, the relationship between empathy and juvenile convictions was studied (see Table 6.1). The probability of a juvenile conviction increased from high to low affective empathy (from 9.8% to 18.5%), but this was again not significant: chi-square (2 df) = 2.35. This probability increased only irregularly from high to low cognitive empathy (from 8.6% to 13.2%), and again this was not significant: chi-square (2 df) = 1.42.

As might have been expected, the probability of being convicted tended to increase with the age searched (considered to be the age on December 31, 2015). Of the 291 G3 males who were interviewed, 275 (94.5%) were searched in the PNC. The average age searched of the 81 who were convicted was significantly greater than that of the 194 who were not convicted: 34.7 compared with 32.6: F (1,273) = 9.43, *p* = .002. Of the 260 G3 females who were interviewed, 255 (98.1%) were searched in the PNC. The average age searched of the 28 who were convicted was greater, but not significantly greater, than that of the 227 who were not convicted: 35.1 compared with 33.4: F (1,273) = 2.49.

Affective and cognitive empathy scores were not significantly correlated with either age interviewed or age searched. For the 274 G3 males with BES scores, age interviewed correlated −.026 with the affective score and −.011 with the cognitive score. For the 267 G3 males with BES scores who were searched, age searched correlated .057 with the affective score and −.072 with the cognitive score. For the 258 G3 females with BES scores, age interviewed correlated −.037 with the affective score and −.035 with the cognitive score. For the 253 G3 females with BES scores who were searched, age searched correlated .008 with the affective score and −.036 with the cognitive score.

In the light of the relationship between age searched and the probability of conviction, the relationship between empathy and the probability of conviction was investigated in logistic regression analyses, controlling for age searched. One-tailed *p*-values were used in light of the clear directional predictions. Table 6.2 shows that, even after controlling for age searched, the affective and cognitive

Table 6.2 Empathy versus convictions in logistic regression analyses

	B	*SE*	*P*
Males – affective	−.024	.022	.138
Age searched	.074	.027	.003
Males – cognitive	−.043	.034	.099
Age searched	.071	.027	.005
Females – affective	−.095	.033	.002
Age searched	.059	.038	.058
Females – cognitive	−.122	.054	.012
Age searched	.060	.039	.064
Juvenile convictions			
Males – affective	−.049	.029	.046
Age searched	.011	.035	.373
Males – cognitive	−.020	.045	.323
Age searched	.006	.035	.428

Note: *p*-values one-tailed in light of directional predictions.

empathy scores of G3 females still significantly predicted their probability of conviction. Also, after controlling for age searched, the affective and cognitive empathy scores of G3 males still did not significantly predict their probability of conviction, although the *p*-value for cognitive empathy was (just) less than .10.

Since all G3 males were searched after their 18th birthday, it was not surprising that age searched was not significantly related to juvenile convictions. Of the 81 G3 males who were interviewed, searched, and convicted, 36 were convicted as juveniles. The average age searched of these 36 G3 males was not significantly different from that of the remaining 239 who were interviewed and searched: 33.5 compared to 35.2: $F(1,273) = .09$. Table 6.2 shows that the affective empathy scores of G3 males were significantly related to juvenile convictions in these analyses. However, the cognitive empathy scores were not significantly related.

Self-reported offending

Not surprisingly, the mean score of the 291 G3 males on the 10-point self-reported offending (SRO) scale was significantly greater than that of the 260 G3 females: 2.57 compared to 1.18; $F(1,549) = 78.67$, $p < .0001$. The SRO scores were highly skewed. Of the G3 males, 105 scored 0–1, 100 scored 2–3, and 86 scored 4–10. Of the G3 females, 105 scored 0, 80 scored 1, and 75 scored 2–8.

Table 6.3 shows that SRO scores were significantly related to the probability of being convicted. For G3 males, this probability increased from 14.1% of those scoring 0–1 to 46.3% of those scoring 4 or more: chi-square (2 df) = 22.51, $p < .0001$. For G3 females, this probability increased from 3.8% of those scoring 0 to 19.4% of those scoring 2 or more: chi-square (2 df) = 10.92, $p = .004$.

Table 6.3 Self-reported offending versus convictions and empathy

Males					*Females*				
(a) Convictions									
SRO	*NC*	*C*	*T*	*% C*	*SRO*	*NC*	*C*	*T*	*% C*
0–1	85	14	99	14.1	0	100	4	104	3.8
2–3	65	29	94	30.9	1	69	10	79	12.7
4+	44	38	82	46.3	2+	58	14	72	19.4
T	194	81	275	29.5	T	227	28	255	11.0
(b) Affective Empathy									
Score	*NS*	*S*	*T*	*% S*	*Score*	*NS*	*S*	*T*	*% S*
H	46	16	62	25.8	H	52	16	68	23.5
M	97	48	145	33.1	M	85	35	120	29.2
L	47	20	67	29.9	L	47	23	70	32.9
T	190	84	274	30.7	T	184	74	258	28.7
(c) Cognitive Empathy									
Score	*NS*	*S*	*T*	*% S*	*Score*	*NS*	*S*	*T*	*% S*
H	43	16	59	27.1	H	53	16	69	23.2
M	104	41	145	28.3	M	86	33	119	27.7
L	43	27	75	38.6	L	45	25	70	35.7
T	190	84	274	30.7	T	184	74	258	28.7

Notes: SRO = Self-reported offending; NC = Not convicted; C = Convicted; T = Total; S = High SRO score; NS = Lower SRO score; H = High empathy score; M = Medium empathy score; L = Low empathy score (see Table 1).

For comparison with Table 6.1, Table 6.3 also shows the relationship between empathy scores and high SRO scores (defined as 4 or more for G3 males and 2 or more for G3 females). Except for affective empathy of G3 males, the probability of a high SRO score was highest for the low empathy scorers and lowest for the high empathy scorers. However, none of these relationships between empathy and high SRO scores was statistically significant. The chi-square values (2 df) were as follows: affective empathy of males, 1.11; cognitive empathy of males, 2.80; affective empathy of females, 1.49; and cognitive empathy of females, 2.76.

The SRO score was not significantly related to age at interview for G3 males ($r = .104$) or G3 females ($r = -.045$). Nevertheless, for comparison with the results for convictions shown in Table 6.2, logistic regression analyses were carried out to investigate to what extent empathy scores were related to high SRO scores independently of the age at interview. Table 6.4 shows that, for G3 males, low cognitive empathy was almost significantly related to high SRO scores, but low affective empathy was not significantly related. However, for G3 females, low affective empathy and low cognitive empathy were both significantly related to high SRO scores (see Note 1).

Table 6.4 Empathy versus high SRO scores in logistic regression analyses

	B	*SE*	*P*
Males – affective	−.007	.021	.376
Age interviewed	.042	.033	.101
Males – cognitive	−.046	.032	.078
Age interviewed	.042	.033	.102
Females – affective	−.042	.023	.033
Age interviewed	−.058	.038	.063
Females – cognitive	−.077	.037	.018
Age interviewed	−.059	.038	.061

Note: SRO = Self-reported offending; *p*-values one-tailed in light of directional predictions.

Conclusions

Our analyses show that affective and cognitive empathy were clearly and consistently related to convictions and self-reported offending for G3 females. They were rather inconsistently related to convictions and self-reported offending for G3 males. Future analyses should seek to explain this gender difference.

In contrast to the conclusions of previous meta-analyses, cognitive empathy was not more strongly related to offending than was affective empathy. For G3 males, affective empathy was significantly related to juvenile convictions and cognitive empathy was almost significantly related to high SRO scores. For females, affective and cognitive empathy were both significantly related to convictions and high SRO scores in logistic regression analyses. It may be that case-control comparisons of prisoners and control groups produce different results from community samples.

It would be desirable to investigate the extent to which the relationship between empathy and offending holds up after controlling for other variables that are related to both empathy and offending, and especially after controlling for earlier risk factors for offending. The commonly accepted criteria for a causal effect of a variable X on offending are that (1) X is related to offending, (2) X occurs before offending, and (3) the relationship between X and offending holds up after controlling for other variables.

Future longitudinal research, with repeated measures of empathy and offending, is ideally needed to investigate whether within-individual changes in empathy are reliably followed by within-individual changes in offending. It might then be possible to draw convincing conclusions about the causal effects of empathy on offending.

Note 1

Because the G3 children are not all independent, it might be desirable (ideally) to adjust the variance of effect sizes to take account of the clustering of G3 children in G2 families. It is easiest to do this by referring to the standardised mean difference d.

Clustering has no material effect on the value of d but it increases the variance of d (see e.g. Hedges & Hedberg, 2007). This variance is increased by [1 + (n – 1)*ICC], where n is the number of individuals in a cluster (e.g. the average number of children in a family) and ICC is the intraclass correlation. This correction has been known for many years and has been called the design effect (e.g. Kish, 1965) or the variance inflation factor (e.g. Donner, Birkett, & Buck, 1981). A similar adjustment could be made to effect sizes that are mathematically related to d, including the variance of B in regression analyses and the variance of Ln(OR).

For convictions of G3 males, the ICC was .27, implying that the SE should be increased by 7.1%. For convictions of G3 females, the ICC was .08, implying that the SE should be increased by 2.0%. It is not surprising that the clustering of convictions in families was greater for G3 males, because convictions of G3 females were much less prevalent. For dichotomised self-report scores, the ICC was .14 for G3 males (implying that the SE should be increased by 3.5%) and .13 for G3 females (implying that the SE should be increased by 3.0%). However, these corrections were not made because they would have had negligible effects on the results. The significant relationships with empathy for G3 females would have become slightly less significant, and the non-significant relationships with empathy for G3 males would still have been non-significant.

Acknowledgements

For funding the CSDD, we are very grateful to the Home Office, the Department of Health, the Department of Education, the Rayne Foundation, the Barrow Cadbury Trust, and the Smith-Richardson Foundation. For carrying out criminal record searches, we are very grateful to Gwen Gundry in the 1960s and 1970s, Lynda Morley in the 1980s, Sandra Lambert in the 1990s, Debbie Wilson in the 2000s, Owen Thomas in 2011–12, and Lisa Robinson in 2017.

References

Auty, K. M., Farrington, D. P., & Coid, J. W. (2017). The intergenerational transmission of criminal offending: Exploring gender-specific mechanisms. *British Journal of Criminology, 57*, 215–237.

Donner, A., Birkett, N., & Buck, C. (1981). Randomization by cluster. *American Journal of Epidemiology, 114*, 906–914.

Farrington, D. P. (1995). The development of offending and antisocial behaviour from childhood: Key findings from the Cambridge study in delinquent development. *Journal of Child Psychology and Psychiatry, 36*, 929–964.

Farrington, D. P. (2003). Key results from the first 40 years of the Cambridge study in delinquent development. In T. P. Thornberry & M. D. Krohn (Eds.), *Taking stock of delinquency: An overview of findings from contemporary longitudinal studies* (pp. 137–183). New York: Kluwer, Plenum.

Farrington, D. P. (2018). Origins of violent behavior over the life span. In A. T. Vazsonyi, D. J. Flannery, & M. DeLisi (Eds.), *The Cambridge handbook of violent behavior and aggression* (2nd ed., pp. 3–30). Cambridge: Cambridge University Press.

Farrington, D. P. (2019). The Cambridge study in delinquent development. In D. Eaves, C. D. Webster, Q. Haque, & J. Eaves-Thalken (Eds.), *Risk rules: A practical guide to structured professional judgment and violence prevention* (pp. 225–233). Hove, East Sussex: Pavilion Publishing.

Farrington, D. P., Coid, J. W., Harnett, L., Jolliffe, D., Soteriou, N., Turner, R., & West, D. J. (2006). *Criminal careers up to age 50 and life success up to age 48: New findings from the Cambridge study in delinquent development* (Research Study No. 299). London: Home Office.

Farrington, D. P., Coid, J. W., & West, D. J. (2009). The development of offending from age 8 to age 50: Recent results from the Cambridge study in delinquent development. *Monatsschrift fur Kriminologie und Strafrechtsreform* [*Journal of Criminology and Penal Reform*], *92*, 160–173.

Farrington, D. P., & Crago, R. V. (2016). The concentration of convictions in two generations of families. In A. Kapardis & D. P. Farrington (Eds.), *The psychology of crime, policing and courts* (pp. 7–23). Abingdon: Routledge.

Farrington, D. P., &. Malvaso, C. G. (2019). Physical punishment and offending in two successive generations of males. In I. Bryce, Y. Robinson, & W. Petherick (Eds.), *Child abuse and neglect: Forensic issues in evidence, impact and management* (pp. 203–224). London: Academic Press.

Farrington, D. P., & McGee, T. R. (2019). The integrated cognitive antisocial potential (ICAP) theory: New empirical tests. In D. P. Farrington, L. Kazemian, & A. R. Piquero (Eds.), *The Oxford handbook of developmental and life-course criminology* (pp. 173–192). New York: Oxford University Press.

Farrington, D. P., Piquero, A. R., & Jennings, W. G. (2013). *Offending from childhood to late middle age: Recent results from the Cambridge study in delinquent development.* New York: Springer.

Farrington, D. P., Ttofi, M. M., & Crago, R. V. (2017). Intergenerational transmission of convictions for different types of offenses. *Victims and Offenders*, *12*, 1–20.

Farrington, D. P., Ttofi, M. M., & Crago, R. V. (2018). Intergenerational transmission of self-reported offending in the Cambridge study in delinquent development. In V. I. Eichelsheim & S. G. A. van de Weijer (Eds.), *Intergenerational continuity of criminal and antisocial behaviour: An international overview of studies* (pp. 115–136). Abingdon: Routledge.

Farrington, D. P., Ttofi, M. M., Crago, R. V., & Coid, J. W. (2015). Intergenerational similarities in risk factors for offending. *Journal of Developmental and Life-Course Criminology*, *1*, 48–62.

Farrington, D. P., & West, D. J. (1981). The Cambridge study in delinquent development (United Kingdom). In S. A. Mednick & A. E. Baert (Eds.), *Prospective longitudinal research* (pp. 137–145). Oxford: Oxford University Press.

Farrington, D. P., & West, D. J. (1990). The Cambridge study in delinquent development: A long-term follow-up of 411 London males. In H. J. Kerner & G. Kaiser (Eds.), *Kriminalitat: Personlichkeit, lebensgeschichte und verhalten* [*Criminality: Personality, behavior and life history*] (pp. 115–138). Berlin: Springer.

Hedges, L. V., & Hedberg, E. C. (2007). Intraclass correlations for planning group randomized experiments in rural education. *Journal of Research in Rural Education*, *22*, 1–15.

Jolliffe, D., & Farrington, D. P. (2004). Empathy and offending: A systematic review and meta-analysis. *Aggression and Violent Behavior*, *9*, 441–476.

Jolliffe, D., & Farrington, D. P. (2006). Development and validation of the basic empathy scale. *Journal of Adolescence*, *29*, 589–611.

Jolliffe, D., & Farrington, D. P. (2007). Examining the relationship between low empathy and self-reported offending. *Legal and Criminological Psychology*, *12*, 265–286.

Jolliffe, D., & Farrington, D. P. (2014). Self-reported offending: Reliability and validity. In G. J. N. Bruinsma & D. Weisburd (Eds.), *Encyclopedia of criminology and criminal justice* (pp. 4716–4723). New York: Springer.

Kish, L. (1965). *Survey sampling*. New York: Wiley.

Piquero, A. R., Farrington, D. P., & Blumstein, A. (2007). *Key issues in criminal career research: New analyses of the Cambridge study in delinquent development*. Cambridge: Cambridge University Press.

van Langen, M. A. M., Wissink, I. B., van Vugt, E. S., van der Stouwe, T., & Stams, G. J. J. M. (2014). The relation between empathy and offending: A meta-analysis. *Aggression and Violent Behavior*, *19*, 179–189.

West, D. J. (1969). *Present conduct and future delinquency*. London: Heinemann.

West, D. J. (1982). *Delinquency: Its roots, careers and prospects*. London: Heinemann.

West, D. J., & Farrington, D. P. (1973). *Who becomes delinquent?* London: Heinemann.

West, D. J., & Farrington, D. P. (1977). *The delinquent way of life*. London: Heinemann.

7 Empathy and reoffending in a UK probation sample

Darrick Jolliffe and David P. Farrington

Introduction

Empathy is typically defined as both a cognitive ability to accurately identify the emotions of other people, and an affective trait which facilitates the actual experience of the emotions of others (Cohen & Strayer, 1996). Across numerous domains including criminology and psychology, low empathy is consistently identified as a potentially important explanation for criminal or antisocial behaviour. For example, the well-known concept of psychopathy, a constellation of psychological and behavioural traits linked to an increased likelihood of perpetrating serious violence and harm, has "lack of empathy" as one of its core features (Hare, 2003). In addition, many evidence-based interventions designed to reduce reoffending have the development of empathy as a key component (Wastell, Cairns, & Haywood, 2009).

Theoretically, those with low empathy are believed to be more likely to offend. This is because they lack accurate information about the emotional impact of their antisocial behaviour on others (low cognitive empathy), and because they fail to experience the emotional reaction that occurs in others as a result of their criminal behaviour (low affective empathy). Two systematic reviews and meta-analyses comparing the empathy of offenders and non-offenders have produced similar results, suggesting that low empathy is related to offending, but with important caveats (Jolliffe & Farrington, 2004; van Langen et al., 2014). These included that the relationship between low empathy and offending was significantly influenced by the measure of empathy,[1] and also that the definition of "offenders" in the primary studies needed to be expanded to help understand the potential link between low empathy and offending. This was because, in almost all primary studies included in both systematic reviews, offenders were those serving time in prison.

In delineating the link between low empathy and criminal behaviour, it is important to consider how both empathy and behaviour are measured. The Basic Empathy Scale (Jolliffe & Farrington, 2006) has been shown to be a valid and reliable tool to measure both cognitive and affective empathy. The evidence in support of this measure is growing, but its use amongst people who have been convicted of a criminal offence is somewhat limited (although see Pechorro et al., this volume).

A full explication of the approaches that can be used to measure offending is beyond the scope of this chapter (see Jolliffe & Farrington, 2014), but it is well-known that prisoners are not representative all those committing offences. In addition, prisoners may score low on measures of empathy because they have committed offences of a sufficient number or seriousness to be sent to prison, or because the experience of imprisonment can erode empathy (Sykes, 1958/2007). These alternative explanations of the "low empathy – offending" link would have very different implications for understanding the importance of empathy as a cause of offending, and of empathy enhancement as a method of reducing reoffending.

First detailed by Blumstein et al. (1986), the criminal career approach encourages the separation of important aspects of offending, such as prevalence (the proportion committing an offence), frequency (the number of offences), the age of first offence, etc. This approach facilitates a more nuanced view of offending than the typical dichotomy of prisoner versus control used in most previous empathy and offending research. It could be that low empathy is associated with certain criminal career features (i.e. the prevalence of certain offence types), but not others (i.e. the probability of reoffending).

Relatively few studies have examined the relationship between low empathy and criminal career features or reoffending. Lauterbach and Hosser (2007) used a shortened version of the Interpersonal Reactivity Index (Davis, 1983)[2] to evaluate the empathy of 839 first-time imprisoned young male offenders (mean age 20.7, *SD* = 2.0) from five prisons in Germany. The IRI is a measure of empathy which has four subscales: Empathy Concern (a measure of the concern one has for others), Empathic Fantasy (a measure of how engaged one becomes with fictional characters), Personal Distress (a measure of distress from emotional situations) and Perspective Taking (a measure of one's ability to understand another's point of view). The authors found that those who self-reported three or more previous violent offences scored significantly lower on the empathy subscales, and also that the Perspective Taking Scale was positively correlated with socio-economic status. Logistic regression was used to predict the violent reoffending of the 577 young males who had been released for at least 24 months, and the results showed that, controlling for measures of IQ, socio-economic status, age and length of detention, low Perspective Taking significantly predicted violent reoffending.

Bok and Hosser (2013) re-examined the relationship between low empathy and reoffending using the same sample of first-time imprisoned young males. Just under half of the young men (47%) were in prison for violent offences, with most of the remainder having committed property (41%) offences. Controlling for age, IQ, SES, and the duration of imprisonment, the type of offence was significantly related to empathy, with property offenders scoring significantly higher on empathy than violent offenders. When the reoffending of this sample was examined 5 years after release (and controlling for the same potential confounds), the results suggested that low Perspective Taking and Empathic Fantasy significantly predicted reoffending. Interestingly, low empathy was not significantly associated with an increased likelihood of violent reoffending.

The purpose of this chapter is to examine the relationship between low empathy and measures of offending in a group of male offenders on probation. In addition, the role that low empathy might have on reoffending is also explored.

Research questions

1 Is low empathy related to important criminal career parameters for male and female offenders?
2 Is low empathy related to measures of reoffending for male and female offenders?

The current study

Participants for this study were recruited from five probation offices in England as part of a study about the experience of probation (Turnbull, McSweeney, & Jolliffe, 2014). Individuals were approached as they left probation supervision meetings that were part of a community sentence that they were serving. This sentence was either served entirely in the community or partially served in the community after a period of incarceration (licence). Over 50 days, 1,000 potential participants were approached by the research team and asked to take part in the study by completing a questionnaire and also to give permission for their criminal records to be released.

The questionnaire asked about basic demographic information such as name, date of birth, ethnicity and gender (to locate the individual in criminal records), and about the type of community sentence they were serving (community or licence). Participants were also asked to complete the Basic Empathy Scale (Jolliffe & Farrington, 2006), a 20-item measure of affective and cognitive empathy.

The Police National Computer (PNC) database provided the criminal records for this study. The PNC is the national database for offences and convictions held and updated by the police in the UK. Briefly, the extracts of the PNC contain basic demographic information about the offender (for example, age at index offence, ethnicity) and information about criminal offending (e.g. index offence) and offending history (e.g. age at first offence). The criminal records of participants were extracted approximately 18 months after initial contact with them. This allowed for a 12-month follow-up reoffending period (plus six months for convictions to be placed on the criminal records).

Of the 1,000 individuals approached, 300 were ineligible (i.e. because they had been on probation for three months or less) and 237 individuals refused to take part. The most common reason given for not taking part was lack of time, but there was also reports of disinterest (i.e. not interested in completing this questionnaire, couldn't be bothered), and mistrust (i.e. not wanting to give personal details, not trusting the researchers). Out of the 463 people who agreed to participate and were eligible, 299 males and 40 females completed a sufficient number of items to produce a cognitive or affective empathy scale score and had their criminal records located. Because of the small numbers, the female sample is not considered further.

Analytic approach

As a result of the clear directional hypothesis with regard to low empathy and offending, and the benefits of dichotomisation, such as, addressing non-linearity (Farrington & Loeber, 2000) males were separately dichotomised into those with high empathy (highest 75%) and low empathy (lowest 25%). For example, of the 299 males who completed half or more of the BES affective items, 76 or 25.4% were categorised as the low affective empathy group, and of the 297 who completed half or more of the BES cognitive items 73 (24.6%) were categorised as the low cognitive empathy group. There was a clear association between the low affective empathy and low cognitive empathy groups in males. About 40% (30/76) of those who were in the low affective empathy group were also in the low cognitive group, compared to 20% (43/220) who were in the low cognitive/high affective empathy group. This results in an odds ratio (OR) of 2.7, 1.5–4.7, $p < .001$. The odds ratio is a measure of effect centred around 1.0, and as a rule of thumb an odds ratio of 2.0 (or 0.5), which is equivalent to the doubling (or halving) of the risk is considered to indicate a strong effect (Cohen, 1996).

Empathy and demographic and criminal history

Table 7.1 shows the relationship between empathy and the demographic and criminal history characteristics of the male sample. For example, the average age of the males in the sample was 32.6 (*SD* = 10.7). However, when the sample was separated into those with low affective empathy (LAE) and those with high affective empathy (HAE), those with LAE were found to be significantly younger (29.6 compared to 33.3, OR = 1.9, 1.6–1.3). Those in the low cognitive empathy (LCE) group were also found to be significantly younger. Interestingly, there was a significant relationship between ethnicity and affective empathy, with a higher proportion of White individuals in the LAE group (*OR* = 2.5, 1.1–10.0). Similarly, those on a licence were significantly more likely to be in the LCE group (*OR* = 2.0, 1.1–3.3).

The proportion of those with certain index offence categories was compared to empathy categories. For example, 18.9% of the sample had an index offence of "Other" (which included fraud, other motoring offences, vandalism, etc); 17.1% of the LAE group had this index offence compared to 19.5% of the HAE group. This difference (*OR* = 0.8, 0.4–1.7) was not significant. Those who had a drug offence were over-represented in the HAE group (not significant), and those who had an index offence of serious theft were over-represented in the LAE group (*OR* = 2.5, 1.7–5.0). There was no evidence that those with violent or sexual index offences were more likely to be in the LAE group.

Table 7.1 Low empathy and the background of the sample

	M (sd)	*Low Aff*	*Norm Aff*	*LCI*	*OR*	*UCI*	*% Low Cog*	*% Norm Cog*	*LCI*	*OR*	*UCI*
Av. Age at Index Offence	32.6 (10.7)	29.6 (9.4)	33.3 (11.1)	1.6	1.9	2.3	29.3 (10.2)	33.2 (10.8)	1.6	2.0	2.5
Ethnicity	*%*	*% Low Aff*	*% Norm Aff*	*LCI*	*OR*	*UCI*	*% Low Cog*	*% Norm Cog*	*LCI*	*OR*	*UCI*
White	83.8	92.1	80.7	1.1	2.5	10	84.4	82.2	0.4	0.8	1.7
Sentence Type	*%*	*% Low Aff*	*% Norm Aff*	*LCI*	*OR*	*UCI*	*% Low Cog*	*% Norm Cog*	*LCI*	*OR*	*UCI*
Licence	29%	36.1	27.6	0.8	1.4	2.5	40.6	26.9	1.1	2.0	3.3
Index Offence Category	*%*	*% Low Aff*	*% Norm Aff*	*LCI*	*OR*	*UCI*	*% Low Cog*	*% Norm Cog*	*LCI*	*OR*	*UCI*
Other	18.9	17.1	19.5	0.4	0.8	1.7	12.3	21.2	0.2	0.5	1.1
Theft	10.4	13.2	9.5	0.7	1.4	3.3	11	10.8	0.4	1.0	2.5
Serious Theft	8.5	11.8	7.2	1.7	2.5	5	12.3	7.2	0.8	1.7	5.0
Drug Offences	9.5	5.3	10.9	0.2	0.5	1.4	9.6	9.5	0.4	1.0	2.5
Sexual	10.5	7.9	10.9	0.3	0.7	1.7	2.7	12.6	0.1	0.2	0.8
Violence	42	44.7	42.1	0.7	1.1	2	52.1	38.7	1.1	1.7	3.3
Previous Offending	*%*	*% Low Aff*	*% Norm Aff*	*LCI*	*OR*	*UCI*	*% Low Cog*	*% Norm Cog*	*LCI*	*OR*	*UCI*
Previous Convictions	92.1	97.4	90.1	0.9	4.0	17	97.3	90.2	0.9	3.3	16.7
Previous Prison Sentences	53.4	59.2	51.6	0.8	1.4	2.5	61.6	50.4	0.9	1.7	2.5
Previous Serious Violence	5.4	7.9	4.5	0.6	2.0	5.0	5.5	5.4	0.3	1.0	3.3
Previous Violence	68.4	75.0	66.4	0.9	1.4	2.5	68.5	68.3	0.6	1.0	1.7
Previous Sex Offending	9.0	6.6	9.0	0.3	0.7	2.0	4.1	10.3	0.1	0.4	1.3

(Continued)

Table 7.1 (Continued)

	M (sd)	*Low Aff*	*Norm Aff*	*LCI*	*OR*	*UCI*	*Low Aff*	*Norm Aff*	*LCI*	*OR*	*UCI*
Age of First Conviction	19.7 (5.5)	17.8 (5.5)	20.5 (8.7)	1.4	1.9	2.3	18.0 (5.2)	20.3 (8.8)	1.3	1.7	2.0
OGRS	50.5 (25.0)	57.9 (22.4)	47.9 (25.5)	1.8	2.1	2.5	56.6 (22.6)	49.0 (25.6)	1.3	1.8	2.1
Measure of Frequency	*%*	*% Low Aff*	*% Norm Aff*	*LCI*	*OR*	*UCI*	*% Low Cog*	*% Norm Cog*	*LCI*	*OR*	*UCI*
Long Criminal Careers	25.1	22.4	26	0.4	0.8	1.4	13.7	28.1	0.2	0.4	0.8
High number of Prev. Conv	23.1	30.3	20.6	0.9	1.7	3.3	27.4	22.3	0.7	1.3	2.5
High number of Prev. Prison	15.4	21.1	13.5	0.9	1.7	3.3	23.3	13.4	1.1	2.0	3.3
High number of Prev. Viol	15.7	15.8	15.7	0.5	1.0	2.0	20.5	14.3	0.8	1.7	3.3

Those with an "Other" offence appeared to be over-represented in the HCE category while those with serious theft appeared more likely to be in the LCE category. Interestingly, those with sexual offences were significantly more likely to come from the high cognitive empathy (HCE) group (*OR* = 0.2, 0.1–0.8), while LCE was significantly associated with an index offence of violence (*OR* = 1.7, 1.1–3.3).

Low affective empathy appeared to be related to having previous convictions. For example, while 92.1% of the sample had previous convictions, 97.4% of the LAE group had previous convictions compared to 90.1% of the HAE group (*OR* = 4.0, 0.9–16.7). The results were similar for LCE (*OR* = 3.3, 0.9–16.7). No other comparisons were statistically significant, but it was noteworthy that previous sexual offending appeared more common in the HCE group (*OR* = 0.4, 0.1–1.3).

In addition to prevalence, it was also considered important to compare low empathy to measures of frequency of offending. The measures available were the number of previous convictions, the number of previous prison sentences and the number of previous violent offences. As these constructs were highly skewed, these were all dichotomised, as far as possible, into the "worst" 25% and the remaining 75%. For example, 23.1% of the total sample had a high number of previous convictions (33 or more), but this proportion was higher in the LAE group (30.3%) compared to the HAE group (20.6%). This difference just failed to reach significance (*OR* = 1.7, 0.9–3.3). The results were similar when these groups were compared on the proportion who had experienced a high number of previous prison sentences (*OR* = 1.7, 0.9–3.3). However, the results did suggest that LCE was significantly associated with a higher number of previous prison sentences (*OR* = 2.0, 1.1–3.3). Generally, the odds ratios were in the expected direction, with both lower affective and cognitive empathy being associated with greater criminal experience.

The Offender Group Reconviction Scale (OGRS) is an actuarial risk assessment device that predicts the probability of reoffending (from 0 to 100) one year after release. This actuarial estimate is based on the offender's gender, age at index offence and a measure of their speed of accruing convictions across their criminal career (Howard et al., 2009). The average OGRS score of the males in this sample was 50.5 (*SD* = 25.0), suggesting that these individuals had about a 50% chance of reoffending over the next 12 months. Those who had LAE and LCE had significantly higher OGRS scores, suggesting that the low empathy groups were significantly more likely to reoffend than those in the high empathy groups.

Reoffending

Table 7.2 shows measures of actual reoffending compared to low empathy for this sample. Overall, 49.8% of the men reoffended in the 12-month follow-up period. The percentage of those in the LAE group who reoffended was similar to those in the HAE group (52.6% compared to 48.9%), and this was also the case when those in the LCE group were compared to those in the HCE group (53.4% compared

Table 7.2 Low empathy and measures of reoffending

Males	*%*	*% Low Aff*	*% Norm Aff*	*LCI*	*OR*	*UCI*	*% Low Cog*	*% Norm Cog*	*LCI*	*OR*	*UCI*
Reoffending	49.8	52.6	48.9	0.7	1.1	2.0	53.4	49.1	0.7	1.3	2.0
Prison	33.6	32.5	33.9	0.4	0.9	2.0	23.1	37.3	0.2	0.5	1.1
High No. Reoff	28.2	27.5	28.4	0.4	1.0	2.0	20.5	31.8	0.2	0.6	1.3
Quick Time to Reoff	24.8	30.0	22.9	0.6	1.4	3.3	20.5	27.3	0.3	0.7	1.7
Types of Reoffence											
Other	52.3	62.5	48.6	0.8	1.7	5.0	51.3	52.7	0.5	0.9	2.0
Theft	16.8	17.5	16.5	0.4	1.1	2.5	23.1	14.5	0.7	1.7	5.0
Serious Theft	4.0	7.5	2.8	0.6	3.3	10.0	7.7	2.7	0.6	3.3	10.0
Drug Offences	8.1	10.0	7.3	0.4	1.4	5.0	5.1	9.1	0.1	0.5	2.5
Sexual	4.7	0.0[4]	6.4	0.01	0.2	3.0	2.6	5.5	0.1	0.5	3.3
Violence	14.1	2.5	18.3	0.01	0.1	0.9	10.3	15.5	0.2	0.7	2.0

to 49.1%). There was also little difference in the percentages of the LAE and HAE samples that were re-sentenced to prison, committed a high number of reoffences, and reoffended earlier.[3] Surprisingly, those in the HCE group appeared somewhat more likely to be re-sentenced to prison, to commit a high number of reoffences and to reoffend quickly.

There was some limited evidence of an association between LAE and reoffending with certain offence types. Those who reoffended with an "Other" offence, and with a drug offence appeared to be over-represented in the LAE group. Those who committed Serious Theft were over-represented in both the LAE and LCE groups with large odds ratios ($OR = 3.3$ for both) but these differences were not significant, likely because of small numbers. Similarly, those who committed Theft and may have been over-represented in the LCE group.

Very counterintuitively, however, there was evidence that those who committed a violent or sexual reoffence tended to be in the high empathy groups (both affective and cognitive) as opposed to the low empathy groups. In fact, none of those who reoffended with a sexual offence came from the LAE group and those with LAE were significantly less likely to reoffend with a violent offence.

Discussion

The results of this study suggested that LAE and LCE, generally, were related to measures of past offending in the expected direction. That is, those who had any previous convictions, previous serious violence, a high number of previous convictions and previous prison sentences appeared to have lower affective empathy. Similarly, those whose index offence was Serious Theft also had significantly lower affective empathy than other offenders. Those with previous convictions, those on licence, and those with an index offence of violence all had significantly lower cognitive empathy, as did those with a high number of previous prison sentences. In addition, the relation between low empathy and the strongest summary measure of the likelihood of reoffending (OGRS) was also in the expected direction, with those in the LAE and LCE groups having significantly higher predicted likelihoods of reoffending. However, there was only very limited evidence that LAE or LCE may have been associated with certain types of reoffending (Serious Theft), and violence or sexual offences were more common among high empathy groups.

The results of this study suggested that those who had an index sex offence, a history of sexual offending, or who reoffended with a sexual offence did not have low empathy compared to other offenders. In fact, there was evidence that these offenders may have had higher cognitive empathy. While this may be a result of how this sample was recruited and impression management (see later), this could also be because elevated cognitive empathy (compared to other offenders) is a true characteristic of sexual offenders. A heightened ability to read the emotions of others could be used by sex offenders in the commission of their offences (i.e. to groom potential victims).

Limitations and directions for future research

Individuals on probation were approached to complete these questionnaires by research assistants, and only those who agreed, who completed a sufficient number of empathy items, and whose criminal records could be located (based on the details they provided) were included. This likely resulted in a unique and non-representative sample. No inducements were offered for completing the questionnaire making it possible that this recruitment method resulted in a select group of offenders, potentially with higher empathy. Furthermore, while previous research has shown the BES to be unrelated to measures of social desirability (and less prone than other measures; Jolliffe & Farrington, 2006) it is still possible, especially in combination with the method of recruitment, that the empathy questionnaire was completed either as the offender wanted to be seen, or as they wanted to see themselves. This might explain why sex offenders, the offending group who carry the greatest stigma (Ricciardelli & Moir, 2013) scored higher on some measures of empathy.

It is perhaps not surprising that the BES was not strongly associated with reoffending. Typically, the best predictors of reoffending are static measures of previous criminal behaviour such as those included in the OGRS score (Farrington, Jolliffe, & Johnstone, 2008), rather than dynamic (changeable) features such as impulsiveness or empathy. Also, the key test of empathy's potential importance as a causal risk factor could only be evaluated if changes in empathy were compared to changes in offending (Murray et al., 2009). If increases in empathy were consistently associated with reductions in offending, this would provide strong evidence of empathy's importance as a causal risk factor.

Perhaps the most significant limitation of this study is the relatively short follow-up period. While 49.8% of the sample had reoffences recorded within the 12-month follow-up period, it is likely that most of these were dealt with in Magistrates court, which typically deals with less serious offending. However, those who commit serious offence are likely to be remanded to the Crown Court and may not have had their reconviction recorded within the 18-month follow-up period. Currently, the average time between an offence taking place and the outcome of a case is 51 weeks in Crown Courts in England and Wales (OpenJustice.gov.uk). This means that any serious offences committed by those in the current study that were committed later than 27 weeks after the start of the study would not be recorded within the current study. This estimate also assumes that this conviction would immediately show up on the PNC, which would be unlikely to be the case. This limitation may have had a particular impact on the results of this study as low empathy would be expected to be related to more serious reoffending, and the ability of this study to detect this serious reoffending was limited.

In addition, while this was a sample of probationers who were serving their sentence in the community, over 92% had previous convictions with an average of 26 previous convictions per offender; about 70% had previous offences for violence, each with an average of 4 previous violent offences, while 6% had previously committed serious violence. Over 9% of the sample had previously committed a sex offence and these offenders had an average of 6 previous sex offences per offender. In addition, over 50% of the sample had previously served time in prison, with an average of 12 previous prison sentences per offender. It is quite possible that the criminal history of these offenders lowered their threshold to be candidates for remand to the Crown Court.

Clearly, much more research on the relationship between empathy and offending is needed. In the absence of prospective longitudinal studies, in which empathy is assessed before the onset of offending, it is not possible to determine whether empathy is causally related to offending or simply a correlate. Low empathy was related to many forms of previous offending in the current study, but this could equally be interpreted as low empathy influencing these forms of offending, or low empathy being an outcome of previous offending. Similarly, those who had previously been to prison and who had been to prison more often had lower empathy (particularly cognitive), which could equally indicate that low empathy is associated with more serious forms of offending, or that experiencing prison reduces empathy. This temporal ambiguity again, calls into question the potential efficacy of empathy enhancement as a tool to reduce future offending.

In order to better understand the potential link between low empathy and offending, prospective longitudinal studies with multiple measures of empathy and offending are needed, similar to the seminal work of White et al. (1994) for impulsivity. Using a multi-trait, multisource assessment as part of the Pittsburgh Youth Study, a prospective longitudinal study, the authors identified two forms of impulsivity, behavioural and cognitive. Behavioural impulsivity, or an under-controlled temperament, was associated with later self-reported delinquency, controlling for socio-economic status and IQ, but cognitive impulsivity, a form of mental control, was not.

Administering multiple measures of empathy, including questionnaire methods and autonomic methods (e.g. galvanic skin response to videos), and using multiple information sources (self, parent), would allow for a much more comprehensive understanding of the structure of empathy. In addition, multiple measure of offending such as self-report, parent-report, teacher-report, and official records would allow for a much greater understanding of how empathy might relate to different forms of criminal and antisocial behaviour.

Conclusions

The results of this study suggested that low empathy was related to current and past offending in the expected direction. In addition, low empathy was related to a validated measure of the likelihood of future offending. However, low empathy did not appear to be related to reoffending. While limitations in the research approach adopted here may partially explain these results, clearly much more research on low empathy and offending is needed. Until the results of careful prospective longitudinal studies, which measure low empathy and offending, are available, it is not possible to confidently categorise empathy as a cause of offending, and therefore a viable target for intervention or a correlate of offending.

Notes

1 A weak measure of empathy erroneously increased the link between low cognitive empathy and offending in both reviews.
2 Concerns have been raised about the extent to which this device measures empathy (as opposed to sympathy) and the relationship between this measure and social desirability (Jolliffe & Farrington, 2006).
3 As before, the number of reoffences was dichotomised into those 25% with the highest number of reoffences and the remaining 75% and the time to reoffence was dichotomised into the 25% who reoffended the earliest compared to the remaining 75%.
4 The odds ratio was calculated using the Haldane-Anscombe correction.

References

Blumstein, A., Cohen, J., Roth, J. A., & Visher, C. A. (1986). *Criminal careers and career criminals*. Washington, DC: National Academies Press.

Bok, E. M., & Hosser, D. (2013). Empathy as a predictor of recidivism among young adult offenders. *Psychology, Crime & Law, 20*, 101–115.

Cohen, D., & Strayer, J. (1996). Empathy in conduct-disordered and comparison youth. *Developmental Psychology, 32*, 988–998.

Cohen, P. (1996). Childhood risks for young adult symptoms of personality disorder: Method and substance. *Multivariate Behavioral Research, 31*, 121–148.

Davis, M. H. (1983). Measuring individual differences in empathy: Evidence for a multidimensional approach. *Journal of Personality and Social Psychology, 44*, 113–126.

Farrington, D. P., Jolliffe, D., & Johnstone, L. (2008). *Assessing violence risk: A framework for practice*. Glasgow: Risk Management Authority. Retrieved from www.rmascotland.gov.uk/ViewFile.aspx?id=374

Farrington, D. P., & Loeber, R. (2000). Some benefits of dichotomization in psychiatric and criminological research. *Criminal Behaviour and Mental Health, 10*, 100–122.

Hare, R. D. (2003). *Hare psychopathy checklist-revised (PCL-R)*. Toronto: Multi-Health Systems.

Howard, P., Francis, B., Soothill, K., & Humphreys, L. (2009). *OGRS 3: The revised offender group reconviction scale*. Research Summary 7/09. London: Ministry of Justice.

Jolliffe, D., & Farrington, D. P. (2004). Empathy and offending: A systematic review and meta-analysis. *Aggression & Violent Behavior, 9*, 441–476.

Jolliffe, D., & Farrington, D. P. (2006). The development and validation of the basic empathy scale. *Journal of Adolescence, 29*, 589–611.

Jolliffe, D., & Farrington, D. P. (2014). The reliability and validity of self-reports of offending. In *Encyclopaedia of criminology* (pp. 4716–4723). New York: Springer.

Lauterbach, O., & Hosser, D. (2007). Assessing empathy in prisoners – a shortened version of the interpersonal reactivity index. *Swiss Journal of Psychology, 66*, 91–101.

Murray, J., Farrington, D. P., & Eisner, M. P. (2009). Drawing conclusions about causes from systematic reviews of risk factors: The Cambridge quality checklists. *Journal of Experimental Criminology, 5*, 1–23.

Ricciardelli, R., & Moir, M. (2013). Stigmatized among the stigmatized: Sex Offenders in Canadian penitentiaries. *Canadian Journal of Criminology and Criminal Justice, 55*, 353–386.

Sykes, G. M. (1958/2007). *The society of captives*. Princeton, NJ: Princeton University Press.

Turnbull, P., McSweeney, T., & Jolliffe, D. (2014). *The experience of probation and reoffending*. London: Ministry of Justice Research Report.

van Langen, M. A. M., Wissink, I. B., van Vugt, E. S., van der Stouwe, T., & Stams, G. J. J. M. (2014). The relation between empathy and offending: A meta-analysis. *Aggression and Violent Behavior, 19*, 179–189.

Wastell, C. A., Cairns, D., & Haywood, H. (2009). Empathy training, sex offenders and re-offending. *Journal of Sexual Aggression, 15*, 149–159.

White, J. L., Moffitt, T. E., Caspi, A., Bartusch, D. J., Needles, D. J., & Stouthamer-Loeber, M. (1994). Measuring impulsivity and examining its relationship to delinquency. *Journal of Abnormal Psychology, 103*, 192–205.

8 Empathy and psychopathy

How are they related in men and women?

Henriette Bergstrøm, Darrick Jolliffe, and David P. Farrington

Introduction

> Psychopathy is an empathy disorder.
>
> (Soderstrom, 2003, p. 249)

Psychopathy is a constellation of psychological traits and behaviours that has been consistently associated with an increased likelihood of criminal and antisocial behaviour, but particularly violence (Hare, 2003). While a number of tools have been developed to assess this latent construct, the Psychopathy Checklist tools of Robert Hare (including the screening version [PCL:SV; Hart, Cox, & Hare, 1995], the youth version [PCL:YV; Forth, Kosson, & Hare, 2003], and the child version (APSD; Frick & Hare, 2001) are the most widely used. Originally, the PCL tools were designed to measure two distinct, but correlated, factors. The first (Factor 1) included features such as deceitfulness, callousness, and a lack of remorse and empathy, while the second (Factor 2) comprised features such as impulsiveness, sensation seeking, aggressiveness and criminality.

Subsequent factor analytic studies have broken this factor structure down further into four facets termed "interpersonal" (facet 1), "affective" (facet 2), "lifestyle" (facet 3), and "antisocial" (facet 4). Each of these factors consists of traits, or symptoms, reflecting the factor's name and description (Hare, 2003). For example, facet 2, which measures the affective features of psychopathy consists of traits/symptoms such as being callous and lacking in empathy as well as an inability to feel guilt. Facet 4, on the other hand, is scored based on the individual's actual antisocial or criminal behaviour. Ratings using the PCL tools are typically based on both a semi-structured interview and available collateral records, with each item scored using a three-point scale (0 – item doesn't apply, 1 – item applies somewhat, 2 – item definitely applies).

The PCL may be the most common measure of psychopathy, but these tools have been criticised for being too focused on behaviours (e.g. Skeem & Cooke, 2010). Other conceptualizations of psychopathy also exist (e.g. Triarchic Model of Psychopathy; Patrick, Fowles, & Krueger, 2009; Elemental Psychopathy

Assessment, EPA; Lynam, Gaughan, Miller, Miller, Mullins-Sweat, & Widiger, 2011), and while there are variations between these measures and the PCL approach, all of these tools emphasise the assessment of inner dispositions, and commonly a lack of empathy and normative affective reactions are considered a key component. In fact, a lack of empathy is often considered the defining feature of psychopathy (Soderstrom, 2003).

Empathy is commonly defined as the ability to understand another's emotions (cognitive empathy) and/or actually experience the emotions of another (affective empathy), and this concept has also been associated with antisocial and criminal behaviour (e.g. Jolliffe & Farrington, 2004). Much like the situation with psychopathy, there are a number of methods of assessing empathy including peer reports (Kaukiainen et al., 1999), responses to vignettes (Cohen & Strayer, 1996) and questionnaires (e.g. Jolliffe & Farrington, 2006), each having their benefits and limitations. Questionnaire measures are by far the most common, however, and systematic reviews comparing questionnaire measures of empathy to crime and antisocial behaviour note a relationship of a strong to moderate size (r = .50 to r = .80; Jolliffe & Farrington, 2004; Vachon et al., 2014; van Langen et al., 2014).

While the lack of empathy amongst those high on psychopathic traits has been consistently noted in the literature (e.g. Brook & Kosson, 2013; de Ruigh, Jansen, Vermeiren, & Popma, 2019; Pajevic, Vukosavjelic-Gvozden, Stavanovic, & Neumann, 2018; Pfabigan et al., 2014), this is typically based on descriptive accounts of the behaviour of so-called psychopaths, such as their commission of particularly heinous crimes, or the psychopath's callous description of such offences. For example, item 5 of the PCL:SV prompts scorers that those who score high on this item would be:

> individuals who have little affective bonding with others and are unable to appreciate the emotional consequences (positive or negative) of their actions. As a result, they may appear cold and callous, unable to experience strong emotions, and indifferent to the feelings of others. Alternatively, they may express their emotions, but these emotional expressions are shallow and labile. The verbal and nonverbal aspects of their emotion may appear inconsistent.
>
> (Hart, Cox, & Hare 1995, p. 30)

Given the central importance of "a lack of empathy" in psychopathy, it is important to further develop the understanding of the relationship between these two concepts using a more precise tool to measure empathy. There are relatively few studies that have compared measures of psychopathy (either amongst those who may be psychopathic such as prisoners, or those in the community) with actual measures of empathy.

Empathy and psychopathy

Domes, Hollerbach, Vohs, Mokros, and Habermeyer (2013) separated a group of German prisoners (N = 90) into three groups according to their psychopathy levels using the PCL-R. The researchers also administered a comprehensive multi-component measure of empathy (IRI; Davis, 1983) and also included a control group ($N = 28$) of non-prisoners. Davis' (1983) IRI scale consists of four inter-related constructs: personal distress, fantasy, empathic concern (EC), and perspective taking (PT). Of these, the EC scale is often treated as a measure of affective empathy and the perspective taking scale is often treated as a measure of cognitive empathy (Davis, 1983). However, these scales have been criticised for being measures of sympathy (as opposed to affective empathy, which is about emotional congruence), and general perspective taking (as opposed to cognitive empathy, which is about the ability to understand another's emotions; Jolliffe & Farrington, 2006). Interestingly, the results from Domes et al. (2013) suggested that the controls did not have higher scores on the EC or PT scales compared to the prisoners. In addition, there was no difference in empathy between those who scored low, medium or high on the PCL-R.

Also using young prisoners, Flight and Forth (2007) examined the relationship between psychopathy and empathy using a sample of 51 young male prisoners in Canada. Psychopathy was measured using the PCL-YV, and empathy was measured using the total score of the IRI. The IRI was found to be significantly and negatively related to the PCL-YV total score ($r = -.55$), and also significantly related to the each of the facet scores (F1: Interpersonal ($r = -.26$) the F2: Affective ($r = -.53$) F3: Lifestyle ($r = -.37$) and the F4: Antisocial ($r = -.40$)).

Empathy and measures of psychopathy in community populations

Mullins-Nelson, Salekin, and Leistico (2006) undertook a study of psychopathy and empathy using a sample of 174 American undergraduate students (75% female). The participants completed the Psychopathic Personality Inventory-Short Form (PPI-SF; Lilienfeld, 2004 in Mullins-Nelson et al., 2006), which is a 24-item self-report measure of psychopathy comprised of two factors: PPI-SF-I measures stress immunity, social potency, fearlessness, and cold-heartedness, while PPI-SF-II measures impulsive nonconformity, blame externalisation, Machiavellian egocentricity, and carefree non-planfulness. Empathy was measured using the EC and PT scales of the IRI (Davis, 1983).

Males scored significantly higher than females on the overall measure of psychopathy, but females scored significantly higher than males on the EC scale. Males and females did not differ on the PT scale. When the scales of the PPI were compared to empathy for males and female separately it was found that, for males, the PPI-SF-I scale was positively related to the EC scale ($r = .31$), but not significantly related to PT ($r = .10$), while both the EC ($r = -.35$) and PT scales ($r = -.29$) were significantly negatively related to the PPI-SF-II scale. For females, neither the EC scale nor the PT scale was significantly related to the PPI-SF-I scale, but both ($r = -.41$; $r = -.30$) were related to the PPI-SF-II scale.

White (2014) used a sample of 539 American undergraduates (75.5% female) to explore the relation between psychopathy and empathy in a community sample. The Levenson Primary and Secondary Psychopathy Scales (LPSP; Levenson,

Kiehl, & Fitzpatrick, 1995) were used to measure psychopathy. The LPSP is a 26-item self-report instrument for assessing psychopathic tendencies in community samples. The 16-item primary psychopathy scale corresponds to Factor 1 of the PCL-R (affective and interpersonal traits), whereas the 10-item secondary scale corresponds to Factor 2 of the PCL – R (irresponsible, impulsive, antisocial traits). Empathy was measured using the EC and PT scales of the IRI. Overall the results suggested that the primary psychopathy scale was significantly negatively related to both the EC scale ($r = -.58$) and the PT scale ($r = -.40$) as was the secondary psychopathy scale (EC, $r = -.36$; PT, $r = -.33$).

In their study conducted with 374 community participants aged 19–49 (61% female) in Portugal, Almeida et al. (2015) used the self-report Triarchic Measure of Psychopathy (TriPM; Patrick in Almeida et al., 2015), to measure psychopathy, and the IRI (Davis, 1983) to measure empathy. The TriPM instrument encompasses three subscales that assess Boldness, Meanness, and Disinhibition. The results showed that the EC measure of the IRI (sympathy) was significantly and negatively related to the Boldness scale ($r = -.17$), and the Meanness scale ($r = -.50$), but only weakly related to the Disinhibition scale ($r = -.11$). The PT scale of the IRI was not significantly related to the Boldness scale ($r = -.10$), but was negatively related to the Meanness ($r = -.40$) and Disinhibition scales ($r = -.31$). Importantly, the Meanness scale includes items (e.g. 'How other people feel is important to me', 'I don't mind if someone I dislike gets hurt', and 'it doesn't bother me to someone else in pain'), which could be considered measures of sympathy, and the relationship with the IRI -EC scale could be considered tautological.

When studying empathy and psychopathy, it is important to avoid tautology. For example, comparing overall PCL scores, which include within them an assessment of empathy with a measure of empathy is potentially tautological. It is therefore important to examine the PCL facet scores and compare these to measures of empathy as this provides a less biased picture of the relationship between these two concepts.

Overall, the previous research suggests that empathy and psychopathy are related, but the magnitude of this relationship appears to vary somewhat, and there may be a number of potential sources of this variation. For example, while the work of Mullins-Nelson et al. (2006) examined the relationship separately for males and females, much other work did not. This is particularly problematic but not surprising, as, traditionally in the field of criminology, gender and sex has often been overlooked (Loeber, Jennings, Ahonen, Piquero, & Farrington, 2017), and this is also the case in the field of psychopathy (Verona & Vitale, 2018). Gender is a social construction based on biological sex, cultural values, and the overall zeitgeist (Lorber, 1994), and women have traditionally been viewed as more caring and empathetic compared to men (Lorber, 1994). Women have also been found to be less likely to score high on psychopathic traits (Verona & Vitale, 2018), and are generally found to be more empathetic than men (e.g. Brody, 1985; Lennon & Eisenberg, 1987; Rueckert & Naybar, 2008). Whether this is a biological difference or it develops through social learning (Brody, 1985) is currently debated. In their overarching review of female psychopathy, Verona and Vitale (2018) concluded that the affective deficiencies in psychopathy were similar for men and women.

Additional variation may arise from the weak measure of empathy that was used in these studies. As previously mentioned, the IRI appears to provide measures of sympathy and general perspective taking as opposed to actual affective and cognitive empathy. Also, the IRI has been noted to be related to social desirability (Jolliffe & Farrington, 2006) and this may be a particular problem, as psychopathy is associated with greater untruthfulness and presentational biases. This may certainly explain the results of Domes et al. (2013), in which prisoners and controls did not differ on either the EC or PT scales.

When examining the relationship between psychopathy and empathy it is also important to have a measure of empathy that clearly separates affective and cognitive empathy. This is because the hypothesised deficiencies in psychopathy might not be equally related to affective and cognitive empathy. It has been proposed that people who are high on psychopathic traits may not have cognitive empathy impairments (Dadds et al., 2009). People high on psychopathic traits are known for their ability to manipulate others and to use other people's emotions for selfish gains (Kirkman, 2005; Pagliaro, 2009). Non-deficient or even superior cognitive empathy might therefore be integral to the interpersonal traits of psychopathy (Dadds et al., 2009).

It is also possible that there is not a relationship between psychopathy and empathy. Null findings are often disregarded, which contributes to bias in the knowledge base (Kepes, Banks, & Oh, 2014). These findings should not be dismissed within the larger literature although they may add to the complexities of both psychopathy and empathy. Despite some mixed findings (depending on samples and measures), there is overall empirical support to suggest that persons who are high on psychopathic traits often have empathy deficiencies.

The current study

As this chapter has shown, the assumed "straightforward" relationship, where people who are high on psychopathic traits have impaired affective empathy but might retain their ability for cognitive empathy (Dadds et al., 2009), is challenged in the overall literature. There is therefore a need for more research on these relationships. This is the first ever study of which we are aware that has compared psychopathy, as measured by the PCL-SV, with a true measure of empathy in a community sample. It is expected that psychopathy may be inversely related to affective empathy, as this is the most consistent finding in the literature. However, it may be that the impairment will be more pronounced for affective than for cognitive empathy.

Recognising the diverse construct that is psychopathy and the findings of past research (e.g. Flight & Forth, 2007), the current study will also investigate how the components of psychopathy are potentially differently related to empathy. Within the PCL-R tradition, Factor 1 (interpersonal/affective) and facet 2 (affective) includes measures of lack of empathy amongst other traits (Hare, 2003), which means that it is reasonable to assume that there will be a fairly strong inverse relationship between Factor 1 and empathy as well as between facet 2 and empathy because of the potential for construct overlap. Factor 2 (lifestyle/antisocial) and facet 4 (antisocial) measure antisociality (Hare, 2003), and past research has shown a robust inverse relationship between empathy and delinquency (Jolliffe & Farrington, 2007).

Finally, since the literature indicates that there are gender differences in the relationship between psychopathy and empathy, these will be investigated throughout. The current study is unique as the sample consists of comparable group sizes between men and women in a community setting. This allows for more equal comparisons of groups that has not been possible in past studies (e.g. Mullins-Nelson et al., 2006).

Methodology

Design and sample

The current study analyses data from the Cambridge Study in Delinquent Development (CSDD). The CSDD is a long-running prospective longitudinal study following 411 males for more than half a century. The CSDD has contributed greatly to the understanding of a wide range of criminological and psychological phenomena. The original 411 males have been referred to as generation 2 ("G2"), while their parents were referred to as Generation 1 ("G1"). Because of the longevity of the CSDD, it has also been possible to interview the children of the G2 males. These children have been referred to as generation 3 ("G3"). Only children above the age 18 (born ≤ 1995) at the time of the interview were eligible for inclusion. 653 (out of 691 known children) were eligible, and 551 were willing and able to participate in the study (see Farrington et al., 2015). The response rate for the G3 children was therefore 84.4%. In contrast to the G2 males, the G3 children consisted of both women and men; 291 males and 260 females make up G3 of the CSDD. The G3 children completed a social interview at the average age of 25. This interview was comprehensive and measured a wide range of variables; most interestingly for the current study, it included measures of psychopathy and empathy.

Measures

There are two measures used in the current study, both completed in a face-to-face interview.

Psychopathy: the Hare Psychopathy Checklist: Screening Version (PCL:SV) (Hart et al., 1995) is a screening version of the full Hare Psychopathy Checklist-Revised (Hare, 2003). It was developed as a means of conducting quicker assessments of psychopathic traits in forensic populations where a cut-off score is provided for clinical/forensic decision making to conduct a full PCL-R assessment. While this recommended cut-off score is 18 (out of 24), it is recognised that a score above 16 is an indication of a person high on psychopathic traits. The PCL-R (Hare, 2003) consists of 20 items. Each item is measured on a 3-point ordinal scale, where the higher the score, the better the item (trait/behaviour) applies. The PCL:SV uses the same ordinal scale (0, 1, 2), but the measure consists of 12 items. As with the PCL-R (Hare, 2003), the PCL:SV loads onto 2 factors (Factor 1: interpersonal/affective; Factor 2: "social deviance" lifestyle/antisocial), and 4 facets (facet 1: interpersonal; facet 2: affective; facet 3: lifestyle; and facet 4: antisocial).

Empathy: the Basic Empathy Scale (Jolliffe & Farrington, 2006) is a 20-item measure of both cognitive and affective empathy that has been used extensively (see Basto-Pereira & Farrington, this volume).

Analyses

The main analytical strategy will focus on descriptive statistics and bivariate correlations. In line with the recommendations of Farrington and Loeber (2000), both empathy and psychopathy will be dichotomised into high and low. For empathy, the approximately worst quarter on both affective and cognitive empathy were identified and labelled "low" on the respective empathy scales.

For females, the PCL:SV total cut-off score was 6 (high = score of 6+), the Factor 1 cut-off score was 3 (high = score of 3+), and the Factor 2 cut-off score was 4 (high = score of 4+). At the facet level for females, high was a score of 2+ for facet 1, 2, and 4, and 3+ for facet 3.

For males, the PCL:SV total cut-off score was 10 (high = score of 10+). The Factor 1 high group had a score of 5+, and for Factor 2 the high group had a score of 6+. At a facet level for males, high was a score of 3+ for all facets.

To further investigate the relationship between empathy and psychopathy, odds ratios will also be calculated. The aim here is to investigate whether or not the relationships hold for those high on psychopathic traits and symptoms.

Results

Descriptive statistics

Table 8.1 presents the overall descriptive statistics for psychopathic traits as measured by the PCL:SV separately for men and women. As can be seen from the average scores, the sample is overall low on psychopathic traits (Hart et al., 1995).

Correlations

Table 8.2 presents the bivariate correlations for men and women separately for psychopathic traits and cognitive and affective empathy. As can be seen from the table, men had few significant relationships between psychopathy and empathy. Factor 1 and Factor 2 were negatively related to cognitive empathy ($r = -.12$, $p < .05$). Facet 2 was significantly negatively related to both cognitive and affective empathy.

Table 8.1 Descriptive statistics for psychopathic traits of men and women

	Men *Mean (SD)*	*Women* *Mean (SD)*	*Cohen's* d
PCL:SV total	4.55 (4.14)	2.32 (2.93)	.62
Factor 1 (interpersonal/affective)	1.96 (2.09)	.93 (1.54)	.56
Facet 1 (interpersonal)	.78 (1.12)	.44 (.91)	.33
Facet 2 (affective)	1.18 (1.36)	.49 (.87)	.60
Factor 2 (lifestyle/antisocial)	2.59 (3.83)	1.39 (1.67)	.41
Facet 3	1.21 (1.19)	.77 (.99)	.40
Facet 4	1.38 (1.44)	.62 (.92)	.63

Table 8.2 Bivariate correlations between psychopathic traits and empathy for men and women

	Men		*Women*	
	Cognitive	*Affective*	*Cognitive*	*Affective*
PCL:SV total	−.05	−.05	−.18**	−.22**
Factor 1	−.12*	−.12*	−.14*	−.18**
Facet 1	−.01	.00	−.07	−.05
Facet 2	−.18**	−.18**	−.17**	−.26**
Factor 2	.02	.02	−.20**	−.23**
Facet 3	.06	.04	−.16**	−.24**
Facet 4	−.01	.01	−.18**	−.16**

Note: *Tests are one-tailed.* *$p < .05$, **$p < .01$.

The impairment in empathy was more consistent for women who were higher on psychopathy, with all measures of empathy significantly and negatively related to all measures of psychopathy, except for facet 1.

Odds ratios

Table 8.3 provides an overview of the odds ratios between psychopathy and empathy for both men and women. As can be seen from the table, the strongest effect is seen between facet 2 (affective) and cognitive and affective empathy. For women, being high on facet 2 increases the odds of being low on empathy more than 2.5 times. In addition to providing a 95% confidence interval in Table 8.3, we also carried out one sided Fisher's exact tests were also carried out to investigate significant differences.

Discussion

The relationship between psychopathy and empathy

Empathy, or our ability to understand and "feel" others' emotions (Jolliffe & Farrington, 2006) has traditionally been believed to be diminished amongst those

Table 8.3 Odds ratio between high/low psychopathic traits and high/low empathy

	Men		*Women*	
	Cognitive	*Affective*	*Cognitive*	*Affective*
PCL:SV total	1.09 (.50; 2.38)	.55 (.22; 1.40)	1.92 (.90; 4.10)[a]	1.92 (.90; 4.10)
Factor 1	1.86 (.92; 3.75)[a]	.99 (.46; 2.15)	2.1 (1.00; 4.43)*	2.10 (1.00; 4.43)*
Facet 1	.91 (.35; 2.37)	.39 (.11; 1.35)	1.05 (.42; 2.63)	.65 (.23; 1.79)
Facet 2	1.67 (.89; 3.16)	1.46 (.76; 2.79)	2.58 (1.22; 5.45)*	2.98 (1.41; 6.30)*
Factor 2	.72 (.30; 1.75)	.63 (.25; 1.58)	2.29 (1.05; 5.01)*	2.29 (1.05;5.01)*
Facet 3	.47 (.19; 1.16)[a]	.88 (.39; 1.95)	1.75 (.91; 3.39)	2.19 (1.14; 4.21)*
Facet 4	1.10 (.60; 2.07)	.95 (.49; 1.84)	1.89 (.90; 3.94)	1.89 (.90; 3.94)

Note: *95% confidence interval in brackets. Fisher exact tests (one tailed) *$p < .05$, **$p < .001$,* a *Close to significance with* $p \leq .07$

high on psychopathy (e.g. Soderstrom, 2003). The inverse relationship has also been included as part of measures of psychopathy (e.g. Hare, 2003; Hart et al., 1995), thus raising concerns about tautology. The current study does, however, show that it is not just the Factor 1/facet 2 that may be inversely related to empathy. We will discuss this in more depth below under 4.2 "Measurements". Interestingly, it seems that the inverse relationships are most consistently significant for women across all the components of the psychopathic personality. The results for women also indicate that the impairment is stronger for affective empathy than for cognitive empathy. This is in accordance with past research (Mullins-Nelson et al., 2006).

Measurement

Tautology is at times a concern when studying psychopathy (e.g. Bergstrøm, Larmour, & Farrington, 2018; Cooke, 2014). Since Factor 1 (specifically facet 2) includes an item that aims to measure lack of empathy, one might worry that studies on the relationship between empathy and psychopathy might have tautology issues. However, when one looks at how empathy is measured in the PCL:SV (Hart et al., 1995; description above), a lack of empathy is just one of the components of one item. In addition to the lack of understanding of emotions, the item also refers to shallow emotional expressions and lacking in normative attachment, which could be outcomes of lacking empathic relationships.

The BES is a reliable and valid tool to assess cognitive and affective empathy, and these concepts somewhat overlap with what the item "Lacks Empathy" assesses using the PCL-SV. If one cannot experience emotions or has a shallow emotional internal life, then their ability to understand and experience the emotions of others will be diminished. However, the BES is a questionnaire measure of empathy and to complete this accurately insight into one's emotions are needed, and those higher on psychopathy may be less likely to have such insight. Similarly, questionnaire measures are open to presentational bias, something that has been noted amongst those who score higher on psychopathy.

Future research

Future research should use prospective longitudinal studies. It is here recommended to replicate the Dadds et al. (2009) study using this design. The fields of both empathy research and psychopathy need such studies across developmental periods with both genders (starting as young as possible). This will inform the development of both constructs as well as how their relationships will differ across time.

Acknowledgements

For funding the CSDD, we are very grateful to the Home Office, the Department of Health, the Department for Education, the Rayne foundation, the Barrow Cadbury Trust, and the Smith-Richardson Foundation.

References

Almeida, P. R., Seixas, M. J., Ferreira-Santos, F., Vieira, J. B., Paiva, T. O., Moreira, P. S., & Costa, P. (2015). Empathic, moral and antisocial outcomes associated with distinct components of psychopathy in healthy individuals: A triarchic model approach. *Personality and Individual Differences*, *85*, 205–211.

Bergstrøm, H., Larmour, S. R., & Farrington, D. P. (2018). The usefulness of psychopathy in explaining and predicting violence: Discussing the utility of competing perspectives. *Aggression and Violent Behavior*, *42*, 84–95.

Blonigen, D. M., Sullivan, E. A., Hicks, B. M., & Patrick, C. J. (2012). Facets of psychopathy in relation to potentially traumatic events and posttraumatic stress disorder among female prisoners: The mediating role of borderline personality disorder traits. *Personality Disorders: Theory, Research, and Treatment*, *3*, 406–414.

Brody, L. R. (1985). Gender differences in emotional development: A review of theories and research. *Journal of Personality*, *53*, 102–149.

Brook, M., & Kosson, D. S. (2013). Impaired cognitive empathy in criminal psychopathy: Evidence from a laboratory measure of empathic accuracy. *Journal of Abnormal Psychology*, *122*(1), 156–166.

Cohen, D., & Strayer, J. (1996). Empathy in conduct-disordered and comparison youth. *Developmental Psychology*, *32*, 988–998.

Cooke, D. J. (2014). Psychopathy and offending. In G. Bruinsma & D. Weisburd (Eds.), *Encyclopedia of criminology and criminal justice* (pp. 4126–4134). New York: Springer.

Dadds, M. R., Hawes, D. J., Frost, A. D. J., Vassallo, S., Bunn, P., Hunter, K., & Merz, S. (2009). Learning to "talk the talk": The relationship of psychopathic traits to deficits in empathy across childhood. *The Journal of Child Psychology and Psychiatry*, *50*, 599–606.

Davis, M. H. (1983). Measuring individual differences in empathy: Evidence for a multidimensional approach. *Journal of Personality and Social Psychology*, *44*, 113–126.

de Ruigh, E. L., Jansen, L. M. C., Vermeiren, R., & Popma, A. (2019). Psychopathic traits and empathic functioning in detained juveniles: Withdrawal response to empathic sadness. *International Journal of Forensic Mental Health*, *31*(5), online first.

Domes, G., Hollerbach, P., Vohs, K., Mokros, A., & Habermeyer, E. (2013). Emotional empathy and psychopathy in offenders: An experimental study. *Journal of Personality Disorders*, *27*, 67–84.

Farrington, D. P., & Bergstrøm, H. (2018). Family background and psychopathy. In C. J. Patrick (Ed.), *Handbook of psychopathy* (2nd ed., pp. 354–379). New York: Guilford.

Farrington, D. P., & Loeber, R. (2000). Some benefits of dichotomization in psychiatric and criminological research. *Criminal Behaviour and Mental Health, 10*, 100–122.

Flight, J. I., & Forth, A. E. (2007). Instrumentally violent youths: The roles of psychopathic traits, empathy, and attachment. *Criminal Justice and Behavior, 34*, 739–751.

Forth, A. E., Kosson, D., & Hare, R. D. (2003). *The Hare psychopathy checklist: Youth version*. Toronto: Multi Health Systems.

Frick, P. J., & Hare, R. D. (2001). *Antisocial process screening device: APSD*. Toronto: Multi Health Systems.

Hare, R. D. (2003). *The Hare psychopathy checklist-revised* (2nd ed.). Toronto: Multi Health Systems.

Hart, S. D., Cox, D. N., & Hare, R. D. (1995). *Hare PCL:SV psychopathy checklist: Screening version*. Toronto: Multi Health Systems.

Jolliffe, D., & Farrington, D. P. (2004). Empathy and offending: A systematic review and meta-analysis. *Aggression and Violent Behavior, 9*, 441–476.

Jolliffe, D., & Farrington, D. P. (2006). Development and validation of the basic empathy scale. *Journal of Adolescence, 29*, 589–611.

Jolliffe, D., & Farrington, D. P. (2007). Examining the relationship between low empathy and self-reported offending. *Legal and Criminological Psychology, 12*, 265–286.

Kaukiainan, A., Björkqvist, K., Lagerspetz, K., Österman, K., Salmivalli, C., Rothberg, S., & Ahlbom, A. (1999). The relationship between social intelligence, empathy, and three types of aggression. *Aggressive Behavior, 25*, 81–89.

Kirkman, C. A. (2005). From soap opera to science: Towards gaining access to the psychopaths who live amongst us. *Psychology and Psychotherapy, 78*, 379–396.

Lennon, R., & Eisenberg, N. (1987). Gender and age differences in empathy and sympathy. In N. Eisenberg & J. Strayer (Eds.), *Empathy and its development* (pp. 195–217). Cambridge: Cambridge University Press.

Levenson, M. R., Kiehl, K. A., & Fitzpatrick, C. M. (1995). Assessing psychopathic attributes in a noninstitutionalized population. *Journal of Personality and Social Psychology, 68*, 151–158.

Loeber, R., Jennings, W. G., Ahonen, L., Piquero, A. R., & Farrington, D. P. (2017). *Female delinquency from childhood to young adulthood: Recent results from the Pittsburgh girls study. Springer briefs in criminology*. Cham: Springer.

Lorber, J. (1994). *Paradoxes of gender*. New Haven, CT: Yale University Press.

Lynam, D. R., Gaughan, E. T., Miller, J. D., Miller, D. J., Mullins-Sweatt, S., & Widiger, T. A. (2011). Assessing the basic traits associated with psychopathy: Development and validation of the Elemental Psychopathy Assessment. *Psychological Assessment, 23*, 108–124.

Mullins-Nelson, J. L., Salekin, R. T., & Leistico, A. M. R. (2006). Psychopathy, empathy, and perspective-taking ability in a community sample: Implications for the successful psychopathy concept. *International Journal of Forensic Mental Health, 5*, 133–149.

Kepes, S., Banks, G. C., & Oh, I. S. (2014). Avoiding bias in publication bias research: The value of "null" findings. *Journal of Business and Psychology, 29*, 183–203.

Pagliaro, M. J. L. (2009). *Survivors of psychopaths: An investigation of victimization experiences, coping, and social support* (Unpublished MA thesis). Carleton University, Ottawa.

Pajevic, M., Vukosavjelic-Gvozden, T., Stavanovic, N., & Neumann, C. S. (2018). The relationship between the dark tetrad a two-dimensional view of empathy. *Personality and Individual Differences, 123*, 125–130.

Patrick, C. J., Fowles, D. C., & Krueger, R. F. (2009). Triarchic conceptualization of psychopathy: Developmental origins of disinhibition, boldness, and meanness. *Development and Psychopathology*, *21*, 913–938.

Pfabigan, D. M., Seidel, E. M., Wucherer, A. M., Keckeis, K., Derntl, B., & Lamm, C. (2014). Affective empathy differs in male violent offenders with high- and low- trait psychopathy. *Journal of Personality Disorders*, *29*, 42–61.

Rueckert, L., & Naybar, N. (2008). Gender differences in empathy: The role of the right hemisphere. *Brain and Cognition*, *67*, 162–167.

Skeem, J. L., & Cooke, D. J. (2010). Is criminal behavior a central component of psychopathy? Conceptual directions for resolving the debate. *Psychological Assessment*, *22*, 433–445.

Soderstrom, H. (2003). Psychopathy as a disorder of empathy. *European Child & Adolescent Psychiatry*, *12*, 249–252.

Vachon, D. D., Lynam, D. R., & Johnson, J. A. (2014). The (non) relation between empathy and aggression: Surprising results from a meta-analysis. *Psychological Bulletin*, *140*, 751–773.

van Langen, M. A. M., Wissink, I. B., van Vugt, E. S., van der Stouve, T., & Stams, G. J. J. M. (2014). The relation between empathy and offending: A meta-analysis. *Aggression and Violent Behavior*, *19*, 179–189.

Verona, E., & Vitale, J. (2018). Psychopathy in women: Assessment, manifestations and etiology. In C. J. Patrick (Ed.), *Handbook of psychopathy* (2nd ed., pp. 509–528). New York: Guilford.

White, B. A. (2014). Who cares when nobody is watching? Psychopathic traits and empathy in prosocial behaviors. *Personality and Individual Differences*, *56*, 115–121.

9 Correlates of affective and cognitive empathy among incarcerated male and female youth offenders

Pedro Pechorro, Darrick Jolliffe, and Cristina Nunes

Introduction

Empathy has long been considered an important contributing factor for antisocial, aggressive and criminal behaviour (Jolliffe & Farrington, 2004). Defined as an affective response to the emotions of another person (e.g. Hoffman, 1987), or the cognitive skill of identifying the emotions of another person (e.g. Hogan, 1969), the acknowledgement that empathy comprises both affective and cognitive components was noted over 100 years ago (Southard, 1918). Only relatively recently, however, has this separation been operationalised in tools designed to measure empathy (e.g. Davis, 1983), and integrated into theoretical understanding of behaviour (Dadds et al., 2009).

Gender differences in empathy can be observed at very early ages. For example, in an experimental study with three- to four-month-old babies, girls demonstrated a superior ability to discriminate facial expressions compared to boys (McClure, 2000). In addition, reviews have established that these early differences in empathy appear to persist through childhood and adolescence. That is, generally, girl's behaviour is more empathetic than those of age similar boys, and in a range of situations, girl's behaviour is closer to social norms (Chaplin & Aldao, 2013).

Interestingly, research has shown that the gender gap in empathy may vary across the life-course, with puberty a particularly crucial period in the widening of this (Lam, Solmeyer, & McHale, 2012). After this developmental stage the differences in empathy between the genders remain through the life course, with women continuing to show higher empathy levels than men (Beadle & de la Vega, 2019). While there may be absolute change in the level of empathy, with both males and females becoming more empathic with age, there is also relatively stability. That is, those who score lowest on measures of empathy during childhood tend to score lowest as adults (Michalska, Kinzler, & Decety, 2013). The observed variation in empathy between males and females has been proposed to explain the universal finding that males are much more likely that females to be involved in antisocial and criminal behaviour, particularly that which involves violence (Broidy, Cauffman, Espelage, Mazerolle, & Piquero, 2003). This is despite evidence for recent increases in the prevalence of female antisocial behaviour (e.g. Tracy, Kempf-Leonard, & Abramoske-James, 2009).

A number of psychological and criminological theories which link empathy and antisocial behaviour have been proffered (Hanson, 2003; Hoffman, 1987), but most all theoretical interpretations can be distilled into their suggestion that individuals with low empathy are more likely to act in an antisocial or aggressive manner. Sufficient empathy is understood to act as an emergency handbrake for antisocial behaviour. For those lacking empathy the distress, the fear and alarm evident in others as a result of one's aggressive, antisocial or violent behaviour is not experienced or understood, and is therefore not aversive or a "cost" of antisocial behaviour. Individuals with low empathy are therefore free of these aversive experiences, and ultimately, may fail to understand the connection between their behaviour and the emotional consequences of these behaviours on others.

Generally, the research evidence has been supportive of the theoretical relationship between low empathy and increased antisocial and criminal behaviour (Jolliffe & Farrington, 2004). For example, in their systematic review of 39 studies which compared levels of empathy between offenders or non-offenders van Langan, Wissink, van Vugt, van der Stouwe, and Stams (2014) found low cognitive empathy to be strongly related to offending ($d = .43$), with affective empathy being somewhat less strongly associated ($d = .19$). It is important to note, however, that the authors attributed the elevated effect size between cognitive empathy and offending to the use of a particular cognitive empathy measure which possessed limited construct validity. Interestingly, another systematic review of 106 effect sizes which compared empathy to aggression (broadly defined), found the relationship to be less strong. For example, the overall effect was found to be $r = -.11$, and to range from $r = -.20$ for verbal aggression to $r = -.09$ for sexual aggression (Vachon et al., 2014).

One of the key challenges for evaluating the link between empathy and behaviour is the operationalisation of empathy. While a number of questionnaire measures of empathy exist, the Basic Empathy Scale (BES; Jolliffe & Farrington, 2006) has become one of the most widely used (Basto-Pereira & Farrington, this volume). This scale, and the affective and cognitive factor structure of this scale, has been validated in several countries, including those in Europe, North America and Asia.

Despite the considerable amount of research regarding empathy and offending, only one previous study has examined empathy measured using the BES amongst detained juveniles (van der Helm et al., 2012). In this study, the BES was administered to 59 juveniles (mean age 17.4) detained in a youth correctional facility in the Netherlands, and the results were compared to those of a validation sample of similarly aged boys. The results suggested that the detained boys had significantly lower affective and cognitive empathy. In addition, cognitive empathy was found to be positively associated with the boy's perception of support and positive group atmosphere and negatively related to the boy's perceptions of repression.

There are a number of reasons that the empathy of detained juveniles is an important area for further study. First, the systematic reviews of Jolliffe and

Farrington (2004) and van Langan et al. (2014) both showed that the difference between offenders and non-offenders was significantly greater for young as opposed to older offenders. This greater disparity between young offenders and young non-offenders may mean that empathy is a more important potential cause of offending amongst the young. Second, prospective longitudinal studies have consistently shown that those who are the most criminal at early ages tend to have extensive criminal careers (Moffitt & Caspi, 2001). If empathy is causally related to offending and can be changed by appropriate interventions then an intervention delivered to young offenders could significantly reduce a potentially lengthy criminal career. Third, a period of detention for a young person offers both an opportunity for empathy enhancing intervention to be delivered, but equally a pitfall of a closed repressive environment which may erode empathy.

Another glaring limitation of previous research in this area is the absence of studies of empathy in female offenders. With important exceptions (Watt, Frausin, Dixon, & Nimmo, 2000) studies tend to focus on males or combine males and females together in "mixed" samples. This is particularly problematic in light of recent calls for more gender-specific interventions (van Voorhis, 2012).

The main aim of the present study was to examine correlates of the BES among a Portuguese sample of male and female youth offenders.

Method

Procedure

Questionnaires were administered to all youths by a research associate who assisted those who had issues with literacy and answered any questions the youths had. This study can be described as quantitative, non-experimental, and cross-sectional (Bachman & Schutt, 2014). The data were analysed using SPSS v25 (IBM Corp., 2018). Pearson correlations and partial-correlations were used to analyse associations between scale variables, Spearman correlations, and point-biserial were used to analyse associations of scale variables with ordinal variables and nominal dichotomous variables (Leech, Barrett, & Morgan, 2015). ANOVA was used to compare the male and female participants in terms of affective and cognitive empathy scores.

Participants

The sample was composed of 270 participants ($M = 16.38$ years, $SD = 1.26$ years, range = 12–19 years) recruited from the Portuguese juvenile detention centres. Of this total, 216 participants ($M_{males} = 16.40$ years, $SD = 1.28$ years, range = 12–19 years) formed male sample and 54 participants ($M_{females} = 16.28$ years, $SD = 1.20$ years, range = 14–18 years) formed the female sample. The participants were mainly white Europeans (males = 55.6%, females = 59.3%) from an urban background (males = 93.5%, females = 98.1%). Detention into a juvenile detention centre for the maximum length of three years is the strictest sanction a Portuguese court can impose on youths, and youths can be tried as adults for crimes committed after they have turned 16 years of age.

Measures

The Basic Empathy Scale (BES; Jolliffe & Farrington, 2006) is a 20-item self-report measure designed to assess affective and cognitive empathy in youths. The Portuguese validation of the BES was used (Pechorro, Ray, Salas-Wright, Maroco, & Gonçalves, 2015).

The Antisocial Process Screening Device – Self-report (APSD-SR; Frick & Hare, 2001) is a multidimensional 20-item measure designed to assess psychopathic traits in adolescents. The Portuguese validation of the APSD-SR was used (Pechorro, Hidalgo, Nunes, & Jiménez, 2016).

The Youth Psychopathic Traits Inventory (YPI; Andershed, Kerr, Stattin, & Levander, 2002) is a 50-item self-report measure designed to assess the core personality traits of the psychopathic personality constellation in youths aged 12 years old and up. The YPI has three dimensions: the Grandiose-Manipulative dimension, the Callous-Unemotional dimension, and the Impulsive-Irresponsible dimension. The Portuguese version of the YPI was used (Pechorro, Ribeiro da Silva, Andershed, Rijo, & Gonçalves, 2016).

The Inventory of Callous-Unemotional Traits (ICU; Essau, Sasagawa, & Frick, 2006) is a 24-item self-report scale designed to assess callous and unemotional traits in youths. Using confirmatory factor analysis, it was possible to identify three independent factors, namely: Callousness (11 items), Uncaring (8 items), and Unemotional (5 items). The Portuguese validation of the ICU was used (Pechorro et al., in press).

The Reactive-Proactive Aggression Questionnaire (RPQ; Raine et al., 2006) is a self-report measure appropriate for use with youths in late adolescence and young adults that distinguishes between reactive and proactive aggression. The Portuguese validation of the RPQ was used (Pechorro, Ayala-Nunes, Kahn, & Nunes, 2018).

The Narcissistic Personality Inventory – 13 (NPI-13; Gentile et al., 2013). This scale was developed specifically to maintain a three-factor structure: Leadership/Authority (LA; four items), Grandiose Exhibitionism (GE; five items), and Entitlement/Exploitativeness (EE; four items). The Portuguese adaptation of the NPI-13 was used (Pechorro, Gentile, Ray, Nunes, & Gonçalves, 2016).

The Social Anxiety Scale for Adolescents (SAS-A; La Greca & Lopez, 1998) has three dimensions: the Fear of Negative Evaluation subscale, the Social Avoidance and Distress subscale and the Social Avoidance and Distress – General subscale. The Portuguese validation of the SAS-S was used (Pechorro, Ayala-Nunes, Nunes, Maroco, & Gonçalves, 2016).

Conduct Disorder diagnostic was assessed using the official diagnostic criteria of the *Diagnostic and Statistical Manual of Mental Disorders* (*DSM-5*; American Psychiatric Association, 2013). A Conduct Disorder (CD) scale was also created based on the 15 items used to assess CD.

In addition, a questionnaire was constructed to describe the socio-demographic and criminal characteristics of the participants. This questionnaire included variables such as participants' age, ethnic group, geographic classification of residence (rural vs. urban), level of schooling completed, socio-economic status, age of criminal onset, age of first problem with the law, age of first detention, criminal charges, crime seriousness classification, general and violent recidivism, drug and alcohol use, unprotected sex, CD symptoms, and taking of psychiatric medication. The Sellin – Wolfgang Index of Crime Seriousness (ICS; Wolfgang, Figlio, Tracey, & Singer, 1985) guided the delinquency seriousness classification of the official court reports. Socio-economic status (SES) was measured by considering both parental level of education and profession, appropriate to the Portuguese context (Simões, 2000).

Results

We compared the male and female participants in terms of the BES Affective ($M_{\text{males}} = 16.35$, $SD = 8.52$; $M_{\text{females}} = 23.94$, $SD = 7.93$) and BES Cognitive scores ($M_{\text{males}} = 22.56$, $SD = 7.31$; $M_{\text{females}} = 27.15$, $SD = 6.35$). ANOVA results indicated that females scored significantly higher on both affective empathy ($F = 35.205$, $p < .001$) and cognitive empathy ($F = 17.846$, $p < .001$).

Table 9.1 presents the correlations of the BES to the other measures for the male and female samples. For males there was evidence that low affective empathy was associated with measures of higher callous unemotional traits such as the Antisocial Process Screening Device – Self-Report CU subscale ($r = -.39$), the Youth Psychopathic Traits Inventory CU ($r = -.29$), and each of the subscales of the Inventory of Callous Unemotional Traits. Interestingly, higher affective empathy in males was related to increased social anxiety. Similar to low affective empathy, low cognitive empathy in males was also associated with increases in measures of callous-unemotional traits (ASPD-SR and ICU). Cognitive empathy in males was not associated with the YPI total score, but was positively associated with greater irresponsibility/impulsiveness on this measure ($r = .14$). All measures of narcissism were significantly associated with higher cognitive empathy in males, while higher cognitive empathy was also positively associated with a measure of reactive aggression ($r = .14$) and the social anxiety measure of fear of negative emotions ($r = .18$).

As the number of females in this sample was relatively small ($n = 54$) statistical significance may not be the best measure of a meaningful association (Cohen, 1996). For this reason, all values of greater than .20 were considered important. This is because a correlation of .20 is equivalent to a 10% difference in proportions (Farrington & Loeber, 1989). For females (like males), low affective empathy was significantly associated with increases in measures of callous-unemotional traits such as the ASPD-SR ($r = -.24$) and YPI CU ($r = -.42$), but unlike males, low affective empathy was associated with higher Leadership-Authority narcissism ($r = -.21$). There was a positive relationship identified between the affective empathy of females and scores on the Reactive-Proactive Aggression questionnaire,

Table 9.1 Correlations of the BES with other measures

Males/Females	*BES Affective*	*BES Cognitive*
APSD-SR total	−.12/.10	−.05/.13
APSD-SR Impulsivity	.08/.18	.09/.11
APSD-SR Narcissism	.03/.20	.08/.17
APSD-SR CU	−.39***/−.24	−.34***/−.01
YPI total	−.16*/−.10	.07/.20
YPI II	−.07/−.02	.14*/.25
YPI GM	−.08/.05	.04/.21
YPI CU	−.29***/−.42**	−.01/−.00
ICU total	−.40***/−.06	−.29***/.07
ICU Callousness	−.22**/.06	−.06/.06
ICU Uncaring	−.37***/−.14	−.36***/.11
ICU Unemotional	−.40***/−.09	−.35***/−.06
NPI-13 total	.04/−.09	.30***/.14
NPI-13 LA	−.06/−.21	.23**/.10
NPI-13 GE	.11/−.05	.23**/.08
NPI-13 EE	.03/.06	.29***/.21
RPQ total	.01/.26	.11/.18
RPQ Reactive	.09/.28*	.14*/.17
RPQ Proactive	−.04/.21	.07/.17
SAS-A total	.36***/.09	.13/−.07
SAS-A General	.28***/.01	−.05/−.39**
SAS-A New	.23**/.11	.06/−.08
SAS-A FNE	.34***/.11	.18*/.09

Note. BES = Basic Empathy Scale; APSD-SR = Antisocial Process Screening Device – Self-Report; APSD-SR CU = Callous-Unemotional; YPI = Youth Psychopathic Traits Inventory; YPI II = Impulsive-Irresponsible; YPI GM = Grandiose-Manipulative; YPI CU = Callous-Unemotional; ICU = Inventory of Callous-Unemotional Traits; BIS-11 = Barratt Impulsiveness Scale version 11; NPI-13 = Narcissistic Personality Inventory 13-item short version; NPI-13 LA = Leadership-Authority; NPI-13 GE = Grandiose-Exhibitionism; NPI-13 EE = Entitlement-Exploitativeness; RPQ = Reactive-Proactive Aggression Questionnaire; SAS-A = Social Anxiety Scale for Adolescents; SAS-A FNE = Fear of Negative Evaluation dimension

***$p < .001$; **$p < .01$; *$p < .05$

and higher cognitive empathy in females was associated with higher scores on the YPI, particularly the Irresponsibility Impulsiveness scale and the Grandiose Manipulative scale, as well as the Entitlement/Exploitativeness scale of the NPI-13. Unlike males, higher cognitive empathy in females was associated with lower scores on the measure General social anxiety.

Because of the overlap between cognitive and affective empathy for males ($r = .48$, $p < .001$) and females ($r = .27$, $p < .05$), it was considered important to examine the independent relationship between affective empathy and the other measures controlling for cognitive empathy (and vice versa). Table 9.2 presents the partial correlations of the BES with other measures for the male and female samples.

For males, there was again evidence that low affective empathy was related to increases in callous-unemotional traits with various measures (e.g. ASPD-CU,

Table 9.2 Partial correlations of the BES with other measures

Males/Females	*BES Affective*	*BES Cognitive*
APSD-SR total	−.12/.07	.02/.11
APSD-SR Impulsivity	.04/.15	.06/.06
APSD-SR Narcissism	−.01/.16	.08/.12
APSD-SR CU	−.27***/−.25	−.19*/.07
YPI total	−.22**/−.16	.17*/.22
YPI II	−.16*/−.09	.20**/.27*
YPI GM	−.12/−.01	.09/.19
YPI CU	−.33***/−.43***	.16*/.12
ICU total	−.31***/−.08	−.12/.08
ICU Callousness	−.22**/.04	.05/.04
ICU Uncaring	−.25***/−.18	−.22**/.15
ICU Unemotional	−.28***/−.09	−.20**/−.04
NPI-13 total	−.13/−.14	.32***/.18
NPI-13 LA	−.21**/−.24	.30***/.17
NPI-13 GE	.01/−.08	.20**/.10
NPI-13 EE	−.12/−.00	.31***/.20
RPQ total	−.04/.22	.12/.13
RPQ Reactive	.03/.24	.11/.10
RPQ Proactive	−.09/.17	.11/.12
SAS-A total	.35***/.12	−.05/−.10
SAS-A General	.32***/.09	−.15*/−.39**
SAS-A New	.22**/.14	−.06/−.12
SAS-A FNE	.30***/.08	.02/.06

Note. BES = Basic Empathy Scale; APSD-SR = Antisocial Process Screening Device – Self-Report; APSD-SR CU = Callous-Unemotional; YPI = Youth Psychopathic Traits Inventory; YPI II = Impulsive-Irresponsible; YPI GM = Grandiose-Manipulative; YPI CU = Callous-Unemotional; ICU = Inventory of Callous-Unemotional Traits; BIS-11 = Barratt Impulsiveness Scale version 11; NPI-13 = Narcissistic Personality Inventory 13-item short version; NPI-13 LA = Leadership-Authority; NPI-13 GE = Grandiose-Exhibitionism; NPI-13 EE = Entitlement-Exploitativeness; RPQ = Reactive-Proactive Aggression Questionnaire; SAS-A = Social Anxiety Scale for Adolescents; SAS-A FNE = Fear of Negative Evaluation dimension

***$p < .001$; **$p < .01$; *$p < .05$

$r = -.27$), and all of the subscales of the Inventory of Callous-Unemotional Traits, however these were somewhat attenuated to the uncontrolled comparisons. Interestingly, the relation between affective empathy and the YPI was somewhat higher when controlling for cognitive empathy. Similar to the uncontrolled results, higher affective empathy in males was associated with increases in social anxiety and these were of a similar magnitude. Dissimilar to the uncontrolled results however, males who scored lower on affective empathy demonstrated significantly higher Leadership Authority narcissism.

When the relation between the cognitive empathy of males was compared to the various measures, controlling for affective empathy, many results were similar to the uncontrolled comparisons. For example, significant relationships were identified between cognitive empathy and measures of callous-unemotional traits such as the ASPD-SR CU and the Uncaring and Unemotional scales of the ICU.

Unlike the uncontrolled results, however, there was a significant positive relationship identified between the YPI total and cognitive empathy, and this was driven by the Impulsive-Irresponsible and the Callous Unemotional dimensions of this measure. Again, higher scores on cognitive empathy in males were associated with higher scores on the measures of narcissism, but unlike the uncontrolled results lower scores on cognitive empathy were related to increases in General social anxiety.

When the independent influence of affective empathy was examined for females, noticeable relationships were identified between this and higher CU traits as assessed by the ASPD-SR CU and the YPI-CU, which was similar to the uncontrolled results. Females higher on affective empathy also tended to score higher on Leadership-Authority narcissism and higher on total and reactive aggression. Controlling for affective empathy, increased cognitive empathy of females was related to increases in the YPI, particularly the Impulsive-Irresponsible scale. Like the uncontrolled results, low cognitive empathy was associated with significant increases in General Social Anxiety for females.

Table 9.3 presents the correlations of the BES with criminal and clinical variables of the male and female samples. For males, low affective empathy was significantly related to increased crime seriousness as well as an increased conduct disorder, particularly the Overt component of CD. There was however, only one

Table 9.3 Correlations of the BES with other variables

Males/Females	*BES Affective*	*BES Cognitive*
Age Crime Onset	.04/−.04	−.05/−.19
Age 1st Problem w/ Law	−.01/−.08	−.10/−.30*
Age First Detention	.02/−.20	−.05/−.21
No. Criminal Charges	−.07/−.03	−.05/−.04
Crime Seriousness	−.15*/.04	−.04/.01
Three Year Recidivism	−.09/−.01	−.06/−.04
Violent Recidivism	−.13/.11	−.01/.01
CD Symptoms total	−.14*/.16	.09/.28*
CD Aggression	−.15*/.11	.08/.20
CD Destruction	−.06/.10	−.02/−.05
CD Deceitfulness	−.11/.19	.09/.19
CD Rules Violations	−.07/.03	.06/.31*
CD Overt	−.15*/.11	.08/.20
CD Covert	−.11/.15	.07/.31*
CD Diagnostic	−.06/.09	.07/.19
Alcohol Use	−.05/.09	.01/.06
Cannabis	−.12/.01	.03/.10
Hard Drugs	−.02/.10	.04/.19
Unprotected Sex	.06/.12	.15*/.18
Psychiatric Medication	.11/.00	.04/−.07
Socio-economic Status	.01/−.19	.11/−.00

Note. BES = Basic Empathy Scale; CD = Conduct Disorder

***$p < .001$; **$p < .01$; *$p < .05$

significant correlation between cognitive empathy and the many measures for males, and this was a positive relationship with unprotected sex.

There were no significant relationships identified between affective empathy and the criminal and clinical variables for females. However, females with lower cognitive empathy tended to have later ages of first problems with the law and first detention while also demonstrating significantly lower levels of conduct disorder, particularly rule violations and covert behaviours.

Discussion

The results of the comparisons between the BES and the other measures suggested some interesting and important relationships which have both theoretical and practical implications. Furthermore, males and female appeared to be similar with regard to some of these relationships, but important differences were also evident. In line with much previous research (e.g. Munoz et al., 2011; Pardini, 2011; Pechorro et al., 2015), this study found a strong negative relationship between low affective empathy and higher callous-unemotional traits for both males and females. However, these correlations were not sufficiently large to suggest that these concepts were redundant. Interestingly, when cognitive empathy was controlled, low affective empathy was associated with low CU traits in females, suggesting the inter-play between cognitive and affective empathy may be more dynamic for females as opposed to males.

Previous results with regard to the relation between cognitive empathy and callous-unemotional traits have been equivocal (Lui et al., 2016). In this study, low cognitive empathy was related to greater CU traits in males only, but even this depended on the measure of CU traits. For males, and when affective empathy was controlled, there was a positive relationship between cognitive empathy and CU as measured by the YPI. This is likely because the YPI CU scales assesses aspects of manipulativeness and grandiosity, skills which might be facilitated by a greater understanding of another's emotions.

For both males and females there were indications that higher empathy could be associated with some other non-desirable characteristics. For example, higher affective empathy in females was associated with more aggression, particularly reactive aggression, and high affective empathy in males was associated with greater social anxiety. In both cases, these relationships may be a result of deficiencies in emotional regulation such that other's emotions are experienced as overwhelming or personally distressing, increasing aggressive reactions in the case of females and profound social anxiety in males (e.g. Jonason & Kroll, 2015). Similarly, higher cognitive empathy was associated with greater psychopathy (as measured by the YPI) and greater narcissism for both males and females. The relation between cognitive empathy and psychopathy has been identified in previous research (e.g. Dadds et al., 2009), and likely reflects the way in which a greater understanding of other's emotions can be used to deceive and manipulate. The link between narcissism and cognitive empathy has also been identified in previous research (e.g. Di Pierro et al., 2018), with some research suggesting that narcissistic individuals who have some concern for others (e.g. affective empathy) may use alternative strategies (e.g. manipulating others, self-aggrandisement) which require cognitive empathy to reach social goals, thus accounting for the relation between high cognitive empathy and narcissism.

This research has some important limitations which need to be considered when interpreting the results. First, this study is correlational, and as such no confident conclusions may be drawn about the ordering of empathy and the other variables that were studied. For example, low affective empathy may predict increased crime seriousness in males, or increased crime seriousness may erode empathy. These equally valid interpretations would have important implications for selecting potential interventions designed to reduce crime seriousness. Second, the nature of this sample, by definition, includes those young people who are the most seriously criminal justice involved in Portugal, and as such the results may not generalise to those at less advanced stages of their criminal careers. Third, and also because of this sample includes only those in prison, it fails to account for the potential impact that the experience of incarceration might have on empathy and the other characteristics under investigation. There is certainly evidence that certain the experience of prison can erode empathy (Jolliffe & Haque, 2017).

Conclusions

The Basic Empathy provided a useful addition to commonly used measures with forensic samples. The results also demonstrated that males and females, while similar in some respects with regard to their relationships between empathy and the other measures, important differences were also identified, and these should be considered when developing appropriate interventions to reduce the likelihood of future offending. Similarly, this research highlighted that the very common intervention goal of increasing cognitive or affective empathy to reduce offending may have quite negative outcomes for the person receiving the intervention (e.g. increasing social anxiety) and others (e.g. increased aggression/ psychopathy). Future research should continue to attempt to disentangle empathy from other potentially important constructs by using methods which allow for examinations of potential changes in empathy over time, and to examine how changes in empathy might be related to later desirable and non-desirable outcomes.

Acknowledgements

This study was partially conducted at the Psychology Research Centre (PSI/01662), School of Psychology, University of Minho, and supported by the Portuguese Foundation for Science and Technology and the Portuguese Ministry of Science, Technology and Higher Education (UID/PSI/01662/2019) and the project CIP (UID/PSI/04345/2020), through the national funds (PIDDAC)

We wish to thank the following Portuguese juvenile detention centres for their collaboration: Bela Vista, Mondego, Navarro de Paiva, Olivais, Padre António Oliveira, Santo António, and Santa Clara.

References

American Psychiatric Association. (2013). *Diagnostic and statistical manual of mental disorders* (5th ed.). Washington, DC: American Psychiatric Association.

Andershed, H., Kerr, M., Stattin, H., & Levander, S. (2002). Psychopathic traits in non-referred youths: Initial test of a new assessment tool. In E. Blaauw & L. Sheridan (Eds.), *Psychopaths: Current international perspectives* (pp. 131–158). Haag: Elsevier.

Bachman, R., & Schutt, R. (2014). *The practice of research in criminology and criminal justice* (5th ed.). London: Sage.

Beadle, J. N., & de la Vega, C. E. (2019). Impact of aging on empathy: Review of psychological and neural mechanisms. *Frontiers in Psychiatry, 10*, 331. doi:10.3389/fpsyt.2019.00331

Broidy, L., Cauffman, E., Espelage, D. L., Mazerolle, P., & Piquero, A. R. (2003). Sex differences in empathy and its relation to juvenile offending. *Violence and Victims, 18*, 503–516.

Chaplin, T. M., & Aldao, A. (2013). Gender differences in emotion expression in children: A meta-analytic review. *Psychological Bulletin, 139*, 735–765. doi:10.1037/a0030737

Cohen, P. (1996). Childhood risk for young adult symptoms of personality disorder: Method and substance. *Multivariate Behavioral Research, 31*, 121–148. doi:10.1207/s15327906mbr3101_7

Dadds, M. R., Hawes, D. J., Frost, A. D. J., Vassallo, S., Bunn, P., Hunter, K., & Merz, S. (2009). Learning to "talk the talk": The relationship of psychopathic traits to deficits in empathy across childhood. *The Journal of Child Psychology and Psychiatry, 50*, 599–606. doi: 10.1111/j.1469-7610.2008.02058.x

Davis, M. H. (1983). Measuring individual differences in empathy: Evidence for a multidimensional approach. *Journal of Personality and Social Psychology, 44*, 113–126.

di Pierro, R., di Sarno, M., Emanuele, P., di Mattei, V. E., & Madeddu, F. (2018). The role of identity instability in the relationship between narcissism and emotional empathy. *Psychoanalytic Psychology, 35*, 237–243. doi:10.1037/pap0000159

Essau, C., Sasagawa, S., & Frick, P. (2006). Callous-unemotional traits in a community sample of adolescents. *Assessment, 13*, 454–469. doi:10.1177/1073191106287354

Farrington, D. P., & Loeber, R. (1989). RIOC and phi as measures of predictive efficiency and strength of association in 2X2 tables. *Journal of Quantitative Criminology, 5*, 201–213. doi:10.1007/BF01062737

Frick, P., & Hare, R. (2001). *The antisocial process screening device (APSD): Technical manual*. Toronto: Multi-Health Systems.

Gentile, B., Miller, J., Hoffman, B., Reidy, D., Zeichner, A., & Campbell, W. (2013). A test of two brief measures of grandiose narcissism: The narcissistic personality inventory-13 and the narcissistic personality inventory-16. *Psychological Assessment, 25*, 1120–1136. doi:10.1037/a0033192

Hanson, K. R. (2003). Empathy deficits of sexual offenders: A conceptual model. *Journal of Sexual Aggression, 9*, 13–23.

Hoffman, M. L. (1987). The contribution of empathy to justice and moral judgement. In N. Eisenberg & J. Strayer (Eds.), *Empathy and its development* (pp. 47–80). Cambridge: Cambridge University Press.

Hogan, R. (1969). Development of an empathy scale. *Journal of Consulting and Clinical Psychology, 33*, 307–316.

IBM Corp. (2018). *IBM SPSS statistics for windows* (version 25). Armonk, NY: IBM Corp.

Jolliffe, D., & Farrington, D. P. (2004). Empathy and offending: A systematic review and meta-analysis. *Aggression and Violent Behavior, 9*, 441–476. doi:10.1016/j.avb.2003.03.001

Jolliffe, D., & Farrington, D. (2006). Development and validation of the basic empathy scale. *Journal of Adolescence, 29*, 589–611. doi:10.1016/j.adolescence.2005.08.010

Jolliffe, D., & Haque, Z. (2017). *Have prisons become dangerous places?* Research Report Runnymede Trust. Retrieved from www.runnymedetrust.org/uploads/PressReleases/Prisons%20report%20v3%20final%20typesetter.pdf

Jonason, P. K., & and Kroll, C. H. (2015). A multidimensional view of the relationship between empathy and the dark triad. *Journal of Individual Differences, 36*, 150–156. doi:10.1027/1614-0001/a000166

La Greca, A., & Lopez, N. (1998). Social anxiety among adolescents: Linkages with peer relations and friendships. *Journal of Abnormal Child Psychology, 26*, 83–94. doi:10.1023/A:1022684520514

Lam, C. B., Solmeyer, A. R., & McHale, S. M. (2012). Sibling relationships and empathy across the transition to adolescence. *Journal of Youth and Adolescence, 41*, 1657–1670. doi:10.1007/s10964-012-9781-8

Leech, N., Barrett, K., & Morgan, G. (2015). *IBM SPSS for intermediate statistics: Use and interpretation* (5th ed.). New York: Routledge.

Lui, J. H. L., Barry, C. T., & Sacco, D. F. (2016). Callous-unemotional traits and empathy deficits: Mediating effects of affective perspective-taking and facial emotion recognition. *Cognition and Emotion, 30*, 1049–1062. doi:10.1080/02699931.2015.1047327

McClure, E. B. (2000). A meta-analytic review of sex differences in facial expression processing and their development in infants, children, and adolescents. *Psychological Bulletin, 126*, 424–453. doi: 10.1037/0033-2909.126.3.424

Michalska, K. J., Kinzler, K. D., & Decety, J. (2013). Age-related sex differences in explicit measures of empathy do not predict brain responses across childhood and adolescence. *Developmental Cognitive Neuroscience, 3*, 22–32. doi:10.1016/j.dcn.2012.08.001

Moffitt, T. E., & Caspi, A. (2001). Childhood predictors differentiate life-course persistent and adolescence-limited antisocial pathways among males and females. *Development and Psychopathology, 13*, 355–375. doi:10.1017/S0954579401002097

Munoz, L. C., Qualter, P., & Padgett, G. (2011). Empathy and bullying: Exploring the influence of callous-unemotional traits. *Child Psychiatry and Human Development, 42*, 183–196.

Pardini, D. A. (2011). Perceptions of social conflicts among incarcerated adolescents with callous-unemotional traits: "You're going to pay. It's going to hurt, but I don't care". *Journal of Child Psychology and Psychiatry, 52*, 248–255. doi:10.1111/j.1469-7610.2010.02336.x

Pechorro, P., Ayala-Nunes, L., Kahn, R., & Nunes, C. (2018). The reactive-proactive aggression questionnaire: Measurement invariance and reliability among a school sample of Portuguese youths. *Child Psychiatry & Human Development, 49*, 523–533. doi: 10.1007/s10578-017-0772-6

Pechorro, P., Ayala-Nunes, L., Nunes, C., Maroco, J., & Gonçalves, R. (2016). The social anxiety scale for adolescents: Measurement invariance and psychometric properties among a school sample of Portuguese youths. *Child Psychiatry and Human Development, 47*, 975–984. doi:10.1007/s10578-016-0627-6

Pechorro, P., Braga, T., Hawes, S., Gonçalves, R., Simões, M., & Ray, J. (in press). The Portuguese version of the inventory of callous-unemotional traits self-report and its short form among a normative sample of community youths. *Child Psychiatry and Human Development*. doi:10.1007/s10578-018-0835-3

Pechorro, P., Gentile, B., Ray, J., Nunes, C., & Gonçalves, R. (2016). Adaptation of the narcissistic personality inventory among Portuguese juvenile offenders. *Psychology, Crime & Law, 22*, 495–511. doi:10.1080/1068316X.2016.1168421

Pechorro, P., Hidalgo, V., Nunes, C., & Jiménez, L. (2016). Confirmatory factor analysis of the antisocial process screening device: Self-report among incarcerated male juvenile offenders. *International Journal of Offender Therapy and Comparative Criminology*, *60*, 1856–1872. doi:10.1177/0306624X15588903

Pechorro, P., Ray, J., Salas-Wright, C., Maroco, J., & Gonçalves, R. (2015). Adaptation of the basic empathy scale among a Portuguese sample of incarcerated juvenile offenders. *Psychology, Crime & Law*, *21*, 699–714. doi:10.1080/1068316X.2015.1028546

Pechorro, P., Ribeiro da Silva, D., Andershed, H., Rijo, D., & Gonçalves, R. A. (2016). The youth psychopathic traits inventory: Measurement invariance and psychometric properties among Portuguese youths. *International Journal of Environmental Research and Public Health*, *13*, 852. doi:10.3390/ijerph13090852

Raine, A., Dodge, K., Loeber, R., Gatzke-Kopp, L., Lynam, D., Reynolds, C., & Liu, J. (2006). The reactive – proactive aggression questionnaire: Differential correlates of reactive and proactive aggression in adolescent boys. *Aggressive Behavior*, *32*, 159–171. doi:10.1002/ab.20115

Simões, M. R. (2000). *Investigações no âmbito da Aferição Nacional do Teste das Matrizes Progressivas Coloridas de Raven* [*Investigations in the context of the national standardization of the Raven coloured progressive matrices test*]. Lisboa: Fundação Calouste Gulbenkian.

Southard, E. E. (1918). The empathic index in the diagnosis of mental diseases. *Abnormal Psychology*, *8*, 199–214.

Tracy, P. E., Kempf-Leonard, K., & Abramoske-James, S. (2009). Gender differences in delinquency and juvenile justice processing: Evidence from national data. *Crime & Delinquency*, *55*, 171–215. doi:10.1177/0011128708330628

Vachon, D. D., Lynam, D. R., & Johnson, J. A. (2014). The (non)relation between empathy and aggression: Surprising results from a meta-analysis. *Psychological Bulletin*, *140*, 751–773.

van der Helm, G. H. P., Stams, G. J. J. M., van der Stel, J. C., van Langen, M. A. M., & van der Laan, P. H. (2012). Group climate and empathy in a sample of incarcerated boys. *International Journal of Offender Therapy and Comparative Criminology*, *56*, 1149–1160.

van Langan, M. A. M., Wissink, I. B., van Vugt, E. S., van der Stouwe, T., & Stams, G. J. J. M. (2014). The relation between empathy and offending: A meta-analysis. *Aggression and Violent Behavior*, *19*, 179–189.

van Voorhis, P. (2012). On behalf of women offenders: Women's place in the science of evidence-based practice. *Criminology and Public Policy*, *11*, 111–145. doi:10.1111/j.1745-9133.2012.00793.x

Watt, M. C., Frausin, S., Dixon, J., & Nimmo, S. (2000). Moral intelligence in a sample of incarcerated females. *Criminal Justice and Behavior*, *27*, 330–355.

Wolfgang, M., Figlio, R., Tracey, P., & Singer, F. (1985). *The national survey of crime severity*. Washington, DC: U.S. Department of Justice, Criminal Justice Reference Service.

10 The relationship between empathy, clinical problems, and reoffending in a sample of Canadian male offenders

Christopher J. Koegl

Introduction

Effective, evidence-based correctional treatment is built on the premise that programmes and services should address risk and need factors that have a demonstrated connection with antisocial behaviour. One of the most well-known paradigms for identifying and responding to such factors is the Risk-Need-Responsivity framework (RNR; Andrews & Bonta, 2010). Formalised in Canada in the 1990s, RNR prioritises eight risk factors: criminal history, antisocial personality pattern, antisocial cognition, criminal associates, family/marital, school/work, leisure/recreation, and substance use. Of these, the first four are considered to be the most important and have robust relationships with criminal offending (e.g. Serin, Lloyd, Helmus, Derkzen, & Luong, 2013; Wooditch, Tang, & Taxman, 2014). Empathy, although often thought to be at the core of the offender-victim relationship, is not explicitly incorporated in the "big four" or the "central eight" RNR risk factors despite the fact that, in practice, empathy-training features prominently in correctional treatment programs, particularly those targeted at sex offenders (Morrow, 2019; Yates, 2009).

Previous meta-analyses have demonstrated a moderate statistical relationship between low cognitive empathy and criminal offending ($d = -.48$, Jolliffe & Farrington, 2004; $d = -.43$, van Langen, Wissink, van Vugt, van der Stouwe, & Stams, 2014). It follows that helping offenders to develop a better understanding of the subjective experiences of others may help to decrease their reoffending potential. Unfortunately, research examining individual-level change variables in relation to offending is sparse, generally speaking (Serin, Lloyd, Helmus, Derkzen, & Luong, 2013), but this is especially true with respect to empathy. What is needed, in addition to continued research on traditional RNR factors, is a greater focus on the broader set of dynamic factors that are theoretically tied to the offending cycles of persistent offenders. In an attempt to address this gap in the literature, this chapter explores the relationship between empathy, as measured by the Basic Empathy Scale (BES; Jolliffe & Farrington, 2006), and a range of offender variables in a sample of incarcerated men receiving treatment at the Ontario Correctional Institute (OCI) in Canada.

The Ontario Correctional Institute (OCI)

The Institute functions as a 220-bed provincial correctional treatment centre for adult male offenders serving sentences of less than two years. In order to be eligible for transfer to OCI, inmates (referred to as "residents") must submit a formal application that declares their willingness to actively participate in treatment and live in the general offender population comprised of both sex and non-sex offenders. Prospective residents must also not manifest acute mental health symptoms (e.g. psychoses, active suicidal behaviours) and demonstrate that they are able to function in a dormitory setting without posing a security risk. If these gross criteria are met, they are transferred to the intake and assessment unit at OCI where they will participate in a structured clinical interview, complete a battery of standardised measures, and undergo behavioural observation by correctional officers who identify treatment needs and further assess their readiness for treatment. After approximately six to eight weeks, a determination is made by a team of senior staff representing psychology, social work, health care and correctional officers about whether the resident should be transferred to the treatment side of the Institute. If successful, individuals are moved to one of five living units until the expiry of their sentence where they will receive a range of core and intensive clinical programmes tailored to their criminogenic needs. Residents who are not willing to fully engage in programmes, or who are violent or disruptive to the treatment milieu, can be transferred out of the Institute at any time.

OCI provides core programming that targets antisocial thinking styles, poor self-regulation and problem-solving skills, and intensive programmes focussed on the specific needs of substance abusers and sex offenders. Roughly one third of all new admissions are residents who have committed a sexual offence, most of which involve crimes against children. In addition to clinical intervention services, OCI also offers educational upgrading through a structured school program, volunteer-led programs (e.g. Alcoholics Anonymous, Narcotics Anonymous), faith and aboriginal-focussed supports, vocationally based institutional work assignments, and regular opportunities for physical recreation. The overarching model of supervision that permeates all programming is "relationship custody" which seeks to build respectful, trusting relationships among staff and inmates. Accordingly, residents are exposed to treatment inputs throughout their day, even when they are not attending structured clinical programmes.

Study aims

The BES was first implemented as a standardised *intake* measure in 2013 to better understand the relationship between empathy and existing demographic, clinical and criminal offending information. In addition to the BES, residents complete standardised measures on the assessment unit that provide a comprehensive picture of their risk, need and responsivity profile at admission to the Institute. Beginning in 2014, the BES was incorporated into a package of *discharge* measures given to residents who successfully completed their sentence and were released from the Institute. This was done to assess whether their overall experience at OCI produced measurable changes in empathy, and whether these changes were related to reoffending post-release. Because the Institute does not provide treatment modules specifically targeted at empathy-building, it was an open question as to whether there would be observed changes in BES scores from pre- to post-treatment. Taken together, this study had four aims, which were to:

1 Measure the statistical relationship between BES intake scores and a range of demographic, psychological, and criminal offending variables;
2 Assess whether empathy scores changed from admission to discharge;
3 Determine whether pre-to-post empathy change scores predicted reoffending, controlling for other risk, and need variables; and
4 Examine whether these relationships were similar for sex and non-sex offenders.

Method

Sampling frame

Study participants were drawn from the total pool of inmates attending OCI between June 2013 and April 2018. Because the BES was distributed as part of the standard package of questionnaires administered for treatment planning, the BES pre-treatment completion rate was nearly perfect (n = 1028/1040 or 98.9%) and only excluded a very small number (n = 12) of residents who could not complete measures due to literacy problems. Discharge measures, which were used to calculate pre-post change scores, were obtained from 461 of 479 (96.2%) residents who successfully completed their sentence at OCI. To measure the association between BES change scores and two-year recidivism status (calculated in 2018), all of the 253 residents who completed pre and post measures between 2014 and 2016 were selected for analysis.

Standardised measures

The following self-reported, standardised intake measures were administered to residents during the assessment phase of their stay at OCI to support RNR-focussed treatment planning:

1 **Barratt Impulsiveness Scale** (BIS; Stanford et al., 2009): 30 items scored on a four-point scale where 1 = "rarely/never" and 4 = "almost always" to yield a total score ranging from 30 to 120; higher BIS scores indicate higher levels of personality and behavioural aspects of impulsivity.
2 **Basic Empathy Scale** (BES; Jolliffe & Farrington, 2006): 20 items scored on a five-point scale where 1 = "strongly disagree" and 5 = "strongly agree" to yield a total score ranging from 20 to 100. Higher BES scores are indicative of having more empathy. The scale was be broken down further into two subscales measuring cognitive (9 items) and affective empathy (11 items) as per Jolliffe and Farrington (2006).

3 **Criminogenic Cognitions Scale** (CCS; Tangney et al., 2012): A 25-item scale rated on a four-point scale where 1 = "strongly agree" and 4 = "strongly disagree" to yield a total score between 25 and 100. Items are counter-balanced so that high scores reflect higher/more criminogenic thinking. (Please note that the CCS and the BIS were implemented at OCI in 2014, approximately one year after the BES, resulting in about 200 fewer cases for analyses for each of these two measures.)

4 **Personality Assessment Inventory** (PAI; Morey, 1991): A 344-item multi-scale measure of psychological functioning. Each item is scored on a four-point scale ranging from 0 (false) to 3 (very true) to yield 18 non-overlapping scales measuring psychiatric problems (e.g. anxiety, depression), treatment considerations (e.g. aggression), and interpersonal traits (e.g. warmth, dominance). The tool also contains validity scales that measure random, inconsistent, and overly positive or negative reporting across items; (PAI scores were excluded from analyses if respondents exceeded thresholds for any of the four validity scales.)

5 **Psychology Intake Form** (PIF; Ontario Correctional Institute, 2010): 10-page, in-house questionnaire that captures a wide range of historical and current psychosocial functioning information related to education, employment, financial status, accommodation, relationships and children, childhood experiences, physical and mental health, criminal history and offending pattern, substance use and abuse, and current problems requiring treatment. Many of the questions are "yes/no" or multiple-choice format, although the PIF also captures detailed, open-ended information for some questions.

6 **Shipley-2** (Shipley, Gruber, Martin, & Klein, 2009): a standardised measure of intellectual ability that includes a 20-item abstract thinking test, whereby higher scores reflect better cognitive ability. This measure was used primarily to control for differences in intellectual ability in multivariate analyses.

Historical criminal offending, two-year recidivism, and criminal risk information

Information about each resident's criminal history was gathered from the provincial offender data management system. The complete list of 1028 study participants was submitted to the research and statistics unit within the Ministry of the Solicitor General, resulting in a 100% retrieval rate. Electronic records were coded to produce two criminal offending variables for each person: 1) number of prior criminal convictions, and 2) whether each person was convicted of a new criminal offence within two years of being released from the Institute.

In addition to official criminal conviction records, it was also possible to capture pre-admission risk assessment information based on the *Level of Service Inventory, Ontario Revision* (LSI-OR; Andrews, Bonta, & Wormith, 1995). The LSI-OR is a risk-needs assessment tool completed by classification officers to assist in placement and treatment decisions. The LSI-OR assesses a range of static and dynamic risk factors across 43 items (each rated dichotomously) to yield a total risk score ranging from 0 to 43. Research on the LSI-OR has shown it to be both reliable and valid for use with offender populations in Ontario (Girard & Wormith, 2004).

Study participants

The average age of the 1028 men who completed pre/assessment measures was 36.0 years (*SD* = 11.5). Over three-quarters (76.2%) of the sample was white, 12.0% were indigenous, 5.4% were black, and 6.5% were of other racial origin. For marital status, 60.7% were single, 26.1% were married and 13.2% were either widowed, separated or divorced. At the time of their admission to OCI, participants were facing a range of educational, vocational, and economic challenges: 54.9% did not complete high school, 57.0% had no job to return to upon release, 29.3% were receiving welfare, and 31.2% reported having unstable housing. More than half (51.5%) of the men were fathers and 46.8% reported that they were financially supporting others (e.g. children, partners, extended family members).

The average number of prior convictions for the sample was 16.4 (*SD* = 18.8), the average sentence length was 531.3 days (*SD* = 143.6) and the average length of stay at OCI was 237.1 days (*SD* = 123.5). In terms of the most serious offence leading to their incarceration at OCI, 31.8% involved a sexual offence (e.g. sexual assault, sexual interference), 18.6% involved violence (e.g. assault, robbery), 19.3% were sentenced for a property offence (e.g. theft, fraud), 15.5% involved a drug-related crime (e.g. possession, trafficking), and 14.8% were convicted of another offence. According to LSI-OR risk scores at admission, 61.4% were classified as "high" or "very high" risk to reoffend (i.e. had total scores of 20 or higher).

Results

The relationship between empathy and current and childhood problems

The Psychology Intake Form allows residents to identify current problems in addition to others they may have experienced during childhood. To facilitate comparisons, the BES total score was subdivided into three groups as follows: "low", representing the bottom 25% (*M* = 60.2, range = 43–66, *n* = 254); "moderate", representing the middle 50% (*M* = 71.6, range = 67–76, *n* = 516); and "high", representing the top 25% (*M* = 81.4, range = 77–94, *n* = 258) of cases based on the distribution of BES total empathy scores. Comparisons were performed for 15 childhood problems (*n* = 954) and 20 current problems (*n* = 952). Table 10.1 shows the results for comparisons where there were statistically significant differences across empathy groups. Odds ratios, based on 2×2 tables comparing the upper and lower quartiles for each variable were also calculated to assist in the interpretation of results.

Looking first at childhood problems, individuals in the low empathy group were more than twice as likely (*OR* = 2.35) to report having criminal siblings than individuals in the high empathy group. Conversely, individuals with high empathy were more than 70% likely to report being anxious, depressed, or a victim of repeated bullying, compared to persons with low empathy. For current problems,

Table 10.1 Percentage of residents with current and childhood problems by total empathy group

	PROBLEM DOMAIN	TOTAL EMPATHY GROUP			χ^2 (df = 2)	OR
		LOWER 25%	MIDDLE 50%	UPPER 25%		
CHILD	Criminal siblings	19.4	15.2	9.3	9.79**	2.35
	Stress/anxiety	48.9	51.7	62.4	10.25**	1.73
	Depression	48.5	53.5	62.4	9.63**	1.76
	Victim of repeated bullying	22.8	30.0	34.6	8.17*	1.79
CURRENT	Lack of concern for others	25.3	20.1	14.8	8.22*	1.96
	Criminal family, spouse, partner	16.5	10.0	8.4	9.02*	2.14
	Criminal friends	50.2	49.8	36.7	12.51**	1.74
	Stress/anxiety	60.3	66.3	76.8	15.16***	2.18
	Depression	51.5	56.9	63.7	7.30*	1.66
	Anger	29.5	31.6	43.9	13.62***	1.87
	Problem relationships: romantic partner	23.2	31.0	40.1	15.75***	2.21
	Problem relationships: family/friends	33.3	32.0	41.8	6.70*	1.43

Notes: ****p* < .001, ***p* < .01, **p* < .05; the chi-square statistic was based on 3 groups; the odds ratio (OR) statistic was calculated using data for the lower and upper empathy groups only; OR = adjusted odds ratio (i.e. for ease of interpretation, the inverse of the OR was calculated for negative relationships).

residents with high empathy were more likely to report feeling anxious, depressed, and angry compared to residents with low empathy. Residents with high empathy also reported more problematic relationships with romantic partners and their families and friends. For the more criminogenic variables, individuals with low empathy were more likely to identify that they had a lack of concern for others or to identify that they had criminal associations with their friends, family and their spouses/partners.

These analyses were rerun separately for affective and cognitive empathy. As before, each subscale was broken down into three groups based on their respective total scores. For *affective empathy* these were: "low", representing the bottom 25% (*M* = 28.4, *SD* = 2.9, range = 9–31, *n* = 226); "moderate", representing the middle 50% (*M* = 34.1, *SD* = 1.4, range = 32–36, *n* = 564); and "high", representing the top 25% (*M* = 39.1, *SD* = 1.9, range = 37–45, *n* = 238). For *cognitive empathy* these were: "low", representing the bottom 25% (*M* = 29.5, *SD* = 3.5, range = 16–33, *n* = 239); "moderate", representing the middle 50% (*M* = 37.5, *SD* = 2.2, range = 34–41, *n* = 554); and "high", representing the top 25% (*M* = 44.4, *SD* = 2.3, range = 42–53, *n* = 235).

Table 10.2 shows the associations between childhood and current problems in relation to affective and cognitive empathy. While the directionality of relationships found for the total empathy score did not change, analyses revealed that 11/12 problems remained significantly associated with affective empathy, but only five were still significantly associated with cognitive empathy. For example,

Table 10.2 Percentage of residents with current and childhood problems by empathy group

	PROBLEM DOMAIN	AFFECTIVE EMPATHY GROUP			χ^2 (df = 2)	OR	COGNITIVE EMPATHY GROUP			$\chi2$ (df = 2)	OR
		LOWER 25%	MIDDLE 50%	UPPER 25%			LOWER 25%	MIDDLE 50%	UPPER 25%		
CHILD	Criminal siblings	**19.6**	**14.5**	**10.6**	**7.15***	**2.06**	**18.4**	**15.7**	**9.1**	**8.09***	**2.25**
	Stress/anxiety	**41.6**	**54.2**	**64.5**	**23.27*****	**2.56**	54.9	52.6	55.3	0.60	1.02
	Depression	**45.7**	**53.5**	**65.9**	**18.49*****	**2.30**	51.0	55.0	56.6	1.49	1.26
	Victim of repeated bullying	**20.5**	**29.0**	**39.2**	**18.31*****	**2.49**	27.7	29.3	31.1	0.57	1.18
CURRENT	Lack of concern for others	**29.1**	**17.9**	**16.1**	**14.83****	**2.13**	20.4	20.7	18.3	0.75	1.15
	Criminal family, spouse, partner	**16.8**	**9.5**	**9.7**	**8.93***	**1.89**	**11.2**	**13.1**	**6.8**	**6.05***	**1.71**
	Criminal friends	50.0	47.8	40.6	4.49	1.47	**51.5**	**48.8**	**37.0**	**11.08****	**1.81**
	Stress/anxiety	**58.2**	**66.6**	**78.8**	**21.51*****	**2.67**	65.0	67.4	69.9	1.12	1.25
	Depression	**52.3**	**56.1**	**65.0**	**7.79***	**1.69**	53.9	58.6	57.1	1.37	1.14
	Anger	**28.6**	**32.8**	**42.9**	**10.70****	**1.87**	**30.1**	**32.8**	**41.1**	**6.61***	**1.62**
	Problem relationships: romantic partner	**23.6**	**31.7**	**38.2**	**10.91****	**2.00**	**23.8**	**31.1**	**38.8**	**11.16****	**2.03**
	Problem relationships: family/friends	**34.5**	**32.0**	**41.9**	**6.60***	**1.37**	34.0	32.6	41.1	4.97	1.36

Notes: ***$p < .001$, **$p < .01$, *$p < .05$; the chi-square statistic was based on 3 groups; the odds ratio (OR) statistic was calculated using data for the lower and upper empathy groups only; *OR* = adjusted odds ratio (i.e. for ease of interpretation, the inverse of the OR was calculated for negative relationships).

comparing the lower and upper quartile groups, persons with high affective empathy had more than a twofold odds of experiencing anxiety or depression, or being a victim of repeated bulling during childhood. The high empathy group was also more than two and a half times more likely to be currently experiencing stress or anxiety. Across the five problem areas that were still significantly associated with cognitive empathy, the magnitude of the odds ratios changed only slightly, suggesting that affective empathy was driving the associations shown in Table 1 with respect to the total empathy score.

The relationship between empathy, current psychological problems, and criminal risk

The association between empathy and a range of psychological and criminal offending and risk variables was examined by calculating Pearson correlation coefficients for continuous variables. Means for the trichotomised empathy groups were also compared using ANOVA procedures to yield F-tests for statistical testing. Table 10.3 shows the results for variables where there were significant differences across levels of the BES total score. The first group of four "connectedness" variables describe individual characteristics of the residents that were most related to empathy. Not surprisingly, individuals with lower empathy were *less* likely to exhibit warmth, which the PAI manual describes as 'the extent to which a person is empathic, engaging or rejecting and mistrustful in interpersonal relationships' (Morey, 1991, p. 21); *more* likely to feel non-supported which is defined as a 'perceived lack of social support, tapping both the availability and quality of the respondent's social relationships' (p. 20); and exhibit *more* feelings of paranoia which is characterised as 'a vigilance in monitoring the environment for potential harm, a tendency to be resentful and to hold grudges, and a readiness to spot inequities in the way that the respondent has been treated by others' (p. 16).

A second group of variables that was significantly associated with BES scores pertains to antisocial traits: low empathy was related to higher criminogenic cognitions ($r = -.30$) and higher levels of antisocial features which is defined in the PAI as a constellation of defining factors of antisocial personality and psychopathy ranging from 'indicators of egocentricity, adventuresomeness, and poor empathy to items addressing antisocial attitudes and behaviors' (p. 18). In addition to associations with higher impulsivity and aggression, low empathy was also significantly correlated with higher LSI-OR risk scores and having more prior convictions.

Table 10.4 shows the associations between the continuous connectedness and antisocial variables and affective and cognitive empathy. All of the bivariate correlations were statistically significant at $p < .001$ (two-tailed) with the exception of the associations between affective empathy and the Barratt Impulsivity total score ($r = -.094$, $p < .05$), and cognitive empathy and the number of prior convictions ($r = -.101$, $p < .01$). Looking at the Pearson coefficients, there were stronger associations between the three connectedness variables and cognitive empathy compared to affective empathy. Likewise, cognitive empathy was more strongly associated with criminal thinking and impulsivity.

Table 10.3 Total empathy, current psychological problems, and criminal risk variables

	PROBLEM DOMAIN	*Pearson Correlation*	*TOTAL EMPATHY GROUP*			*F-value* (df)
			LOWER 25% M (SD)	*MIDDLE 50%* M (SD)	*UPPER 25%* M (SD)	
CONNECTEDNES	Warmth (PAI)	**+0.339**	**39.7** (10.9)	**44.3** (9.6)	**48.6** (9.8)	**40.55** (2, 850)
	Non-Support (PAI)	**−0.218**	**62.3** (13.2)	**57.6** (12.7)	**55.5** (12.4)	**15.12** (2, 850)
	Paranoia (PAI)	**−0.174**	**63.1** (11.3)	**59.8** (10.7)	**58.8** (12.6)	**8.46** (2, 850)
ANTISOCIAL	Criminogenic Cognitions (CCS-tot)	**−0.299**	**53.4** (9.2)	**50.0** (8.4)	**46.7** (9.4)	**23.59** (2, 650)
	Antisocial Features (PAI)	**−0.214**	**72.9** (12.9)	**68.9** (12.1)	**66.8** (12.8)	**12.89** (2, 850)
	Barratt Impulsivity total score (BIS-tot)	**−0.163**	**77.7** (12.9)	**73.2** (12.3)	**72.5** (14.7)	**8.13** (2, 650)
	Aggression (PAI)	**−0.161**	**61.1** (14.8)	**58.3** (13.9)	**55.5** (15.3)	**7.87** (2, 850)
	Total risk score (LSI-OR)	**−0.152**	**22.9** (9.4)	**22.2** (8.9)	**19.0** (9.7)	**13.41** (2, 1023)
	Number of prior convictions	**−0.135**	**19.5** (20.9)	**16.9** (19.0)	**12.3** (15.0)	**9.89** (2, 1025)

Notes: All Pearson correlations and F-statistics are significant at $p < .001$; *M* and (*SD*) are given in each cell for the three empathy groups.

Table 10.4 Affective and cognitive empathy, current psychological problems, and criminal risk variables

PROBLEM DOMAIN		*AFFECTIVE EMPATHY*					*COGNITIVE EMPATHY*				
		Pearson Correlation (r)	*GROUP*			*F-value* (df)	*Pearson Correlation* (r)	*GROUP*			*F-value* (df)
			LOWER 25% M (SD)	*MIDDLE 50%* M (SD)	*UPPER 25%* M (SD)			*LOWER 25%* M (SD)	*MIDDLE 50%* M (SD)	*UPPER 25%* M (SD)	
CONNECTEDNES	Warmth (PAI)	.261	**40.6** (11.3)	**44.9** (9.57)	**46.5** (10.69)	**17.62***** (2, 850)	.346	**39.9** (10.3)	**43.8** (9.7)	**49.2** (10.3)	**41.97***** (2, 850)
	Non-Support (PAI)	−.156	**61.2** (13.9)	**57.7** (12.3)	**56.2** (12.92)	**7.96 ***** (2, 850)	−.238	**62.2** (13.3)	**58.8** (12.7)	**53.4** (11.7)	**25.58***** (2, 850)
	Paranoia (PAI)	−.128	**62.6** (11.4)	**59.8** (10.9)	**59.4** (12.4)	**5.10 **** (2, 850)	−.185	**63.0** (10.7)	**60.8** (10.8)	**56.8** (12.5)	**14.82***** (2, 850)
ANTISOCIAL	Criminogenic Cognitions (CCS-tot)	−.233	**52.9** (9.7)	**50.0** (8.5)	**47.1** (9.2)	**15.48***** (2, 650)	−.298	**53.3** (8.0)	**50.6** (8.8)	**45.7** (9.2)	**29.70***** (2, 650)
	Antisocial Features (PAI)	−.221	**73.5** (13.2)	**68.8** (11.8)	**66.5** (13.1)	**15.93 ***** (2, 850)	−.140	**72.2** (12.5)	**69.5** (12.1)	**66.7** (13.4)	**8.90***** (2, 850)
	Barratt Impulsivity Total Score (BIS-tot)	−.094	**76.3** (13.7)	**73.6** (12.4)	**73.0** (14.5)	**2.83** (2, 650)	−.210	**77.7** (12.5)	**74.5** (12.6)	**70.3** (14.4)	**12.20***** (2, 650)
	Aggression (PAI)	−.140	**60.5** (14.9)	**58.5** (14.0)	**55.3** (15.3)	**6.38**** (2, 850)	−.142	**60.4** (14.5)	**59.1** (14.2)	**54.4** (14.9)	**9.59***** (2, 850)
	Total Risk Score (LSI-OR)	−.149	**22.9** (9.2)	**22.0** (9.1)	**19.2** (9.8)	**10.31***** (2, 1025)	−.112	**22.7** (8.9)	**22.1** (9.2)	**19.3** (9.7)	**7.68***** (2, 1025)
	Prior convictions	−.131	**18.7** (20.5)	**16.4** (17.9)	**18.8** (16.4)	**3.50*** (2, 1025)	−.101**	**18.6** (19.9)	**17.2** (19.9)	**12.5** (13.9)	**7.36***** (2, 1025)

Notes: All Pearson correlations are significant at P < .001 unless noted in the text; ***$p < .001$, **$p < .01$, *$p < .05$; *M* and (*SD*) are given in each cell for the three empathy groups.

Changes in empathy from pre- to post-treatment

Between 2014 and 2018, 461 residents completed the BES at both admission and discharge. As noted earlier, even though the Institute does not offer a specific treatment module dedicated to increasing empathy, it was still possible that residents could improve empathy indirectly, or as a result of interacting with staff and other residents. To test this possibility, differences in BES admission and discharge empathy scores were compared using a series of paired samples t-tests (Table 10.5).

For the entire sample, total ($t = -5.18$, $df = 460$, $p < .001$), affective ($t = -3.65$, $df = 460$, $p < .001$), and cognitive ($t = -5.41$, $df = 460$, $p < .001$) empathy scores were significantly higher at discharge compared to their corresponding scores at admission. This held true for the sex-offender group for the total score ($t = -4.97$, $df = 198$, $p < .001$), affective empathy ($t = -3.85$, $df = 198$, $p < .001$), and cognitive empathy ($t = -4.77$, $df = 198$, $p < .001$), and for the non-sex offender group for total empathy ($t = -2.51$, $df = 261$, $p < .013$), cognitive empathy ($t = -3.01$, $df = 261$, $p < .003$), but *not* affective empathy ($t = -1.46$, $df = 261$, $p < .145$). Statistical tests also revealed that sex-offenders had higher total, affective and cognitive empathy at both admission and discharge compared to non-sex offenders.

Change in empathy as a predictor of two-year recidivism status

Building on the findings in the preceding section, pre-to-post change scores were calculated for the total, cognitive and affective empathy variables for the 253 cases with corresponding two-year recidivism data. These change scores were then trichotomised, as before, to yield three change score groups (i.e. "low", "moderate", and "high", representing 25%, 50%, and 25% of cases, respectively). The cut-off scores for these low, moderate and high groups were −20 to −3, −2 to 6, and 7 to 30 for total empathy; −16 to −3, −2 to 4, and 5 to 24 for affective empathy; and −14 to −2, −1 to 3, and 4 to 19 for cognitive empathy.

These trichotomised change score variables were then cross-tabulated with the dichotomous two-year reconviction variable for sex (n = 97) and non-sex offenders (n = 156) to yield six chi-square test statistics. The results of these tests

Table 10.5 Changes in BES scores empathy from admission to discharge

BES MEASURE		*NON-SO* **(n = 262)**		*SO* **(n = 199)**		*TOTAL* **(n = 461)**	
		M	SD	M	SD	M	SD
PRE/ADMISSION	**TOTAL**	**70.55**	(8.01)	**72.65**	(8.88)	**71.46**	(8.45)
	Affective	36.75	(5.47)	38.08	(5.77)	37.32	(5.63)
	Cognitive	33.80	(3.79)	34.58	(4.32)	34.14	(4.04)
POST/DISCHARGE	**TOTAL**	**71.81**	(7.30)	**75.65**	(7.72)	**73.47**	(7.71)
	Affective	37.26	(5.02)	39.68	(5.28)	38.30	(5.27)
	Cognitive	34.55	(3.32)	35.97	(3.51)	35.16	(3.47)

indicated that neither of the three change scores predicted reoffending for the non-sex offender group. However, total and cognitive empathy change scores were significant predictors of recidivism for sex-offenders: for total empathy change, the percentage of low, moderate and high change groups convicted of a new offence at follow-up was 25.0%, 19.5% and 0%, respectively ($\chi^2[2] = 8.42$, $p < .015$); for cognitive empathy change, the comparable figures were 40.0%, 9.8% and 3.8%, respectively ($\chi^2[2] = 13.80$, $p < .001$).

To determine whether these associations remained significant after controlling for covariates, the following variables were entered into logistic regression models to predict conviction status for sex offenders only: continuous BES change score, age at admission, Shipley-2 Abstract Reasoning score (as a proxy for IQ), number of previous convictions (to control for criminal potential), and the BES admission score (to control for pre-existing differences in empathy). Two models were fitted: Model 1 tested the predictive power of the *total* empathy change score; Model 2 tested the predictive power of the *cognitive* empathy change score.

Table 10.6 shows that, when controlling for potential confounds, changes in empathy from admission to discharge remained a significant predictor of reoffending among sex offenders. This was true for the total change score ($Exp(B) = .830$, $p < .009$), indicating that a one-point increase in empathy from admission to

Table 10.6 Empathy change score predictors of 2-year recidivism status (sex offenders only; n = 97)

MODEL 1: TOTAL EMPATHY	*B*	*SE*	*Wald*	*df*	*P-value*	*Exp(B)*	*90% CI Exp(B)*	
							Lower	*Upper*
TOTAL empathy change score	**–.186**	**0.72**	**6.76**	**1**	**.009**	**0.83**	**0.74**	**0.93**
Age	–0.05	0.04	1.84	1	.176	0.95	0.89	1.01
Number of previous convictions	**0.12**	**0.04**	**11.06**	**1**	**.001**	**1.12**	**1.06**	**1.19**
Shipley-2 Abstract Thinking	–0.04	0.02	3.43	1	.064	0.96	0.92	1.00
Admission TOTAL empathy score	0.03	0.06	0.19	1	.665	0.97	0.88	1.08
MODEL 2: COGNITIVE EMPATHY	*B*	*SE*	*Wald*	*df*	*P-value*	*Exp(B)*	*90% CI Exp(B)*	
							Lower	*Upper*
COGNITIVE empathy change score	**–0.25**	**0.13**	**3.92**	**1**	**.048**	**0.78**	**0.63**	**0.96**
Age	–0.05	0.04	1.47	1	.225	0.95	0.89	1.02
Number of previous convictions	**0.10**	**0.03**	**10.33**	**1**	**.001**	**1.11**	**1.05**	**1.17**
Shipley-2 Abstract Thinking	**–0.04**	**0.02**	**3.64**	**1**	**.057**	**0.96**	**0.92**	**0.99**
Admission COGNITIVE empathy score	0.05	0.13	0.12	1	.726	1.05	0.84	1.30

discharge corresponded to a 20% decrease in the likelihood of reconviction within two years. The same was found for cognitive empathy (*Exp(B)* = .779, $p < .048$), where a one-point improvement corresponded to a 28% decrease in the odds of reconviction.

Discussion

One of the aims of this study was to examine the relationship between empathy and demographic, clinical, criminogenic and criminal offending variables in men participating in treatment at the Ontario Correctional Institute. It was possible to undertake this analysis given the large number of cases available, near-perfect response rates, and high data quality across multiple sources, over an extended period of time. The analysis of empathy in an offender population using the BES is the first of its kind in Canada. Although preliminary, the results are largely consistent with the extant literature and suggest that improvements in empathy can lead to lower levels of offending for some offenders.

Overall, empathy was related to a range of mental health and antisocial indicators. Specifically, lower empathy was associated with: 1) more prior convictions and higher LSI-OR criminal risk scores; 2) elevated levels of criminal traits (i.e. antisocial features, criminogenic cognitions, aggression, impulsivity); 3) more problematic interpersonal relationships and criminal associations (i.e. with friends, family members, spouses); and 4) a lack of connectedness with others (i.e. higher paranoia, less perceived support).

It was also found that higher empathy was related to a greater likelihood of having mood or anxiety problems in either childhood or adulthood. This finding was surprising because it is often assumed that having more empathy is an unambiguously good thing (i.e. being able to assume another person's perspective does not carry a burden of risk). One potential explanation is that individuals who are more "outwardly oriented" may be more susceptible to internalising negative features or events in their environment. Such an interpretation is consistent with studies that have found a positive relationship between social anxiety and empathy in adolescents (Pechorro, Ayala-Nunes, Nunes, Maroco, & Gonçalves, 2016) and adults (Tibi-Elhanany & Shamay-Tsoory, 2011). Having said this, given that the data in the present study were cross-sectional, it is possible that the mood and anxiety problems led to higher levels of empathy. Future research should therefore determine the directionality of this relationship.

Analyses were performed to examine whether the pattern of results (based on the total empathy score) would extend to each of its subscales, affective and cognitive empathy. Looking at the differences in effect sizes between affective and cognitive empathy (Tables 2 and 4) revealed some interesting differences. Results showed that affective empathy, and not cognitive empathy, was more strongly associated with stress/anxiety and depression, in both childhood and adulthood. Likewise, individuals with lower affective empathy were more likely indicate that they lacked concern for other people, and they also had higher levels of antisocial features, as measured by the PAI. On the other hand, cognitive empathy appeared to be more strongly associated with indices of connectedness (i.e. warmth, non-support, and paranoia), and criminogenic cognitions. This might be expected given the cognitive nature of these constructs, especially the latter which explicitly focuses on antisocial thinking. Lower cognitive empathy was also associated with higher impulsivity – a finding which is consistent with prior research (e.g. Reniers, Corcoran, Drake, Shryane, & Völlm, 2011).

Looking at subgroups of offenders, it was found that sex-offenders had higher levels of total, affective and cognitive empathy compared to non-sex offenders at admission and discharge. Sex offenders also showed statistically significant improvements on the BES total score, affective and cognitive subscales, whereas non-sex offenders only showed gains in total and cognitive empathy. When empathy change scores were used to predict two-year recidivism status, it was found that improvements in total and cognitive empathy (i.e. higher/positive change scores) predicted reoffending, but only among sex offenders. Moreover, these change scores remained significant predictors even when controlling for initial levels of empathy and other individual factors. The finding that cognitive empathy, and not affective empathy, predicted recidivism post-treatment is consistent with previous research (Bock & Hosser, 2014; Brown, Harkins, & Beech, 2012; O'Brien & Daffern, 2017).

Despite the positive findings of this study, some limitations should be noted. The first of these concerns generalisability. The sample consisted of men serving their sentences in an open correctional treatment setting. As a result of multiple assessment/gating processes, this means that individuals exhibiting more violence and/or acute mental health and addictions problems were under-represented in the sample. Second, due to the dynamic nature of programming offered at the Institute, it was not possible to quantify treatment dosage or perform a treatment component analysis for study participants. Having these data would have made it possible to understand which programs, services or mechanisms led to the improvements in empathy. On this point, it would be valuable to gather qualitative information from OCI residents in the future to understand *how* and *why* their empathy changed so that such information can be incorporated into subsequent program development.

Conclusions

As is the case with any intervention designed to address specific risk factors, part of the challenge is not only understanding what the most relevant risk factors are, but also identifying specific mechanisms of change (Kroner & Yessine, 2013), and determining which clients will benefit the most from the intervention (Taxman, Thanner, & Weisburd, 2006). This study suggests that sex offenders are more likely to benefit from interventions that are designed to increase empathy, and in particular, cognitive empathy. The study also suggests that, even though there were significant changes in BES cognitive and total empathy for non-sex offenders, other factors (e.g. drug addiction, criminal associates) likely play a larger role in affecting their potential to reoffend. This is not to say that empathy is unimportant for non-sex offenders. It remains possible that higher doses of empathy training may reduce recidivism and/or produce positive spinoff effects in other, non-criminal domains (e.g. parenting). Future research should explore these possibilities.

Acknowledgements

I would like to thank Michael Kirk, Supervisor, Statistical Analysis Unit Research, Analytics, and Innovation Branch at the Ministry of the Solicitor General for his help in retrieving risk and criminal offending records.

References

Andrews, D. A., & Bonta, J. L. (2010). *The psychology of criminal conduct* (5th ed.) New Providence, CT: Matthew Bender & Company.

Andrews, D. A., Bonta, J., & Wormith, J. S. (1995). *The level of service inventory: Ontario revision*. Toronto: Ontario Ministry of Community Safety & Correctional Services.

Bock, E. M., & Hosser, D. (2014). Empathy as a predictor of recidivism among young adult offenders. *Psychology, Crime & Law*, *20*(2), 101–115.

Brown, S., Harkins, L., & Beech, A. R. (2012). General and victim-specific empathy: Associations with actuarial risk, treatment outcome, and sexual recidivism. *Sexual Abuse*, *24*(5), 411–430.

Girard, L., & Wormith, J. S. (2004). The predictive validity of the level of service inventory-Ontario revision on general and violent recidivism among various offender groups. *Criminal Justice and Behavior*, *31*(2), 150–181.

Jolliffe, D., & Farrington, D. P. (2004). Empathy and offending: A systematic review and meta-analysis. *Aggression and Violent Behavior*, *9*, 441–476.

Jolliffe, D., & Farrington, D. P. (2006). Development and validation of the basic empathy scale. *Journal of Adolescence*, *29*, 589–611.

Kroner, D. G., & Yessine, A. K. (2013). Changing risk factors that impact recidivism: In search of mechanisms of change. *Law and Human Behavior*, *37*(5), 321.

Morey, L. C. (1991). *Personality assessment inventory (PAI)*. New York: Wiley.

Morrow, E. P. (2019). Cognitive, affective, and general empathy in individuals convicted of a sexual offense: A meta-analysis. *Sexual Abuse*. Retrieved July 10, 2019. doi:10.1177/1079063219858062

O'Brien, K., & Daffern, M. (2017). Treatment gain in violent offenders: The relationship between proximal outcomes, risk reduction and violent recidivism. *Psychiatry, Psychology and Law*, *24*(2), 244–258.

Ontario Correctional Institute. (2010). *Psychology intake form*. Brampton, ON: Ministry of the Solicitor General.

Pechorro, P., Ayala-Nunes, L., Nunes, C., Maroco, J., & Gonçalves, R. A. (2016). The social anxiety scale for adolescents: Measurement invariance and psychometric properties among a school sample of Portuguese youths. *Child Psychiatry & Human Development*, *47*(6), 975–984.

Reniers, R. L., Corcoran, R., Drake, R., Shryane, N. M., & Völlm, B. A. (2011). The QCAE: A questionnaire of cognitive and affective empathy. *Journal of Personality Assessment*, *93*(1), 84–95.

Serin, R. C., Lloyd, C. D., Helmus, L., Derkzen, D. M., & Luong, D. (2013). Does intra-individual change predict offender recidivism? Searching for the holy grail in assessing offender change. *Aggression and Violent Behavior*, *18*(1), 32–53.

Shipley, W. C., Gruber, C. P., Martin, T. A., & Klein, A. M. (2009). *Shipley-2 manual*. Los Angeles, CA: Western Psychological Services.

Stanford, M. S., Mathias, C. W., Dougherty, D. M., Lake, S. L., Anderson, N. E., & Patton, J. H. (2009). Fifty years of the Barratt impulsiveness scale: An update and review. *Personality and individual Differences*, *47*(5), 385–395.

Tangney, J. P., Stuewig, J., Furukawa, E., Kopelovich, S., Meyer, P. J., & Cosby, B. (2012). Reliability, validity, and predictive utility of the 25-item criminogenic cognitions scale (CCS). *Criminal Justice and Behavior*, *39*(10), 1340–1360.

Taxman, F. S., Thanner, M., & Weisburd, D. (2006). Risk, need, and responsivity (RNR): It all depends. *Crime & Delinquency*, *52*(1), 28–51.

Tibi-Elhanany, Y., & Shamay-Tsoory, S. G. (2011). Social cognition in social anxiety: First evidence for increased empathic abilities. *The Israel Journal of Psychiatry and Related Sciences*, *48*(2), 98–106.

van Langen, M. A., Wissink, I. B., van Vugt, E. S., van der Stouwe, T., & Stams, G. J. J. M. (2014). The relation between empathy and offending: A meta-analysis. *Aggression and Violent Behavior*, *19*(2), 179–189.

Wooditch, A., Tang, L. L., & Taxman, F. S. (2014). Which criminogenic need changes are most important in promoting desistance from crime and substance use? *Criminal Justice and Behavior*, *41*(3), 276–299.

Yates, P. M. (2009). Is sexual offender denial related to sex offence risk and recidivism? A review and treatment implications. *Psychology, Crime & Law*, *15*(2–3), 183–199.

11 Enhancing empathy amongst mentally disordered offenders with music therapy

Stella Compton-Dickinson and Darrick Jolliffe

Introduction

The risk of violence is high amongst mentally disordered offenders (MDOs), particularly amongst those who have co-morbid diagnoses of schizophrenia and personality disorder (Harris, Rice, & Quinsey, 1993). In the United Kingdom, the criminal justice system commits such offenders to high secure hospitals where the aim is to provide treatment for these mental illnesses, and therefore reduce the risk of future violence. The recovery model seeks to enable the mentally ill who have committed offences, to move towards reducing the impact of their mental illness on their daily functioning (Shepherd, Boardman, & Slade, 2008). In order to achieve this goal, evidence-based treatments for incarcerated seriously MDOs are needed (Kellett, Hall, & Compton Dickinson, 2018).

Forensic multi-disciplinary psychiatric treatment in the United Kingdom involves concurrent treatments delivered at appropriate points within a structured treatment pathway. These treatments commonly emphasise the importance of improving inter-personal relations with due consideration of the high prevalence of early trauma in these patients (Adshead, 2012). One such evidence-based approach involves psychological and creative arts therapies, which are designed to engage patients with the non-verbal creative medium of art, music, or drama. These can help to assist the therapist in uncovering repressed, dissociated and/or difficult to talk about issues with the patient in a creative and unique manner. The development of empathy, or the ability to share and understand the emotions of others (e.g. Jolliffe & Farrington, 2006), in these patients, is an important treatment goal of these interventions.

This chapter describes a small-scale exploratory evaluation in which the development of empathy was a central goal of a cognitive analytic music therapy delivered in a high-secure hospital in England. In order to evaluate this, a small patient-choice randomised controlled trial was conducted, in which nine patients received Group Cognitive Analytic Music Therapy (G-CAMT) and six received standard multi-disciplinary treatment (SMDC). The main outcome of interest of this study was change in empathy,[1] measured using the Basic Empathy Scale, a reliable and valid measure of affective and cognitive empathy (Jolliffe &

Farrington, 2006). Change in engagement, with the treatment process and with others, measured using the Disengagement scale of the Multiscale Dissociation Inventory (MDI; Briere, 2002), was also included in the current study. See Compton-Dickinson, 2015; Kellett et al., 2018, for more details about the full study.

Music therapy

In the UK, music therapy (MT) is a Health Professions and Care Council (HCPC) registered profession, which requires a master's degree training with clinical placements. The evidence that MT may be beneficial for those with mental disorders has developed over the past 20 years from initial qualitative psychoanalytic case studies (Glyn, 2009) to randomised controlled trials (RCTs; Talwar et al., 2006), and meta-analyses (Chen, Leith, Aarø, Manger, & Gold, 2016). For example, Gold, Voracek, and Wigram (2004) conducted a meta-analysis to examine the effects of MT for children and adolescents with psychopathology. They identified 11 evaluations in which the impact of MT was compared to standard care and showed that MT was associated with significant treatment benefits, particularly for those with behavioural and developmental disorders. Similarly, Maratos et al. (2008) conducted a systematic review of all RCTs in which MT (plus standard care) was compared to standard care alone, for the treatment of depression. Five RCTs were identified but the heterogeneity of the samples and the variation in what constituted standard care prevented a meta-analysis from being conducted. Interestingly, however, four of the five evaluations reported greater reduction in the symptoms of depression among those randomised to music therapy compared to those in the standard care conditions.

There is also emerging evidence that MT may be beneficial for improving the mental health of those who have committed criminal offences. Chen et al. (2016) conducted a systematic review and meta-analysis of high-quality evaluations (i.e. RCTs or quasi-experiments) to examine the impact of MT on offenders' functioning and mental health. Five evaluations were identified ($n = 409$, mostly men) and overall MT was found to be associated with significant increases in self-esteem and social functioning compared to standard treatment. MT was also associated with significant reductions in depression and anxiety, but only in those studies in which 20 or more sessions of MT were delivered.

Cognitive analytic music therapy

Music therapy in the United Kingdom generally focuses on introducing clinically based musical improvisation as a potential active ingredient for developing a therapeutic relationship between the clinician and patient, and further, obtaining the desired psychological and relational change. Music therapists are trained in musical improvisational techniques, culture-specific musical styles and make careful use of the aspects of melody, harmony, rhythm, pitch, timbre and duration that make up the components of jointly created musical improvisation. Pre-recorded music is often used as a safe introduction to psychologically based music therapy through which the patient's creative abilities can then develop to jointly creating improvisation. This can then progress to collaborative song writing. This jointly created and spontaneous music making, which can include rap song, can be tailored to fit the mood of the moment and the therapeutic goals (Souflas & Compton Dickinson, 2011).

This therapeutic process can be understood from the perspective of Vygotsky's (1978) activity theory in which a scaffolded approach of non-didactic learning from the more experienced other, in this case the trained music therapist, occurs. This involves a collaborative approach, of watching, listening, mirroring, sharing and then exploring the musical interactions. This theoretical stance underpins the dialogical nature of both cognitive analytic psychotherapy (Ryle & Kerr, 2002), as well as the developmental theoretical concepts that are frequently applied in music therapy (Trevarthen, 2007). These concepts have been integrated within the development process of G-CAMT to create an easy to implement model of music therapy. For greater detail of the model's iterative development see Compton Dickinson and Hakvoort (2017).

Music therapy and the development of empathy

The development of the ability to share and/or understand other's emotions (i.e. affective and cognitive empathy), are key treatment goals for those who have committed offences, and MDOs are no exception (Gannon, King, Miles, Lockerbie, & Willis, 2011). This is because many MDOs have committed serious violent and sexual interpersonal offences, which are indicative of a lack of empathy (NOMS, 2015). In addition, and as previously mentioned, many MDOs also have concurrent personality disorders, and a lack of empathy is a primary presenting feature of some personality disorders such as Schizoid, Antisocial and Narcissistic personality disorder (NOMS, 2015).

Empathy development in MDOs may be facilitated by assisting these patients to re-connect with, and recognise their own emotions. One way this may be achieved is when patients safely and gradually discover how to relate to others, initially non-verbally, through jointly creating music together within a safe clinical environment. It is proposed that the effects of collaboratively developed musical improvisation could form a creative bridge which could promote affective and cognitive integration through mindful thoughts and feelings. Tinnin (1990) hypothesised that music could create a bridging effect within the brain itself, as the musical vibration is transmitted across the corpus callosum between the left and right hemispheres of the brain. Blood and Zatorre (2001) used positron emission topography to study the neural mechanisms activated amongst those experiencing intensely pleasurable music. Their findings showed that as the music "chill" factor intensified, the cerebral blood flow increased to the amygdala, orbital cortex and ventral medial pre-frontal cortex.

These areas of the brain, typically associated with emotional rewards such as food, sex and drugs, have also been identified as key areas in the neural underpinnings of empathy (Jankowiak-Siuda, Rymarczyk, & Grabowska, 2011). For example, neuroimaging and electrophysiology studies suggest that affective mirroring, the basis for affective empathy, involves the inferior parietal and the inferior frontal lobe of the brain, while cognitive empathy was associated with activation in a number of areas such as the medial prefrontal cortex, the temporo-parietal junction, and the superior temporal sulcus (Jankowiak-Siuda et al., 2011).

Music therapy and engagement

Another important treatment goal of MT is to increase the engagement of the individual with others around them, and also the wider treatment process (Kellett et al., 2018). There is evidence to suggest that exposure to MT is associated with offender's increased awareness of the mental states of others (Chen et al., 2016), and also that exposure to MT is associated with an increased likelihood of engagement with other interventions such as cognitive behaviour therapy (Dingle, Gleadhill, & Baker, 2008).

The current study

The current study aims to explore the levels of affective and cognitive empathy in a group of MDOs and evaluate the impact that a form of music therapy, G-CAMT, may have on these levels over time. This study was conducted at one high secure hospital in England and potential participants were identified by both hospital nurses and the lead researcher. Potential participants were considered suitable for G-CAMT if they were male, aged 18–64, had a primary diagnosis of mental illness, had committed a violent or sexual index offence and had an IQ of 70 or above. Out of a potential pool of 102 patients, 35 did not meet the inclusion criteria, and 47 refused or were unable to commit, leaving 20 participants.

Because of the small numbers of participants identified and who gave consent to be a part of this exploratory study the evaluation approach was limited. The G-CAMT "treatment" group comprised those who consented to be allocated to either the G-CAMT or the standard multidisciplinary care (SMDC) group, as well as those who expressed a preference to receive G-CAMT (and who were available at the times that G-CAMT was to be delivered). While not a "comparison group" (i.e. because the small sample size meant it was not possible to equate groups on known or unknown characteristics), it was possible to follow-up another group of MDOs in the same institution who had not received G-CAMT (the SMDC group).

A total of 10 patients comprised the G-CAMT group and 10 comprised the SMDC group at the start of the study. However, complete pre- and post- measures were only available for 9 patients who received G-CAMT and 6 who received SMDC. This study only reports on the impact of G-CAMT on empathy at baseline, at the end of the delivery of G-CAMT (16 weeks) and at a follow-up point, 24 weeks after beginning G-CAMT (8 weeks after the completion of G-CAMT). For more details on the full study see Compton Dickinson, 2015). Empathy was measured using the Basic Empathy Scale (Jolliffe & Farrington,

2006) which is a reliable and valid tool measuring both affective (11 items; i.e. the extent to which one shares emotions with others) and cognitive empathy (9 item, i.e. the extent to which one understands the emotions of others). The BES has been used to measure the empathy of offenders previously (e.g. Heynen, van der Helm, Stams, & Korebrits, 2016; Pechorro, Ray, Salas-Wright, Maroco, & Gonçalves, 2015), but this is the first study of which we are aware in which the empathy of MDOs has been measured and followed up over time using the BES. Disengagement was measured using the Disengagement scale of the Multiscale Dissociation Inventory (MDI; Briere, 2002), which is a 5-item Likert-scored scale which measures the extent to which one is consciously aware or engaged with the current moment.

Ethical approval was granted by the local ethics committee through the integrated research application system (IRAS).

Sample at baseline

Table 11.1 shows the demographic and criminal history features of the G-CAMT group and the SMDC group. Generally, both groups were about age 40, White British, and had extensive criminal histories, having over 15 previous offences. In both groups, almost all had a diagnosis of schizophrenia and had committed serious violence as their index offence.

Table 11.2 shows the means and standard deviation of affective and cognitive empathy for the G-CAMT and SMDC groups at baseline using the BES, and also the Disengagement Scale of the MDI. Because of the small sample sizes, no tests of statistical significance were used, but the standardised mean differences (Cohen's d) were calculated to assist interpretation. A helpful way to interpret the standardised mean effect size is by first converting the standardised mean effect size *d* into a phi correlation (*r*; Lipsey & Wilson, 2001, p. 199). This results in

Table 11.1 Demographics of sample

	G-CAMT	*SMDC*
	$n = 9$	$n = 6$
Av. Age	$M = 40.0$ ($SD = 8.9$)	$M = 39.0$ ($SD = 14.8$)
% White British	77	83
Av. No. Previous Offences	$M = 15.4$ ($SD = 9.6$)	$M = 15.5$ ($SD = 12.1$)
Av. Length of Incarceration (Years)	$M = 6.6$ ($SD = 5.3$)	$M = 5.3$ ($SD = 3.8$)
Mental Disorder		
% Schizophrenia Diagnosis	100	83
Index Offence		
% Murder/Manslaughter	67	33
% Other Violence	22	50
% Sex Offence	11	16

Table 11.2 Empathy levels and disengagement for sample at baseline

	G-CAMT	*SMDC*	
	***M* (*SD*)**	***M* (*SD*)**	***d***
Affective Empathy	34.56 (6.71)	37.00 (4.56)	–0.41
Cognitive Empathy	32.44 (3.54)	33.33 (4.50)	–0.23
Total Empathy	67.00 (7.84)	70.33 (7.89)	–0.42
Disengagement	9.44 (3.71)	8.83 (1.83)	0.20

an *r* value of approximately half that of d, and this value of *r* or phi is, in turn, equal to the difference in proportions between the two groups or time periods (Farrington & Loeber, 1989). Therefore, Cohen's d of −.41 for the comparison of the G-CAMT group and the SMDC group for affective empathy would suggest that the SMDC group had about 20% more affective empathy at baseline. The G-CAMT group had lower cognitive empathy at baseline as well, and this group also appeared to be more disengaged than the SMDC group.

Delivery of G-CAMT

G-CAMT was delivered once a week for a period of 16 weeks with each session lasting for 90 minutes. A single follow-up session took place eight weeks after the end of the treatment. G-CAMT is a manualised intervention which progresses through four stages.[2]

Mindfulness (sessions 1–4)

This stage involves encouraging the men to be present in the moment and being supportive as each patient explores various sounds to find a particular note or instrument that "feels" right to him. As the stages progress this could become his "sound print". Furthermore, patients are encouraged to use breathing and grounding techniques to support mind-body connection and to manage anxieties.

Emotional regulation (sessions 5–8)

At this stage individuals are encouraged to reflect on their emotions during and after they have been developing or co-developing music. Men are prompted to make statements such as 'I feel like . . .'; 'I feel as if . . .'; 'Our/my music makes me feel like . . .'; or, 'Our/my music reminds me of . . .'. It is important that the therapist ensure that all understand that individuals may have unique and different feelings about the same piece of music, and about each person's own contribution to it. At this point the therapist attempts to make links between the expressive qualities of the music and each individual's emotions. By validating a sense of ownership of each individual's internal experience it is hoped that the participant may verbalise this emotional experience.

Distress Tolerance (sessions 9–12)

This stage introduces conflict resolution, as each participant is supported in discovering how to tolerate inter-individual differences of feelings and perceptions. At times group members may agree to differ when it comes to certain views or perceptions about the music. This is a stage when verbal and musical dialogue may become more extended and reciprocal. Individual differences and group "storming" (where an individual attempts to overwhelm the group) can be worked through in the group improvisations. The music therapist must provide safety and emotional containment to ensure that a satisfactory musical resolution is reached. The aim of this stage is for each individual to discover that they can tolerate individual differences and tolerate feelings of frustration.

Interpersonal effectiveness (sessions 13–16)

The final stage of G-CAMT is about encouraging the men to discover a sense of harmony with others in more than just the musical sense. Individuals learn to negotiate choices, to respect each other's distress and unique life experiences. The value of the group process becomes apparent as each individual prepares to end his treatment. At this stage there may be considerable distress, as "endings" may be linked on an unconscious level to a prior death, loss or previous offending. Each member of the group, and the music therapist, are encouraged to reflect on how they chose to express feelings about the end of G-CAMT in a closure letter which some may choose to read aloud in the final session.

Standard multi-disciplinary care

The G-CMAT group were also eligible to receive the standard treatments and supports that were available to all. Table 11.3 shows the proportion (prevalence) of men who engaged with other interventions and support, and the average number of hours that they engaged with these for the 24 weeks of this evaluation (from the first assessment to the final follow-up) for both the G-CAMT group ($n = 9$) and the SMDC group ($n = 6$).

Those in the G-CAMT group were less likely to have engaged with psychology and less likely to have taken part in physical activities and off ward activities.

Table 11.3 Other interventions and support received

	G-CAMT (n = 9)	*Av. Hrs.*	*SMDC (n = 6)*	*Av. Hrs.*
	(%)	*M (SD)*	*(%)*	*M (SD)*
Psychology	44	10 (23.6)	83	41 (32.1)
Physical Activities	44	21 (31.8)	83	59 (45.4)
Other Music Therapy	33	10 (16.9)	33	15 (23.2)
Other Activities	100	98 (58.2)	100	59 (49.4)
Off-ward Activities	44	34 (27.6)	83	29 (22.5)

In addition, those in the G-CAMT group who did receive or attend the various supports received fewer hours of psychology, physical activities and other music therapy, but received more hours of other activities and off-ward activities.

Results

Table 11.4 shows the average affective, cognitive and total empathy scores for the G-CAMT and standard care group at baseline (B), completion (C, 16 weeks), and at Follow-up (F; 24 weeks). Figure 11.1 illustrates the change over time for affective empathy for both groups and Figure 11.2 illustrates the change over time for cognitive empathy for both groups. For example, the average affective empathy score for the G-CAMT group was 34.6 at baseline, and had risen to an average of 36.4 by completion. This is equivalent to a standardised mean difference of $d = .28$, or about a 14% increase in affective empathy.

Overall, the levels of both affective and cognitive empathy increased by similar magnitudes for both the G-CAMT and SMDC groups over equivalent time period. For the G-CAMT group there was a slight increase in cognitive empathy from completion to the follow-up 8 weeks later, and there were no increases in affective empathy over this time period. However, for the SMDC group affective empathy increased slightly from 16 weeks to follow-up (24 weeks), but cognitive empathy increased markedly ($d = .58$) over this time period. This is equivalent to about a 29% increase in cognitive empathy.

The level of disengagement of the G-CAMT group increased slightly from baseline to completion and follow-up. However, the levels for the SMDC group increased markedly over the equivalent time period before decreasing, but by the 24-week follow-up, a considerable increase in disengagement of $d = .49$ (or about 25%) was evident.

Table 11.4 Change in empathy for G-CAMT and SMDC groups

G-CAMT (n = 9)	*Baseline (B)*	*Completion (C)*	*Follow-up (F)*	*B v C*	*C v F*	*B v F*
	M (SD)	*M* (SD)	*M* (SD)	*d*	*d*	*d*
Aff. Empathy	34.56 (6.71)	36.44 (6.91)	36.44 (6.71)	0.28	0.0	0.28
Cog. Empathy	32.44 (3.54)	33.89 (7.10)	34.44 (4.69)	0.26	0.09	0.48
Total Empathy	67.00 (7.84)	70.33 (12.71)	70.89 (9.28)	0.31	0.05	0.45
Disengagement	9.44 (3.71)	10.11 (4.26)	10.44 (5.55)	0.17	0.07	0.21
SMDC (n = 6)	**Baseline (B)**	**16 weeks**	**24 weeks**			
	M (SD)	**M** (SD)	**M** (SD)			
Aff. Empathy	37.00 (4.56)	38.67 (6.38)	39.33 (6.74)	0.31	0.09	0.39
Cog. Empathy	33.33 (4.50)	34.67 (3.83)	36.50 (2.66)	0.33	0.58	0.91
Total Empathy	70.33 (7.89)	73.33 (8.64)	75.83 (7.31)	0.36	0.32	0.73
Disengagement	8.83 (1.83)	11.83 (3.06)	9.83 (2.23)	1.19	–0.75	0.49

Discussion

Those who have committed serious offences and been detained in secure hospitals as a result of suffering from mental disorders pose considerable challenge for those responsible for their care and rehabilitation. The development of empathy in this group is a key treatment goal as, theoretically, increases in the ability to understand and/or share the emotions of another should facilitate interpersonal connection, and therefore reductions in later offending behaviour. There is developing evidence that music therapy may be beneficial in reducing the severity of the symptoms of some mental disorders (e.g. Maratos et al., 2008), and in increasing the social functioning of those who have committed offences (Chen et al., 2016), but this is the first study of which we are that empirically examines the impact of music therapy on the empathy of offenders detained in a secure hospital.

The results of this exploratory study suggested that affective and cognitive empathy increased for both the group that received the innovative 16-week music therapy (G-CAMT), but also, and at a similar level, for the group who received the standard multi-disciplinary care that was on offer. Interestingly, the cognitive empathy of the SMDC group continued to increase, but increases for the G-CAMT group were less evident after the delivery of G-CAMT ended. Also, and perhaps counterintuitively, the levels of disengagement of both groups increased over the duration of the investigation, and this was greater amongst the SMDC group.

These results could be read to suggest that G-CAMT provided no additional benefit to SMDC in terms of developing empathy, however, we believe this to be unlikely. This is because there was evidence that the G-CAMT group was more treatment resistant at the commencement of the evaluation, and also were more psychopathic.[3] For example, the G-CAMT group had been in the secure hospital for much longer, and also had much lower affective and cognitive empathy at the commencement of the study than the SMDC group. The G-CAMT group was also more disengaged at the beginning of the study. With the G-CAMT group and SMDC group showing similar increases in affective and cognitive empathy for the duration of the delivery of G-CAMT, and a slower rate of increased disengagement, this suggests that the G-CAMT group showed greater "distance-travelled" in their treatment journey.

There are a number of potential explanations for the finding that cognitive empathy increased from 16 to 24 weeks in the SMDC group, but not in the G-CAMT group, and this includes the previous suggestion that the G-CAMT group may have been more challenging. In addition, because of practical limitations G-CAMT was delivered for 16 weeks but was then discontinued. However, there was no discontinuity in what was provided for the SMDC group. It could be that the continuity of the standard care fostered more cognitive empathy development, and/or it could be that the relatively abrupt end of G-CAMT resulted in limited further empathy increases past the date of last delivery.

The results may also partially be explained by the G-CAMT group engaging more honestly and openly with the empathy questionnaire. That is, the SDMC group may have been more motivated to complete the BES in a way that demonstrated improvements, while the G-CAMT group, who had been actively challenged to consider their emotions and the emotions of others, may have completed the BES more truthfully. The considerable variation evident in disengagement for the SMDC group may suggest that there may have been more presentation bias amongst this group.

It is important to recall that this was not a controlled study and very likely the G-CAMT group and the SMDC differed on a number of individual and criminal history factors which were unmeasured and may contribute to understanding the changes in empathy that were observed.

Conclusion

The results of this study suggest that the levels of empathy of offenders detained in secure hospitals can increase, and G-CAMT is a promising approach in achieving this. Future empirical studies should aim to replicate these results in secure hospitals using evaluations with high methodological quality such as RCTs and quasi-experiments and with much larger samples. In addition, it would be desirable to compare the potential changes in empathy associated with G-CAMT to changes in behaviour of this group, such as engagement with other treatments, or even reoffending. G-CAMT is a promising intervention for a challenging group, but much more research of higher quality is needed to establish this as an evidence-based intervention.

Notes

1 A number of other outcomes were examined in the full study.
2 See Table 1 in Kellett Hall and Compton Dickinson (2018) for full details of the manualised stages.
3 See Compton Dickinson (2015) for full details.

References

Adshead, G. (2012). "Mirror, mirror": Parallel processes in forensic institutions. In J. Adlam, A. Aiyebuisi, P. Kleinot, A. Motz, & C. Scanlon (Eds.), *The therapeutic milieu under fire: Security and insecurity in forensic mental health. Forensic focus 34* (pp. 97–116). London: Jessica Kingsley Publications.

Blood, A. J., & Zatorre, R. J. (2001). Intensely pleasurable responses to music correlate with activity in brain regions implicated in reward and emotion. *Proceedings of the National Academy of Sciences, 98*, 11818–11823.

Briere, J. (2002). *Multiscale dissociation inventory professional manual*. Odessa, FL: Psychological Assessment Resources.

Chen, X. J., Leith, H., Aarø, L. E., Manger, T., & Gold, C. (2016). Music therapy for improving mental health problems of offenders in correctional settings: Systematic review and meta-analysis. *Journal of Experimental Criminology, 12*, 1–20. doi:10.1007/s11292-015-9250-y.

Compton Dickinson, S. J. (2015). *A feasibility trial of group cognitive analytic music therapy in secure hospital settings*. Unpublished manuscript. Anglia Ruskin University. Retrieved from http://hdl.handle.net/10540/581523

Compton Dickinson, S. J., & Hakvoort, L. (2017). *The clinician's guide to forensic music therapy: Treatment manuals for group cognitive analytic music therapy and music therapy anger management*. London: Jessica Kingsley Publishers.

Dingle, G. A., Gleadhill, L., & Baker, F. A. (2008). Can music therapy engage patients in group cognitive behaviour therapy for substance abuse treatment? *Drug and Alcohol Review*, *27*, 190–196.

Farrington, D. P., & Loeber, R. (1989). RIOC and phi as measures of predictive efficiency and strength of association in 2X2 tables. *Journal of Quantitative Criminology*, *5*, 201–213.

Gannon, T. A., King, T., Miles, H., Lockerbie, L., & Willis, G. (2011). Good lives sexual offender treatment for mentally disordered offenders. *British Journal of Forensic Practice*, *13*, 153–168. doi:10.1108/14636641111157805

Gold, C., Voracek, M., & Wigram, T. (2004). Effects of music therapy for children and adolescents with psychopathology: A meta-analysis. *Journal of Child Psychology and Psychiatry, and Allied Disciplines*, *45*(6), 1054–1063. doi:10.1111/j.1469-7610.2004.t01-1-00298.x

Glyn, J. (2009). Two's company, three's a crowd. In H. Odell-Miller & E. Richards (Eds.), *Supervision of music therapy: A theoretical and practical handbook* (pp. 67–82). London: Routledge.

Harris, G. T., Rice, M. E., & Quinsey, V. L. (1993). Violent recidivism of mentally disordered offenders: The development of a statistical prediction instrument. *Criminal Justice and Behavior*, *20*, 315–335.

Heynen, E. J. E., van der Helm, G. H. P., Stams, G. J. J. M., & Korebrits, A. M. (2016). Measuring empathy in a German youth prison: A validation of the German version of the basic empathy scale (BES) in a sample of incarcerated juvenile offenders. *Journal of Forensic Psychology Practice*, *5*, 336–346.

Jankowiak-Siuda, K., Rymarczyk, K., & Grabowska, A. (2011). How we empathize with others: A neurobiological perspective. *Medical Science Monitor*, *17*, RA18–RA24.

Jolliffe, D., & Farrington, D. P. (2006). Development and validation of the basic empathy scale. *Journal of Adolescence*, *29*, 589–611.

Kellett, S., Hall, J., & Compton Dickinson, S. J. (2018). Group cognitive analytic music therapy: A quasi-experimental feasibility study conducted in a high secure hospital. *Nordic Journal of Music Therapy*, *28*, 224–255. doi:10.1080/08098131.2018.1529697

Lipsey, M. W., & Wilson, D. B. (2001). *Practical meta-analysis*. Thousand Oaks, CA: Sage.

Maratos, A., Gold, C., Wang, X., & Crawford, M. (2008). Music therapy for depression. *Cochrane Database of Systematic Reviews*. retrieved from http://onlinelibrary.wiley.com/doi/9.10.02/14651858.CD004517.pub2/abstract

National Offender Management Service. (2015). *Working with offenders with personality disorder: A practitioner's guide*. London: Ministry of Justice.

Pechorro, P., Ray, J. V., Salas-Wright, C. P., Maroco, J., & Gonçalves, R. A. (2015). Adaptation of the basic empathy scale among a Portuguese sample of incarcerated juvenile offenders. *Psychology, Crime & Law*, *7*, 699–714.

Ryle, A., & Kerr, I. (2002). *Introducing cognitive analytic therapy*. Chichester: Wiley.

Shepherd, G., Boardman, J., & Slade, M. (2008). *Making recovery a reality*. London: Sainsbury Centre for Mental Health.

Souflas, P., & Compton Dickinson, S. J. (2012). Rapping round the system: A young Black man's journey through a high secure hospital. In S. Hadley & G. Yancy (Eds.), *Therapeutic uses of rap and hip hop* (pp. 353–373). New York: Routledge.

Talwar, N., Crawford, M., Maratos, A., Nur, U., McDermott, O., & Procter, S. (2006). Music therapy for in-patients with schizophrenia: Exploratory randomised controlled trial. *British Journal of Psychiatry*, *189*, 405–409.

Tinnin, L. (1990). Mental unity, altered states of consciousness and dissociation. *Dissociation*, *3*, 154–59.

Trevarthen, C. (2007). Moving experiences: Perceiving as action with a sense of purpose. In G. J. Pepping & M. A. Grealy (Eds.), *Closing the gap: The scientific writings of David N. Lee* (pp. 1–75). London: Lawrence Erlbaum.

Vygotsky, L. S. (1978). *Mind in society: The development of higher psychological processes*. Cambridge, MA: Harvard University Press.

Part III

Aggression and bullying

12 Cognitive empathy as a moderator in the relation between negative emotionality traits and schoolchildren's aggressive behaviours

Noelia Sánchez-Pérez and Carmen González-Salinas

Introduction

Aggressive behaviour has been defined as the observable manifestation of any act intended to cause harm, pain, or injury in another (Zirpoli, 2008). At school, these behaviours can include acts such as physical violence, relational aggression, and bullying. Research evidence has shown that when aggressive children grow older they are more likely to exhibit hyperactive-distractible behaviours in class (Ladd, 2006), to have an elevated risk of depression when entering adolescence (Kaltiala-Heino, Rimpelä, Marttunen, Rimpelä, & Rantanen, 1999; Swearer, Song, Cary, Eagle, & Mickelson, 2001), and to tend to exhibit more overt and covert delinquency (Vitaro, Brendgen, & Tremblay, 2002). On the other hand, children who are victims of aggressive acts, particularly those repeated over time, are at increased risk of developing a number of internalising problems such as depression, anxiety and low self-esteem (Cook, Williams, Guerra, Kim, & Sadek, 2010; Hawker & Boulton, 2000).

Given the consequences of aggressive behaviours for children's development, researchers have tried to ascertain which individual characteristics might act as risk factors for aggressive acts. A number of research findings have confirmed the relevance of two characteristics: negative emotional reactivity (Dodge, Lochman, Harnish, Bates, & Pettit, 1997; Eisenberg et al., 2009b; Xu, Farver, & Zhang, 2009) and empathic abilities (Jolliffe & Farrington, 2004; Miller & Eisenberg, 1988; Sánchez-Pérez, Fuentes, Jolliffe, & González-Salinas, 2014). These characteristics have often been studied separately, but the complex nature of aggressive acts is probably better captured when their potential interactions are taken into account.

Negative emotionality and aggressive behaviours

Temperament has been defined as individual differences in emotional reactivity and self-regulation (Rothbart & Derryberry, 1981; Rothbart, Ahadi, & Evans,

2000). These reactive and self-regulatory systems have been related to behaviour, particularly aggression. Concerning self-regulation, low effortful control has been negatively associated with children's aggression and delinquency (Eisenberg, Chang, Ma, & Huang, 2009a; Eisenberg et al., 2009b; Rathert, Fite, & Gaertner, 2011). Also impulsivity, a trait reflecting low self-regulation, has been repeatedly related to children's higher likelihood of aggression (Dodge et al., 1997; Eisenberg et al., 2009b; Halperin et al., 1995).

Regarding negative reactivity, previous studies have found that children's proneness to negative emotionality was positively related to aggressive behaviours (Dodge et al., 1997; Eisenberg et al., 2009b; Xu et al., 2009). However, the construct of negative emotionality encompasses a set of temperamental traits such as anger, fear, sadness, and discomfort, each of which may contribute differently to the manifestation of aggressive behaviours in school. In the case of anger proneness, it is well-established that individuals with high scores on measures of anger reactivity are more likely to behave aggressively (Fung, Gerstein, Chan, & Engebretson, 2015; Hubbard, McAuliffe, Morrow, & Romano, 2010; Wilkowski & Robinson, 2010; Xu et al., 2009). Fearless children have also been shown to be more prone to engage in antisocial acts and aggression, likely because they are less sensitive to punishment. However, children who are fearful also tend to act out with impulsive forms of aggression, typically explosive and uncontrolled (Vitiello & Stoff, 1997). Studies addressing the association of sadness and discomfort with aggressive behaviours have not been so numerous and have yielded inconsistent results. For example, Bohnert, Crnic, and Lim (2003) found that there was no significant correlation between sadness expression and aggressive behaviours, whereas Zeman, Shipman, and Suveg (2002) showed that adolescents' expressions of sadness were inversely related to aggression. There is much more limited evidence for the relationship between discomfort and aggressive behaviour, with studies finding an association with antisocial (Rothbart, Ahadi, & Hershey, 1994), but not aggressive behaviour (Embregts, Didden, Schreuder, Huitink, & van Nieuwenhuijzen, 2009).

Empathy and aggressive behaviours

There has been increasing evidence supporting empathy as a developmental protection factor in childhood because of its positive relation to prosocial behaviour (Barchia & Bussey, 2011; Krevans & Gibbs, 1996; Masten, Morelli, & Eisenberger, 2011; Roberts & Strayer, 1996; Sze, Gyurak, Goodkind, & Levenson, 2012), and negative association with aggressive behaviours (Björkqvist, Österman, & Kaukiainen, 2000; Blair, 2018; Eisenberg, Eggum, & Di Giunta, 2010; Eisenberg & Miller, 1987; Jolliffe & Farrington, 2004; Richardson, Hammock, Smith, Gardner, & Signo, 1994).

Furthermore, longitudinal studies showed that adolescents' perspective taking (a variable closely related to the concept of cognitive empathy; Carlo, Mestre, Samper, Tur, & Armenta, 2010) and affective empathy, negatively predicted later aggressive behaviours (Stavrinides, Georgiou, & Theofanous, 2010). However, the negative relation between empathy and aggression has not always been consistently identified; a meta-analysis found non-significant effect sizes for the relation between affective empathy and offending (van Langen, Wissink, van Vugt, van der Stouwe, & Stams, 2014), and another one concluded that empathy and aggression were only weakly correlated (Vachon, Lynam, & Johnson, 2014).

Negative emotionality, empathy, and aggressive behaviours

Pakaslahti (2000) proposed that the evaluation of social problem-solving alternatives could be affected by a person's emotional state (Petty, Wegener, & Fabrigar, 1997). Particularly anger, in combination with lack of empathy, might serve as a trigger for aggressive behaviour (Crick & Dodge, 1994; Miller & Eisenberg, 1988). However, research considering both negative reactivity traits and empathy in connection with aggressive behaviours in childhood is still quite limited. In addition, those studies conducted did not examine the possible interaction effects of negative emotionality and empathy. Among the few studies conducted, Strayer and Roberts (2004) found that 5-year-olds with higher levels of anger behaved more aggressively, and empathy was negatively associated with both aggression and anger. However, the authors did not analyse the potential interaction between empathy and anger on aggressive behaviours. Similarly, Fung et al. (2015) investigated the associations between proactive and reactive aggression, anger, and empathy in a sample of secondary school students. Although the authors found different anger and empathic profiles depending on the kind of aggression, the potential interaction between anger and empathy on the manifestation of aggression was not analysed.

Given the aforementioned gaps in the literature, the major objective of this study was to jointly consider the association of negative emotionality traits and empathic abilities with aggressive behaviours exhibited by children at school, taking into account the potential interactions of these individual characteristics.

Method

Participants

Originally, 386 families were contacted to take part in the research and 225 agreed to participate (58.30%). However, 40 children were excluded because they had a clinical diagnosis and/or learning problems, 20 parents later removed their child from the study, and 24 parents did not complete the questionnaires. The final sample, therefore, was composed of 141 families, with children (78 boys, 76 girls) aged between 6 and 12 years (M = 8.75; SD = 1.71); most of them lived with both parents (91.3%). No child was diagnosed with clinical and/or learning difficulties.

The mothers were aged 21 to 58 years (M = 38.36, SD = 6.11); 38.9% were educated up to elementary school level, 50.1% to high school, and 11% to university level. The fathers' ages ranged from 26 to 57 years (M = 41.43, SD = 5.73), and their educational level was distributed as follows: 33.4% elementary school, 56.8% high school, and 9.8% university degree. Regarding family monthly incomes, 25% of the parents reported less than 750 € per month, 29.5% reported between 751 and 1200 €, 24.3% between 1201 and 1600 €, 9.8% between 1601 and 2000 €, 10.6% between 2001 and 3000€, and 0.8% of the parents reported more than 3000 €.

Measures

Negative emotionality. Children's negative emotionality was measured by parental report using the Spanish version of the Temperament in Middle Childhood Questionnaire (TMCQ; Simonds & Rothbart, 2006). Parents evaluated the extent to which each statement described his/her child's behaviour within the previous 6 months. The scale ranged from 1 (almost always untrue) to 5 (almost always true), with an additional option of "Not applicable". For the purposes of this study we selected the following negative emotionality scales: anger, discomfort, fear, and sadness. Anger (7 items) was defined as the amount of negative affect related to interruption of ongoing tasks or goal blocking; Discomfort (10 items) refers to negative affect associated with the sensory qualities of stimulation, including intensity, rate or complexity of light, movement, sound, and texture; Fear (9 items) refers to the unease, worry or nervousness related to anticipated pain or distress and/or potentially threatening situations; and Sadness (10 items) was defined as lowered mood and energy related to the exposure to suffering, disappointment, and object loss. Cronbach's alphas for the scales in this sample were .83, .72, .77, and .78, respectively.

Empathy. Parents reported on their children's cognitive and affective empathy via the Spanish version of the Basic Empathy Scale (BES; Sánchez-Pérez et al., 2014). The items of the BES-parent report (BES-PR) were taken from the original BES self-report (Jolliffe & Farrington, 2006) and reworded in third person, retaining the original content. Parents rated the extent to which they agreed or disagreed with each statement using a Likert-type scale that ranged from 1 (strongly disagree) to 5 (strongly agree), with an additional option of "Not Applicable" ($\alpha = .72$ for both empathy scales).

Aggressive behaviours. Children's aggressive behaviours at school was measured by having Teachers complete the aggression scale included in the Behaviour Assessment System for Children (BASC; Reynolds & Kamphaus, 2004; Spanish version developed by González et al., 2004). This scale provided a measure of the frequency of aggression, ranging from 1 (never) to 4 (almost always), with which children showed the tendency to act in a hostile manner, verbally or physically, which threatened others ($\alpha = .95$; 14 items).

Procedure

The Ethics Committee of the University of Murcia approved the study. The Head Teachers of the two schools were given letters describing the research project and provided with consent forms to distribute to the families. Parents who decided to enrol in the study received the temperament, empathy and socio-demographic questionnaires, along with the instructions to complete them at home. Once completed, families returned them to school. Teachers were given the questionnaire by one of our staff members and once completed, teachers returned to them personally.

Statistical analyses and data transformation

The first step was to compute *t*-test analyses to examine potential sex differences between boys and girls. To reduce multicollinearity among the independent variables-centred scores were calculated. Lastly, multiple regression analyses were run with aggressive behaviours as the dependent variable and negative emotionality traits and empathic abilities as the independent variables. Interactions between the independent factors were tested.

Results

Potential sex differences between the variables under study

Independent *t*-tests revealed that boys ($M = 1.66$; $SD = .67$) exhibited a higher frequency of aggressive behaviours than girls ($M = 1.43$; $SD = .45$), $t(121.27) = 2.41$, $p = .018$, however, they did not differ in parental reports of anger $t(139) = 37$, $p = .714$, discomfort, $t(139) = -1.84$, $p = .077$, fear, $t(139) = -.42$, $p = .679$, sadness, $t(139) = -.64$, $p = .521$, cognitive empathy, $t(139) = -.31$, $p = .754$, and affective empathy, $t(139) = -.62$, $p = .539$. Given the significant differences between boys and girls on the dependent variable, we took gender into account for all further analyses.

Negative emotionality traits and cognitive empathy in predicting aggressive behaviours at school

Gender, cognitive empathy and negative emotionality traits (anger, fear, sadness, and discomfort) were regressed on aggressive behaviours at school (see Table 12.1). The model, including anger and cognitive empathy was significant, $R^2_a = .09$, $F(4,136) = 4.29$, $p = .003$. The main effect of cognitive empathy, and the anger x cognitive empathy interaction were significant, $\beta = -.16$, $p = .046$, and $\beta = -.19$, $p = .026$, respectively. The regression analysis including children's fear and cognitive empathy was also significant; $R^2_a = .08$, $F(4,136) = 4.27$, $p = .003$, with a significant interaction involving fear and cognitive empathy; $\beta = -.19$, $p = .025$. The model testing the contribution of sadness and cognitive empathy also resulted in a significant result ($R^2_a = .08$, $F(4,136) = 2.36$, $p = .003$), with a significant sadness x cognitive interaction, $\beta = -.18$, $p = .029$. The interactions between children's anger, fear, and sadness, and cognitive empathy can be seen in Figures 1, 2, and 3, respectively.

Table 12.1 Multiple regression analyses including interaction effects between empathy and negative emotionality traits to predict children's aggressive behaviours at school.

	R^2_a	*B*	*SE B*	*β*	t	p
Model: Cognitive empathy*Anger	.09**					
Sex		−.18	.09	−.16	−1.99	.049
Cognitive empathy		−.17	.09	−.16	−2.01	.046
Anger		.06	.06	.07	.92	.361
Cognitive empathy*Anger		−.27	.12	−.19	−2.25	.026
Model: Cognitive empathy*Fear	.08**					
Sex		−.23	.09	−.21	−2.57	.011
Cognitive empathy		−.16	.09	−.15	−1.77	.080
Fear		.04	.06	.06	.78	.438
Cognitive empathy*Fear		−.28	.12	−.19	−2.26	.025
Model: Cognitive empathy*Sadness	.08**					
Sex		−.19	.09	−.17	−2.05	.042
Cognitive empathy		−.15	.09	−.14	−1.65	.101
Sadness		.06	.07	.07	.80	.426
Cognitive empathy*Sadness		−.27	.12	−.18	−2.21	.029
Model: Cognitive empathy*Discomfort	.07**					
Sex		−.20	.09	−.18	−2.16	.035
Cognitive empathy		−.15	.09	−.14	−1.65	.101
Discomfort		.03	.07	.03	.34	.737
Cognitive empathy* Discomfort		−.25	.14	−.15	−1.78	.077
Model: Affective empathy*Anger	.05*					
Sex		−.21	.09	−.19	−2.31	.023
Affective empathy		−.09	.08	−.09	−1.08	.281
Anger		.05	.06	.07	.84	.403
Affective empathy*Anger		−.19	.11	−.15	−1.82	.072
Model: Affective empathy*Fear	0.4					
Sex		−.23	.09	−.21	−2.49	.014
Affective empathy		−.08	.08	−.08	−.95	.345
Fear		.06	.06	.09	1.09	.278
Affective empathy*Fear		−.11	.09	−.09	−1.12	.266
Model: Affective empathy*Sadness	.05*					
Sex		−.23	.09	−.20	−2.46	.015
Affective empathy		−.07	.08	−.07	−.89	.375
Sadness		0.9	.07	.10	1.19	.235
Affective empathy*Sadness		−.17	.11	−.13	−1.50	.135
Model: Affective empathy*Discomfort	0.4					
Sex		−.23	.09	−.21	−2.46	.015
Affective empathy		−.08	.08	−.08	−1.00	.321
Discomfort		.07	.07	.08	.97	.334
Affective empathy* Discomfort		−.15	.12	−.11	−1.27	.208

$^{*}p < 0.05$; $^{**}p < 0.005$

Concerning the regression analysis including discomfort and cognitive empathy, although the general model resulted significant, $R^2_a = .07$, $F(4,136) = 3.71$, $p = .007$, there were no significant main or interaction effects (see Table 1).

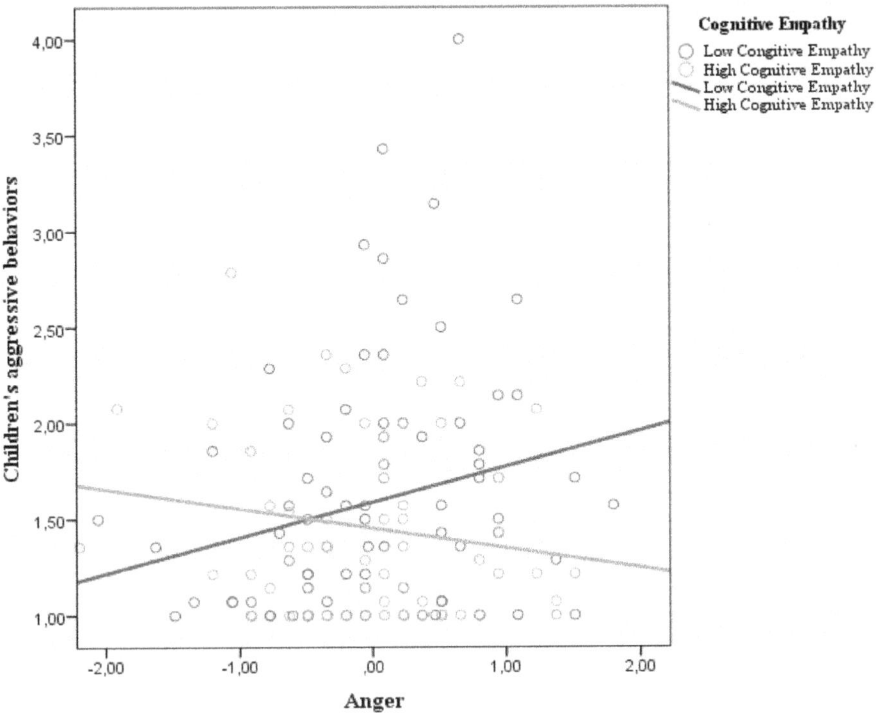

Figure 12.1 Interaction effects between children's anger and cognitive empathy to explain aggressive behaviours at school.

Negative emotionality traits and affective empathy in predicting aggressive behaviours at school

Gender, affective empathy and negative emotionality traits (anger, fear, sadness, and discomfort) were regressed on aggressive behaviours at school, with a main effect of sex on aggressive behaviours as the only significant result (see Table 13.1).

Discussion

Children who exhibit aggressive behaviours at school are at an increased risk for a range of personal difficulties, poor social and school adjustment, and enduring patterns of aggression (Broidy et al., 2003; Kim-Cohen et al., 2005; Nansel, Haynie, & Simonsmorton, 2003; Yoon, Barton, & Taiariol, 2004). Previous literature focusing on the contribution of dispositional characteristics to the variance of children's aggressive behaviours, such as negative emotionality reactivity and empathy abilities, had often produced inconsistent results. The present study

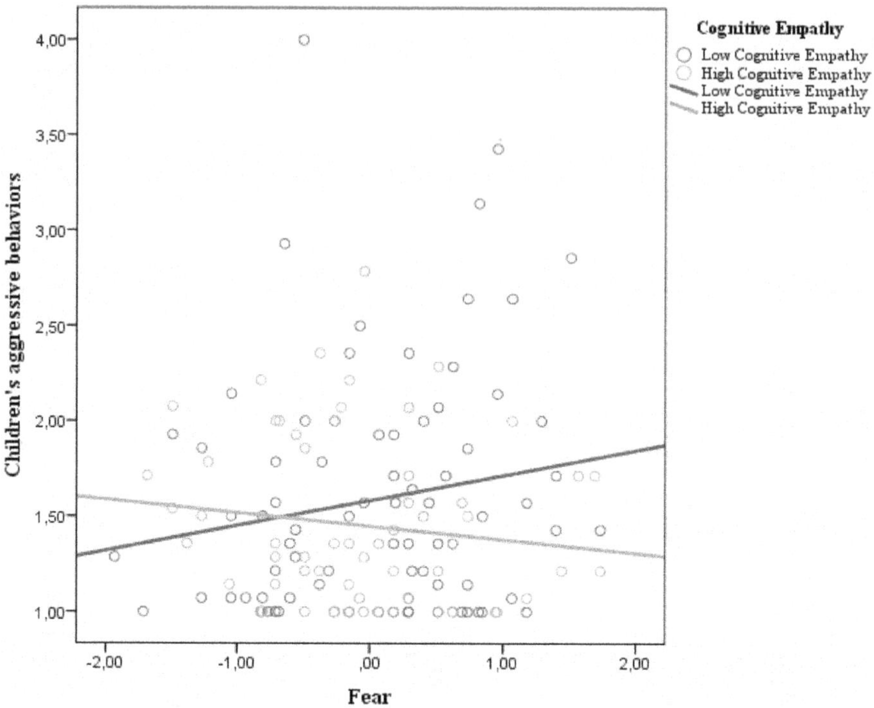

Figure 12.2 Interaction effects between children's fear and cognitive empathy to explain aggressive behaviours at school.

aimed to shed light on this inconsistency by jointly analysing these two individual characteristics and taking into consideration their possible interaction effects.

As a central finding, although the main effects of negative reactivity traits and empathic abilities were not significant in most cases, the interaction effects between cognitive empathy and anger, fear, and sadness, respectively, did significantly predict aggressive behaviours at school.

The first model tested included cognitive empathy and anger proneness as dispositional factors contributing to the variance of children's aggressive behaviours. A main effect of cognitive empathy was found, so that children less able to understand other's feelings (as reported by their parents), exhibited more frequent teacher-reported aggressive behaviours. This finding is consistent with previous studies (Barchia & Bussey, 2011; Eisenberg & Miller, 1987; Fung et al., 2015; Hubbard et al., 2002; Sánchez-Pérez et al., 2014; Wilkowski & Robinson, 2010). Following the social deficit theory (Crick & Dodge, 1994; Dodge, 2014), children with lower cognitive empathy would ignore important information in social situations, over-interpret others' intentions as hostile in ambiguous situations, and consequently react aggressively (Dodge & Coie, 1987).

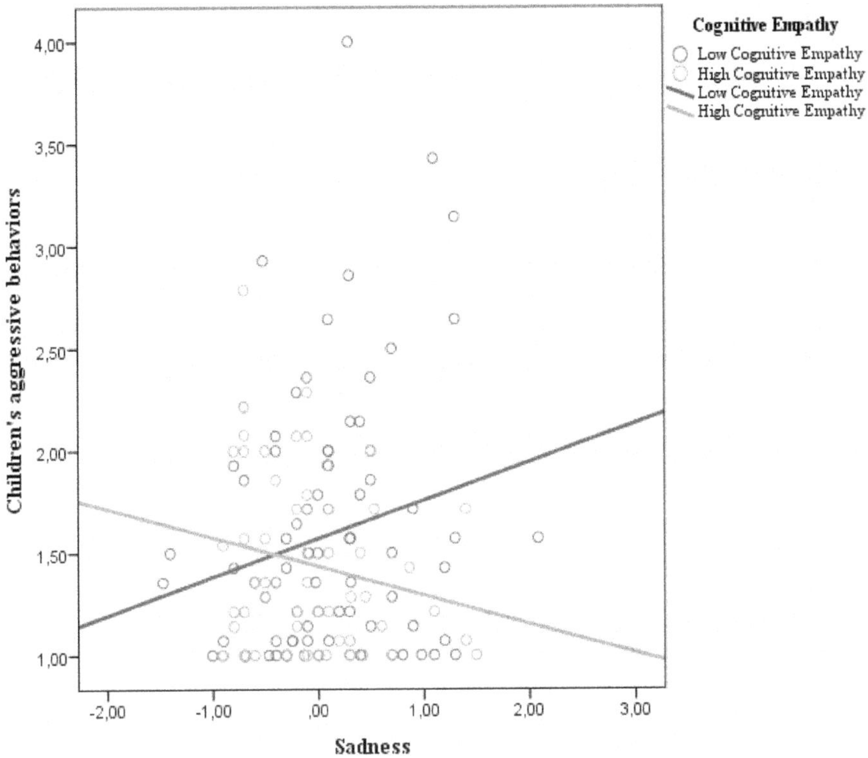

Figure 12.3 Interaction effects between children's sadness and cognitive empathy to explain aggressive behaviours at school.

Additionally, the interaction effects found between cognitive empathy and anger proneness suggested that for children exhibiting poorer cognitive empathy abilities, higher levels of anger were associated with more aggressive behaviours. However, for children with better cognitive empathy abilities, their level of anger did not affect the frequency of children's aggressive behaviours in the classroom. In other words, schoolchildren with high negative affect related to goal blocking were at an increased risk of displaying aggressive behaviours when their capacity to understand others' feelings was compromised. As noted by Pakaslahti (2000), angry children with low cognitive empathy abilities may tend to make hostile attributions of the other children's behaviours and intentions (Forgas, 1995; Graham, Hudley, & Williams, 1992) and, as a result, they are more likely to behave aggressively. The comprehension of others' feelings would likely buffer the manifestation of aggression. Although we have not distinguished the kind of aggression exhibited by children in our study, this explanation is especially suitable for reactive rather than proactive aggression because anger is considered a component of reactive aggression (Hubbard et al., 2010), and deficits in social information-processing may explain reactive but not proactive aggression (Austin, Bondü, & Elsner, 2017).

A similar interaction was found between fear and cognitive empathy. As proposed by Vitiello and Stoff (1997), fearful children are probably at risk of expressing an impulsive, explosive, and uncontrolled aggression. Our results suggested that aggression is more likely among fearful children with poorer abilities to understand other's feelings.

Research focusing on sadness and aggressive behaviours is more scarce, with findings showing no significant association between children's sadness and aggression (Bohnert et al., 2003; Kim, Walden, Harris, Karrass, & Catron, 2007). Our study has similarly failed to show a main effect of sadness on aggression but interestingly, the interaction between cognitive empathy and sadness suggested that this negative emotion was also positively associated with aggressive behaviour in children low in cognitive empathy. Although we are unaware of previous research reporting similar findings for typically developing children, research carried out on clinical samples has found that children with mood disorders such as depression, tend to show hostile attributional biases and lower use of assertive responses (Quiggle, Garber, Panak, & Dodge, 1992), while also exhibiting disruptive behaviours (Weisbrot & Ettinger, 2002).

Finally, the analyses of discomfort did not demonstrate any significant results, in consonance with the work by Embregts et al. (2009). Defined as negative emotionality aroused by sensory qualities of stimulation, the concept is non-social in nature and probably has little to do with social behaviours such as aggression.

Unexpectedly, affective empathy did not show a main or interaction effect in predicting children's aggressive behaviours in the classroom. An explanation for these results might come from the age period studied, as the critical review published by Lovett and Sheffield (2007), found no consistent relationship between affective empathy and aggression for children, but did identify a negative relationship for adolescents. Therefore, sharing other's feelings might constitute a relevant factor for explaining aggression in older students but it might play little role during school years.

Although the influence of gender on the manifestation of aggressive behaviours at school was not a main focus of this study, the statistical analyses showed that being male was a significant predictor of aggression in all models tested. Our results are consistent with previous meta-analysis (i.e. Archer, 2004) confirming that direct aggression was more common in males than females across ages and cultures. Although alternative explanations can be suggested, following a social cognitive approach of gender role development (Bussey & Bandura, 1999), boys, but less so girls, receive implicit (or explicit) communication that aggressive reactions are appropriate throughout the socialisation processes, as these are often considered a set of instrumental behaviours that suit the masculine role.

This study has a number of strengths, including a more fine-grained approach than that of previous research, in which the different components of negative emotionality and empathy were studied. In addition, this study examined both main and interaction effects to better capture the complexity of the potential causes of aggressive behaviours. Despite these strengths, the main limitation of this study was that the data used were concurrent, which therefore does not facilitate drawing conclusions regarding the direction of the effects. In this sense, longitudinal studies are required to disentangle the temporal cause and effect relations. A second limitation comes from the lack of differentiation between proactive and reactive aggression. These forms of aggression have been associated with different physiological and personality profiles (Bobadilla, Wampler, & Taylor, 2012). Future research should consider how negative reactivity and empathy may differently relate to proactive versus reactive aggression. A third limitation comes from the low explanatory power of the models tested, as represented by the R^2_a, suggesting that there are additional factors involved in children's aggressive behaviours which should be considered. This may include factors such as parental involvement, and children's perceptions about their school and class climate, or the class approval of students' aggressive behaviours (Farrell, Henry, Mays, & Schoeny, 2011).

Acknowledgements

This study was supported by the Spanish Ministry of Economy and Competitiveness (project PSI2017–84556-P, FEDER funds). We thank the participating children, their parents, teachers, and the administrative authorities of the participating schools for their cooperation.

References

Archer, J. (2004). Sex differences in aggression in real-world settings: A meta-analytic review. *Review of General Psychology, 8*(4), 291–322.

Austin, G., Bondü, R., & Elsner, B. (2017). Longitudinal relations between children's cognitive and affective theory of mind with reactive and proactive aggression. *Aggressive Behaviour, 43*(5), 440–449.

Barchia, K., & Bussey, K. (2011). Predictors of student defenders of peer aggression victims: Empathy and social cognitive factors. *International Journal of Behavioural Development, 35*(4), 289–297.

Björkqvist, K., Österman, K., & Kaukiainen, A. (2000). Social intelligence- empathy= aggression? *Aggression and Violent Behaviour, 5*(2), 191–200.

Blair, R. J. R. (2018). Traits of empathy and anger: Implications for psychopathy and other disorders associated with aggression. *Philosophical Transactions of the Royal Society B: Biological Sciences, 373*(1744).

Bobadilla, L., Wampler, M., & Taylor, J. (2012). Proactive and reactive aggression are associated with different physiological and personality profiles. *Journal of Social and Clinical Psychology, 31*(5), 458–487.

Bohnert, A. M., Crnic, K. A., & Lim, K. G. (2003). Emotional competence and aggressive behaviour in school-age children. *Journal of Abnormal Child Psychology, 31*(1), 79–91.

Broidy, L. M., Nagin, D. S., Tremblay, R. E., Bates, J. E., Brame, B., Dodge, K. A., . . . Laird, R. (2003). Developmental trajectories of childhood disruptive behaviors and adolescent delinquency: A six-site, cross-national study. *Developmental Psychology, 39*(2), 222.

Bussey, K., & Bandura, A. (1999). Social cognitive theory of gender development and differentiation. *Psychological Review, 106*(4), 676.

Carlo, G., Mestre, M. V., Samper, P., Tur, A., & Armenta, B. E. (2010). Feelings or cognitions? Moral cognitions and emotions as longitudinal predictors of prosocial and aggressive behaviors. *Personality and Individual Differences*, *48*(8), 872–877.

Cook, C. R., Williams, K. R., Guerra, N. G., Kim, T. E., & Sadek, S. (2010). Predictors of bullying and victimization in childhood and adolescence: A meta-analytic investigation. *School Psychology Quarterly*, *25*(2), 65.

Crick, N. R., & Dodge, K. A. (1994). A review and reformulation of social information-processing mechanisms in children's social adjustment. *Psychological Bulletin*, *115*(1), 74.

Dodge, K. A. (2014). A social information processing model of social competence in children. In *Cognitive perspectives on children's social and behavioral development* (pp. 85–134). New York: Psychology Press.

Dodge, K. A., & Coie, J. D. (1987). Social-information-processing factors in reactive and proactive aggression in children's peer groups. *Journal of Personality and Social Psychology*, *53*(6), 1146.

Dodge, K. A., Lochman, J. E., Harnish, J. D., Bates, J. E., & Pettit, G. S. (1997). Reactive and proactive aggression in school children and psychiatrically impaired chronically assaultive youth. *Journal of Abnormal Psychology*, *106*(1), 37.

Eisenberg, N., Chang, L., Ma, Y., & Huang, X. (2009a). Relations of parenting style to Chinese children's effortful control, ego resilience, and maladjustment. *Development and Psychopathology*, *21*(2), 455–477.

Eisenberg, N., Eggum, N. D., & di Giunta, L. (2010). Empathy-related responding: Associations with prosocial behavior, aggression, and intergroup relations. *Social Issues and Policy Review*, *4*(1), 143–180.

Eisenberg, N., & Miller, P. A. (1987). The relation of empathy to prosocial and related behaviors. *Psychological Bulletin*, *101*(1), 91–119.

Eisenberg, N., Valiente, C., Spinrad, T. L., Cumberland, A., Liew, J., Reiser, M., Zhou, Q., & Losoya, S. H. (2009). Longitudinal relations of children's effortful control, impulsivity, and negative emotionality to their externalizing, internalizing, and co-occurring behavior problems. *Developmental Psychology*, *45*(4), 988–1008. https://doi.org/10.1037/a0016213

Embregts, P. J., Didden, R., Schreuder, N., Huitink, C., & van Nieuwenhuijzen, M. (2009). Aggressive behavior in individuals with moderate to borderline intellectual disabilities who live in a residential facility: An evaluation of functional variables. *Research in Developmental Disabilities*, *30*(4), 682–688.

Farrell, A. D., Henry, D. B., Mays, S. A., & Schoeny, M. E. (2011). Parents as moderators of the impact of school norms and peer influences on aggression in middle school students. *Child Development*, *82*(1), 146–161.

Forgas, J. P. (1995). Mood and judgment: The affect infusion model (AIM). *Psychological Bulletin*, *117*(1), 39.

Fung, A. L., Gerstein, L. H., Chan, Y., & Engebretson, J. (2015). Relationship of aggression to anxiety, depression, anger, and empathy in Hong Kong. *Journal of Child and Family Studies*, *24*(3), 821–831.

González, J., Fernández, S., Pérez, E., & Santamaría, P. (2004). *Adaptación española del sistema de evaluación de la conducta en niños y adolescentes: BASC*. Madrid: TEA Ediciones.

Graham, S., Hudley, C., & Williams, E. (1992). Attributional and emotional determinants of aggression among African-American and Latino young adolescents. *Developmental Psychology*, *28*(4), 731.

Halperin, J. M., Newcorn, J. H., Matier, K., Bedi, G., Hall, S., & Sharma, V. (1995). Impulsivity and the initiation of fights in children with disruptive behaviour disorders. *Journal of Child Psychology and Psychiatry*, *36*(7), 1199–1211.

Hawker, D. S., & Boulton, M. J. (2000). Twenty years' research on peer victimization and psychosocial maladjustment: A meta-analytic review of cross-sectional studies. *The Journal of Child Psychology and Psychiatry and Allied Disciplines*, *41*(4), 441–455.

Hubbard, J. A., McAuliffe, M. D., Morrow, M. T., & Romano, L. J. (2010). Reactive and proactive aggression in childhood and adolescence: Precursors, outcomes, processes, experiences, and measurement. *Journal of Personality*, *78*(1), 95–118.

Hubbard, J. A., Smithmyer, C. M., Ramsden, S. R., Parker, E. H., Flanagan, K. D., Dearing, K. F., . . . Simons, R. F. (2002). Observational, physiological, and self-report measures of children's anger: Relations to reactive versus proactive aggression. *Child Development*, *73*(4), 1101–1118.

Jolliffe, D., & Farrington, D. P. (2004). Empathy and offending: A systematic review and meta-analysis. *Aggression and Violent Behavior*, *9*(5), 441–476.

Jolliffe, D., & Farrington, D. P. (2006). Development and validation of the basic empathy scale. *Journal of Adolescence*, *29*(4), 589–611.

Kaltiala-Heino, R., Rimpelä, M., Marttunen, M., Rimpelä, A., & Rantanen, P. (1999). Bullying, depression, and suicidal ideation in Finnish adolescents: School survey. *BMJ: British Medical Journal*, *319*(7206), 348–351.

Kim, G., Walden, T., Harris, V., Karrass, J., & Catron, T. (2007). Positive emotion, negative emotion, and emotion control in the externalizing problems of school-aged children. *Child Psychiatry and Human Development*, *37*(3), 221–239.

Kim-Cohen, J., Arseneault, L., Caspi, A., Tomás, M. P., Taylor, A., & Moffitt, T. E. (2005). Validity of DSM-IV conduct disorder in 4$1/2$ – 5-year-old children: A longitudinal epidemiological study. *American Journal of Psychiatry*, *162*(6), 1108–1117.

Krevans, J., & Gibbs, J. C. (1996). Parents' use of inductive discipline: Relations to children's empathy and prosocial behavior. *Child Development*, *67*(6), 3263–3277.

Ladd, G. W. (2006). Peer rejection, aggressive or withdrawn behavior, and psychological maladjustment from ages 5 to 12: An examination of four predictive models. *Child Development*, *77*(4), 822–846.

Lovett, B. J., & Sheffield, R. A. (2007). Affective empathy deficits in aggressive children and adolescents: A critical review. *Clinical Psychology Review*, *27*(1), 1–13.

Masten, C. L., Morelli, S. A., & Eisenberger, N. I. (2011). An fMRI investigation of empathy for "social pain" and subsequent prosocial behavior. *Neuroimage*, *55*(1), 381–388.

Miller, P. A., & Eisenberg, N. (1988). The relation of empathy to aggressive and externalizing/antisocial behavior. *Psychological Bulletin*, *103*(3), 324–344.

Nansel, T. R., Haynie, D. L., & Simonsmorton, B. G. (2003). The association of bullying and victimization with middle school adjustment. *Journal of Applied School Psychology*, *19*(2), 45–61.

Pakaslahti, L. (2000). Children's and adolescents' aggressive behavior in context: The development and application of aggressive problem-solving strategies. *Aggression and Violent Behavior*, *5*(5), 467–490.

Petty, R. E., Wegener, D. T., & Fabrigar, L. R. (1997). Attitudes and attitude change. *Annual Review of Psychology*, *48*(1), 609–647.

Quiggle, N. L., Garber, J., Panak, W. F., & Dodge, K. A. (1992). Social information processing in aggressive and depressed children. *Child Development*, *63*(6), 1305–1320.

Rathert, J., Fite, P. J., & Gaertner, A. E. (2011). Associations between effortful control, psychological control and proactive and reactive aggression. *Child Psychiatry & Human Development, 42*(5), 609.

Reynolds, C. R., & Kamphaus, R. W. (2004). *BASC: Sistema de evaluación de la conducta en niños y adolescentes: Manual*. Spain: TEA Ediciones.

Richardson, D. R., Hammock, G. S., Smith, S. M., Gardner, W., & Signo, M. (1994). Empathy as a cognitive inhibitor of interpersonal aggression. *Aggressive Behavior, 20*(4), 275–289.

Roberts, W., & Strayer, J. (1996). Empathy, emotional expressiveness, and prosocial behavior. *Child Development, 67*(2), 449–470.

Rothbart, M. K., Ahadi, S. A., & Evans, D. E. (2000). Temperament and personality: Origins and outcomes. *Journal of Personality and Social Psychology, 78*(1), 122.

Rothbart, M. K., Ahadi, S. A., & Hershey, K. L. (1994). Temperament and social behavior in childhood. *Merrill-Palmer Quarterly (1982–)*, 21–39.

Rothbart, M. K., & Derryberry, D. (1981). Development of individual differences in temperament. In M. E. Lamb & A. L. Brown (Eds.), *Advances in developmental psychology* (Vol. 1). Hillsdale, NJ: Lawrence Erlbaum.

Sánchez-Pérez, N., Fuentes, L. J., Jolliffe, D., & González-Salinas, C. (2014). Assessing children's empathy through a Spanish adaptation of the basic empathy scale: Parent's and child's report forms. *Frontiers in Psychology, 5*.

Simonds, J., & Rothbart, M. K. (2006). *Temperament in middle childhood questionnaire*. Retrieved from http://www.bowdoin.edu/~sputnam/rothbart-temperament-questionnaires/

Stavrinides, P., Georgiou, S., & Theofanous, V. (2010). Bullying and empathy: A short-term longitudinal investigation. *Educational Psychology, 30*(7), 793–802.

Strayer, J., & Roberts, W. (2004). Empathy and observed anger and aggression in five-year-olds. *Social Development, 13*(1), 1–13.

Swearer, S. M., Song, S. Y., Cary, P. T., Eagle, J. W., & Mickelson, W. T. (2001). Psychosocial correlates in bullying and victimization: The relationship between depression, anxiety, and bully/victim status. *Journal of Emotional Abuse, 2*(2–3), 95–121.

Sze, J. A., Gyurak, A., Goodkind, M. S., & Levenson, R. W. (2012). Greater emotional empathy and prosocial behaviour in late life. *Emotion, 12*(5), 1129.

Vachon, D. D., Lynam, D. R., & Johnson, J. A. (2014). The (non) relation between empathy and aggression: Surprising results from a meta-analysis. *Psychological Bulletin, 140*(3), 751.

van Langen, M. A., Wissink, I. B., van Vugt, E. S., van der Stouwe, T., & Stams, G. (2014). The relation between empathy and offending: A meta-analysis. *Aggression and Violent Behavior, 19*(2), 179–189.

Vitaro, F., Brendgen, M., & Tremblay, R. E. (2002). Reactively and proactively aggressive children: Antecedent and subsequent characteristics. *Journal of Child Psychology and Psychiatry, 43*(4), 495–505.

Vitiello, B., & Stoff, D. M. (1997). Subtypes of aggression and their relevance to child psychiatry. *Journal of the American Academy of Child & Adolescent Psychiatry, 36*(3), 307–315.

Weisbrot, D. M., & Ettinger, A. B. (2002). Aggression and violence in mood disorders. *Child and Adolescent Psychiatric Clinics of North America, 11*(3), 649–672.

Wilkowski, B. M., & Robinson, M. D. (2010). The anatomy of anger: An integrative cognitive model of trait anger and reactive aggression. *Journal of Personality, 78*(1), 9–38.

Xu, Y., Farver, J. A. M., & Zhang, Z. (2009). Temperament, harsh and indulgent parenting, and Chinese children's proactive and reactive aggression. *Child Development*, *80*(1), 244–258.

Yoon, J. S., Barton, E., & Taiariol, J. (2004). Relational aggression in middle school: Educational implications of developmental research. *The Journal of Early Adolescence*, *24*(3), 303–318.

Zeman, J., Shipman, K., & Suveg, C. (2002). Anger and sadness regulation: Predictions to internalizing and externalizing symptoms in children. *Journal of Clinical Child and Adolescent Psychology*, *31*(3), 393–398.

Zirpoli, T. J. (2008). *Behavior management: Applications for teachers*. Upper Saddle River, NJ: Pearson, Merrill Prentice Hall.

13 Low cognitive empathy and its relationship to relational, online, and physical aggression in young adults in Australia

Tara Renae McGee, Darrick Jolliffe, Li Eriksson, Christine E.W. Bond, and David P. Farrington

Introduction

Researchers have been examining the empirical association between low empathy and aggression for over 50 years. This pursuit is based on an understanding that those who have higher empathy, and therefore a greater capacity to understand or vicariously experience the negative emotional reactions of others caused by their own aggression, will be less likely to continue such behaviour or be aggressive in the future. It therefore follows that, if heightened empathy inhibits negative social behaviours such as aggression, then those exhibiting these negative social behaviours may have lower levels of empathy.

While reviews of the relationship between empathy and aggression had been undertaken previously (e.g. Feshbach, 1987; Feshbach, 1978), the first systematic attempt to synthesise this knowledge was conducted by Miller and Eisenberg (1988). This research included studies where empathy was measured using picture/story methods, facial or gesture responses to emotional stimuli, and questionnaire measures. The primary studies included in this review operationalised aggression as the intensity and duration of an aversive stimuli (noise or "shock") that a research participant was willing to administer, teacher ratings of aggression, the type of criminal offences committed, and aggressive responses. The samples included school students, incarcerated delinquents, college students, forensic psychiatric patients, and abusive and non-abusive mothers.

Overall the results identified a small to moderate relationship between low empathy and aggression. For example, in the nine studies in which empathy was measured using picture/story methods the correlation with aggression was $r = -.11$, but in the five studies in which empathy was measured using facial or gesture methods the correlation with aggression was only $r = -.06$. The relationship was found to be strongest in the nine studies where empathy was measured using questionnaires ($r = -.18$). In addition, Miller and Eisenberg (1988) also reviewed studies in which empathy was compared to externalising and antisocial behaviours such as: behavioural ratings by parents or correctional staff, aggression based on experimental paradigms, or self-report scales of psychopathology.

In the 13 studies examined, the correlations between measures of empathy and externalising behaviour were estimated to be between $r = -.13$ to $r = -.20$.

Although this seminal review clearly established an empirical link between empathy and aggression, particularly for children, it was also limited in some regards. Most notably this review conflated measures of affective empathy (i.e. the ability to vicariously experience the emotions of others) with measures of sympathy (i.e. a general fellow feeling, regardless of the emotion; Jeffrey, 2016; Southard, 1919). The delineation of these concepts is important, as the relationship between aggression and emotional congruence may differ in important ways from the relationship between aggression and feeling general emotions.

In their systematic review and meta-analysis of 106 effect sizes comparing measures of empathy (predominantly self-reports) with a range of measures of aggression (self-report, archival criminal records, laboratory-based, or group membership such as "criminals"), Vachon, Lynam, and Johnson (2014) found the relationship between empathy and aggression to be small to moderate ($r = -.11$). The authors suggested that this estimate was fairly consistent across the various forms of aggression, including verbal aggression ($r = -.20$) and physical aggression ($r = -.12$), and while numerous potential moderators were investigated, such as the method of measuring empathy, the measure of aggression, and demographic features (such as age, gender, and ethnicity), most had only a limited impact on the magnitude of the estimated relationship. Interestingly, only education moderated the empathy – aggression relationship, with those study participants who had lower levels of education showing no relationship between these constructs.

These reviews of empathy and aggression, along with those examining low empathy and criminal behaviour (e.g. Jolliffe & Farrington, 2004; van Langen et al., 2014) appear to establish that low empathy and direct forms of aggression are related, but perhaps at a lower magnitude than might be theoretically expected. However, the relationship between low empathy and equally harmful but more subtle forms of aggression, such as so-called indirect, social or relational aggression, is still unclear. These aggressive behaviours are broadly defined as those '. . . that attack a victim's actual or perceived social relations with others, often (though not always) in a way that avoids direct confrontation' (Card, Stucky, Sawalani, & Little, 2008, p. 1186). While the terms indirect, social, and relational aggression are often used interchangeably, there are important distinctions between these (for a discussion, see Archer, 2001; Archer & Coyne, 2005). In the current study, we focus on relational aggression which is defined as any behaviour that causes harm by damaging relationships or feelings of acceptance and love. Previous research has suggested that there are limited gender differences in the prevalence of relational aggression (Burton, Hafetz, & Henninger, 2007; Smits, Doumen, Luyckx, Duriez, & Goossens, 2011; Werner & Crick, 1999). However, examinations of the relationship between low empathy and relational aggression have suggested that low cognitive empathy may predict later relational aggression (Batanova & Loukas, 2011).

Like direct forms of aggression, relational, social, and indirect aggression could be related to low empathy, in that those who perpetrate behaviours which clearly cause distress to a victim may be deficient in their ability to vicariously experience or understand the emotions of others. Alternatively, successful relational aggression could derive from a combination of empathic deficits and intact or even enhanced social intelligence, broadly defined as 'the ability to understand other people and how they will react to different social situations' (Silvera, Martinussen, & Dahl, 2001, p. 313). These abilities could be used to manipulate the victim or encourage others to take part in this aggression by maliciously spreading rumours or undermining peer relationships (Björkqvist, Österman, & Kaukiainen, 2000).

The link between empathy, social intelligence, and aggression (physical, indirect, and verbal) was explored in a sample of 526 Finnish school children (274 girls and 252 boys) aged 10, 12, and 14 (Kaukiainen et al., 1999). Using peer-estimations of empathy (e.g. helps classmate in trouble) and social intelligence (e.g. notices easily if others lie) the researchers found that social intelligence was significantly and positively related to *indirect* aggression in both males and females, but was not related to the *direct* forms of aggression. However, low empathy was significantly related to all forms of aggression when controlling for social intelligence. In interpreting the results of this study, it is important to note that the affective and cognitive components of empathy were not treated separately. This is problematic, as the authors themselves noted that the concepts of cognitive empathy and social intelligence overlap, and that this social/emotional understanding could act as a facilitator of "successful" indirect aggression.

Additional research with young adults has found relatively consistent between-gender differences in the relations between affective empathy and more direct forms of aggression, but less consistent differences between genders in the relation between cognitive empathy and indirect aggression. For example, in their study of over 300 American university students (mean age 22.8 years; 61.5% female), Warren, Richardson, and McQuillin (2011) used the self-reported Interpersonal Reactivity Index (IRI; Davis, 1983) to measure empathy and compared this to measures of physical, indirect, and relational aggression. They found that males scored significantly higher than females on measures of physical aggression, but not on measures of indirect or relational aggression. Overall the results suggested that both cognitive empathy (measured using the Perspective Taking scale) and affective empathy (measured using the Empathic Concern scale) were negatively related to both physical and indirect aggression. This study also found that indirect and relational aggression were likely to be measuring the same underlying construct and were used equally by both males and females. An additional noteworthy finding in the context of the current study is that indirect aggression was more strongly associated with poor perspective taking (low cognitive empathy) than was relational aggression.

Similarly, Loudin, Loukas, and Robinson (2003) conducted a study of relational aggression and empathy using three hundred 19–25-year-old (67.7% females) American university students. Empathy was measured using the IRI and compared with peer estimated direct aggression (Crick, 1996) and relational aggression (Werner & Crick, 1999). The results suggested that low Empathic Concern (affective empathy) was significantly related to overt aggression in females ($r = -.16$), but not in males. Perspective Taking (cognitive empathy) was significantly and negatively associated with relational aggression for both males and females.

Online aggression and cyberbullying are relatively new and understudied forms of aggression. These are defined as intentional harm carried out through electronic means to a person who perceives such acts as offensive, derogatory, harmful or unwanted (Grigg, 2010). Kokkinos, Antoniadou, and Markos (2014) conducted a study of 430 Greek university students' (mean age 20.3, 58% female) involvement in online aggression and compared this to empathy, as well as to other important explanatory factors such as social skills (a component of social intelligence) and impulsiveness (acting without considering the consequences of one's actions). Cognitive empathy was assessed using the Eight Question Empathy scale (EQ-8; Loewen et al., 2010). Males reported engaging in significantly more online aggression than females, while also showing significantly lower cognitive empathy and higher impulsivity. Males and females did not differ on social skills. Overall, cyber-aggression was significantly predicted by gender, lower social skills, and higher impulsivity, but not by cognitive empathy. In contrast, a study of 1282 university students in Spain found that the capacity for understanding others' emotions (cognitive empathy assessed as part of emotional intelligence) was related to lower levels of cyberbullying perpetration (Martínez-Monteagudo et al., 2019).

When examining the relationship between cyberbullying and self-control in 208 university students in Hong Kong, it was found that the impact of self-control on cyberbullying did not differ between males and females (Wong et al., 2018). Rather than being differentiated on the basis of self-control, male cyberbullying was best explained by previous victimisation, and female cyberbullying by disinhibition (Wong et al., 2018). These relationships stand in contrast to findings that show that the gender gap in crime is accounted for by self-control (Burton, Cullen, Evans, & Dunaway, 1998).

There is clearly a need for further research in which measures of both affective and cognitive empathy are compared to not only more traditional measures of aggression such as physical and relational, but also online aggression, for both males and females. It would also be important to control for other potential explanatory variables such as impulsiveness (or self-control) and social intelligence. It could be that certain factors may be related to specific forms of aggression differently for males and females, in which case gender-specific interventions may be desirable.

This is the first research of which we are aware that examines the relationship between affective and cognitive empathy and different forms of in-person aggression (physical and relational) and online aggression. Furthermore, this research aims to add to knowledge by examining potential gender differences in these relationships while also considering the roles of the potentially important explanatory variables of social intelligence and self-control.

Research Questions:

1. To what extent are there gender differences in affective empathy, cognitive empathy, physical, relational, and online aggression, as well as self-control and social intelligence?
2. To what extent are the types of empathy, self-control, and social intelligence related to the types of aggression? To what extent do these relationships vary with gender?
3. To what extent do the types of empathy predict various forms of aggression, controlling for self-control, and social intelligence? To what extent do these relationships vary with gender?

Methods

The undergraduate criminology students who participated in this study were enrolled at a large public university in Australia. The university at which the study was conducted had almost 50,000 students enrolled in 2017. Participants were recruited using a convenience sampling strategy in which students attending a criminological theory course were invited to participate in a research project on aggression. Participants were provided the incentive of receiving course credit for taking part in research projects such as this. The completion of this survey contributed partially towards this. Students who did not wish to participate were given the option of completing another short research task to gain the course credit.

The data were collected across 2016 and 2017. Students were provided with a link to the online survey by the course convenor, which was posted on the course website. The survey was administered through Qualtrics. In compliance with Australian National Ethical Guidelines, the survey had a coversheet that outlined the nature of the research project, provided assurances that participant anonymity would be maintained, and provided contact details for the Principal Researcher and the University Ethics Committee. A total of 765 participants fully completed the questionnaire. The majority identified as female (72.5% versus 27.5% male) and reported being born in Australia (76.6% versus 23.4% not born in Australia). Participants were on average 21.5 years of age ($SD = 4.6$).

Measures

Aggression

The aggressive behaviour of the participants was assessed with the 56-item Self-Report of Aggression and Social Behavior Measure (SRASBM) (Linder et al., 2002; Morales & Crick, 1998). In addition to the original 56 items, 15 additional items about the use of online aggression on social media platforms such as Facebook, Instagram, and Twitter were added (contact lead author for these items). The SRASB was designed to assess the qualities of adult social interaction in intimate relationships with both friends and romantic partners. Responses ask about "the previous year" and are recorded on a seven-point Likert scale ("not at all true" (1) to "very true" (7)). In this study, we focus on the *use of aggression* across three domains: physical aggression (6 items); indirect aggression (16 items); and online aggression (15 items). Subscale scores were calculated by computing the mean of all the items in the subscale, with higher scores indicating higher levels of aggression. The internal consistency and validity of the SRASBM has been demonstrated by a number of previous studies (see for example Linder et al., 2002; Murray-Close et al., 2010). In this study, the subscales all showed high levels of internal consistency: relational aggression (Cronbach's α = .89); online aggression (Cronbach's α = .90); and physical aggression (Cronbach's α = .85);

Independent variables

Low empathy

Empathy was measured using the 20-item Basic Empathy Scale (BES) (Jolliffe & Farrington, 2006). The affective empathy subscale of the BES measures the participants' capacity to mirror or experience another's feelings, while the cognitive empathy scale assesses the capacity to identify and understand another's feelings. In this study, we reverse coded the scores so that a high score indicates *low empathy*.

Low self-control

Low self-control was assessed using Grasmick's 24-item scale (Grasmick et al., 1993), which includes items about impulsive behaviour, risk seeking behaviour, preference for physical activities, self-centredness, preference for simple tasks, and temper control. Items are scored on 4-point Likert scale, from *strongly disagree* (1) to *strongly agree* (4). Higher scores indicate *lower levels of self-control* and the score was calculated by summing all the item scores together (Cronbach's α = .84).

Low social intelligence

The 21-item social intelligence scale (Silvera et al., 2001) measures aspects of social information processing, social skills, and social awareness, and respondents are asked to indicate the extent to which an item is *poor description* of them (1) to an *accurate description* (7). Items worded in the opposite direction in this scale were reverse coded so that higher scores indicate *lower social intelligence* (Cronbach's α = .86).

Results

Table 13.1 shows the comparisons between males and females on the variables included in this study. For example, males scored an average of 1.89 (*SD* = 0.86) on the measure of relational aggression, while females scored an average of 1.85 (*SD* = 0.72). This was a non-significant difference and the measure of effect

Table 13.1 Gender differences in aggression, empathy, self-control, and social intelligence.

	Males	*Females*	*t*	p	*D*
	n = *220*	n = *555*			
	M (SD)	*M (SD)*			
Aggression					
Relational aggression	1.89 (0.86)	1.85 (0.72)	0.62	n.s.	0.05
Online aggression	1.55 (0.77)	1.40 (0.59)	2.84	0.005	0.23
Physical aggression	1.85 (1.08)	1.35 (0.66)	7.68	0.001	0.63
Low Empathy					
Cognitive empathy	19.27 (4.95)	17.48 (4.52)	4.76	0.001	0.39
Affective empathy	31.27 (7.14)	24.34 (6.88)	12.31	0.001	1.01
Low Self-Control					
Total score	54.08 (9.17)	51.40 (9.47)	3.52	0.001	0.29
Low Social Intelligence					
Total score	69.07 (16.22)	67.45 (15.29)	1.29	n.s.	0.10
Age					
Average Age	21.89 (4.36)	21.36 (4.71)	1.41	n.s.	0.11

(Cohen's d) of 0.05 suggests very limited differences in gender in the use of relational aggression. However, males scored significantly higher than females on the measures of online aggression and physical aggression. Males also demonstrated significantly lower cognitive empathy, and particularly lower affective empathy than females, and lower self-control, while there were no significant gender differences in levels of social intelligence or age.

Table 13.2 shows the correlations between the variables included in the study. The pattern of significant and strong inter-relationships between the three types of aggression was similar for males and females, with the strongest relationships existing between relational aggression and online aggression (r = .81 males; r = .75 females). This is perhaps unsurprising given that online aggression may be considered a specific type of relational aggression. The results also showed that low cognitive empathy was significantly related to all three types of aggression for both males and females, while low affective empathy was only significantly related to physical aggression in males, but to both online and physical aggression in females. The magnitude of the significant correlations between aggression and low empathy for males and females ranged from relatively weak (r = .13 for online aggression versus low affective empathy among females) to quite strong (r = .37 for online aggression versus low cognitive empathy among males).

Low self-control and low social intelligence were significantly related to all types of aggression for both males and females with the strongest relationship being between low self-control and physical aggression for males (r = .52), and the weakest for low social intelligence versus relational aggression for females (r = .23). A weak but significant correlation was found between age and online

Table 13.2 Correlation matrix for aggression, empathy, low self-control, and social intelligence (males above diagonal and females below)

Females \ *Males*	*Relational aggression*	*Online aggression*	*Physical aggression*	*Low cognitive empathy*	*Low affective empathy*	*Low self-control*	*Low social intelligence*	*Age*
Relational aggression		.81**	.67**	.27**	.08	.46**	.31**	.01
Online aggression	.75**		.61**	.37**	.02	.32**	.28**	.01
Physical aggression	.61**	.66**		.28**	.25**	.52**	.26**	.02
Low cognitive empathy	.23**	.29**	.25**		.20**	.21**	.61**	–.02
Low affective empathy	.04	.13**	.16**	.48**		.28**	–.04	.05
Low self-control	.48**	.38**	.36**	.31**	.17**		.27**	–.17*
Low social intelligence	.23**	.28**	.24**	.56**	.18**	.37**		–.10
Age	–.07	–.09*	.01	–.09*	.01	–.15**	–.04	

$^{*}p < .05$; $^{**}p < .01$; $^{***}p < .001$

aggression for females, suggesting that younger females were somewhat been more likely to commit online aggression.

Many of the explanatory variables were significantly related to one another for both males and females. For males the largest correlation was between low cognitive empathy and low social intelligence (r = .61), followed by low affective empathy and low self-control (r = .28), and low self-control any low social intelligence (r = −.27). For females, the largest correlation was also between low cognitive empathy and low social intelligence (r = .56), followed by low cognitive empathy versus low affective empathy (r = .48). Importantly, none of the correlations between the explanatory variables were so high that multicollinearity would be an issue.

In order to examine whether low cognitive or affective empathy independently predicted the different types of aggression a series of stepwise regression models were performed. Separate regression models for males (Table 13.3) and females (Table 13.4) for each type of aggression (relational, online, and physical) were performed. The explanatory variables included were cognitive empathy, affective empathy, self-control, social intelligence, and age.

Table 13.3 shows that for males, relational, online and physical aggression were all significantly predicted only by low cognitive empathy and low self-control, while for females (Table 13.4) these were also the only significant independent predictors of online and physical aggression. Relational aggression by females was also predicted by low self-control, low cognitive empathy, and high affective empathy.

In order to explore whether increasing cognitive empathy might reduce aggression, the relationship between low cognitive empathy, low self-control, and aggression was investigated further by creating four mutually exclusive groups based on levels of cognitive empathy and self-control (High Self-Control/High

Table 13.3 Regression models predicting three types of aggression – males

Relational Aggression	*B*	*SE*	*Beta*	*F Change*	*Sig F Change*
Adj R Sq = .234					
Low Self-Control	0.039	0.006	0.418	54.7	0.0001
Low Cognitive Empathy	0.032	0.011	0.186	9.0	0.001
Online Aggression				*F Change*	*Sig F Change*
Adj R Sq = .190					
Low Cognitive Empathy	0.049	0.01	0.316	32.6	0.0001
Low Self-Control	0.021	0.005	0.255	16.1	0.0001
Physical Aggression				*F Change*	*Sig F Change*
Adj R Sq = .298					
Low Self-Control	0.057	0.007	0.486	78.4	0.0001
Low Cognitive Empathy	0.04	0.013	0.181	9.4	0.001

Table 13.4 Regression models predicting three types of aggression – females

Relational Aggression	*B*	*SE*	*Beta*	*F Change*	*Sig F Change*
Adj R Sq = .239					
Low Self-Control	0.034	0.003	0.452	163.19	0.0001
Low Cognitive Empathy	0.022	0.007	0.137	5.08	0.025
Low Affective Empathy	–0.011	0.004	–0.103	5.98	0.015
Online Aggression	*B*	*SE*	*Beta*	*F Change*	*Sig F Change*
Adj R Sq = .190					
Low Self-Control	0.02	0.003	0.321	94.09	0.0001
Low Cognitive Empathy	0.025	0.005	0.192	22.28	0.0001
Physical Aggression	*B*	*SE*	*Beta*	*F Change*	*Sig F Change*
Adj R Sq = .298					
Low Self-Control	0.022	0.003	0.311	81.05	0.0001
Low Cognitive Empathy	0.022	0.006	0.148	12.82	0.0001

Cognitive Empathy; High Self-Control/Low Cognitive Empathy; Low Self-Control/High Cognitive Empathy; Low Self-Control Low Empathy). Because of the relatively small number of males, the scores on the measures of cognitive empathy and low self-control were dichotomised into high versus low based on the 50% of individuals who scored the lowest. For females the lowest 25% constituted the low group, while the remaining 75% comprised the high group. For consistency, the three types of aggression were also dichotomised into the worst 25% compared to the remaining 75%, separately for males and females.

Table 13.5 shows the prevalence of the three types of aggression amongst those with high or low self-control and high or low cognitive empathy. For example, of the 210 males, 61 (29.0%) had both high self-control and high cognitive empathy, and of these 13.1% were high on relational aggression. In comparison, 36.1% (22) of the 61 males who scored low on self-control and low on cognitive empathy scored high on relational aggression (*OR* = 3.7, *p* < .01). Similarly, 360 (64.8%) females were high on both self-control and cognitive empathy, and of these 16.1% were high on relational aggression, compared to 57.4% (27/47) who were low on both self-control and cognitive empathy (*OR* = 7.0, *p* < .001).

For males, the results (top of Table 13.5; Figure 13.1) show that those with low self-control were more likely to be high on relational, online and physical aggression. Amongst males with high self-control, there was no significant difference in the prevalence of relational (13.1% compared to 14.0%; *OR* = 1.1, n.s.), or online aggression (16.4% compared to 18.6%; *OR* = 1.1, n.s.) for those with low or high cognitive empathy, respectively. For physical aggression (11.5% compared to 20.9%, n.s.) this difference was also not significant, but the odds ratio of 2.0 is equivalent to a small to moderate effect size (Chen, Cohen, & Chen, 2010) and suggests that cognitive empathy may be important in reducing the likelihood of physical aggression amongst those with high self-control.

Table 13.5 Comparison of high/low self-control and high/low cognitive empathy with aggression

Males	*Relational Agg (%)*	*N*	*Online Agg (%)*	*N*	*Physical Agg (%)*	*N*	*Total N*
High SC/High C Emp	13.1	8	16.4	10	11.5	7	61
High SC/Low C Emp	14.0	6	18.6	8	20.9	9	43
Low SC/High C Emp	37.8	17	35.6	16	31.1	14	45
Low SC/Low C Emp	36.1	22	34.4	21	39.3	24	61
Total	25.2	53	26.2	55	25.7	54	210
Females	*Relational Agg (%)*	*N*	*Online Agg (%)*	*N*	*Physical Agg (%)*	*N*	*Total N*
High SC/High C Emp	16.1	58	15.3	55	17.2	62	360
High SC/Low C Emp	20.3	14	23.2	16	24.6	17	69
Low SC/High C Emp	51.9	41	44.3	35	46.8	37	79
Low SC/Low C Emp	57.4	27	66.0	31	53.2	25	47
Total	25.2	140	24.7	137	25.4	141	555

SC – self-control; C Emp – Cognitive empathy

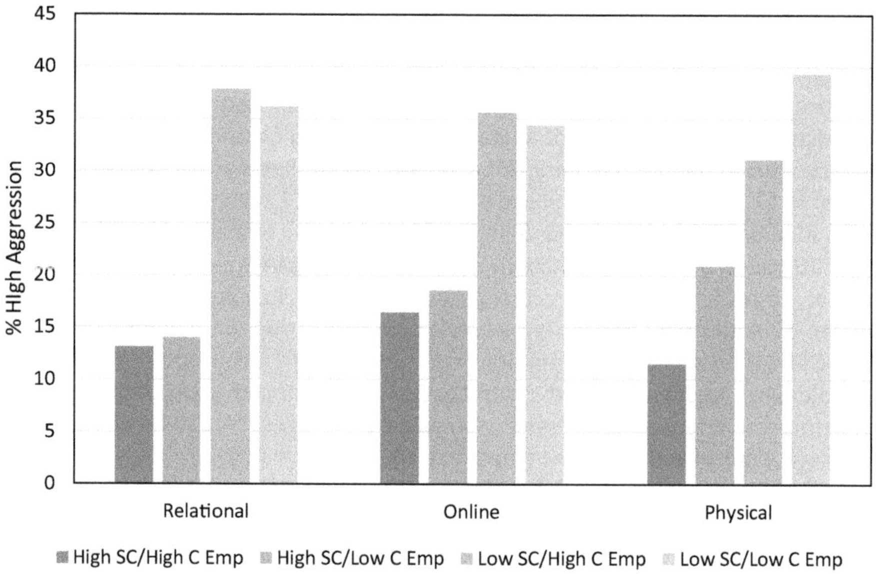

Figure 13.1 Self-control and cognitive empathy for males

Amongst males with low self-control, there was no evidence that the prevalence of relational (36.1% compared to 37.8%; *OR* = 0.9, n.s.) or online aggression (35.6% compared to 34%; *OR* = 1.0, n.s.), was significantly increased amongst those with low as opposed to high levels of empathy. Males who had low self-control and low cognitive empathy appeared more likely to be high on physical aggression compared to those who had low self-control but high cognitive empathy (39.3% compared to 31.1% OR = 1.5, n.s.), but this difference was not significant.

For females, the results (bottom of Table 13.5; Figure 13.2) show that those with low self-control were more likely to be high on relational, online and physical aggression. Amongst females with high self-control, there was no significant difference in the prevalence of relational (16.1% compared to 20.3%; *OR* = 1.3, n.s.) or online aggression (15.3% compared to 23.2%; *OR* = 1.2, n.s.) for those with low or high cognitive empathy, respectively. For physical aggression (17.2% compared to 24.6%, n.s) this difference was also not significant, but the odds ratio of 1.6, which is equivalent to a small effect size (Chen, Cohen, & Chen, 2010), suggests that cognitive empathy may be important.

Amongst females with low self-control there was no evidence that the prevalence of relational (57.4% compared to 51.9%; *OR* = 1.3, n.s.) or physical aggression (53.2% compared to 46.8%; *OR* = 1.3, n.s.), was significantly increased amongst those with low as opposed to high levels of empathy. However, females who had low self-control and low cognitive empathy were significantly more likely to be high on online aggression compared to those who had low self-control but high cognitive empathy (66.0% compared to 44.3%; *OR* = 2.4, $p < .05$).

Discussion

The purpose of this study was to examine whether low affective or cognitive empathy was associated with relational, online or physical aggression in a sample of university students. The results suggested that males and females differed in their levels of online and physical aggression (males higher), but not in relational aggression,

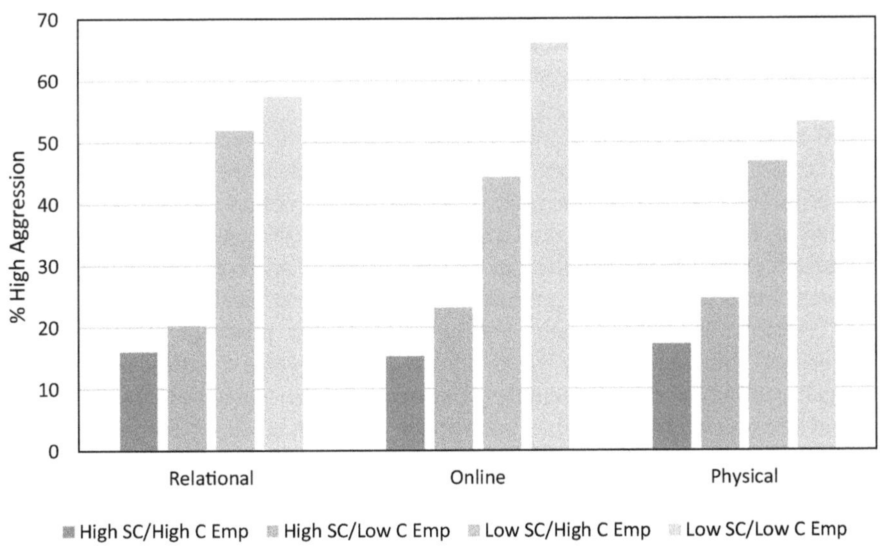

Figure 13.2 Self-control and cognitive empathy for females

which is consistent with the findings of similar research (Burton et al., 2007; Smits et al., 2011; Warren et al., 2011; Werner & Crick, 1999). Also, consistent with previous research (e.g. Baez et al., 2017) females self-reported higher levels of empathy than males, while males reported lower self-control. In the present study, males and females did not differ significantly in their level of social intelligence.

For males, relational, online and physical aggression were found to be independently predicted by both low self-control and low cognitive empathy, and this was also true for online and physical aggression amongst females. For females, relational aggression was predicted by low self-control, low cognitive empathy, and high affective empathy.

The results of the multivariate analyses indicate the importance of low self-control and low cognitive empathy in explaining all three types of aggression could suggest that interventions and approaches to increase both self-control and cognitive empathy might reduce these forms of aggression. However, when this was examined more closely, the relative importance of high self-control, as opposed to high cognitive empathy was evident. That is, those who had higher levels of self-control had lower levels of aggression, in many cases regardless of their levels of cognitive empathy. The only exception to this was physical aggression amongst males (in which higher cognitive empathy was associated with less physical aggression), and online aggression amongst females (in which higher cognitive empathy was associated with less online aggression).

The fact that greater cognitive empathy, or an increased ability to understand the emotions of another person, may not have an appreciable impact on reducing the likelihood of some forms of aggression is surprising given previous findings (e.g. Loudin et al., 2003; Warren, Richardson, & McQuillin, 2011). The current research suggested that low self-control, or acting without considering the consequences of one's actions, had a much stronger association with aggression than did cognitive empathy. When applying these findings to a prevention setting, it would seem that a multimodal approach that targets both self-control and cognitive empathy is likely to have most success as it is the interaction of these factors that appears to be important.

All types of aggression examined in this study were predicted by low cognitive empathy and low self-control. There is a well-established body of literature that links empathy with various forms of aggression, such as a criminal offending (Jolliffe & Farrington, 2004; van Langen et al., 2014). The current study is unique because it examines the relationship between affective and cognitive empathy and different forms of in-person aggression (physical and relational) and online aggression. Notably, affective empathy was not a significant predictor of any form of aggression, with one exception; high affective empathy was a significant predictor of relational aggression for females. Experiencing the fear or distress of others would be expected to be aversive, but perhaps very high levels result in one becoming emotionally overwhelmed and acting aggressively (Hatfield & Dula, 2014).

When exploring the joint role of low cognitive empathy and low self-control, the interaction of these factors significantly predicted relational, online, and physical aggression. These effects were the same for both males and females.

It could be argued that high levels of cognitive empathy are predictive of relational aggression, with a better understanding of other people's emotions allowing for the commission of relationally aggressive behaviours. We did not find this relationship in the current study; instead our findings are more consistent with prospective longitudinal research that showed that low cognitive empathy was related to future relational aggression (Batanova & Loukas, 2011; Loudin et al., 2003; Warren et al., 2011).

Limitations

It is important to note that this research was cross-sectional, and as such the directionality of aggression, self-control, and cognitive empathy could not be established. In addition, this was a convenience sample of university students. Future research should look at these associations using prospective longitudinal data from population-based samples. Future research in this area can also add to the knowledge generated here by examining to whom (peers or partners) the various types of aggressive behaviours (relational, online, are physical) are directed towards. There is also scope to examine the various dimensions of low self-control, moral disengagement, and social intelligence in more detail. Each of these scales had a number of subscales, and for self-control in particular it would be useful to better understand which elements of low self-control may be limiting low cognitive empathy in driving certain forms of aggressive behaviour.

References

Archer, J. (2001). A strategic approach to aggression. *Social Development*, *10*(2), 267–271.

Archer, J., & Coyne, S. M. (2005). An integrated review of indirect, relational, and social aggression. *Personality and Social Psychology Review*, *9*(3), 212–230.

Baez, S., Flichtentrei, D., Prats, M., Mastandueno, R., Garcia, A. M., Cetkovich, M., & Ibanez, A. (2017). Men, women . . . who cares? A population-based study on sex differences and gender roles in empathy and moral cognition. *PLoS One*, *12*(6), e0179336.

Batanova, M. D., & Loukas, A. (2011). Social anxiety and aggression in early adolescents: Examining the moderating roles of empathic concern and perspective taking. *Journal of Youth and Adolescence*, *40*(11), 1534–1543.

Björkqvist, K., Österman, K., & Kaukiainen, A. (2000). Social intelligence – empathy = aggression? *Aggression and Violent Behavior*, *5*(2), 191–200.

Burton, L. A., Hafetz, J., & Henninger, D. (2007). Gender differences in relational and physical aggression. *Social Behavior and Personality*, *35*(1), 41–50.

Burton, V. S., Cullen, F. T., Evans, T. D., & Dunaway, R. G. (1998). Gender, self-control, and crime. *Journal of Research in Crime & Delinquency*, *35*(2), 123–147.

Card, N. A., Stucky, B. D., Sawalani, G. M., & Little, T. D. (2008). Direct and indirect aggression during childhood and adolescence: A meta-analytic review of gender differences, intercorrelations, and relations to maladjustment. *Child Development*, *79*(5), 1185–1229.

Chen, H., Cohen, P., & Chen, S. (2010). How big is a big odds ratio? Interpreting the magnitudes of odds ratios in epidemiological studies. *Communications in Statistics – Simulation and Computation*, *39*(4), 860–864.

Crick, N. R. (1996). The role of overt aggression, relational aggression, and prosocial behavior in the prediction of children's future social adjustment. *Child Development, 67*(5), 23217–22327.

Davis, M. (1983). Measuring individual differences in empathy: Evidence for a multidimensional approach. *Journal of Personality and Social Psychology, 44*(1), 113–126.

Feshbach, N. D. (1978). Studies of empathic behavior in children. In B. A. Maher (Ed.), *Progress in experimental personality research* (Vol. 8, pp. 1–47). New York: Academic Press.

Feshbach, N. D. (1987). Parental empathy and child adjustment/maladjustment. In N. Eisenberg & J. Strayer (Eds.), *Empathy and its development* (pp. 271–291). New York: Cambridge University Press.

Grasmick, H. G., Tittle, C. R., Bursik, R. J., & Arneklev, B. J. (1993). Testing the core empirical implications of Gottfredson and Hirschi's general theory of crime. *Journal of Research in Crime and Delinquency, 30*(1), 5–29.

Grigg, D. W. (2010). Cyber-aggression: Definition and concept of cyberbullying. *Australian Journal of Guidance and Counselling, 20*(2), 143–156.

Hatfield, J., & Dula, C. (2014). Impulsivity and physical aggression: Examining the moderating role of anxiety. *The American Journal of Psychology, 127*(2), 233–243. doi:10.5406/amerjpsyc.127.2.0233

Jeffrey, D. (2016). Empathy, sympathy and compassion in healthcare: Is there a problem? Is there a difference? Does it matter? *Journal of the Royal Society of Medicine, 109*(12), 446–452.

Jolliffe, D., & Farrington, D. P. (2004). Empathy and offending: A systematic review and meta-analysis. *Aggression and Violent Behavior, 9*(5), 441–476.

Jolliffe, D., & Farrington, D. P. (2006). Development and validation of the basic empathy scale. *Journal of Adolescence, 29*(4), 589–611.

Kaukiainen, A., Björkqvist, K., Lagerspetz, K., Österman, K., Salmivalli, C., Rothberg, S., & Ahlbom, A. (1999). The relationships between social intelligence, empathy, and three types of aggression. *Aggressive Behavior, 25*, 81–89.

Kokkinos, C. M., Antoniadou, N., & Markos, A. (2014). Cyber-bullying: An investigation of the psychological profile of university student participants. *Journal of Applied Developmental Psychology, 35*(3), 204–214.

Linder, J. R., Crick, N. R., & Collins, W. A. (2002). Relational aggression and victimization in young adults' romantic relationships: Associations with perceptions of parent, peer, and romantic relationship quality. *Social Development, 11*(1), 70–86.

Loewen, P. J., Lyle, G., & Nachshen, J. S. (2010). *An eight-item form of the empathy quotient (EQ) and an application to charitable giving.* Retrieved from http://individual.utoronto.ca/loewen/Research_files/Eight%20Question%20ES_final.pdf

Loudin, J. L., Loukas, A., & Robinson, S. (2003). Relational aggression in college students: Examining the roles of social anxiety and empathy. *Aggressive Behavior, 29*(5), 430–439.

Martínez-Monteagudo, M. C., Delgado, B., Inglés, C. J., & García-Fernández, J. M. (2019). Cyberbullying in the university setting: Relationship with family environment and emotional intelligence. *Computers in Human Behavior, 91*, 220–225.

Miller, P. A., & Eisenberg, N. (1988). The relation of empathy to aggressive and externalizing/antisocial behavior. *Psychological Bulletin, 103*(3), 324–344.

Morales, J. R., & Crick, N. R. (1998). *Self-report measure of aggression and victimization.* Minneapolis, MN: University of Minnesota. Unpublished measure.

Murray-Close, D., Ostrov, J. M., Nelson, D. A., Crick, N. R., & Coccaro, E. F. (2010). Proactive, reactive, and romantic relational aggression in adulthood: Measurement, predictive validity, gender differences, and association with intermittent explosive disorder. *Journal of Psychiatric Research*, *44*(6), 393–404.

Silvera, D. H., Martinussen, M., & Dahl, T. I. (2001). The Tromsø social intelligence scale, a self-report measure of social intelligence. *Scandinavian Journal of Psychology*, *42*, 313–319.

Smits, I., Doumen, S., Luyckx, K., Duriez, B., & Goossens, L. (2011). Identity styles and interpersonal behavior in emerging adulthood: The intervening role of empathy. *Social Development*, *20*(4), 664–684.

Southard, E. E. (1919). The empathic index in the diagnosis of mental disease. *The Journal of Abnormal Psychology*, *13*, 199–214.

Vachon, D. D., Lynam, D. R., & Johnson, J. A. (2014). The (non)relation between empathy and aggression: Surprising results from a meta-analysis. *Psychological Bulletin*, *140*, 751–773.

van Langen, M. A. M., Wissink, I. B., van Vugt, E. S., van der Stouwe, T., & Stams, G. J. J. M. (2014). The relation between empathy and offending: A meta-analysis. *Aggression and Violent Behavior*, *19*(2), 179–189.

Warren, P., Richardson, D. S., & McQuillin, S. (2011). Distinguishing among nondirect forms of aggression. *Aggressive Behavior*, *37*(4), 291–301.

Werner, N. E., & Crick, N. R. (1999). Relational aggression and social-psychological adjustment in a college sample. *Journal of Abnormal Psychology*, *108*(4), 615–623.

Wong, R. Y. M., Cheung, C. M. K., & Xiao, B. (2018). Does gender matter in cyberbullying perpetration? An empirical investigation. *Computers in Human Behavior*, *79*, 247–257.

14 Empathy in Polish and Spanish children and adolescents

Validation of the Basic Empathy Scale and its relation to bullying, cyberbullying, and other antisocial behaviours

Izabela Zych, David P. Farrington, Darrick Jolliffe, and Estera Twardowska-Staszek

Introduction

Empathy has been widely studied in certain geographic areas, but the number of studies in other non-Western geographic areas is still low. To our knowledge, there are no validated instruments to study empathy in Poland. Research in many different countries showed that empathy is related to high prosociality and low antisocial behaviours (e.g. Jolliffe & Farrington, 2004, 2006). Thus, studying empathy in Poland and comparing the results to other countries can be an important step in understanding and decreasing antisocial behaviour in Poland and internationally, including bullying, cyberbullying and other problem behaviours. This chapter describes the psychometric properties of the BES in Poland and in Spain, together with the relation between empathy and antisocial behaviours in both countries.

Chapter 2 of this book shows that the original study where the BES was created and validated has received almost 800 citations (Basto-Pereira & Farrington, 2021). Thus, it is likely that the BES is the most popular measure of empathy in the world. Validating the BES in Poland would therefore be especially useful, as this would allow the results in Poland to be compared to the research about empathy as measured using the BES, and compare this to other countries.

The factor structure of the BES

The original version of the BES includes 20 items, 11 measuring affective empathy and 9 measuring cognitive empathy (Jolliffe & Farrington, 2006). This is the most commonly used structure, and many studies have found a good fit of different datasets to this two-factor 20-item version (Albeiro et al., 2009; D'Ambrosio et al., 2009; Cavojova et al., 2012; Jolliffe & Farrington, 2006; Pechorro, Ray, Salas-Wright, Maroco, & Goncalves, 2015). Nevertheless, several studies found that different versions showed a better fit to their data. Two-factor models with fewer items were found to have a better fit in some studies, including a 12-item version (Heynen et al., 2016), a 16-item version (Geng et al., 2012) and an 18-item version (Pechorro et al., 2015) in the incarcerated female subsample (Sánchez-Pérez et al., 2014). Confirmatory factor analyses of shorter versions generally find a better fit compared to the 20-item version.

A study that validated a three-factor 20-item model that divided the items into scales called emotional contagion, cognitive empathy and emotional disengagement (Herrera-López et al., 2017) also found a very good fit. Although a three-factor version can potentially be very useful, findings are difficult to compare to the studies that used a two-factor structure (i.e. cognitive and affective empathy). Moreover, almost all of the positive worded items of the affective empathy factor in the original version formed the emotional contagion factor and almost all of the negative worded items formed the emotional disengagement factor, but the content of these items was similar. Thus, more studies are needed to check if there might be a response bias, or if negative worded items form a factor because they are difficult to understand.

New developments in psychometrics show that combining positive and negative worded items in the same questionnaire might decrease the psychometric properties of the measure. This was tested through a repeated measure study with three versions of a self-efficacy questionnaire including positive worded items only, negative worded items only, or a combination of positive and negative worded items (Suárez-Alvarez et al., 2018). No difference regarding acquiescence response bias was found among these three versions. Nevertheless, the version which combined positive and negative worded items showed the worst reliability, the worst fit indices in a confirmatory factor analysis and the worst discrimination indices.

Building upon previous studies, this chapter focuses on the psychometric properties of the BES in Polish and Spanish children and adolescents. First, analyses are conducted based on the original 20-item two-factor model. Given that it is reasonable to suggest that the psychometric properties of a short version of the BES with positive worded items only could have stronger psychometric properties than the longer versions that combine both positive and negative worded items, a short 12-item positive worded version was also tested.

Empathy and antisocial behaviours

Measuring empathy using instruments with strong psychometric properties, such as the BES, is important for several reasons. Given that empathy has been shown to be related to both desirable and undesirable human behaviours, measuring empathy in novel samples could help develop a greater understanding of whether empathy may or may not be part of the causal chain which might explain these behaviours. If empathy is consistently implicated as a potential cause, then empathy enhancement should form a central component of strategies or interventions to promote greater prosocial behaviour.

There are many studies focused on the antisocial behaviour of young people, and these studies typically focus on offences such as theft, violence and substance use (see, for example, Farrington, Loeber, Stouthamer-Loeber, van Kammen, & Schmidt, 1996). While some may consider school bullying a less serious form of "offending", longitudinal research has consistently shown that school bullying is a strong predictor of later criminal offending controlling for other childhood risk factors (Ttofi, Farrington, Loesl, & Loeber, 2011). Bullying, defined as frequent and long-term aggressive behaviours perpetrated by some students on their peers who cannot defend themselves easily (Smith et al., 2002), is one of the most frequently studied antisocial behaviours in schools. Cyberbullying is an emerging type of antisocial behaviour that can be defined as bullying perpetrated through electronic devices (Patchin & Hinduja, 2006). It is important to decrease these problem behaviours given their serious detrimental consequences (see Zych, Farrington, Llorent, & Ttofi, 2017 for a review).

Some studies have found that empathy was related to prosocial behaviours. Among them, two meta-analyses which focused on the bystanders of bullying showed that children with high empathy were more likely to defend a victim of bullying (Nickerson, Aloe, & Werth, 2015; Zych, Ttofi et al., 2019). In addition, research has shown that inducing empathy by presenting children with an emotional story was found to be related to higher levels of cooperation with others (Batson & Moran, 1999).

Research has also shown that low empathy is related to different problematic behaviours. Among them, it was found that offending was related to lower empathy (Jolliffe & Farrington, 2004; van Langen, Wissink, van Vugt, van der Stouwe, & Stams, 2014). Also, a meta-analysis by Zych, Ttofi et al. (2019) showed that the perpetrators of school bullying tended to score lower on measures of empathy. Another meta-analysis concluded that cognitive and affective empathy was also relatively low amongst cyberbullies (Zych, Baldry et al., 2019). Furthermore, a systematic review of meta-analyses of the protective factors against bullying and cyberbullying confirmed these results (Zych, Farrington, & Ttofi, 2019). However, while these results are compelling, they derive from studies typically conducted in the US and UK, so there are other geographic areas where these relations still need to be discovered. Moreover, the number of studies about emerging antisocial behaviours such as cyberbullying are still limited.

A meta-analysis conducted by Teding van Berkhout and Malouff (2016) found that empathy can be successfully increased. This, in turn, might increase the likelihood of prosocial behaviours and decrease the likelihood of antisocial behaviours, although more research on the topic is still needed. To begin this journey, validated instruments and international comparisons regarding the relation between empathy and antisocial behaviours can be very useful. For this reason, the following chapter describes the psychometric properties of the BES in Spain and in Poland, together with the relation between empathy and antisocial behaviours in both countries.

Method

Participants

Participants were selected in both Spanish and Polish Primary and Secondary Schools. Sample selection was performed to maximise the comparability between Poland and Spain. Thus, the age and gender characteristics of the participants in both countries were similar.

The Polish sample included 1,052 students enrolled in four Primary (Grades 4 to 7, $n = 580$) and two Secondary Schools (Grades 2 and 3, $n = 472$) in the Lesser Poland geographic area. Thus, participants were aged 9 to 16 years ($M = 12.53$, $SD = 1.98$), and 54.4% were females. Four schools were located in a big city and two schools were located in a town. All the students had a Polish nationality and were Caucasian.

The Spanish sample included 1,483 Primary (Grades 4 and 5, $n = 598$) and Secondary (Grades 1 to 4, $n = 885$) Education students enrolled in eight schools in two big cities and two towns in the south of Spain. As in the Polish sample, participants were aged 9 to 16 ($M = 12.68$, $SD = 2.17$), with 48.1% of females. Spanish nationality was reported by 97.7% of the participants.

Instruments

Empathy was measured using the Basic Empathy Scale (BES; Jolliffe & Farrington, 2006). For the Spanish sample, the Spanish version, validated by Villadangos Fernández, Errasti Pérez, Amigo Vázquez, Jolliffe, and García-Cueto (2016), was used. The Spanish version of the BES included 20 items answered on a 5-point Likert scale ranging from 1 (totally disagree) to 5 (totally agree). The Affective empathy dimension included 11 items ($\alpha = .70$) and the Cognitive empathy dimension included 9 items ($\alpha = .67$). The first Polish version had the same structure as the original and the Spanish versions, but the final Polish and Spanish versions included only 12 positive-worded items, with six focused on affective empathy and six focused on cognitive empathy. The psychometric properties are described in the results section.

Bullying was measured through the European Bullying Intervention Project Questionnaire (EBIP-Q) (Ortega-Ruiz, Del Rey, & Casas, 2016) that included 14 items focused on victimisation (7 items) and perpetration (7 items) about different bullying behaviours, answered on a 5-point Likert scale that ranged from 1 (no) to 5 (more than once). Students were asked to focus on one school year (2016/2017). This questionnaire showed good Cronbach's alphas in Primary (Spain: α victimisation = .85; α perpetration = .79; Poland: all $\alpha = .85$) and Secondary (Spain: α victimisation = .85; α perpetration = .80; Poland: all $\alpha = .85$) Education. A confirmatory factor analysis was conducted showing a good fit to the data of the original 2-factor structure in Spain (S/B chi-square = 558.05; df = 76; $p < .00$; NFI = .95; NNFI = .94; CFI = .95; RMSEA = .068, 90% CI = .062 −.073) and in Poland (S/B chi-square = 796.23, df = 76, NFI = .94, NNFI = .93, CFI = .94, RMSEA = .09). The perpetration scale was used in this study.

The European Cyberbullying Intervention Project Questionnaire (ECIP-Q) (Del Rey et al., 2015) was used to measure cyberbullying. This instrument includes 11 items about cybervictimisation and 11 items about cyber-perpetration with a 5-point Likert scale ranging from 1 (no) to 5 (more than once). Students were asked to focus on one school year (2016/2017). This questionnaire showed excellent Cronbach's alphas in Spain (Primary α victimisation = .76; α perpetration = .67; Secondary α victimisation = .84, α perpetration = .83) and in Poland (cybervictimisation α = .90 and cyber-perpetration α = .89). The two-factor structure was confirmed in Spain (S/B chi-square = 842.24; df = 208; $p < .001$; CFI = .98; RMSEA = .046) and in Poland (S/B chi-square = 981.92, df = 208, NFI = .98, NNFI = .98, CFI = .98, RMSEA = .06). The perpetration scale was used in this study.

The Self-Reported Antisocial Behavior Questionnaire (SRA; Loeber, Stouthamer-Loeber, van Kammen, & Farrington, 1989) was used to measure different antisocial behaviours. This questionnaire included 32 questions about different antisocial behaviours in the past 6 months answered on a 4-point Likert scale ranging from 1 (*Never*) to 4 (*Yes, more than 3 times*). The original version is divided into five scales including damage (5 items focused on breaking things), stealing (9 items on stealing in different contexts), violence (7 items on physical violence towards different people), substance use (6 items on different substance use such as alcohol and drugs), and status offences (5 items on offences such as cheating or running away from home). The current data showed excellent reliability (Spanish Cronbach's α = .90, Polish α = .94) and an excellent fit to this 5-factor structure (Spanish *S/B* χ^2 = 1243.74; *df* = 454; $p < .001$; *NFI* = .97; *NNFI* = .98; *CFI* = .98; *RMSEA* = .036, *90% CI* = .034 – .039; Polish S/B Chi-square = 1021.44, df = 454, $p < .001$, NFI = .98, NNFI = .99, CFI = .99, RMEA = .044, 90% CI = .040 – .047).

Design and procedure

This study was conducted with a cross-sectional design using a pen-and-paper survey in both Polish and Spanish schools. In Spain, data were collected at the end of the 2016/2017 school year and, in Poland, at the beginning of the 2017/2018 school year. An existing Spanish version of the BES was used (Villadangos et al., 2016). Given that there was no Polish version of the BES, the original English version was translated into Polish by the first author who is a Polish native speaker. This version was then reviewed by the last author who is also a Polish native speaker, and further back-translated into English by an official translation service. Minor differences were found, discussed and resolved.

In both Spain and Poland, participants were selected by convenience and head teachers were invited to have their schools participate. Parental consent was also obtained, and the student's participation was voluntary and anonymous. Students were informed about the aims of this project and asked to fill in the questionnaires. They were informed that they had the right to decline or withdraw from the study at any point. This project met all the national and international ethical standards and was approved by the University of Cordoba Ethics Committee. Questionnaires were completed during the regular classroom hours, which were supervised by senior researchers (first author, last author and team members) without any intervention by the teachers. All the students agreed to participate.

Results

The positive worded item version

Confirmatory Factor Analyses were conducted with EQS 6.2 software with a maximum likelihood robust method based on polychoric correlations. Model fit was tested through the combination of different indices including CFI, NFI (higher values show a better fit, with an excellent fit > 95) and RMSEA (lower values show a better fit, with an excellent fit < .05).

The Polish version of the BES, with the original number of items (i.e. 20), and the original factor structure, showed a poor fit to the data (Primary School S/B chi-square = 794.52, df = 169, $p < .01$, CFI = .69, NFI = .64. RMSEA = .09; Secondary School S/B chi-square = 1528.12, df = 169, $p < .01$, CFI = .66, NFI = .63. RMSEA = .14). Thus, a short version, retaining only the 12 positive worded items, was obtained with a good fit (Primary Education S/B chi-square = 177.14, df = 53, $p < .01$, CFI = .97, NFI = .96, RMSEA = .07; Secondary Education S/B chi-square = 203.02, df = 53, $p < .01$, CFI = .94, NFI = .93, RMSEA = .08; total S/B chi-square = 281.48, df = 53, CFI = .97, NFI = .96, RMSEA = 0.07). Details about the item reduction process and psychometric properties are reported elsewhere (Zych, Farrington, Nasaescu, Jolliffe, & Twardowska-Staszek, 2020).

The Spanish data showed an acceptable, but relatively weak fit to the original 20-item structure, with the two factors of cognitive and affective empathy (S/B chi-square = 1622.75, df = 169, $p < .01$, CFI = .85, NFI = .84. RMSEA = .08). To maximise the comparability with the Polish sample and with the aim of identifying a better fit, a short version with 12 positive worded items, identical to the Polish version, was tested. This short version showed a much better fit to the data (S/B chi-square = 232.19, df = 53, $p < .01$, CFI = .98, NFI = .97, RMSEA = .05). Thus, both the Polish and the Spanish versions showed an improved fit with 12 positive worded items (6 for affective and 6 for cognitive empathy). This model is shown in figure 14.1.

As shown in Table 14.1, there were gender differences found for both affective and cognitive empathy in Poland and Spain. Girls scored higher than boys in both empathy subscales and both Spanish and Polish samples. All differences were statistically significant. Table 14.2 shows that students in Primary schools scored higher than those in Secondary schools in both affective and cognitive empathy in both Poland and Spain. All the differences were statistically significant, except for the difference between Primary and Secondary school in Spain in cognitive empathy.

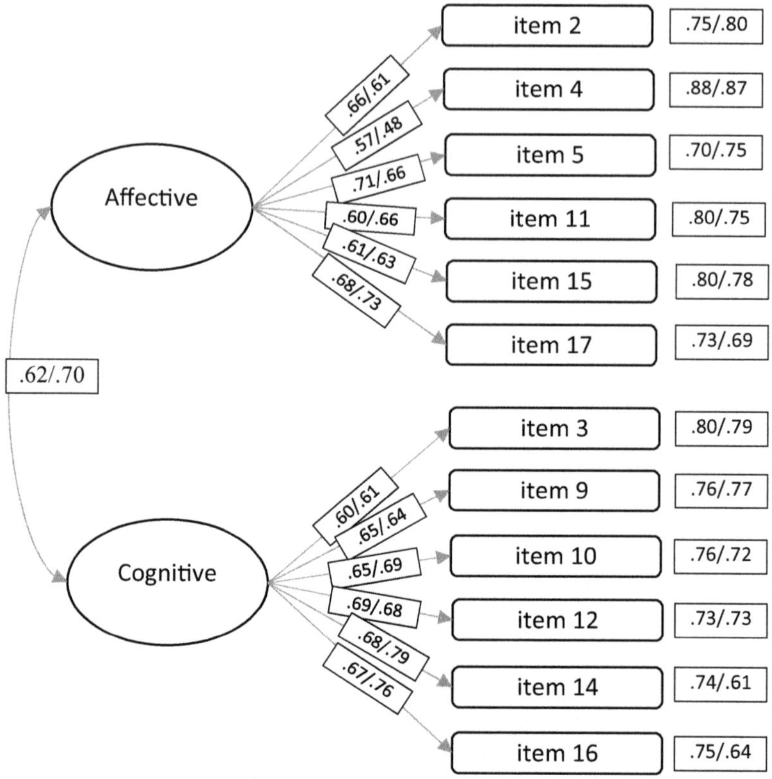

Figure 14.1 Confirmatory factor analysis of the short version of the BES including Spanish and Polish data

Note: Spanish/Polish data

Table 14.1 Gender differences in affective and cognitive empathy in Polish and Spanish samples

	Polish		*t*	*Spanish*		*t*
	Boys *M (SD)*	*Girls*		*Boys*	*Girls*	
Affective	16.70 (5.18)	20.35 (4.80)	11.24**	18.41 (5.62)	21.20 (5.11)	9.66**
Cognitive	21.32 (5.31)	23.22 (4.36)	6.00**	23.80 (4.47)	25.01 (3.97)	5.34**

Empathy and antisocial behaviours in Polish and Spanish participants

Table 14.3 shows the Pearson correlations between affective and cognitive empathy measured using the newly developed scales, and the different antisocial behaviours for both Polish and Spanish participants. As expected, low scores in

Table 14.2 Differences between primary and secondary schools in affective and cognitive empathy in Polish and Spanish samples

	Polish		*t*	*Spanish*		*t*
	Primary M (SD)	*Secondary*		*Primary*	*Secondary*	
Affective	19.12 (5.26)	18.21 (5.27)	2.66**	20.67 (5.43)	19.14 (5.54)	5.13**
Cognitive	22.83 (5.06)	21.85 (4.66)	3.14**	24.66 (4.44)	24.20 (4.14)	1.94

Note: In Spain, Primary school children are aged 9 to 12 and Secondary school students are aged 12 to 16. In Poland, primary school children are aged 9 to 13 and secondary 13 to 15.

$^{**}p < .01$

both affective and cognitive empathy were related to higher scores for all types of antisocial behaviours in both Poland and Spain, although not all of the relations were statistically significant. Interestingly, the strongest association for both the Polish and Spanish sample for low cognitive empathy was to Bullying perpetration ($r = -.154$ Polish, $r = -.126$ Spanish). The strongest association with affective empathy was with substance use for the Polish sample ($r = -.118$), and Damage ($r = -.148$) for the Spanish sample.

Conclusions

Empathy has been widely studied in different geographic areas and contexts. Nevertheless, research about empathy is not equally developed across the world. Studies about empathy in Eastern European countries are still lacking. Thus, the current chapter described the psychometric properties of the BES in Poland, tested a short version of the BES in Poland and in Spain, and studied the relation between empathy and different antisocial behaviours including bullying, cyberbullying, damage, stealing, violence, status offences and substance use.

First, the original factor structure of the BES was tested with the Polish and Spanish datasets. The original model did not show an acceptable fit, and therefore a short version was developed and tested. Both the Spanish and Polish data showed the best fit for a 12-item positively worded version of the BES. In both of the samples, the factor loadings were high and similar amongst the items. Thus, this short version was considered robust as it showed the best psychometric properties in both samples. Given that not all of the validation studies have shown an acceptable fit of the original 20-item structure (e.g. Geng et al., 2012; Heynen et al., 2016; Pechorro et al., 2015; Sánchez-Pérez et al., 2014), a short version such as the one developed in this study could potentially show a better fit across contexts, and therefore be very useful for comparative studies. Nevertheless, more research is needed to confirm this.

As found in previous studies (see, for example, Jolliffe & Farrington, 2006, and other chapters in this book), girls usually score higher than boys on measures of empathy. This was also found in the current study in both the Spanish and Polish samples. Also, participants from primary schools were found to score higher

Table 14.3 Correlations between affective and cognitive empathy and different types of antisocial behaviours

	1	*2*	*3*	*4*	*5*	*6*	*7*	*8*	*9*
1. Affective empathy	1	.553**	−.114**	−.071*	−.074	−.094*	−.088*	−.036	−.118**
2. Cognitive empathy	.457**	1	−.154**	−.149**	−.130**	−.131**	−.139**	−.143**	−.112**
3. Bullying perpetration	−.100**	−.126**	1	.658**	.357**	.331**	.325**	.316**	.287**
4. Cyberperpetration	−.070**	−.070**	.464**	1	.409**	.338**	.321**	.324**	.338**
5. Damage	−.148**	−.123**	.371**	.417**	1	.803**	.749**	.666**	.576**
6. Stealing	−.091**	−.065*	.370**	.377**	.680**	1	.825**	.759**	.650**
7. Violence	−.095**	−.055*	.448**	.352**	.556**	.615**	1	.749**	.613**
8. Status offences	−.103**	−.058*	.305**	.414**	.582**	.649**	.533**	1	.643**
9. Substance use	−.083**	−.026	.226**	.268**	.451**	.459**	.380**	.597**	1

Note: Polish above the diagonal, Spanish below the diagonal

$^{**}p < .01$, $^{*}p < .05$

on the measure of empathy compared to participants in secondary schools. It is possible that younger children have a more positive perception of their empathy compared to adolescents, who might be more critical and doubtful about their personal characteristics.

As expected, high empathy was found to be related to less antisocial behaviour in both the Polish and Spanish samples. Higher scores of each type of antisocial behaviour were related to higher scores in other forms of antisocial behaviour. Also, high scores in all of the forms of antisocial behaviours were related to low empathy. Thus, it is possible that promoting empathy in intervention programmes could be a useful tool to decrease antisocial behaviours. Future studies in different geographic areas, including Spain and Poland, could be useful to confirm this.

With some limitations, such as the use of self-reports only, and samples selected by convenience, this study advances knowledge about the psychometric properties of the BES and the relation between empathy and antisocial behaviour in an understudied population. It shows that the BES is a robust measure which can be used for comparative studies between countries. This chapter might also contribute to research, policy and practice for the prevention of antisocial behaviours, including face to face antisocial behaviours and emerging problems such as cyberbullying.

References

Albeiro, P., Matricardi, G., Speltri, D., & Toso, D. (2009). The assessment of empathy in adolescence: A contribution to the Italian validation of "the basic empathy scale". *Journal of Adolescence*, *32*, 393–408.

Basto-Pereira, M., & Farrington, D. P. (2021). The basic empathy scale: Psychometric properties and contributions to the understanding of antisocial behaviour. In D. Jolliffe & D. P. Farrington (Eds.), *Empathy versus offending, aggression and bullying: Advancing knowledge using the basic empathy scale*. Abingdon: Routledge.

Batson, C. D., & Moran, T. (1999). Empathy-induced altruism in a prisoner's dilemma. *European Journal of Social Psychology*, *29*, 909–924.

Cavojova, V., Sirota, M., & Belovicova, Z. (2012). Slovak validation of the Basic Empathy Scale in pre-adolescents. *Studia Psychologica*, *54*, 195–208.

D'Ambrosio, F., Olivier, M., Didon, D., & Besche, C. (2009). The basic empathy scale: A French validation of a measure of empathy in youth. *Personality and Individual Differences*, *46*, 160–165.

Del Rey, R., Casas, J. A., Ortega-Ruiz, R., Schultze-Krumbholz, A., Scheithauer, H., Smith, P., . . . Guarini, A. (2015). Structural validation and cross-cultural robustness of the European Cyberbullying intervention Project Questionnaire. *Computers in Human Behavior*, *50*, 141–147.

Farrington, D. P., Loeber, R., Stouthamer-Loeber, M., van Kammen, W. B., & Schmidt, L. (1996). Self-reported delinquency and a combined delinquency seriousness scale based on boys, mothers, and teachers: Concurrent and predictive validity for African-Americans and Caucasians. *Criminology*, *34*(4), 493–517.

Geng, Y., Xia, D., & Qin, B. (2012). The basic empathy scale: A Chinese validation of a measure of empathy in adolescents. *Child Psychiatry and Human Development*, *43*, 499–510.

Herrera-López, M., Gómez-Ortiz, O., Ortega-Ruiz, R., Jolliffe, D., & Romera, E. M. (2017). Suitability of a three-dimensional model to measure empathy and its relationship with social and normative adjustment in Spanish adolescents: A cross-sectional study. *BMJ Open*, *7*, e015347.

Heynen, E. E., van der Helm, G. P., Stams, G. M., & Korebrits, A. M. (2016). Measuring empathy in a German youth prison: A validation of the German version of the basic empathy scale (BES) in a sample of incarcerated juvenile offenders. *Journal of Forensic Psychology Practice*, *16*, 336–346.

Jolliffe, D., & Farrington, D. P. (2004). Empathy and offending: A systematic review and meta-analysis. *Aggression and Violent Behavior*, *9*, 441–476. doi:10.1016/j.avb.2003.03.001

Jolliffe, D., & Farrington, D. P. (2006). Development and validation of the basic empathy scale. *Journal of Adolescence*, *29*, 589–611.

Loeber, R., Stouthamer-Loeber, M., van Kammen, W., & Farrington, D. (1989). Development of a new measure of self-reported antisocial behavior for young children: Prevalence and reliability. In M. W. Klein (Ed.), *Cross-national research in self-reported crime and delinquency* (pp. 203–225). London: Kluwer.

Nickerson, A. B., Aloe, A. M., & Werth, J. M. (2015). The relation of empathy and defending in bullying: A meta-analytic investigation. *School Psychology Review*, *44*, 372–390.

Ortega-Ruiz, R., Del Rey, R., & Casas, J. A. (2016). Evaluar el bullying y el ciberbullying: Validación espanola del EBIP-Q y del ECIP-Q Evaluation of bullying and cyberbullying: Spanish validation of EBIP-Q and ECIP-Q. *Psicología Educativa*, *22*, 71–79.

Patchin, J. W., & Hinduja, S. (2006). Bullies move beyond the schoolyard: A preliminary look at cyberbullying. *Youth Violence and Juvenile Justice*, *4*, 148–169.

Pechorro, P., Ray, J. V., Salas-Wright, C. P., Maroco, J., & Goncalves, R. A. (2015). Adaptation of the basic empathy scale among a Portuguese sample of incarcerated juvenile offenders. *Psychology, Crime & Law*, *21*, 699–714.

Sánchez-Pérez, N., Fuentes, L. J., Jolliffe, D., & González-Salinas, C. (2014). Assessing children's empathy through a Spanish adaptation of the basic empathy scale: Parent's and child's report forms. *Frontiers in Psychology*, *5*, 1438.

Smith, P. K., Cowie, H., Olafsson, R. F., & Liefooghe, A. P. (2002). Definitions of bullying: A comparison of terms used, and age and gender differences, in a fourteen-country international comparison. *Child Development*, *73*, 1119–1133.

Suárez-Alvarez, J., Pedrosa, I., Lozano Fernández, L. M., García-Cueto, E., Cuesta, M., & Muñiz, J. (2018). Using reversed items in Likert scales: A questionable practice. *Psicothema*, *30*, 149–158.

Teding van Berkhout, E., & Malouff, J. M. (2016). The efficacy of empathy training: A meta-analysis of randomized controlled trials. *Journal of Counseling Psychology*, *63*, 32–41.

Ttofi, M. M., Farrington, D. P., Loesl, F., & Loeber, R. (2011). The predictive efficiency of school bullying versus later offending: A systematic/meta-analytic review of longitudinal studies. *Criminal Behaviour and Mental Health*, *21*, 80–89.

van Langen, M. A., Wissink, I. B., van Vugt, E. S., van der Stouwe, T., & Stams, G. J. J. M. (2014). The relation between empathy and offending: A meta-analysis. *Aggression and Violent Behavior*, *19*, 179–189.

Villadangos Fernández, J. M., Errasti Pérez, J. M., Amigo Vázquez, I., Jolliffe, D., & García-Cueto, E. (2016). Characteristics of Empathy in young people measured by the Spanish validation of the Basic Empathy Scale. *Psicothema*, *28*, 323–329.

Zych, I., Baldry, A. C., Llorent, V. J., & Farrington, D. P. (2019). Are children involved in cyberbullying low on empathy? A systematic review and meta-analysis of research on empathy in different cyberbullying roles. *Aggression and Violent Behavior*, *45*, 83–97.

Zych, I., Farrington, D. P., Llorent, V. J., & Ttofi, M. M. (2017). *Protecting children against bullying and its consequences*. New York: Springer.

Zych, I., Farrington, D. P., Nasaescu, E., Jolliffe, D., & Twardowska-Staszek, E. (2020). Psychometric properties of the Basic Empathy Scale in Polish children and adolescents. *Current Psychology*, Online First.

Zych, I., Farrington, D. P., & Ttofi, M. M. (2019). Protective factors against bullying and cyberbullying: A systematic review of meta-analyses. *Aggression and Violent Behavior*, *45*, 4–19.

Zych, I., Ttofi, M. M., & Farrington, D. P. (2019). Empathy and callous – unemotional traits in different bullying roles: A systematic review and meta-analysis. *Trauma, Violence, & Abuse*, *20*, 3–21.

15 Risk factors for cyberbullying

The mediating role of empathy in adolescents in Italy in a one-year follow-up study

Anna Sorrentino, Anna Costanza Baldry†, Darrick Jolliffe, and David P. Farrington

Introduction

Because of the proliferation of devices to access the internet, and even more since smartphones have become readily available, the method and forms of communication between young people have progressively been transformed. Besides its many positive aspects, this new electronic way of communicating can lead to increased opportunities for antisocial behaviour for some, and considerable interpersonal and health problems for others (Baldry, Sorrentino, & Farrington, 2019; Gámez-Guadix, Orue, Smith, & Calvete, 2013; Hemphill & Heerde, 2014; Kowalski et al., 2014; Kowalski & Limber, 2013; Kubiszewski, Fontaine, Potard, & Auzoult, 2015; Wang, Nansel, & Iannotti, 2011). In extreme cases, the impact of this negative online behaviour can even lead to victims' suicidal ideation or suicide (van Geel, Vedder, & Tanilon, 2014). This so-called cyberbullying is a problem affecting children and youngsters all around the world (WHO, 2010).

The causes, correlates and consequences of school bullying have been the subject of considerable research efforts for well over four decades, but cyberbullying is a relatively new phenomenon. Cyberbullying is typically defined as a collection of acts, such as sending or posting aggressive or offensive electronic digital messages by a young person (or more than one young person), with the intention of causing harm to another (Li, 2007; Patchin & Hinduja, 2006; Smith et al., 2008; Tokunaga, 2010). There has been a recent increase in research dedicated to attempting to understand these behaviours (Kowalski, Giumetti, Schroeder, & Lattanner, 2014), and while there is not a single "cause" of cyberbullying (Baldry, Farrington, & Sorrentino, 2016), a few factors that relate to a higher probability of perpetrating cyberbullying have been identified. These include being male, lower levels of parental supervision, and the absence of prevention programmes in schools (Baldry et al., 2015; Gaffney, Farrington, Espelage & Ttofi, 2019; Kowalski et al., 2014; Zych et al., 2019). Among individual characteristics, low levels of empathy have been proposed to be risk factors for cyberbullying involvement (Ang & Goh, 2010; Baldry et al., 2015; Zych, Baldry, Farrington, & Llorent, 2018; Zych, Ttofi, & Farrington, 2016). Empathy is typically defined as having both cognitive (i.e. ability to understand the emotions of another person), and affective (i.e. ability to experience the emotions of another person) components.

Early research on the relationship between cognitive and affective empathy and cyberbullying has produced some inconclusive results. For example, some studies reported that cyberbullying perpetration was related to low empathy (e.g. Brewer & Kerslake, 2015; Del Rey et al., 2016), while others did not find any significant relationship between cyberbullying perpetration and levels of empathy (Garaigordobil & Martínez-Valderrey, 2015; Pettalia et al., 2013). However, in their systematic review and meta-analysis of 25 studies, Zych et al. (2018) found that cyberbullies tended to score low on both cognitive and affective empathy. Furthermore, this relationship was identified even when controlling for a number of important covariates.

In addition to this important finding, Zych et al. (2018) also identified some important gaps in the cyberbullying – empathy literature. One of these was that there were few longitudinal studies which examined the relationship between empathy and later cyberbullying. In the absence of longitudinal studies, it is not possible to determine whether low empathy may be a cause of cyberbullying, or whether cyberbullying may result in lower empathy. It is important to understand the direction of this relationship, especially in light of the many prevention programmes which include empathy enhancing components. Another limitation noted by Zych et al. (2018) was that few previous studies disentangled the potential gender differences between empathy and cyberbullying. While some studies (e.g. Del Rey et al., 2016) found that both cognitive and affective empathy negatively predicted cyberbullying and that the effect of empathy on cyberbullying did not change between males and females (controlling for age and nationality), other research has noted differences in the empathy levels of male and female cyberbullies (Zych et al., 2018).

One exception is the study by Festl (2016), conducted in Germany. In this study, the role of empathy and gender on cyberbullying perpetration was examined in a longitudinal study. The results showed that cyberbullying perpetration was negatively related to empathy for both males and females. However, this relationship was not independent of the additional risk factors measured earlier. These risk factors included cyberbullying cognitions, age, previous in-person bullying, previous cyberbullying, media influence, social position and peer influence.

This study aims to fill an important gap in the literature by examining the relationship between cyberbullying, empathy and gender and exploring potential causal relationships using a longitudinal study. The key research questions to be explored are:

1 Do males and females differ in their level or types of cyberbullying?
2 Do males and females differ in their levels of cognitive and/or affective empathy?
3 Does gender mediate the relationship between affective and/or cognitive empathy and later cyberbullying?

Mediation is one of the best methods to disentangle the possible relationship between different risk and protective factors and cyberbullying (Memon, Cheah, Ramayah, Ting, & Chuah, 2018; Pieters, 2017; VanderWeele, 2015; Rucker, Preacher, Tormala, & Petty, 2011).

Method

Participants

The initial sample consisted of 759 students randomly recruited from five schools located in Southern Italy. Overall, 385 students were included in the analyses as they had fully completed the questionnaires from both the initial phase of the research (T1) and the follow-up one year later (T2). The impact of attrition was examined by comparing the demographic features and prevalence of key features of the two samples and cyberbullying for those in the initial sample and final sample. The results did not show any significant differences in any of the variables investigated (see Table 15.1). The main cause of attrition (for just over 300 students) was the student's errors in completing their ID code in the second wave of data collection (see later).

Overall, 47% of those included in the final sample were males and 53% were females, and the age range of this sample was between 10 and 17 years old ($M = 13.23$, $SD = 1.40$). Just over 19% of the students reported at least one profile on a social network, while only 10.3% of these students reported that they personally knew at least half of their online contacts. About 41% of the students reported spending an average of between 2 and 4 hours a day online (see Table 15.1 for details).

Procedure

Approval from the University Departmental Ethics committee was obtained for the procedure, and consent from the custodial adults and the participating students was obtained before the data collection. All participants filled in the online

Table 15.1 Descriptive statistics for the sample

	Overall (n = 759)	*Matched (n = 385)*	*Min*	*Max*
Gender (% male)	47.9	47.0	0	1
Age	$M = 12.20$ ($SD = 1.46$)	$M = 13.23$ ($SD = 1.40$)	10	17
Online between 2 and 4 hours a day	37.9	41.0	0	4
Presence of at least one social network profile	29.1	19.3	0	2
Personally know half or fewer of their "friends" on social network	6.6	10.3	0	4
Experienced cyberbullying at least once	13.2	15.9	0	20
Internet addiction	$M = 10.74$ ($SD = 4.40$)	$M = 11.16$ ($SD = 5.01$)	0	20
Level of cognitive empathy	$M = 9.82$ ($SD = 4.75$)	$M = 10.40$ ($SD = 5.24$)	0	29
Level of affective empathy	$M = 15.21$ ($SD = 6.85$)	$M = 15.88$ ($SD = 7.45$)	0	37

anonymous Tabby Improved Checklist (Baldry, Blaya, & Farrington, 2018) (available at www.tabby.eu), initially in November 2015 (T1) and then again after one year (October 2016, T2). Students were recruited in their own classes, and if they gave consent, class by class they went with their teachers to their school's Computer Technology Room (which all participating schools had), to complete the online questionnaire. To facilitate confidential and therefore more honest responding, each student sat in front of their own PC which was connected to the website questionnaire page. All students were provided with a standardised briefing before commencing questionnaire completion.

Students were instructed to complete the online, anonymous self-report questionnaire reflecting on their own personal online experiences and their use of new communication technologies. They were also assured about the anonymity of the data that they were providing and assured that no one but the researchers would have access to the responses that, once provided, would automatically go into a database for subsequent aggregated analysis.

At this point students were instructed on how to generate an individualised ID code which would allow them to anonymously match their answers provided at T1 with those provided at the point of the follow-up data collection T2. The instructions provided to students were:

> Please insert your personal code which will be the two numbers of the day of your birth, for example 03 if you were born on the 3rd, followed by the last two letters of your surname, and lastly the final 3 numbers of your mobile or home phone number. For example, 03BA362, would indicate a person with the last name Barbara born on the 3rd, with mobile phone number: ++362.

Unfortunately, many students did not follow these instructions consistently at both TI and T2, resulting in the attrition. Students completed the questionnaires in the presence of both a researcher and a classroom teacher. After completing the questionnaire, all students returned to their classes.

Measures

The online Tabby Improved Checklist (Baldry, Blaya, & Farrington, 2018) was developed by analysing the results of a review of the international literature about the risk factors for youngsters' involvement in cyberbullying. Additionally, the checklist asked about the granular detail of these concepts to facilitate an examination of how these risk factors might operate and/or interact at different levels according to an ecological theoretical framework (Baldry et al., 2015). The predictive ability of the risk factors, based on previous analyses of the questionnaire, was also used to inform what was measured, particularly for the individual risk factors for cyberbullying (Baldry, Blaya, & Farrington, 2018; Baldry, Farrington, Blaya, & Sorrentino, 2018).

The Tabby Improved Checklist consisted of 12 scales and a total of 130 items. These included socio-demographic questions, as well as questions about the type of use of the internet (e.g. the number of hours spent online), the presence of a social network profile, and direct knowledge of those who they were in contact with online, as well as other interpersonal and personality dimensions.

For the purposes of the current study, the following dimensions were examined:

(i) *Cyberbullying* was assessed using the scale developed by Willard (2007), which included the following 5 items measuring different types of cyberbullying: 'I sent mean, cruel, or threatening messages online to someone I knew', 'I humiliated someone online by sending or posting offensive material or cruel messages with the aim to damage his/her reputation or friendships', 'I pretended to be someone else, created a fake profile in order to send or post damaging messages about another person', 'I disclosed private information or images online without that person's consent', and 'I was actively engaged in excluding someone from an online group' (α = .72). Students rated their experiences of cyberbullying on 5-point Likert scales ranging from 0 = "it has never happened in this period" to 4 = "it happened several times a week".
(ii) *Empathy* was assessed using the Basic Empathy Scale, which consists of 20 items assessing both cognitive and affective empathy on a 5-point Likert scale ranging from 1 = "Strongly disagree" to 5 = "Strongly agree" (Albiero, Matricardi, Speltri, & Toso, 2009; Jolliffe & Farrington, 2006), (total α = .85; cognitive empathy α = .71; affective empathy α = .65).

Results

To measure participants' involvement in cyberbullying we adopted as classification criterion of once or more often in the previous 6 months. The results can be seen in Table 15.2. For example, 13.3% of the male sample reported so-called "Flaming" (i.e. sending or posting hostile, threatening and mean messages online), compared to 3.9% of females. This was equivalent to an odds ratio (OR) of 3.8

Table 15.2 Gender differences in cyberbullying and empathy

	Male (%)	*Female (%)*	*OR (95% CI)*
Flaming	13.3	3.9	3.8 (1.6–8.6)**
Denigration	6.1	1.0	6.5(1.4–29.9)*
Impersonation	0.6	1.0	0.6 (0.1–6.2)
Outing	5.5	1.5	3.9 (1.1–.14.5)*
Exclusion	12.2	6.9	1.9 (0.9–3.8)†
Total Cyberbullying	23.8	9.8	1.5 (1.1–1.9)**
Total empathy	*M* = 22.12 (*SD* = 8.75)	*M* = 29.01 (*SD* = 9.64)	1.08 (1.06–1.11)***
Cognitive empathy	*M* = 9.05 (*SD* = 4.09)	*M* = 11.11 (*SD* = 4.77)	1.11 (1.06–1.17)***
Affective empathy	*M* = 13.06 (*SD* = 6.03)	*M* = 17.90 (*SD* = 6.61)	1.13 (1.09–1.17)***

Notes: † $p < .10$ * $p < .05$, ** $p < .01$, *** $p < .001$.

(1.6–8.6), suggesting that males were significantly more likely to be involved in flaming. The odds ratio is a measure of effect centred around 1.0, and as a rule of thumb an odds ratio of 2.0 (or 0.5) is considered an important difference (Cohen, 1996). Males were also significantly more likely to report being involved in "Outing" (i.e. disclosing online private information or images without the person's consent), and "Denigration" (i.e. humiliating someone online by sending or posting offensive materials or cruel messages with the aim to damage his/her reputation or friendships) than females. Males appeared somewhat more likely than females to be involved in "Exclusion" (i.e. actively engaging in excluding someone from an online group), but there were no significant male-female differences in reporting "Impersonation" (i.e. pretending to be someone else, by creating a fake profile in order to send or post damaging messages about another person). Overall, just under a quarter of males reported cyberbullying, compared to about 10% of females (OR = 1.5, CI = 1.1–1.9).

The bottom of Table 15.2 shows the results for the comparison of empathy for males and females. Males scored an average of about 22 on the overall empathy scale ($SD = 8.8$) compared to females who scored an average of 29 ($SD = 9.6$). This difference was statistically significant with an odds ratio of 1.08 (1.06–1.11). The difference between males and females appeared to be greater for affective empathy ($OR = 1.13$), than for cognitive empathy ($OR = 1.11$), but in both cases males had significantly lower empathy than females.

Individual risk factors for cyberbullying

The associations between the individual risk factors measured at baseline (T1) and students' involvement in cyberbullying after one year (T2) were investigated. The results showed that being male ($r = .14$, $p < .01$), previous involvement in cyberbullying ($r = .21$, $p < .01$), and low levels of cognitive ($r = .20$, $p < .01$) and affective ($r = .17$, $p < .01$) empathy were significant risk factors for cyberbullying after one year (T2). No significant associations were found between the number of hours spent online a day ($r = .05$, n.s.), having at least one social network profile ($r = .002$, n.s.), and direct knowledge of online contacts ($r = .04$, n.s.) and later cyberbullying at T2.

Mediational model of cognitive and affective empathy and cyberbullying

To test whether gender differences in cyberbullying were mediated by low levels of cognitive empathy, we adopted a regression approach (Baron & Kenny, 1986). Three multiple regression analyses were conducted in order to examine the mediator relationships.

The model and results can be seen in Figure 15.1. Gender was significantly associated with low levels of cognitive empathy at baseline, and also significantly influenced involvement in cyberbullying after one year. Low levels of cognitive empathy predicted cyberbullying involvement at T2.

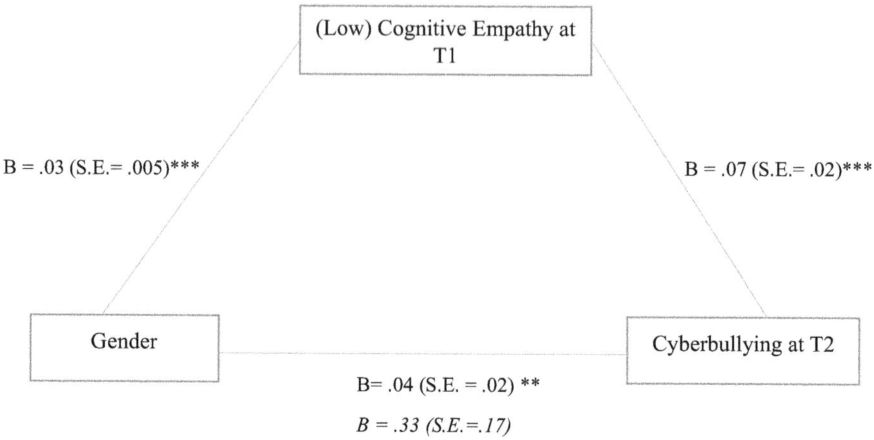

Figure 15.1 Mediation model for cognitive empathy.

Notes: Gender 0 = female; 1 = male. For low Cognitive Empathy answers ranged from 0 = high levels of cognitive empathy to 29 = low levels of cognitive empathy.

The italicised coefficient (.33) is the effect after controlling for the mediator variable.

Sobel Test Z = 2.69, *p* = .007; Bootstrap 95%: LLCI: .0059; ULCI: .0956

Moreover, when gender and cognitive empathy were simultaneously entered as potential predictors of cyberbullying, the effect of gender on cyberbullying involvement in T2 was non-significant, indicating that the association between gender and cyberbullying was mediated by low levels of cognitive empathy at baseline. A Sobel test ($Z = 2.69$, $p = .007$) confirmed the existence of a mediation.

The same approach was adopted to test whether the gender differences in cyberbullying involvement were mediated by low levels of affective empathy (see Figure 15.2). Again, gender was significantly associated with low levels of affective empathy at baseline and also significantly associated with involvement in cyberbullying after one year. Low levels of affective empathy predicted cyberbullying involvement at T2.

When gender and affective empathy were simultaneously entered as predictors, the effect of gender on cyberbullying involvement one year later was not significant. This indicated that the association between gender and cyberbullying was mediated by low levels of affective empathy at baseline. A Sobel test ($Z = 2.40$, $p = .02$) confirmed the existence of a mediation.

Discussion

Cyberbullying is a serious problem affecting children and young people from around the world (Baldry et al., 2016; Zych, Ortega-Ruiz, & Del Rey, 2015). Developing a fuller understanding of the nature and forms of cyberbullying, particularly with regard to gender differences, as well as potential risk factors for

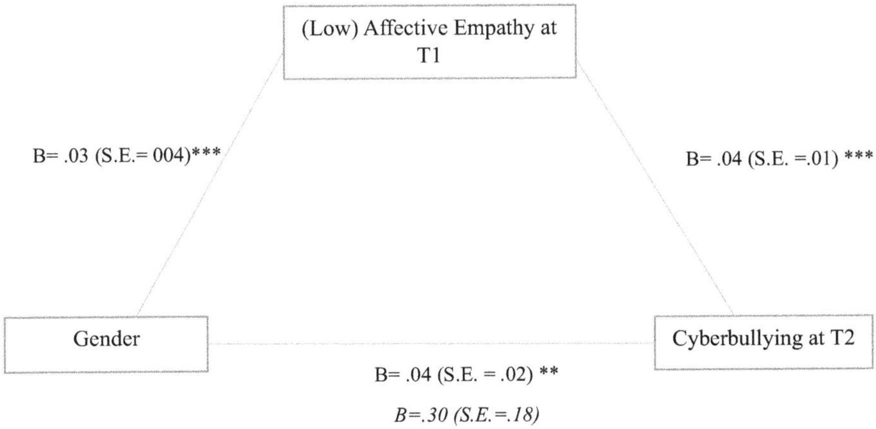

Figure 15.2 Mediation model for affective empathy.

Notes: Gender 0 = female; 1 = male. For low Affective Empathy answers ranged from 0 = high levels of affective empathy to = 34 low levels of affective empathy.

The italicised coefficient (.30) is the effect after controlling for the mediator variable.

Sobel Test $Z = 2.40$ $p = .02$; Bootstrap 95%: LLCI:.0173; ULCI: .0737

cyberbullying, is useful in the development of anti-cyberbullying programmes. Even if the results of the evaluations of existing programmes to reduce cyberbullying have been encouraging (Gaffney, Farrington, Espelage, & Ttofi, 2019), greater and more specific knowledge could help these programmes to become more targeted in their ability to prevent and/or reduce this harmful form of antisocial behaviour (Zych et al., 2018).

The present study was based on a longitudinal study of cyberbullying amongst a sample of several hundred school-aged young people in Italy, and it, examined forms of cyberbullying for males and females as well as the relation between cognitive and affective empathy and cyberbullying one year later. The results showed that, overall, males were more likely to be involved in cyberbullying than females, and this was true of "Flaming", "Denigration", and "Outing", all of which are direct forms of cyberbullying. Interestingly, however, while not statistically significant, it appeared that females may have been more likely than males to be involved in the form of cyberbullying "Impersonation", or pretending to be someone else, by creating a fake profile in order to send or post damaging messages about another person. Future research should examine whether these potential gender differences are replicable, but this appears similar to the results of studies of more traditional bullying in which males have typically been found to be more involved in direct forms of bullying (e.g. physical bullying), while females have typically been found to be more involved in indirect types (e.g. rumour spreading; Jolliffe & Farrington, 2011). This study also found that males and females differed in their levels of empathy, with females having much higher cognitive and affective empathy. These gender differences in empathy have been found in numerous previous studies (e.g. Davis, 1983; Jolliffe & Farrington, 2006).

While gender differences in cyberbullying and empathy may well have been identified in previous research, this study is the first of which we are aware which demonstrated that low levels of cognitive and affective empathy were related to cyberbullying one year later. In addition, mediation analyses were used to disentangle the potential relationships between empathy, gender and later cyberbullying. Conducted separately for cognitive and affective empathy, the results suggested that low cognitive empathy and low affective empathy mediated the relationship between gender and later cyberbullying. This suggests that males' greater prevalence of cyberbullying is at least partly, explained by males significantly lower levels of empathy.

These results, consistent with those of much previous research (i.e. Ang & Goh, 2010; Zych et al., 2018), highlight the importance of including cognitive and affective empathy training modules in interventions designed to prevent or reduce cyberbullying, particularly amongst males.

References

Albiero, P., Matricardi, G., Speltri, D., & Toso, D. (2009). The assessment of empathy in adolescence: A contribution to the Italian validation of the "basic empathy scale". *Journal of Adolescence, 32*(2), 393–408. doi:10.1016/j.adolescence .2008.01.001

Ang, R. P., & Goh, D. H. (2010). Cyberbullying among adolescents: The role of affective and cognitive empathy, and gender. *Child Psychiatry and Human Development, 41*(4), 387–397. doi:10.1007/s10578-010-0176-3

Baldry, A. C., Blaya, C., & Farrington, D. P. (Eds.). (2018). *International perspectives on cyberbullying: Prevalence, risk factors and interventions*. London: Palgrave Macmillan.

Baldry, A. C., Farrington, D. P., Blaya, C., & Sorrentino, A. (2018). The Tabby online project: The threat assessment of bullying behaviour online approach. In A. C. Baldry, C. Blaya, & D. P. Farrington (Eds.), *International perspectives on cyberbullying: Prevalence, risk factors and interventions* (pp. 25–36). London: Palgrave Macmillan.

Baldry, A. C., Farrington, D. P., & Sorrentino, A. (2015). Am I at risk of cyberbullying? A narrative review and conceptual framework for research on risk of cyberbullying and cybervictimization: The risk and needs assessment approach. *Aggression and Violent Behavior, 23*, 36–51. doi:10.1016/j.avb.2015.05.014

Baldry, A. C., Farrington, D. P., & Sorrentino, A. (2016). Bullying and cyberbullying among youngsters: A pattern of disruptive behavior. *Psicologia Educativa, 22*, 19–26. doi:10.1016/j.pse.2016.02.001

Baldry, A. C., Sorrentino, A., & Farrington, D. P. (2019). Cyberbullying and cybervictimization versus parental supervision, monitoring and control of adolescents' online activities. *Children and Youth Services Review, 96*, 302–307. doi:10.1016/j.childyouth.2018.11.058

Baron, R. M., & Kenny, D. A. (1986). The moderator-mediator variable distinction in social psychological research: Conceptual, strategic, and statistical considerations. *Journal of Personality and Social Psychology, 51*, 1173–1182. doi:10.1037/0022-3514.51.6.1173

Brewer, G., & Kerslake, J. (2015). Cyberbullying, self-esteem, empathy and loneliness. *Computers in Human Behavior, 48*, 255–260. doi:10.1016/j.chb.2015.01.073

Cohen, P. (1996). Childhood risks for young adult symptoms of personality disorder: Method and substance. *Multivariate Behavioral Research*, *3*, 121–148. doi:10.1207/s15327906mbr3101_7

Davis, M. H. (1983). The effects of dispositional empathy on emotional reactions and helping: A multidimensional approach. *Journal of Personality*, *51*(2), 167–184. doi:10.1111/j.1467-6494.1983.tb00860.x

Del Rey, R., Lazuras, L., Casas, J. A., Barkoukis, V., Ortega-Ruiz, R., & Tsorbatzoudis, H. (2016). Does empathy predict (cyber) bullying perpetration, and how do age, gender and nationality affect this relationship? *Learning and Individual Differences*, *45*, 275–281. doi:10.1016/j. lindif.2015.11.021

Festl, R. (2016). Perpetrators on the internet: Analyzing individual and structural explanation factors of cyberbullying in school context. *Computers in Human Behavior*, *59*, 237–248. doi:10.1016/j.chb.2016.02.017

Gaffney, H., Farrington, D. P., Espelage, D. L., & Ttofi, M. M. (2019). Are cyberbullying intervention and prevention programs effective? A systematic and meta-analytical review. *Aggression and Violent Behavior*, *45*, 134–153. doi:10.1016/j.avb.2018.07.002

Gámez-Guadix, M., Orue, I., Smith, P. K., & Calvete, E. (2013). Longitudinal and reciprocal relations of cyberbullying with depression, substance use, and problematic internet use among adolescents. *Journal of Adolescent Health*, *53*(4), 446–452. doi:10.1016/j. jadohealth.2013.03.030

Garaigordobil, M., & Martínez-Valderrey, V. (2015). Effects of cyberprogram 2.0 on "face-to-face" bullying, cyberbullying, and empathy. *Psicothema*, *27*, 45–51. doi:10.7334/psicothema2014.78

Hemphill, S. A., & Heerde, J. A. (2014). Adolescent predictors of young adult cyberbullying perpetration and victimization among Australian youth. *Journal of Adolescent Health*, *55*(4), 580–587. doi:10.1016/j.jadohealth.2014.04.014

Jolliffe, D., & Farrington, D. P. (2006). Development and validation of the basic empathy scale. *Journal of Adolescence*, *29*(4), 589–611. doi:10.1016/j.adolescence.2005.08.010

Jolliffe, D., & Farrington, D. P. (2011). Is low empathy related to bullying after controlling for individual and social background variables? *Journal of Adolescence*, *34*(1), 59–71. doi:10.1016/j.adolescence.2010.02.001

Kowalski, R. M., Giumetti, G. W., Schroeder, A. N., & Lattanner, M. R. (2014). Bullying in the digital age: A critical review and meta-analysis of cyberbullying research among youth. *Psychological Bulletin*, *140*(4), 1073–1137. doi:10.1037/a0035618

Kowalski, R. M., & Limber, S. P. (2013). Psychological, physical, and academic correlates of cyberbullying and traditional bullying. *Journal of Adolescent Health*, *53*(1), S13–S20. doi:10.1016/j.jadohealth.2012.09.018

Kubiszewski, V., Fontaine, R., Potard, C., & Auzoult, L. (2015). Does cyberbullying overlap with school bullying when taking modality of involvement into account? *Computers in Human Behavior*, *43*, 49–57. doi:10.1016/j.chb.2014.10.049

Li, Q. (2007). New bottle but old wine: A research of cyberbullying in schools. *Computers in Human Behavior*, *23*(4), 1777–1791. doi:10.1016/j.chb.2005.10.005

Memon, M. A., Cheah, J., Ramayah, T., Ting, H., & Chuah, F. (2018). Mediation analysis issues and recommendations. *Journal of Applied Structural Equation Modeling*, *2*(1), 1–9.

Patchin, J. W., & Hinduja, S. (2006). Bullies move beyond the schoolyard: A preliminary look at cyberbullying. *Youth Violence and Juvenile Justice*, *4*(2), 148–169. doi:10.1177/1541204006286288

Pettalia, J., Levin, E., & Dickinson, J. (2013). Cyberbullying: Eliciting harm without consequence. *Computers in Human Behavior*, *29*, 2759–2765. doi:10.1016/j.chb.2013.07.020

Pieters, R. (2017). Meaningful mediation analysis: Plausible causal inference and informative communication. *Journal of Consumer Research, 44*(3), 692–716. doi:10.1093/jcr/ucx081

Rucker, D. D., Preacher, K. J., Tormala, Z. L., & Petty, R. E. (2011). Mediation analysis in social psychology: Current practices and new recommendations. *Social and Personality Psychology Compass, 5*(6), 359–371. doi:10.1111/j.1751-9004.2011.00355.x

Smith, P. K., Mahdavi, J., Carvalho, M., Fisher, S., Russell, S., & Tippett, N. (2008). Cyberbullying: Its nature and impact in secondary school pupils. *Journal of Child Psychology and Psychiatry, 49*(4), 376–385. doi:10.1111/j.1469-7610.2007.01846.x

Tokunaga, R. S. (2010). Following you home from school: A critical review and synthesis of research on cyberbullying victimization. *Computers in Human Behavior, 26*(3), 277–287. doi:10.1016/j.chb.2009.11.014

VanderWeele, T. J. (2015). *Explanation in causal inference: Methods for mediation and interaction*. New York: Oxford University Press.

van Geel, M., Vedder, P., & Tanilon, J. (2014). Relationship between peer victimization, cyberbullying, and suicide in children and adolescents: A meta-analysis. *JAMA Pediatrics, 168*(5), 435–442. doi:10.1001/jamapediatrics.2013.4143

Wang, J., Nansel, T. R., & Iannotti, R. J. (2011). Cyber and traditional bullying: Differential association with depression. *Journal of Adolescent Health, 48*(4), 415–417. doi:10.1016/j.jadohealth. 2010.07.012

Willard, N. E. (2007). *Cyberbullying and cyber-threats: Responding to the challenge of online social aggression, threats, and distress*. Champaign, IL: Research Press.

World Health Organization. (2010). *mhGAP intervention guide for mental, neurological and substance use disorders in nonspecialized health settings: Mental health gap action programme* (mhGAP). Geneva: World Health Organization.

Zych, I., Baldry, A. C., Farrington, D. P., & Llorent, V. J. (2018). Are children involved in cyberbullying low on empathy? A systematic review and meta-analysis of research on empathy versus different cyberbullying roles. *Aggression and Violent Behavior, 45*, 83–97. doi:10.1016/j.avb.2018.03.004

Zych, I., Farrington, D. P., & Ttofi, M. M. (2019). Protective factors against bullying and cyberbullying: A systematic review of meta-analyses. *Aggression and Violent Behavior, 45*, 4–19. doi:10.1016/j.avb.2018.06.008

Zych, I., Ortega-Ruiz, R., & Del Rey, R. (2015). Systematic review of theoretical studies on bullying and cyberbullying: Facts, knowledge, prevention, and intervention. *Aggression and Violent Behavior, 23*, 1–21. doi:10.1016/j.avb.2015.10.001

Zych, I., Ttofi, M. M., & Farrington, D. P. (2016). Empathy and callous – unemotional traits in different bullying roles: A systematic review and meta-analysis. *Trauma, Violence and Abuse, 20*(1), 3–21. doi:10.1177/1524838016683456

16 A retrospective examination of bullying victimisation during high school

Exploring narcissism deficits and empathy

Jeffrey A. Walsh, Jessie L. Krienert, and Samantha McAdams

Introduction

School bullying is a social concern receiving attention from politicians, the public, education leaders and academics (Feldman et al., 2014). The bullying phenomenon is not new, with an early wave of seminal work dating back to the 1970s (see Olweus, 1978). Media reported bullying incidents have been linked to school shootings and youth suicides, renewing the urgency to better understand bullying dynamics. Estimates suggest between 30 and 40% of youth experience bullying annually (Hicks, Jennings, Jennings, Berry, & Green, 2018). In a national sample of 13,846 high school students, Hertz, Everett Jones, Barrios, David-Ferdon, and Holt (2015) found that approximately 27% of students in grades 9–12 had been victims of in-person bullying, electronic bullying, or some combination of both. Bullying among school age youth, high school in particular, is of paramount importance, in need of greater understanding, intervention, and prevention.

Bullying experiences are a catalyst to adverse psychosocial consequences and outcomes. Empirical literature has examined bullying correlates related to both offending and victimisation including low self-esteem, depression, suicide, eating disorders, early drug and alcohol experimentation, deficits in educational achievement and motivation, relationship conflict, aggression, and more (Copeland et al., 2013; Wolke & Lereya, 2015). The effects of bullying behaviour manifest throughout the life-course as depression, anxiety, suicidality, antisocial personality, heavy drinking behaviour, physical altercations, dating violence, sexual victimisation and the commission of felonies (see Copeland et al., 2013; Wolke et al., 2013; Hertz et al., 2015; Bender & Losel, 2011; Ragatz et al., 2011).

Prior studies of bullying tend to emphasise the role of the bully from a social deficit/social incompetence perspective suggesting bullies are socially and emotionally obtuse and intellectually simple in their responses towards conflict resolution (Hymel & Swearer, 2015; Sutton, Smith, & Swettenham, 1999a). The social incompetence model suggests a deficit in perspective taking and understanding the emotions of others. In other words, bullies may experience low levels of empathy and empathic understanding and fail to connect their antisocial behaviour to the negative emotional responses of victims and victim suffering (Jolliffe & Farrington, 2006). Walsh et al. (2018), in their high school bullying study (n = 2,113), found the deficit/incompetence model may explain bullying victimisation through victim deficits in healthy self-preservation aspects of narcissism, in addition to empathy deficits among bullies.

The impetus for the present study generates from previous unanticipated inverse primary psychopathy findings among victims and the established empirical link between primary psychopathy and narcissism (see Miller, Gaughan, & Pryor, 2008). Although often viewed as undesirable, narcissism has two factors: pathological narcissism and healthy narcissism (Falkenbach, Howe, & Falki, 2013). Empirical investigation has emphasised pathological narcissism neglecting healthy narcissism. This study examines the relationship between bullying, bullying victimisation, and deficits in healthy narcissism and the role of empathy.

The present study, drawing on a foundation of prior bullying research explores new areas and addresses several limitations. First, we utilise a large sample (*n* = 1,206) of university students reflecting on their last two years of high school. High school bullying is the second least studied group in the bulling literature (Cook, Williams, Guerra, Kim, & Sadek, 2010) though this group is associated with the most lethal bullying-related outcomes – school shooting and youth suicides. Second, we examine four bullying participation categories while emphasising the bullied victim role. Much of the extant work emphasises the bully with limited consideration of the victim. Third, we utilise three normed psychometric instruments examining the relationship between empathy, narcissism, including deficits in healthy narcissism, and bullying participation. Finally, we examine bullying and victimisation by gender, and empathy and narcissism (Jolliffe & Farrington, 2006). Understanding the nexus between bullying participation, especially the victim role, empathy, and narcissism, will inform bullying intervention and prevention efforts (Feldman et al., 2014).

Literature review

Bullying

Olweus (1978, 1995) defined bullying behaviour as the repeated exposure over time to negative actions/behaviours on the part of one or more other individuals, with the target of these negative actions/behaviours having difficulty defending himself or herself. School bullying consists of different forms of aggression involving the repeated and systematic abuse of power in a relationship and may be physical, verbal, relational (social isolation), or cyber-aggression (Cook et al., 2010).

Much of the knowledge about bullying is based on young children with less known about bullying among high school aged youth (15–18 years old) which has been explored in just 9% of bullying studies (Cook et al., 2010). Prevalence estimates of bullying vary by methodology though these suggest that between 30 and 40% of youth experience bullying (Hicks et al., 2018). Research consistently finds that males are more frequent bullies than females though differences between males and females as victims are less pronounced and inconsistent (Fanti & Kimonis, 2013; Ragatz et al., 2011; Wienke Totura et al., 2009).

Narcissism

The conceptualisation of narcissism is negative with pathological inclinations towards exploitation, arrogance, preoccupation with power and success, self-enhancing tendencies, grandiosity, inflated-self appraisal, and superiority beliefs (Kostas & Henrick, 2014; Stone, 1998). Pioneering psychoanalyst Heinz Kohut (1966) suggested narcissism was necessary and that, 'healthy narcissism provides us with self-esteem, pride, ambition, creativity, and resilience' (Malkin, 2015, p. 21). Healthy narcissism is characterised by self-preservation attitudes, realistic self-evaluation, and enlightened self-interest with genuine respect for others (Stone, 1998). Deficits in healthy narcissism would offer the converse presenting as low self-esteem, subjugation to others wishes, needs, or demands, feeling undeserving, pessimistic about the future, overly modest, and emotionally fragile. This study hypothesises that bullied victims experience deficits in healthy narcissism lacking adequate self-protective egocentrism, have low self-esteem, deal less effectively with their environment, and consequently are less capable of fending off bullies.

Empathy

Empathy is both an affective trait facilitating the experience of the emotional state of another, as well as a cognitive ability facilitating the understanding of the emotions of another, with the intended end result being prosocial behaviour inhibiting antisocial behaviour (Jolliffe & Farrington, 2006, p. 540). Importantly, empathising and understanding the feelings of another person does not necessarily mean that the response will be either sympathetic, compassionate or prosocial (Lamia, 2010). The association between empathy and bullying remains unclear (van Noorden et al., 2015). Bullies have been characterised as lacking empathy, having low self-esteem, and being unable to comprehend how their actions harm others. Adams, Mebane, and Espelage (2004), examining empathy, bullying, and caring in 263 11–14-year olds, found negative correlations between bullying and both affective and cognitive empathy. Pioneers of the Basic Empathy Scale (BES), Jolliffe and Farrington (2011), found that males and females who bullied had lower scores on both cognitive and affective empathy compared to non-participants. However, other research has found that bullies may feel empathy but instead withhold it; they may be unwilling to empathise rather than unable to. '[B]ullies have an amazing ability to recognize exactly what is going to hurt, manipulate, or control you' (Lamia, 2010, p. 1). For example, Walsh et al. (2018)

found that male bullies scored higher in cognitive empathy than other participant categories in a retrospective high school bullying study ($n = 2,113$).

Methodology

The present study is a cross-sectional retrospective descriptive and exploratory self-report examination of bullying utilising confidential e-survey responses from a large sample of university students (n = 1,206) reflecting on their last two years of high school experiences. Participants were categorised into one of four participation roles: bullies, victims, bully-victims (individuals experiencing both bullying and victimisation), or uninvolved/non-participants. The sample of respondents was examined to identify differences between participation groups, across normed empathy and narcissism scale scores, and by respondent sex.

Instrument – The e-survey consisted of approximately 80 multiple choice and Likert-scale questions subcategorised into four sections: 1) respondent's demographics, 2) questions about bullying via the Olweus Bullying Survey, 3) the Narcissistic Personality Inventory-16 (NPI-16) and the Narcissism Spectrum Scale (NSS), 4) and Jolliffe and Farrington's BES (affective and cognitive). The following section provides a brief description of the instruments.

Bullying

The Olweus Bully/Victim Questionnaire contains a definition of bullying behaviour followed by a series of Likert-scale questions including the global question: During your last two years of high school, how often were you bullied? Response options included: never, once or twice, 2–3 times a month, about once a week, several times a week. A similar series of victimisation questions was asked followed by the global question: How often during your last two years of high school did you take part in bullying another student? The categorisation of bully, victim, or bully-victim relied on the lower-bound cut-point response of "2–3 times a month" (see Ragatz et al., 2011; Solberg & Olweus, 2003; Walsh et al., 2018). Participants who responded never, or did not meet the lower bound, were categorised as uninvolved/non-participants.

Empathy

The BES emphasises the degree to which a person understands and shares the emotions of another (Jolliffe & Farrington, 2011). The BES is a normed and validated 20-item scale with loadings on two factors, factor one measures cognitive empathy and factor two measures affective empathy (Jolliffe & Farrington, 2006). Factor loadings in the present study for the full scale ($\alpha = .877$), cognitive empathy (9 items, $\alpha = .801$), and affective empathy (9 items, $\alpha = .853$) support their use and exceed minimum thresholds. Cognitive empathy is the capacity of one person to comprehend and understand the emotions of another person. Affective empathy is the capacity of one person to experience the emotions of another person.

Narcissism

The Narcissistic Personality Inventory (NPI), originally developed by Raskin and Hall (1979), has been used to measure grandiose and overt aspects of narcissism (Konrath, Meier, & Bushman, 2014). The present study employed the NPI-16, a 16 item sub-clinical questionnaire developed by Ames, Rose, and Anderson (2006) measuring narcissism as a single construct derived from the full NPI 40-item scale. The NPI-16 presents paired questions with the respondent selecting the option in each pairing that best describes them. The factor loading here for the NPI-16 ($\alpha = .747$) supports its use.

A second measure of narcissism, the Narcissism Spectrum Scale (NSS) developed by Malkin, Quirk and Martin (see Malkin, 2015), was also utilised. The NSS is a newer 30-item five-point Likert-scale measure of narcissism. The scale has been validated with various populations across age groups and demographics. The NSS offers three scales capturing narcissism deficits ($\alpha = .787$), healthy narcissism ($\alpha = .761$), and extreme narcissism ($\alpha = .812$).

Analysis plan

The first step of the analysis was to derive descriptive statistics to measure the frequency and prevalence of several respondent characteristics. Descriptive statistics for the full sample and by bullying participation categories (bully, victim, bully-victim, non-participant) are located in Table 16.1. Step 2 of the bivariate analyses, noted in Table 16.2, involved a series of Chi-square tests to identify statistically significant relationships between the bullying participation categories and several respondent characteristics. An ANOVA was used to identify statistically significant relationships between the four bullying participation categories, the empathy full and subscales, as well as the NPI-16 and NSS. These results are also in Table 16.2. The final series of analyses, reported in Tables 16.3–16.6, includes a multivariate analysis, binomial logistic regression, to confirm aspects of the victim relationship, empathy, narcissism, and gender.

Results

The sample consisted of 878 (73%) female students and 328 (27%) male students, representing a slightly higher female response rate than the actual campus population (F 58%, M 42%). As noted in Table 16.1, the majority of the sample was white (78%) reflecting the composition of white students on campus (82%). The majority of respondents identified as heterosexual (85%) and were under 22 years of age (75%). Most respondents reported no high school bullying participation as either bullies or victims (55%), followed by victim only (37%), bully-victim (5%), and bully only (3%).

Table 16.2 highlights the demographic differences across bullying participation categories with significant differences identified by sex of respondent, sexual orientation, and age. Males were significantly more likely to report participation in

Table 16.1 Sample demographics n = 1,206

	Number	*Percent*
Gender		
Female	878	72.8
Male	328	27.2
Age		
18–19	575	47.9
20–21	320	26.7
22 +	305	25.4
Race		
White	943	78.2
Black	77	6.4
Hispanic	81	6.7
Other	105	8.7
Sexual Orientation		
Straight	1022	84.9
Gay	40	3.3
Bisexual	142	11.8
Bully Categories		
Neither Bully or Victim	666	55.2
Bully Only	30	2.5
Victim Only	449	37.2
Bully-Victim	61	5.1
Empathy (mean)	78.60	
Affective Empathy (mean)	41.73	
Cognitive Empathy (mean)	36.85	
Narcissistic Personality Inventory (mean)	3.42	
Narcissism Spectrum Scale		
Narcissism Deficits (mean)	33.17	
Healthy Narcissism (mean)	39.05	
Extreme Narcissism (mean)	25.12	

the bully-victim category (7%) when compared to their female counterparts (4%), χ^2 (3, n = 1,206) = 10.698, p = .013. Females reported more victim only participation (40%) compared to males (31%). Age differences were noted with those in the victim-only category increasing with age, χ^2 (6, n = 1,200) = 17.801, p = .007. No significant race differences were noted in the sample.

Significant differences in respondent scores across the empathy and narcissism scales are noted. Victims reported higher scores on overall empathy followed by the non-participants, bully-victims, and finally bullies with the lowest empathy scores. Differences in subscales show that victims have higher affective empathy followed by bully-victims, non-participants, and then bullies again scoring the lowest on affective empathy. Despite victims again having the highest scores on cognitive empathy and bullies having the lowest, the differences were not significant. These findings comport with most prior findings and do not support the idea

Table 16.2 Demographics by bully categories, n = 1,206

	None		*Bully Only*		*Victim Only*		*Bully Victim*	
	#	%	#	%	#	%	#	%
*Gender								
Male	196	29.4	9	30.0	100	22.3	23	37.7
Female	470	70.6	21	70.0	349	77.7	38	62.3
*Age								
18–19	344	51.9	14	46.7	190	42.6	27	44.3
20–21	159	24.0	12	40.0	137	30.7	12	19.7
22 +	160	24.1	4	13.3	119	26.7	22	36.1
Race								
White	509	76.4	27	90.0	358	79.7	49	80.3
Black	46	6.9	1	3.3	25	5.6	5	8.2
Hispanic	50	7.5	1	3.3	25	5.6	5	8.2
Other	61	9.2	1	3.3	40	8.9	3	4.9
**Sexual Orientation								
Straight	839	96.3	59	98.3	460	92.6	127	94.8
Gay	13	1.5	0	0.0	13	2.6	4	3.0
Bisexual	19	2.2	1	1.7	24	4.8	3	2.2
**Empathy (mean)	77.68		75.81		80.35		77.23	
**Affective Empathy (mean)	36.57		36.05		37.34		36.72	
Cognitive Empathy (mean)	41.15		39.76		42.93		40.10	
**Narcissistic Personality Inventory (mean)	3.49		4.89		2.86		6.00	
Narcissism Spectrum Scale								
** Narcissism Deficit (mean)	32.41		31.47		34.35		33.11	
Healthy Narcissism (mean)	39.15		39.37		39.08		37.74	
**Extreme Narcissism	25.04		27.84		24.51		29.94	

$^{*}p \leq .05$
$^{**}p \leq .001$

that bullies have higher empathy and use it to their bullying advantage. The NPI-16 shows significantly higher scores for bullies and bully-victims, with victims having the lowest scores, even lower than non-participants. Similarly, on the NSS, victims have significant deficits in narcissism compared to the other three categories, including the non-participants, and bully-victims have significantly higher levels of extreme narcissism while victims score the lowest in extreme narcissism.

Multinomial logistic regression

The final step of the analysis includes binomial logistic regression as a discriminant function to explain differences in bullying victimisation compared to non-participants across gender. Results generally support the bivariate findings with a few notable exceptions.

Table 16.3 shows that victims, when compared to non-participants, have significantly more empathy and significantly less narcissism. When examined by gender, both empathy and narcissism fall out of the equation for men, but both remain significant for females. In sum, female victims have significantly less narcissism and significantly more empathy than individuals who have not been bullies or victims of bullying.

Table 16.4 further examines the empathy/narcissism relationship by expanding the basic empathy categories to include the affective and cognitive subscales. For the total sample, affective empathy and narcissism are significant. Victims report lower narcissism and higher affective empathy than those who have not been either bullies or victims, however, no differences were found in cognitive empathy. Examined by gender, no significant differences between victim and non-participants in empathy or narcissism are noted for men, however, female victims have significantly less narcissism when compared to those who are uninvolved but no differences in cognitive or affective empathy.

Switching to the Narcissism Spectrum Scale (NSS) examining narcissism deficits, healthy narcissism, and extreme narcissism, Tables 16.5 and 16.6 show significant

Table 16.3 Logistic regression BES and NPI comparing victims to non-participants by gender (n = 1,206)

	B	*SEB*	*Wald* χ^2	p	*Exp (B)*
Total (n = 763)					
*NPI	−.066	.029	5.150	.023	.936
*Empathy	.020	.008	6.446	.011	1.020
Males (n = 194)					
NPI	−.008	.052	.022	.881	.992
Empathy	.010	.015	.453	.501	1.010
Females (n = 569)					
*NPI	−.090	.035	.6567	.010	.914
*Empathy	.021	.010	4.560	.033	1.021

*$p \leq .05$
**$p \leq .001$

Table 16.4 Logistic regression results BES subscales and NPI comparing victims to non-participants by gender (n = 1,206)

	B	*SEB*	*Wald* χ^2	p	*Exp* (B)
Total (n = 763)					
*NPI	−.064	.029	4.844	.028	.938
*Affective Empathy	.025	.012	4.002	.045	1.025
Cognitive Empathy	.010	.020	.254	.614	1.010
Males (n = 194)					
NPI	−.003	.052	.004	.950	.997
Affective Empathy	.021	.023	.827	.363	1.021
Cognitive Empathy	−.008	.033	.062	.803	.992
Females (n = 569)					
*NPI	−.089	.035	6.464	.011	.914
Affective Empathy	.023	.016	2.068	.150	1.023
Cognitive Empathy	.017	.024	.473	.491	1.017

*$p \leq .05$
**$p \leq .001$

Table 16.5 Logistic regression BES and NSS by gender (n = 1,206)

	B	*SEB*	*Wald* χ^2	p	*Exp* (B)
Total (*n* = 744)					
Empathy	.014	.008	2.913	.088	1.014
*Narcissism Deficit	.039	.012	9.979	.002	1.040
Healthy Narcissism	.002	.017	.010	.919	1.002
Extreme Narcissism	−.004	.012	.102	.749	.996
Males (*n* = 184)					
Empathy	−.006	.017	.127	.722	.994
Narcissism Deficit	.042	.026	2.630	.105	1.042
Healthy Narcissism	.013	.030	.195	.658	1.013
Extreme Narcissism	−.014	.023	.271	.543	.986
Females (*n* = 560)					
Empathy	.019	.010	3.210	.073	1.019
*Narcissism Deficit	.039	.014	7.227	.007	1.039
Healthy Narcissism	−.002	.021	.009	.925	.998
Extreme Narcissism	.000	.014	.000	.993	1.00

*$p \leq .05$
**$p \leq .001$

sex differences in one important aspect of narcissism. In the total sample examining the total empathy scale and the NSS subscales, narcissism deficit is significant. Examined by gender it is the females that show significant narcissism deficits, whereas male victims show no significant difference when compared to those not involved in bullying or victimisation. Empathy is not significant in the total, female, or male categories when included with the NSS scales. Similarly, when examining

Table 16.6 Logistic regression BES subscales and NSS by gender (n = 1,206)

	B	*SEB*	*Wald* χ^2	p	*Exp* (B)
Total (n = 744)					
Affective Empathy	.013	.013	.997	.318	1.013
Cognitive Empathy	.017	.021	.659	.417	1.017
*Narcissism Deficit	.040	.013	9.832	.002	1.040
Healthy Narcissism	.001	.017	.005	.943	1.001
Extreme Narcissism	−.004	.012	.102	.749	.996
Males (n = 184)					
Affective Empathy	.001	.024	.004	.952	1.001
Cognitive Empathy	−.021	.038	.300	.584	.979
Narcissism Deficit	.040	.026	2.314	.128	1.040
Healthy Narcissism	.018	.032	.318	.573	1.018
Extreme Narcissism	−.015	.023	.400	.527	.985
Females (n = 560)					
Affective Empathy	.012	.016	.563	.453	1.012
Cognitive Empathy	.030	.025	1.394	.238	1.030
*Narcissism Deficit	.040	.015	7.439	.006	1.041
Healthy Narcissism	−.003	.021	.025	.874	.997
Extreme Narcissism	.000	.014	.000	.997	1.000

*$p \leq .05$
**$p \leq .001$

the affective and cognitive empathy subscales with the NSS scales across the total, male, and female samples neither empathy measure is significant though female victims have statistically significant scores on deficits in narcissism.

Discussion

While much is known about the psychosocial behavioural consequences of bullying for victims and bullies (see Copeland et al., 2013; Wolke & Lereya, 2015) less is known about the dispositional character and personality trait differences between participant roles. This work corroborates previous findings and preliminary interpretations, refutes others, and presenting new questions and avenues for inquiry. Our findings reveal that female victims scored significantly lower on the NPI-16 and higher on the NSS narcissism deficit scale than all other participation categories including the non-participant/uninvolved group. What has yet to be determined is the causal orientation of this finding. Does bullying victimisation cause deficits in the self-protective features of narcissism due to the psychosocial consequences of being bullied, or do deficits in narcissism present as victimological vulnerability cues to motivated bullies? This is an important question for future research requiring a more complex research design. Further, neither narcissism scale or subscales nor the empathy scales were significant for males. Males are the frequent perpetrators of lethal bullying associated behaviour (suicide and school shootings). Gender differences in bullying experiences remain an important avenue of study along with better understanding of the differences between extreme internalising self-defeating suicidal responses and extreme externalising school shooting responses (Walsh et al., 2018).

Findings revealed that victims have greater empathy than all other roles including the non-participants, affective rather than cognitive, and in the total empathy model including NPI-16 among females rather than males. Extant literature supports that females, especially adolescents, have higher affective empathy than males with biological and sociological explanations offered (Stuijfzand et al., 2016). Future research is necessary to continue to explore gender differences across bullying participation and empathy.

Youth bullying intervention programs tend to emphasise the bully role and neglect the victim role. In addition to introducing bullies to empathy training and perspective taking as courses of action, efforts to alleviate deficits in narcissism by bolstering the qualities of healthy narcissism may be increasingly important and serve to reduce victim vulnerability. Regardless of whether the link is causal or consequential, interventions that strengthen victim's healthy narcissism including characteristics of self-worth, self-esteem, self-confidence and self-assurance should be advantageous to victims' resilience against bullying.

There are several limitations to be noted. This work utilised retrospective self-reporting may have impacted memory recall likely resulting in underreporting. Second, we relied on standardised measures of bullying, narcissism, and empathy and while valid and reliable across a variety of settings they may not have been ideal for this university population. Further, despite anonymity, there are concerns about socially desirable responding considering the attention the bullying narrative has received in society. Despite limitations, we find value added in the results of the study, both the corroboration and clarification of findings as well as the questions yet to be answered. Bullying remains an important social concern and with each new examination we are closer to understanding and identifying opportunities for intervention and prevention.

References

Adams, R. S., Mebane, S. E., & Espelage, D. L. (2004). Empathy, caring, and bullying: Toward an understanding of complex associations. In *Bullying in American schools* (pp. 59–84). London: Routledge.

Ames, D., R., Rose, P., & Anderson, C. P. (2006). The NPI-16 as a short measure of narcissism. *Journal of Research in Personality*, *40*, 440–450.

Bender, D., & Lösel, F. (2011). Bullying at school as a predictor of delinquency, violence and other anti-social behaviour in adulthood. *Criminal Behaviour and Mental Health*, *21*(2), 99–106.

Cook, C. R., Williams, K. R., Guerra, N. G., Kim, T. E., & Sadek, S. (2010). Predictors of bullying and victimization in childhood and adolescence: A meta-analytic investigation. *School Psychology Quarterly*, *25*(2), 65.

Copeland, W. E., Wolke, D., Angold, A., & Costello, E. J. (2013). Adult psychiatric outcomes of bullying and being bullied by peers in childhood and adolescence. *JAMA Psychiatry*, *70*(4), 419–426.

Falkenbach, D. M., Howe, J. R., & Falki, M. (2013). Using self-esteem to disaggregate psychopathy, narcissism, and aggression. *Personality and Individual Differences*, *54*(7), 815–820.

Fanti, K. A., & Kimonis, E. R. (2013). Dimensions of juvenile psychopathy distinguish "bullies," "bully-victims," and "victims". *Psychology of Violence*, *3*(4), 396.

Feldman, M. A., Ojanen, T., Gesten, E. L., Smith-Schrandt, H., Brannick, M., Totura, C. M. W., & Brown, K. (2014). The effects of middle school bullying and victimization on adjustment through high school: Growth modeling of achievement, school attendance, and disciplinary trajectories. *Psychology in the Schools*, *51*(10), 1046–1062.

Hertz, M. F., Everett Jones, S., Barrios, L., David-Ferdon, C., & Holt, M. (2015). Association between bullying victimization and health risk behaviours among high school students in the United States. *Journal of School Health*, *85*(12), 833–842.

Hicks, J., Jennings, L., Jennings, S., Berry, S., & Green, D.-A. (2018). Middle school bullying: Student reported perceptions and prevalence. *Journal of Child and Adolescent Counseling*, 1–14.

Hymel, S., & Swearer, S. M. (2015). Four decades of research on school bullying: An introduction. *American Psychologist*, *70*(4), 293.

Jolliffe, D., & Farrington, D. P. (2006). Examining the relationship between low empathy and bullying. *Aggressive Behavior*, *32*(6), 540–550.

Jolliffe, D., & Farrington, D. P. (2011). Is low empathy related to bullying after controlling for individual and social background variables? *Journal of Adolescence*, *34*(1), 59–71.

Kohut, H. (1966). Forms and transformations of narcissism. *Journal of the American Psychoanalytic Association*, *14*(2), 243–272.

Konrath, S., Meier, B. P., & Bushman, B. J. (2014). Development and validation of the single item narcissism scale (SINS). *PLoS One*, *9*(8), 1–20.

Kostas, F. A., & Henrich, C. C. (2014). Effects of self-esteem and narcissism on bullying and victimization during early adolescence. *Journal of Early Adolescence*, 1–25.

Lamia, M. C. (2010). Do bullies actually lack empathy? *Psychology Today*. Retrieved from http://www.psychologytoday.com/

Malkin, C. (2015). *Rethinking narcissism: The secret to recognizing and coping with narcissists*. New York: Harper.

Miller, J. D., Gaughan, E. T., & Pryor, L. R. (2008). The Levenson self-report psychopathy scale: An examination of the personality traits and disorders associated with the LSRP factors. *Assessment*, *15*(4), 450–463.

Olweus, D. (1978). *Aggression in the schools: Bullies and whipping boys*. Washington, DC: Hemisphere (Wiley). (PDF) Bullying in schools: Facts and intervention. Retrieved December 18, 2018, from www.researchgate.net/publication/228654357_Bullyinginschoolsfactsandintervention

Olweus, D. (1995). Bullying or peer abuse in school: Intervention and prevention. In G. Davies (Ed.), *Psychology, law, and criminal justice: International developments in research and practice* (pp. 248–263). New York: de Gruyter.

Ragatz, L. L., Anderson, R. J., Fremouw, W., & Schwartz, R. (2011). Criminal thinking patterns, aggression styles, and the psychopathic traits of late high school bullies and bully-victims. *Aggressive Behavior*, *37*(2), 145–160.

Raskin, R. N., & Hall, C. S. (1979). A narcissistic personality inventory. *Psychological Reports*, *45*(2), 590–590.

Solberg, M. E., & Olweus, D. (2003). Prevalence estimation of school bullying with the Olweus bully/victim questionnaire. *Aggressive Behavior*, *29*(3), 239–268.

Stone, M. H. (1998). Normal narcissism: An etiological and ethological perspective. In E. F. Ronningstam (Ed.), *Disorders of narcissism: Diagnostic, clinical, and empirical implications* (pp. 7–28). Washington, DC: American Psychiatric Press.

Stuijfzand, S., de Wied, M., Kempes, M., van de Graaf, J., Branje, S., & Meeus, W. (2016). Gebder differences in empathis sadness towards persons of the same-versus other-sex during adolescence. *Sex Roles*, *75*(9), 434–446.

Sutton, J., Smith, P. K., & Swettenham, J. (1999a). Bullying and "theory of mind": A critique of the "social skills deficit" view of anti-social behaviour. *Social Development*, *8*(1), 117–127.

van Noorden, T. H., Haselager, G. J., Cillessen, A. H., & Bukowski, W. M. (2015). Empathy and involvement in bullying in children and adolescents: A systematic review. *Journal of Youth and Adolescence*, *44*(3), 637–657.

Walsh, J. A., Krienert, J. L., Thresher, G., & Potratz, K. (2018). Examining the link between bullying participation, psychopathy and empathy in a large retrospective sample of university students. *Criminal Justice Studies*, *31*(3), 249–266.

Wienke Totura, C. M., MacKinnon-Lewis, C., Gesten, E. L., Gadd, R., Divine, K. P., Dunham, S., & Kamboukos, D. (2009). Bullying and victimization among boys and girls in middle school: The influence of perceived family and school contexts. *The Journal of Early Adolescence*, *29*(4), 571–609.

Wolke, D., Copeland, W. E., Angold, A., & Costello, E. J. (2013). Impact of bullying in childhood on adult health, wealth, crime, and social outcomes. *Psychological Science*, *24*(10), 1958–1970.

Wolke, D., & Lereya, S. T. (2015). Long-term effects of bullying. *Archives of Disease in Childhood*. doi:10.1136/archdischild-2014-306667

17 The relationship between empathy and prison bullying in a sample of Croatian prisoners

Ivana Sekol, Tihomir Vidranski and Darrick Jolliffe

Introduction

Empathy and antisocial behaviour, offending, and bullying

Empathy is defined as an individual's sensitivity to the emotional state or experience (actual or anticipated) of another person (Davis, 1983). It is a two-dimensional construct including affective empathy, or the ability to *experience* the emotions of another person, and cognitive empathy, the ability to *recognise* and *understand* the emotions of another person (Davis, 1980). Considerable research has been devoted to identifying the association between empathy and antisocial or offending behaviour, with studies suggesting that empathy is negatively related to antisocial (Cohen, 1982), aggressive (Carrasco, Barker, Tremblay, & Vitaro, 2006) and delinquent behaviour (Ellis, 1982).

The relationship between empathy and bullying in schools, defined as the repeated oppression, psychological or physical, of a less powerful person by a more powerful one (Farrington, 1993), also suggests that children who bully may have lower empathy than those who do not (Endresen & Olweus, 2002). While there has been much less research on bullying in prison compared to that in schools, there is emerging research highlighting the prevalence and severity of bullying in prison (e.g. Ireland & Ireland 2008), along with the potential causes and correlates of this behaviour, of which empathy has been implicated.

To date, only one study (Ireland, 1999) has explicitly examined the relationship between empathy and bullying amongst prisoners. This study used the Interpersonal Reactivity Index (IRI) constructed by Davis (1983), and found that bullies scored significantly lower on "perspective taking" than other prisoners. Similarly, compared to victims of bullying, bullies also scored significantly lower on "empathetic concern". In related research, López-Pérez, Hanoch, Holt, and Gummerum (2017) found that prisoners who held positive attitudes about bullying scored significantly lower on both "perspective taking" and "empathetic concern" than other prisoners.[1]

Empathy and bullying has also been studied amongst institutionalised individuals by Sekol and Farrington (2016) using a national sample of young people from

Croatian children's homes and correctional institutions. This study employed the Basic Empathy Scale (BES) developed by Jolliffe and Farrington (2006a), and the results demonstrated that male bullies scored significantly lower on overall and affective empathy than non-bullies, but no such differences were found for females. Once other concepts such as personality traits and attitudes were controlled, however, empathy did not independently predict bullying in either sample.

Aims of the study

This chapter is the first to examine the relationship between affective and cognitive empathy and different forms of prison bullying, while also controlling for the impact of other socio-demographic and individual correlates of bullying. It aims to answer the following research questions:[2]

1. Do prisoners who self-report bullying differ on overall, cognitive or affective empathy from those who do not?
2. Does empathy independently predict overall and type-specific bullying after controlling for prisoner demographic characteristics?
3. Do the results differ for males and females?

Method

Participants

A total of 534 prisoners from five Croatian penitentiaries (4 adult males and 1 adult female) and 5 adult male prisons were asked to complete a battery of questionnaires. In Croatia, penitentiaries house those serving sentences of longer than six months and prisons house those with sentences of less than six months or on remand. Both prisons and penitentiaries have maximum and medium security wings. Of the 534 prisoners who were asked to participate in the study, 11 declined and 30 either submitted blank questionnaires or completed the questionnaires randomly. The final sample consisted of 493 prisoners, 48 of whom were female. Female prisoners were on average 39.1 years old (SD = 11.5) and had spent on average 1.6 years in their current facility (SD = 18.8). Their average sentence length was 3.4 years. For the majority of women (87.5 %), this was their first prison sentence. Male prisoners were on average 38.1 years old (SD = 11.1) and had spent on average 2.3 years in their current facility (SD = 35.6). Their average sentence length was 5.4 years (SD = 70.4) and for 54.5% of males this was their first prison sentence. Overall, 401 of 493 prisoners were being held in maximum security wings, while 92 prisoners were being held in medium security wings.

Measures

The Direct and Indirect Prisoner Behaviour Checklist-Revised (DIPC-R ÓIreland, 2002)

Bullying was measured using a modified version of the Direct and Indirect Prisoner Behaviour Checklist (DIPC-R ©Ireland, 2002a) which consists of 58 items assessing whether one is a victim of bullying, another 58 items assessing bullying behaviour and 23 filler items. The items measure six main types of bullying and victimisation, including indirect bullying, physical bullying, coercive bullying, intimidating bullying, verbal and sexual bullying.[3] Given that the DIPC-R results in a dichotomous behavioural classification, its psychometric properties (e.g. alpha coefficients) could not be calculated (Ireland & Power, 2013).

The basic empathy scale (Jolliffe & Farrington, 2006b)

The Basic Empathy Scale was used to measure prisoners' overall, affective and cognitive empathy. In this sample of Croatian prisoners, the Cronbach's alpha for overall empathy was 0.80, for affective empathy was 0.64 and for cognitive empathy 0.81.

Procedure

Ethical approval for the study was granted by the Croatian Ministry of Justice. All prisoners were invited to participate on their wings by the authors of the study. The authors explained the aims of the study, stressed the voluntary nature of participation, and guaranteed the anonymity of those who chose to take part. Prisoners who agreed to participate completed the battery of questionnaires in groups of 7 to 20 prisoners in a communal area, but in a layout that prevented them from seeing each other's answers. A consent statement was provided at the beginning of each questionnaire, but no signature was recorded to maintain anonymity. The authors were present during the completion of the questionnaires to answer any questions that the prisoners may have had. Upon completion, the questionnaires were placed into a large box and shuffled.

Results

Preliminary analyses

In line with this definition provided by Ireland (2002a), prisoners were classified as bullies or victims if they reported at least one behaviour indicative of bullying others or being bullied in the past week. Those who were both bullies and victims (so called bully/victims) were identified in both the male and female sample, but because the aim of this research was to examine whether prisoners who bully differed on empathy from those who do not, bully/victims were included as bullies or victims depending on the analysis.

Slightly over three quarters of females reported being a victim of bullying, while half of the female sample reported bullying others weekly. The prevalence of bullying and victimisation in the male sample was 36.2% and 47.9% respectively. Females were almost significantly more likely than males to be classified as bullies (50.0% vs. 36.2%; $r = 0.15$; $p < 0.10$) and significantly more likely to be classified as victims (77.1% vs. 47.9%; $r = 0.34$; $p < 0.001$). Similarly, females scored significantly higher on overall ($M = 75.02$ vs. $M = 68.58$; $r = 0.30$; $p < 0.001$), affective ($M = 38.86$ vs. 35.13; $r = 0.21$; $p < 0.001$) and cognitive ($M = 36.15$ vs. 33.45; $r = 0.15$; $p < 0.01$) empathy than males. For these reasons the sample was split into males and females for further analyses. Given the small sample size for females the results for this sub-group should be treated with caution. Furthermore, no differences in the prevalence of bullying were found between maximum- and minimum-security prisons ($\chi^2 = 0.60$; $p = 0.44$), so these groups were combined.

Was there a relationship between empathy and overall and type-specific bullying?

Table 17.1 shows the significant zero-order correlates of male and female bullying. While many other prisoner characteristics measured were significantly related to bullying by males, empathy was not.[4] For instance, compared to non-bullies, male bullies were significantly younger and significantly more likely to have been incarcerated for the first time at a younger age, to have used drugs prior to their imprisonment, and to have been incarcerated for burglary, threat, and kidnapping. During their imprisonment, male bullies were also significantly more likely than other prisoners to have spent time in solitary confinement, to have attended a special prison programmes, and to have been subjected to disciplinary proceedings.

As shown on the right-hand side of Table 17.1, female bullies had significantly higher cognitive empathy than non-bullies. Compared to their non-bully counterparts, they were also significantly less likely to be incarcerated for fraud. As indicated by effect sizes larger than 0.20, female bullies appeared younger and were serving longer sentences than non-bullies. Similarly, they were also considerably more likely to have used drugs before their imprisonment, to have attended a special prison programmes, and to have been incarcerated for burglary, murder, illegal possession of drugs and drug dealing.

No females reported physical or coercive bullying and only one female reported intimidating bullying, therefore, only the correlates of female verbal and indirect bullying are shown (Table 17.4). The correlates of male physical and coercive bullying are presented in Table 17.2, while the correlates of male verbal, intimidating and indirect bullying are shown in Table 17.3.

Table 17.2 shows that males who bullied physically had significantly lower affective empathy than other prisoners, while males who bullied coercively had significantly lower overall and affective empathy. Table 17.3 shows that many other prisoner characteristics were related to male verbal, intimidating and indirect bullying, but that empathy was not.

Table 17.1 The relationships between prisoner demographic and personal characteristics and the prevalence of overall bullying

	Males (n = 445)				*Females (n = 48)*			
	B	*NB*	t/χ^2	r	*B*	*NB*	t/χ^2	r
Age	35.75	40.93	–4.63	0.22***	45.80	51.13	–1.70	0.24†
Sentence length	–	–	–	–	49.25	32.04	1.80	0.26†
Age at 1st imprisonment	26.77	30.28	–2.90	0.15**	–	–	–	–
Cognitive empathy	–	–	–	–	37.90	34.56	2.15	0.31*
Used drugs prior to imprisonment	*58.5*	*31.0*	*31.44*	*0.19****	*20.8*	*4.2*	*3.05*	*0.44†*
Spent time in solitary confinement	*27.5*	*17.8*	*5.73*	*0.15**	–	–	–	–
Subjected to disciplinary proceedings	*34.4*	*21.9*	*8.19*	*0.17***	–	–	–	–
Attended special prison programmes	*36.3*	*22.7*	*11.23*	*0.18***	*37.5*	*20.8*	*1.61*	*0.22*
Incarcerated for burglary	*21.7*	*12.3*	*6.81*	*0.19***	*8.3*	*0.0*	*1.63*	*0.21*
Incarcerated for murder	–	–	–	–	*12.5*	*4.2*	*1.10*	*0.31*
Incarcerated for fraud	–	–	–	–	*16.7*	*54.2*	*7.38*	*0.44***
Incarcerated for threat	*2.0*	*0.0*	*5.33*	*0.42**	–	–	–	–
Incarcerated for possession and drug abuse	–	–	–	–	*2.0*	*0.0*	*2.09*	*0.21*
Incarcerated for drug dealing	–	–	–	–	*16.7*	*4.2*	*2.01*	*0.40*
Incarcerated for kidnapping	*1.2*	*0.0*	*3.54*	*0.33†*	–	–	–	–

Notes: B = bullies; NB = non-bullies; in columns B and NB, means are given for continuous variables and percentages are given for the dichotomous variables (in italics); t/χ^2 = t test values for continuous explanatory variables, χ^2 values for dichotomous explanatory variables; r = effect size (Pearson's *r*); in cases where no prisoners reported a certain dichotomous event/behaviour, the Haldane-Anscombe correction was performed to calculate the odds ratio; for all dichotomous variables, odds ratios were calculated first and then transformed into the Pearson's *r*; † = $p < 0.10$; * = $p < 0.05$; ** = $p < 0.01$; *** = $p < 0.001$.

Table 17.2 The relationships between prisoner demographic and personal characteristics and the prevalence of male physical and coercive bullying

	Male physical bullying				*Male coercive bullying*			
	PB	*OP*	t/χ^2	r	*CB*	*OP*	t/χ^2	r
Age	32.18	39.52	–3.30	0.15*	30.96	39.56	–3.74	0.18***
Sentence length	99.86	62.57	2.41	0.13.*	104.4	62.3	2.73	0.15*
Age at 1st imprisonment	22.65	29.42	–2.78	0.42**	*22.6*	*29.4*	*2.78*	0.14*
Overall empathy	–	–	–	–	64.87	68.82	–2.17	0.10*
Affective empathy	32.89	35.30	–2.32	0.12*	32.83	35.28	–2.23	0.11*
Used drugs prior to imprisonment	*64.3*	*39.5*	*6.67*	*0.27***	*65.4*	*39.5*	*6.76*	*0.28****
Spent time in psychiatric hospital	*35.7*	*18.3*	*5.10*	*0.25†*	–	–	–	–
Attempted suicide prior to imprisonment	*12.5*	*4.0*	*3.82*	*0.34**	–	–	–	–
Self-harmed prior to imprisonment	*30.0*	*8.2*	*10.66*	*0.40****	*33.3*	*8.2*	*12.87*	*0.43****
Spent time in solitary confinement	*42.9*	*19.9*	*8.26*	*0.30***	*52.0*	*19.5*	*14.87*	*0.40****
Self-harmed in prison	*26.3*	*8.7*	*6.49*	*0.34**	*33.4*	*8.4*	*12.34*	*0.42****
Subjected to disciplinary proceedings	*57.1*	*24.3*	*14.52*	*0.36****	–	–	–	–
Attended special prison programmes	*46.4*	*26.4*	*5.30*	*0.24†*	*60.0*	*24.4*	*15.37*	*0.16****
Incarcerated for murder	*14.3*	*5.3*	*3.87*	*0.30**	*11.5*	*5.5*	*1.63*	*0.22*
Incarcerated for fraud	*3.6*	*16.5*	*3.33*	*0.42†*	*3.8*	*16.5*	*2.94*	*0.40†*

Notes: PB = physical bullies, OP = other prisoners, CB = coercive bullies, OP = other prisoners; in columns PB, CB and OP, means are given for continuous variables and percentages are given for dichotomous variables (in italics); t/χ^2 = t test values for continuous explanatory variables, χ^2values for dichotomous explanatory variables; *r* = effect size (Pearson's *r*); for all dichotomous variables, odds ratios were calculated first and then transformed into the Pearson's *r*; † = $p < 0.10$; *= $p < 0.05$; ** = $p < 0.01$; *** = $p < 0.001$.

Table 17.3 The relationship between prisoner demographic and personal characteristics and the prevalence of male verbal, intimidating, and indirect bullying

	Male verbal bullying				*Male intimidating bullying*				*Male indirect bullying*[A]			
	VB	*OP*	t/χ^2	r	*INTB*	*OP*	t/χ^2	*r*	*IB*	*NI*	t/χ^2	r
Age	33.91	39.77	–3.55	0.17***	32.23	39.61	–3.58	0.17***	–	–	–	–
Sentence length	90.36	61.00	2.62	0.14**	105.44	61.42	3.15	0.17**	–	–	–	–
Amount of time already served	39.33	25.59	2.31	0.13*	45.62	26.17	2.70	0.15**	–	–	–	–
Age at 1st imprisonment	24.62	29.60	–2.77	0.14**	24.22	29.37	–2.27	0.11*	–	–	–	–
Incarcerated for the 1st time	–	–	–	–	–	–	–	–	68.5	53.4	2.23	0.20†
Used drugs prior to imprisonment	*77.8*	*35.9*	*34.35*	*0.60****	*72.7*	*38.5*	*14.8*	*0.40****	*62.1*	*39.6*	*5.67*	*0.24**
Spent time in psychiatric hospital	*31.5*	*17.8*	*5.64*	*0.20**	*36.4*	*18.1*	*6.57*	*0.25**	–	–	–	–
Self-harmed prior to imprisonment	*20.9*	*7.9*	*7.71*	*0.30***	*25.0*	*8.3*	*7.43*	*0.34***	–	–	–	–
Self-harmed in prison	*19.0*	*8.4*	*4.90*	*0.25****	*28.0*	*8.3*	*10.51*	*0.37***	–	–	–	–
Subjected to disciplinary proceedings	*46.3*	*23.6*	*12.51*	*0.16****	*54.5*	*24.1*	*14.51*	*0.34****	–	–	–	–
Spent time in solitary confinement	–	–	–	–	*39.4*	*19.9*	*6.94*	*0.25***	–	–	–	–
Spends > 6 hrs a day locked up	–	–	–	–	*63.6*	*42.5*	*5.51*	*0.23**	–	–	–	–
Attended special prison programmes	*40.7*	*25.8*	*5.34*	*0.20†*	–	–	–	–	*51.7*	*26.0*	*9.00*	*0.30**
Incarcerated for rape	*7.4*	*2.8*	*3.07*	*0.33†*	–	–	–	–	–	–	–	–
Incarcerated for fraud	*5.6*	*17.1*	*4.80*	*0.33**	–	–	–	–	–	–	–	–
Incarcerated for kidnapping	*3.7*	*0.0*	*14.55*	*0.71****	–	–	–	–	–	–	–	–
Incarcerated for possession of drugs	–	–	–	–	*15.2*	*7.0*	*2.85*	*0.23†*	–	–	–	–
Incarcerated for drug dealing	–	–	–	–	–	–	–	–	*13.8*	*5.3*	*3.56*	*0.30†*
Incarcerated for burglary	–	–	–	–	–	–	–	–	*31.0*	*14.7*	*5.48*	*0.26**
Incarcerated for workplace coercion/corruption	–	–	–	–	–	–	–	–	*3.4*	*0.0*	*14.34*	*0.72****

Notes: Notes: VB = verbal bullies, INTB = intimidating bullies; IB = indirect bullies, OP = other prisoners; [A] = prisoners who bullied directly were excluded from the analyses comparing indirect bullies to other prisoners; in columns VB, INTB, IB and OP, means are given for continuous variables and percentages are given for the dichotomous variables (in italics); t/χ^2 = t test values for continuous explanatory variables, χ^2values for dichotomous explanatory variables; r = effect size (Pearson's r); in cases where no prisoners reported a certain dichotomous event/behaviour, the Haldane-Anscombe correction was performed to calculate the odds ratio; for all dichotomous variables, odds ratios were calculated first and then transformed into the Pearson's r; † = $p < 0.10$; * = $p < 0.05$; ** = $p < 0.01$; *** = $p < 0.001$.

Table 17.4 shows that females who verbally bullied had significantly higher cognitive empathy than other female prisoners, but empathy was unrelated to female indirect bullying. Due to a small sample of female verbal bullies, no logistic regression was conducted for female verbal bullies.

Does empathy independently predict overall and type-specific bullying by males?

To examine whether empathy independently predicted male physical and coercive bullying, two separate logistic regression analyses were conducted. All prisoner demographic characteristics and behaviours that had occurred *prior to imprisonment* which significantly distinguished between male physical and coercive bullies and non-bullies were entered into Block 1. Prisoners' behaviours and measures *during their imprisonment* that were related to male physical or coercive bullying were entered into Block 2, while empathy was entered in Block 3. For details on which variables were entered as predictors in each regression, see Table 17.2.

The results of the logistic regressions demonstrated that, when other prisoner characteristics were controlled for, empathy did not independently predict either male physical or coercive bullying (not shown in tables). However physical bullying by males was predicted by young age (B = – 0.08, SE = 0.035; p = 0.021) and serving a longer sentence (B = 0.01; SE = 0.003; p = 0.037). Male coercive bullying was predicted by younger age (B = – 0.11; SE = 0.040; p = 0.007), serving a longer sentence (B = 0.001; SE = 0.003; p = 0.047) and having spent time in solitary confinement (B = −1.31; SE = 0.582; p = 0.024; POR = 3.72).[5]

Additional exploratory analyses

Additional exploratory analyses were performed to examine whether empathy was related to some other prisoners' characteristics and types of their behaviour within and outside of the prison. For males, affective empathy was positively related to prisoner's current age (r = .15, p = 0.004) and their age at the time of their first imprisonment (r = 0.17; p = 0.001).[6] Affective empathy was also negatively related to the length of their sentences (r = – 0.13; p = 0.032), the likelihood of having spent time in psychiatric hospital prior to imprisonment (r = – 0.11; p = 0.034), the likelihood of having been incarcerated for murder (r = – 0.11; p = 0.036), and the likelihood of substance abuse prior to their imprisonment (r = – 0.11; p = 0.033). Surprisingly, affective empathy was also positively related to the likelihood of having been incarcerated for rape (r = 0.12, p = 0.016).

In the female sample, both affective and cognitive empathy were positively related to the likelihood of having been subjected to disciplinary proceedings during imprisonment (r = 0.39; p = 0.010; and r = 0.31; p = 0.041, respectively). Amongst females, affective empathy was also negatively related to the likelihood of having been incarcerated for theft (r = 0.20, n.s.) and grievous bodily harm (r = – 0.21; n.s.). In the female sample, cognitive empathy was also positively related to self-harming behaviours prior to incarceration (r = 0.25; p = 0.099) and suicide attempts prior to incarceration (r = 0.21; n.s.).

Table 17.4 The relationship between prisoner demographic and personal characteristics and the prevalence of female verbal and indirect bullying

	Female verbal bullying				*Female indirect bullying*[A]			
	VB	*OP*	*t/χ²*	r	*IB*	*OP*	*t/χ²*	r
Age	38.17	49.93	–2.56	0.20*	42.50	49.65	–1.70	0.24†
Age at 1st imprisonment	27.75	41.39	–1.95	0.15†	–	–	–	–
Cognitive empathy	39.83	35.60	1.86	0.27†				
Used drugs prior to imprisonment	–	–	–	–	*25.0*	*10.0*	*1.37*	*0.30**
Spent time in psychiatric hospital	*50.0*	*7.3*	*8.61*	*0.60**	*0.0*	*15.4*	*1.69*	*0.32*
Self-harmed prior to imprisonment	–	–	–	–	–	–	–	–
Self-harmed in prison	*16.7*	*0.0*	*8.98*	*0.65***	–	–	–	–
Subjected to disciplinary proceedings	*33.3*	*14.6*	*1.30*	*0.30*	–	–	–	–
Spent time in solitary confinement	*16.7*	*9.8*	*0.26*	*0.22*	–	–	–	–
Spends > 6 hrs. a day locked up	*20.0*	*66.7*	*5.90*	*0.50*	*31.6*	*0.0*	*3.42*	*0.50†*
Incarcerated for fraud	*16.7*	*38.1*	*1.05*	*0.30*	–	–	–	–
Incarcerated for destroying of public devices	*16.7*	*0.0*	*7.15*	*0.65***	–	–	–	–
Incarcerated for possession of drugs	*33.3*	*0.0*	*14.61*	*0.73****	–	–	–	–
Incarcerated for drug dealing	*33.3*	*7.1*	*3.86*	*0.46**	–	–	–	–
Incarcerated for burglary	–	–	–	–	*12.5*	*2.5*	*1.67*	*0.43**
Incarcerated for theft	*0.0*	*16.7*	*1.17*	*0.27*	*0.0*	*17.5*	*1.64*	*0.34*
Incarcerated for murder	–	–	–	–	*0.0*	*10.0*	*0.87*	*0.20*
Incarcerated for violation of court order re best interest of the child	–	–	–	–	*12.5*	*0.0*	*5.12*	*0.43**
Incarcerated for procuring/pandering	–	–	–	–	*12.5*	*0.0*	*5.12*	*0.43**

Notes: VB = verbal bullies, IB = indirect bullies, OP = other prisoners; [A] = prisoners who bullied directly were excluded from the analyses comparing indirect bullies to other prisoners; in columns VB, INTB, IB and OP, means are given for continuous variables and percentages are given for the dichotomous variables (in italics); t/χ^2 = t test values for continuous explanatory variables, χ^2values for dichotomous explanatory variables; r = effect size (Pearson's r); in cases where no prisoners reported a certain dichotomous event/behaviour, the Haldane-Anscombe correction was performed to calculate the odds ratio; for all dichotomous variables, odds ratios were calculated first and then transformed into the Pearson's r; † = $p < 0.10$; * = $p < 0.05$; ** = $p < 0.01$; *** = $p < 0.001$.

Discussion

This research found somewhat mixed evidence for the suggestion that individuals in prison who bully have low empathy. On the one hand male prisoners who bullied physically and coercively had low affective empathy which is in line with previous research suggesting that affective empathy is inversely related to more overt types of aggressive behaviour such as violent offending (Jolliffe & Farrington, 2004, 2007) and violent school bullying (Jolliffe & Farrington, 2011). However, there was no evidence to suggest that male bullies (regardless of the type of bullying) had low cognitive empathy. This suggests that males who bully physically and coercively may have a reduced ability to experience the emotions of others, but they have no such detriment in their ability to understand emotions. These bullies understand the pain that they cause, but they themselves do not experience these aversive emotions.

Interestingly, males who bullied indirectly, using intimidation and verbally did not show low affective or cognitive empathy, and females who bullied verbally showed significantly higher levels of cognitive empathy. This may suggest that cognitive empathy may help female bullies devise particularly effective methods of bullying and target victims "where it hurts the most". Additional data found that female victims reported that this verbal bullying typically consisted of hurtful comments about one's children or family. This would be particularly painful for female prisoners, especially in a more traditional and family-oriented country such as Croatia.

The somewhat inconsistent findings with regard to low empathy and bullying, together with the fact that low empathy did not independently predict bullying in any of the regression models for males, suggests that empathy may not be causally related to bullying in prisons. This means that interventions designed to increase empathy with the aim of reducing bullying in prison may not be effective, particularly if these interventions focus on increasing the understanding of the emotions of others (i.e. cognitive empathy). In fact, increasing the cognitive empathy of male, but especially female bullies, may have the unintended consequences of increasing the severity of bullying.

The results of logistic regressions indicated that male physical and coercive bullying were independently predicted by being younger and serving a longer sentence and that male coercive bullying was also predicted by disciplinary infractions during imprisonment. This suggests, perhaps not surprisingly, that some of the best predictors of male bullying are those which reflect continuity of overt aggressive behaviour and youth, a well-established correlate of antisocial behaviour (Moffitt, Caspi, Rutter, & Silva, 2001). Very interestingly, further exploratory analyses suggested that many of these factors, such as younger age, serving longer sentences, being incarcerated for the first time at a younger age, an index offence of murder, having spent time in a psychiatric hospital and having abused drugs prior to imprisonment, were significantly associated with lower affective empathy. This explains why affective empathy was not independently related to male bullying, and may further suggest that low affective empathy might be more relevant in explaining antisocial behaviour pre-incarceration rather than within a prison. That is, prisoners' behaviour within the prison setting, especially their bullying behaviour, might be more determined by contextual factors. The special nature of the closed physical and social prison environment, marked by many deprivations and authoritarian relationships between staff and prisoners, likely creates a social system in which the survival of the fittest is a priority and in which bullying is consequently just a normalised survival tool (Bottoms, 1999; Ireland, 2002b; Ireland & Murray, 2005).

Not all of the findings with regard to empathy and behaviour in this study were in the expected direction. For example, females with high cognitive empathy were more likely to have engaged in self-harming behaviour and suicide attempts prior to their imprisonment, while males with high affective empathy were more likely to have been imprisoned for rape. Inconsistent findings have been noted previously when examining the empathy of sex offenders (e.g. Fernandez & Marshall, 2003), but future research should attempt to replicate these findings to determine whether elevations in empathy may be associated with harmful behaviours directed towards oneself and/or others.

There are some methodological limitations that need to be considered when interpreting the results of this study. First, the cross-sectional nature of the study does not allow for the causal order of the observed relationships to be established. For instance, it is impossible to determine whether low affective empathy found in male physical and coercive bullies in zero-order correlations causes their bullying behaviour, or whether their affective empathy is decreased after bullying (Jolliffe & Farrington, 2011). Also, regardless of the fact that the present study was anonymous, its self-reported nature might have caused bias not only in reporting incidents of bullying, but also in prisoners' representation of their empathy.

To overcome these issues a prospective longitudinal study, which would include more individual and contextual explanatory variables and more informants, should be considered. This would allow for the measurement of empathy, and other potentially important variables, before any bullying had taken place, so that causal ordering could be established and the relative importance of these factors could be more clearly established.

Conclusions

This study contributes to prison bullying research, as this is the first study that has examined the relationship between empathy and prison bullying after controlling for other prisoner characteristics and factors which may be related to prison bullying. The key finding, that empathy might better explain pre-incarceration antisocial behaviour than behaviours within the prison walls, has important consequences for interventions designed to reduce prison bullying. Further evidence and replication of this important finding is needed. In addition, the direction and magnitude of the relationship between empathy and certain types of bullying differed between males and females, which also has potentially important practical implications.

Notes

1 'Perspective taking' and 'empathetic concern' are similar to, although not the same as, cognitive and affective empathy respectively of the Basic Empathy Scale (Jolliffe & Farrington, 2006a).
2 No directional hypotheses were set because of the lack of research on the relationship between empathy and bullying in a prison setting.
3 Previous research that was based on the original DIPC-R (©Ireland, 2002a) has used a different classification of the DIPC-R items. For instance, Ireland and Power (2013) distinguished between physical, psychological/verbal, theft-related, and sex-related direct bullying and indirect bullying.
4 Bullies and non-bullies were compared on 43 variables both for overall and type-specific bullying. The number of significant results, however, was in no instance the result of chance alone. For instance, of 43 tests comparing all male physical bullies to other prisoners, 11 were significant, and 1 had an effect size of 0.42 at $p = .10$, which greatly exceeds the number of significant results that would be expected by chance.
5 Since Exp (B) represents a partial odds ratio, which is not a meaningful measure of an effect size for continuous predictors, it is not reported here. Instead, the exact value of statistical significance (p) is shown. For dichotomous predictors, Exp (B) values are reported and referred to as a partial odds ratio (POR).
6 For males, only the results regarding affective empathy are reported here because cognitive empathy was mainly unrelated to other prisoners' characteristics and types of their behaviour. Consequently, the results regarding the relationship between overall empathy and other measures in the male sample were driven by affective empathy.

References

Bottoms, A. E. (1999). Interpersonal violence and social order in prisons. In M. Tonry & J. Petersilia (Eds.), *Crime and justice: A review of research* (Vol. 26, pp. 205–281). Chicago, IL: University of Chicago Press.

Carrasco, M., Barker, E. D., Tremblay, R. E., & Vitaro, F. (2006). Eysenck's personality dimensions as predictors of male adolescent trajectories of physical aggression, theft and vandalism. *Personality and Individual Differences*, *41*(7), 1309–1320. doi:10.1016/j.paid.2006.05.005

Cohen, D. (1982). *Empathy in conduct disordered youth* (Unpublished M. Phil. thesis). Department of Psychology, University of Ottawa, Ottawa.

Davis, M. H. (1980). A multidimensional approach to individual differences in empathy. *JSAS Catalog of Selected Documents in Psychology*, *10*.

Davis, M. H. (1983). Measuring individual differences in empathy: Evidence for a multidimensional approach. *Journal of Personality & Social Psychology*, *44*(1), 113–126. doi:10.1037/0022-3514.44.1.113

Ellis, P. L. (1982). Empathy: A factor in antisocial behavior. *Journal of Abnormal Child Psychology*, *10*(1), 123–134. doi:10.1007/BF00915957

Endresen, I. M., & Olweus, D. (2002). Self-reported empathy in Norwegian adolescents: Sex-differences, age trends, and relationship to bullying. In A. C. Bohart & D. J. Stipek (Eds.), *Constructive and destructive behavior: Implications for family, school, & society* (pp. 147–165). Washington, DC: American Psychological Association. doi:10.1037/10433-000

Farrington, D. P. (1993). Understanding and preventing bullying. In M. Tonry (Ed.), *Crime and justice* (Vol. 12, pp. 381–458). Chicago: University of Chicago Press.

Fernandez, Y. M., & Marshall, W. L. (2003). Victim empathy, social self-esteem, and psychopathy in rapists. *Sexual Abuse*, *15*(1), 11–26. doi:10.1177/107906320301500102

Ireland, J. L. (1999). Provictim attitudes and empathy in relation to bullying behaviour among prisoners. *Legal and Criminological Psychology*, *4*(1), 51–66. doi:10.1348/135532599167789

Ireland, J. L. (2002a). *Direct and indirect prisoner behaviour checklist-revised (DIPC-R)*. Preston: University of Central Lancashire.

Ireland, J. L. (2002b). *Bullying among prisoners: Evidence, research and intervention strategies*. Hove: Brunner-Routledge. doi:10.4324/9781315783239

Ireland, J. L., & Ireland, C. A. (2008). Intra-group aggression among prisoners: Bullying intensity and exploration of victim-perpetrator mutuality. *Aggressive Behavior*, *34*(1), 76–87. doi:10.1002/ab.20213

Ireland, J. L., & Murray, E. G. (2005). Social problem-solving and bullying: Are bullies really impaired problem-solvers? In J. L. Ireland (Ed.), *Bullying amongst prisoners: Innovations for theory and research* (pp. 150–176). Cullompton, Devon: Willan. doi:10.1111/j.1468-2311.2007.00467_3.x

Ireland, J. L., & Power, C. L. (2013). Propensity to support prison gangs: Its relationship to gang membership, victimisation, aggression and other disruptive behaviours. *Psychology, Crime & Law*, *19*(9), 801–816.

Jolliffe, D., & Farrington, D. P. (2004). Empathy and offending: A systematic review and meta-analysis. *Aggression and Violent Behavior*, *9*(5), 441–476. doi:10.1016/j.avb.2003.03.001

Jolliffe, D., & Farrington, D. P. (2006a). Examining the relationship between low empathy and bullying. *Aggressive Behavior*, *32*(6), 540–550. doi:10.1002/ab.20154

Jolliffe, D., & Farrington, D. P. (2006b). Development and validation of the basic empathy scale. *Journal of Adolescence*, *29*(4), 589–611. doi:10.1016/j.adolescence.2005.08.010

Jolliffe, D., & Farrington, D. P. (2007). Examining the relationship between low empathy and self-reported offending. *Legal and Criminological Psychology*, *12*(2), 265–286. doi:10.1348/135532506X147413

Jolliffe, D., & Farrington, D. P. (2011). Is low empathy related to bullying after controlling for individual and social background variables? *Journal of Adolescence*, *34*(1), 59–71. doi:10.1016/j.adolescence.2010.02.001

López-Pérez, B., Hanoch, Y., Holt, K., & Gummerum, M. (2017). Cognitive and affective empathy, personal belief in a just world, and bullying among offenders. *Journal of Interpersonal Violence*, *32*(17), 2591–2604. doi:10.1177/0886260515593300

Moffitt, T. E., Caspi, A., Rutter, M., & Silva, P. (2001). *Sex differences in antisocial behaviour: Conduct disorder, delinquency, and violence in the Dunedin longitudinal study*. Cambridge: Cambridge University Press.

Sekol, I., & Farrington, D. P. (2016). Personal characteristics of bullying victims in residential care for youth. *Journal of Aggression, Conflict and Peace Research*, *8*(2), 99–113. doi:10.1108/JACPR-11-2015-0198

Part IV

Conclusions

18 Empathy and offending, aggression, and bullying

Taking stock and moving forward

Darrick Jolliffe and David P. Farrington

Introduction

As stated in the opening chapter of this book, its main aim is to examine the relationship between empathy, as measured by the Basic Empathy Scale (BES; Jolliffe & Farrington, 2006a), and offending, aggression, and bullying in several different countries. This final chapter takes stock of research on the BES and examines some of the challenges associated with measuring empathy using questionnaires. It then briefly considers what approaches are needed to advance understanding of the relationship between empathy and antisocial behaviour. Finally, the implications of the collective knowledge about empathy and antisocial behaviour for interventions designed to prevent or reduce this behaviour will be examined.

Basto-Pereira and Farrington (2021) reviewed the remarkably widespread use of the BES in many different countries. Encouragingly, psychometric analyses mostly confirmed the affective and cognitive subscales, which were generally moderately correlated (.4 to .6). Furthermore, the internal consistency of these scales was usually quite high, and there was evidence of convergent validity between empathy and factors such as agreeableness and social skills. Generally, females had higher empathy than males, and cognitive empathy was more strongly related to offending than was affective empathy. However, there is a need for studies comparing BES scores with observational or behavioural measures of empathy.

The key findings of the 16 chapters have pushed forward the frontiers of knowledge. For example, there is evidence from an incredibly diverse range of samples that, generally, persons who scored lower on the BES were on average more likely to commit offending, aggression, and bullying. This was found when a parent version of the BES was compared to teacher-rated aggressive behaviour in 9-year-old schoolchildren (Sanchez-Perez & González-Salinas, 2021) when the BES was compared to official and self-reported offending in a community sample in the UK (Farrington & Jolliffe, 2021), when the BES was compared to the reoffending of an incarcerated offender population in Canada (Koegl, 2021) and when the BES was compared to self-reported bullying amongst female and male prisoners in Croatia (Sekol, Vidranski, & Jolliffe, 2021). From relatively "normal" aggressive behaviour amongst children to offending by incarcerated populations, low empathy was important.

The fact that those who act antisocially tend to have lower empathy may not appear to be a new finding, particularly as this is in line with the general theoretical expectation of the link between empathy and antisocial behaviour, but the new results add considerably to the evidence base. The BES is a relatively simple paper and pencil tool of 20 items (9 affective empathy, 11 cognitive empathy) that can be completed in a few minutes. Unlike much longer measures, measures that conflate empathy with sympathy, or instruments that are measuring behaviours supposedly indicative of empathy differences, the BES provides a cogent assessment of the extent to which a person shares or understands the emotions of others. This considerable cross-cultural consistency in results from incredibly diverse populations is very promising in suggesting that the relationship between empathy and antisocial behaviour is very important.

The chapters in this book yield many results that need to be incorporated in and explained by existing theories. For example, the fact that females generally have higher empathy than males is a highly replicable finding, but a key issue is why? Is it, perhaps, a consequence of gender differences in child-rearing, different social interactions, or differences in other individual factors such as impulsivity and psychopathic personality? What should we conclude about the relation between empathy and other demographic factors such as age and ethnic or national origin?

The chapters suggest that gender has some important moderating effects. For example, Farrington and Jolliffe (2021) found that the relation between low empathy and official and self-reported offending was more consistent for females than for males. Why? Sekol, Vidranski, and Jolliffe (2021) reported that low affective empathy was related to physical bullying for males, while high cognitive empathy was related to verbal bullying by females. Why? Sorrentino, Baldry, Jolliffe, and Farrington (2021) suggested that gender differences in cyberbullying might be explained by gender differences in empathy. The explanation of gender differences in antisocial behaviour is a very important topic. For example, previously Choy, Raine, Venables, and Farrington (2017) suggested that gender differences in criminal offending might be explained (at least to some extent) by gender differences in resting heart rate. More research on the explanation of gender differences in antisocial behaviour is clearly needed.

Assessing the BES

The evidence suggests that the BES is a useful instrument to measure empathy, but there were also indications that it may benefit from revision and additional research. For example, Basto-Pereira and Farrington (2021) indicated that more research is needed on the inter-rater reliability of the BES. Similarly, Zych, Farrington, Jolliffe, and Twardowska-Staszek (2021) noted that the negatively worded items resulted in a poor model fit in their large sample of Spanish and Polish primary and secondary school children, and therefore proposed a shortened 12-item version consisting of the positively worded items. Previous researchers have noted that alternative factor structures which separated affective empathy into two components of emotional contagion and emotional disengagement yielded a better fit to the data (Carre, Stefaniak, D'Ambrosio, Bensalah, & Besche-Richard, 2013; Herrera-López, Gómez-Ortiz, Ortega-Ruiz, Jolliffe, & Romera, 2017).

Future developments or revisions of the BES should ensure that the clear distinction between affective and cognitive empathy is maintained. This is because the difference between experiencing the emotions of others and understanding the emotions of others is theoretically significant for developing a deeper understanding of the relation between empathy and various forms of both prosocial and antisocial behaviour. For example, there is some suggestion in bullying research that those who are particularly effective at bullying may have low affective empathy but may have normal levels of cognitive empathy which they use to recruit co-bullies and bully effectively (Jolliffe & Farrington, 2006b). In addition, this separation is also supported by neurological evidence, as studies have found that distinctive neurological pathways and areas of the brain are activated when a person experiences affective empathy (anterior cingulated cortex) compared to cognitive empathy (medial pre-frontal lobe; Singer, 2006).

A benefit of traditional paper and pencil questionnaire measures of empathy such as the BES is that they can provide a reliable and valid picture of empathy quickly and inexpensively for large samples. Similarly, these measures can be completed anonymously or confidentially, which may reduce social desirability bias and impression management (i.e. the aim of conveying a favourable picture of oneself to others) compared to more clinical forms of assessing empathy (Sassenrath, 2019). In fact, it has been demonstrated that the empathy levels of assessors can have a discernible impact on forensic interviews (Vera et al., 2019). Paper and pencil tests can be placed on online survey platforms to reach more heterogeneous audiences and substantially increase samples sizes as well. Research has generally suggested that scores obtained via Internet administration are comparable to those obtained in more traditional paper and pencil formats, but it is also important to confirm the psychometric properties of any paper and pencil test placed on the internet (Meade, Michels, & Lautenschlager, 2007).

Questionnaires assessing concepts such as empathy also have some limitations that need to be borne in mind. For example, all paper and pencil measures benefit from the respondent possessing a degree of literacy, and this may be problematic particularly for more antisocial populations who may, on average, have lower literacy (e.g. Creese, 2016; Totten & Quigley, 2003).[1] While this problem might be overcome by having a researcher read the items aloud and ask for a response, this method has the potential to increase social desirability responding (Sassenrath, 2019). It is a challenge to determine to what extent the questionnaires are assessing the target person's actual empathy compared to the target person's desire to appear empathetic. This could reflect impression management (how participants wish to be viewed by others), but also how participants might be deceiving themselves. Self-deception is an unconscious bias referring to people's beliefs about their positive qualities, such as empathy (Uziel, 2010). Another potential limitation of questionnaires, particularly in the assessment of emotions (including affective empathy), is that an accurate assessment may be influenced by people's ability to identify and describe their own emotions. Ideally, self-reports about empathy need to be validated against ratings of empathy by others (e.g. peers, parents and teachers).

While these are clearly challenges in measuring empathy, the BES fares relatively well in mitigating these problems. For example, with regard to literacy, according to the Flesch-Kincaid reading index (Flesch, 1948), the BES has a US grade level of 4.2, suggesting that it can be understood by those with the reading level of a typical 9- to 10-year-old. The BES is also unique in that it was developed using a sample of 15-year-old adolescents from state schools, and not University students, whose mastery of language, and arguably their desire to answer in a socially desirable way, might be greater. In our own research (e.g. Jolliffe & Farrington, 2006a) and that of others (e.g. Carré et al., 2013), scores on the BES were not related to commonly used measures of social desirability responding in youth and adults. Limited evidence of impression management, however, does not necessarily mean that individuals are not deceiving themselves (self-deception) about their levels of empathy. That said, the strict definition of empathy used in developing the items for the BES (understanding the emotions of others and sharing the emotions of others) may limit self-deception as well, as these qualities are much less obviously desirable compared to items assessing sympathy (e.g. concern for unfortunate others), or the proposed behavioural outcomes of empathy (e.g. helping unfortunate others).

Finally, rather than mediating the relationship between empathy and behaviour, it appears that individual differences in the difficulty of identifying and/or describing one's own feelings (commonly referred to as alexithymia) mirror this relationship, with both high alexithymia and low empathy associated with undesirable social behaviour. That is, it appears that a distance from one's own affective states is also associated with a similar distance from other people's affective states (Grynberg, Luminet, Corneille, Grèzes, & Berthoz, 2010). When scores on the BES and on a measure of alexithymia were related to the personality characteristics referred to as the Dark Triad (Machiavellianism, Narcissism and Psychopathy) in a study of 322 males and females, a unique pattern of relationships was identified. For example, psychopathy was correlated with lower empathy, difficulty in describing feelings, and externally oriented thinking, while narcissism was associated with lower affective empathy and difficulty in identifying feelings (Jonason & Krause, 2013). Similarly, the relationship between low empathy, measured by the BES, and self-reported offending by males and females held when controlling for alexithymia in an unpublished doctoral thesis (Jolliffe, 2005).

This is certainly not to suggest that the BES is the last word in the measurement of empathy, but simply that the focus of the BES, on measuring empathy using a clear definition, appears to mitigate many of the concerns associated with previous (and subsequently) developed questionnaire measures of empathy. Nevertheless, the BES can and should be improved. Ideally, a consortium of researchers from different countries should collaborate to develop and pilot the

BES version 2, and then collaborate on a programme of research on empathy and antisocial behaviour.

Empathy and antisocial behaviour – taking stock

The knowledge summarised in this book has considerably added to the understanding of the relationships between low empathy and offending, aggression, and bullying. Much more research on the nature of these important relationships is needed, but it is very important that any new research is of sufficiently high methodological quality. Unfortunately, studies in this area have tended to replicate rather than innovate, and this has resulted in rather limited advances in knowledge in recent years.

For example, Jolliffe and Farrington (2004) conducted a systematic review and meta-analysis of 35 studies which compared measures of empathy of offenders to those of non-offenders. The key results of this study were that low empathy was related to offending (at least partly driven by a poor measure of cognitive empathy) but that, in studies where other factors were controlled (i.e. intelligence and socio-economic status), these empathy differences diminished or disappeared. Ten years later this research was replicated by van Langen, Wissink, van Vugt, van der Stouwe, and Stams (2014) with 38 primary research studies, and their key findings replicated those published 10 years earlier. That is, low empathy was related to offending, but this was largely driven by a poor measure of cognitive empathy, and in primary research studies which applied more controls the relationship between low empathy and offending was significantly diminished or disappeared completely. Also in 2014, Vachon, Lynam and Johnson published a systematic review of empathy and aggression including 106 effect sizes, which concluded that empathy and aggression (variously defined) were weakly related ($r = -11$; this corresponds to an 11% absolute difference between high and low empathy persons in the percent aggressive in a 2×2 table). They also noted the limitations of a particular measure of cognitive empathy. While there has been an increase in the number of studies included in these reviews, the conclusions are similar, and it is most disappointing that the methodological quality of the primary studies included in these reviews has not substantially increased.

In order to advance understanding in this area, researchers on empathy need to: (a) adopt a consistent definition of empathy; (b) conduct studies that allow for the temporal ordering of empathy and antisocial behaviour; (c) undertake studies which integrate empathy with existing knowledge about factors associated with antisocial behaviour; and (d) carry out studies examining whether low empathy is a cause of antisocial behaviour.

Consistent definition of empathy

Research on empathy cannot move forward without agreement about what empathy is. It is our belief that the definition put forward by Eisenberg and Strayer (1987) as "the understanding and sharing of another's emotional state" is that which is most true to the origins of empathy as a concept and Titchener's (1909) original coining of the term. The BES was developed on this basis (Jolliffe & Farrington, 2021a). Others have adopted definitions which overlap with sympathy, general perspective taking, or the capacity to feel shame or guilt (see Neumann, Chan, Boyle, Wang & Westbury, 2015, for a review of empathy measures), all of which may have very different relationships with antisocial behaviour. Definitions and instruments which include behaviour, such as helping unfortunate others, or acting in an antisocial manner (e.g. Vachon & Lynam, 2016), will be positively associated with antisocial behaviour (and negatively associated with prosocial behaviour), but this is because they are tautological, not because they are "better" measures of empathy. Empathy was originally conceived as an emotional matching of another's affective state and/or the understanding of another's emotional state (Titchener, 1909), but there are not many instruments that currently measure empathy in this way. It is important always to distinguish between affective and cognitive empathy and to compare results obtained with these different types of empathy.

Temporal ordering

Most research on empathy has been cross-sectional and correlational, although several chapters in this book move beyond this (e.g. Jolliffe & Compton-Dickinson, 2021; Jolliffe & Farrington, 2021b; Koegl, 2021; Sorrentino, Baldry, Jolliffe, & Farrington, 2021). Cross-sectional research cannot distinguish between low empathy causing later antisocial behaviour and antisocial behaviour causing later low empathy. Perhaps committing an antisocial act, and viewing the overt consequences for the victim as minimal, may erode a person's ability to understand or share other people's emotions. Similarly, but maybe more likely, the typical punitive response to antisocial behaviour, ranging from being punished by parents or teachers for minor antisocial behaviour to being incarcerated and labelled as an "offender", can ultimately reduce the capacity for empathy (e.g. Obsuth, Eisner, Malti, & Ribeaud, 2015). The critical point is that, while the theoretical relationship between low empathy and antisocial behaviour is strong, the empirical evidence for the directionality of this relationship is almost non-existent. This is an important and often overlooked gap in the area of empathy research, and one that may at least in part explain the limited efficacy of interventions designed to address antisocial behaviour by increasing empathy (e.g. Hanson & Morton-Bourgon, 2005).

Empathy and other factors associated with antisocial behaviour

Probably because of the strong theoretical relationship between low empathy and antisocial behaviour, studies have tended to be fairly narrow in their focus on empathy and antisocial behaviour. However, it is important to evaluate how empathy differences might be related to (or accounted for) by other explanatory factors for which much more methodologically sound evidence exists. For example, while suffering similar definitional issues to empathy, the broad concept of acting without considering the consequences of one's actions (or impulsivity), and its relationship to antisocial behaviour, has been investigated in a number of prospective longitudinal studies in many countries. Collectively these studies have demonstrated that higher levels of impulsivity in childhood predict many forms of later antisocial behaviour (Farrington, 2021b; Farrington & Welsh, 2007).

Furthermore, a systematic review of prospective longitudinal studies that measured impulsiveness early in life showed that this individual difference factor was significantly and strongly associated to official and self-reported violence over 11 years later (Jolliffe & Farrington, 2009). This provides evidence that impulsivity is an important risk factor for antisocial behaviour, but how impulsivity and empathy may relate to one another has rarely been studied (see McGee, Jolliffe, Eriksson, Bond, & Farrington, 2021, for an exception). Persons with high impulsivity may be more likely to act in an antisocial way regardless of their level of empathy, or alternatively high empathy may buffer the impact of high impulsivity. If the former was true, interventions which address impulsivity (and not empathy) may successfully reduce antisocial behaviour, and if the latter was true interventions which target empathy (and not impulsivity) may be successful.

It is important to investigate the relation between empathy and psychopathy. As Bergstrom, Jolliffe, and Farrington (2021) pointed out, affective empathy is one element of one of the four facets (the affective facet 2) of psychopathy in the PCL-SV. They found that all measures of psychopathy (total, factors and facets) were higher for males than for females. For males, only the affective facet 2 was related to low (affective and cognitive) empathy. However, for females, low affective and cognitive empathy were related not only to the effective facet 2, but also to the lifestyle facet 3 and the antisocial facet 4. More research is especially needed on the relation between empathy and psychopathy in childhood, and the possible role of empathy in the development of psychopathy. Unfortunately, most previous research on psychopathy has been based on adults (often convicted criminals) rather than children (but see Farrington, 2005). The chapter by Pechorro, Jolliffe, and Nunes (2021) is important in showing relations between empathy and callous-unemotional traits in young offenders.

There are many other established social, family and individual risk factors for antisocial behaviour and offending such as low socio-economic status, harsh parental discipline, poor parental supervision and low school attainment (see Farrington, 2021b). In addition, there is evidence that the core set of risk factors for offending is remarkably similar across different cultures (e.g. Farrington, 2015; Farrington & Loeber, 1999), and even across different generations (Farrington, Ttofi, Crago, & Coid, 2015). The relative contribution that empathy might make to explaining antisocial behaviour needs to be integrated with this established evidence so that programmes that are designed to prevent and reduce antisocial behaviour are targeting the correct risk factors.

Studying empathy as a cause of antisocial behaviour

Kraemer, Lowe and Kupfer (2005) provide a useful ordering of key concepts when considering the methodological quality of research (see also Kraemer et al., 1997). The definition of a correlate is a variable that has been shown to be associated with a given outcome. From the many chapters in this volume (e.g. Farrington & Jolliffe, 2021) and the bulk of other research on empathy, there is evidence that empathy is a reliable correlate of antisocial behaviour. The definition of a risk factor is a variable that has a clear temporal ordering with an outcome, or one that predicts a later outcome. Considerable research effort, using prospective longitudinal studies, has been invested in identifying the key risk factors for antisocial behaviour. This effort is based on the reasoning that, if these risk factors could be identified, then evidence-based interventions could be developed to target these risk factors and reduce subsequent antisocial behaviour (Farrington, 2021a; Farrington & Welsh, 2007). As previously mentioned, there is only somewhat limited evidence that empathy may be a risk factor for antisocial behaviour (e.g. Koegl, 2021; Şahin, 2012; Stavrinides, Georgiou, & Theofanous, 2010).

However, a risk factor is not necessarily a causal risk factor, which is defined is a risk factor that can change, and when changed, causes a change in the likelihood of the outcome (Kraemer, Lowe, & Kupfer, 2005). Establishing a risk factor can be based on a between-individual comparison, but establishing a causal risk factor should be based on within-individual change (Murray, Farrington, & Eisner, 2009). The major problem with studies of variations between individuals is that it is incredibly difficult to disentangle the effect of the risk factor of interest (e.g. low empathy) from the effects of numerous other risk factors that are correlated with low empathy and that might also influence antisocial behaviour. For example, compared with those who have high empathy, those with low empathy may be more impulsive, less intelligent (etc.) even before they developed low empathy.

There are a number of statistical approaches that could be used to try to draw causal conclusions from between-individual comparisons, such as regression techniques (e.g. Walsh, Krienert, & McAdams, 2021; Sekol, Vidranski, & Jolliffe, 2021) which examine the extent to which the relationship between low empathy and antisocial behaviour holds when controlling for other theoretically relevant variables. However, a more desirable way to examine the causes of antisocial behaviour is to compare within-individual changes in risk factors over time with later within-individual changes in antisocial behaviour over time. This is because, in studies of changes within individuals, all the pre-existing differences between individuals are held constant, making it much more possible to isolate the effect of a factor such as low empathy on antisocial behaviour as an individual's level of empathy changes. This approach was used by Jolliffe et al. (2019) to show that depression and anxiety were not causes of delinquency but were actually consequences of delinquency. Similar conclusions were drawn by Defoe, Farrington, and Loeber (2013). This means that interventions that are designed to address these mental health needs are unlikely to reduce later delinquency. Unfortunately, there is limited evidence regarding whether low empathy is a causal risk factor for offending, and as a result it is not clear that increasing empathy will be reliably associated with later reductions in antisocial behaviour.

As mentioned earlier, Koegl (2021) studied changes in empathy of offenders from admission to release, and showed that these predicted recidivism for sex offenders. More research relating within-individual changes in empathy to later within-individual changes in antisocial behaviour is greatly needed. This research should also seek to test hypotheses about why low empathy leads to antisocial behaviour, and to identify intervening processes.

Implications for interventions

Despite the limited evidence that empathy is a causal risk factor for offending, low empathy continues to be a key component of many intervention programmes, including those designed to reduce school bullying (Gaffney, Ttofi, & Farrington, 2019), criminal reoffending (Ross & Ross, 1995), and in particular, amongst those designed to reduce sexual reoffending (Hanson & Morton-Bourgon, 2005). The results of these interventions are, perhaps unsurprisingly, mixed.

In the future, a more thoughtful and robust approach to evaluating the impact of empathy enhancement interventions is needed. This includes ensuring that potential participants have low empathy (and have the capacity to benefit from empathy enhancement), that the measurement of other factors associated with antisocial behaviour are included so that the relative role of empathy in behaviour change can be established, and that these interventions should be evaluated using methodologically robust evaluation approaches to minimise potential threats to internal validity. Repeated assessments using the BES could be utilised to measure treatment progress, as Koegl (2021) did.

Interventions that are designed to improve empathy as a way of decreasing antisocial behaviour should proceed with extreme caution, and with an appreciation of the serious limitations of the research in this area. For example, all interventions designed to increase empathy should ensure that empathy is measured using an appropriate instrument before the intervention takes place. This would act as a baseline so that any changes in empathy can be monitored, and it should also be used to determine whether those who are given the intervention actually possess empathy deficits. Not everyone who acts antisocially may have low empathy.

Zhou, Gan, Hoo, Chong, and Chu (2018) examined the impact of a six to eight month, two-hour weekly violence prevention programme (VPP) administered to 156 mostly male young offenders in Singapore. The results suggested that the VPP was associated with desirable changes in self-reported measures of aggression, self-control and anger, but not in empathy, as measured by the BES. However, when empathy was examined in greater depth by performing a high/low median split based on empathy levels at the commencement of the intervention, they found that those who were originally low on both affective and cognitive empathy showed significant improvements in empathy over time, while those who were originally high on empathy showed no significant change.

These ceiling effects, and the fact that females are consistently found to have higher empathy than males (e.g. Pechorro et al., 2021), may call into question the likely efficacy of empathy enhancement programmes for females who act antisocially. It is also true that wholesale increases in empathy may not always be desirable. The study by Pechorro et al. (2021) found that elevated affective empathy was associated with increased social anxiety in incarcerated male juvenile offenders in Portugal, and Walsh et al. (2021) showed that those who reported being victims of bullying had high affective empathy. There are also certain categories of individuals (e.g. sex offenders, persistent bullies, those with high psychopathy) who may actually show increased antisocial behaviour as a result of empathy enhancement, particularly that which focuses on helping them to understand the emotions of others, which they could use for manipulative purposes (Jolliffe & Farrington, 2011).

In addition to the baseline (and ideally repeated) measurement of empathy, other variables that are known to be associated with antisocial behaviour should also be measured in future evaluations of empathy enhancement interventions. These might include other known risk factors such as low intelligence, high impulsivity, low socio-economic status (etc.), to help determine the relative role of empathy in explaining antisocial behaviour. For example, Sanchez-Perez and Salinas-Gonzales (2021) found that cognitive empathy might mediate the relationship between anger and aggression in young Spanish males, meaning that angry boys with low cognitive empathy were more likely to be aggressive. Similarly, in their study of 115 Dutch juvenile offenders who received a community-based intervention called Tools4U, van der Stouwe, Asscher, Hoeve, van der Laan, and Stams (2018) found that this intervention was only effective in reducing hostile intent attributions amongst juveniles who scored moderate to high on the affective scale of the BES, not among those who scored low. The identification of these sorts of important relationships suggests that the relevance of empathy in reducing antisocial behaviour may operate, at least in part, indirectly through other variables.

Finally, interventions that are designed to reduce antisocial behaviour by increasing empathy need to be evaluated using robust methodological approaches such as randomised controlled trials (RCTs) or quasi-experiments (Farrington, 2013). RCTs involve randomly allocating individuals or other units (e.g. classrooms in schools) to a treatment (in this case empathy enhancement) and others to no treatment or treatment as usual. With sufficient numbers in each group and a sufficient follow-up period, this approach provides the strongest evidence for the effectiveness of empathy interventions because it controls for the many threats to internal validity, or the confidence that one can have that any later observable differences in antisocial behaviour are the result of the empathy enhancement and are not attributable to extraneous factors such as pre-existing differences between the groups (i.e. the group that does better were better to begin with), or regression to the mean (i.e. the natural tendency for those high on a measure, such as antisocial behaviour, to reduce over time). Quasi-experiments use statistical approaches to approximate the control of an RCT, but in practice these may miss important factors that may not have been measured (Jolliffe & Hedderman, 2015).

There have been relatively few RCTs that have examined whether empathy enhancement might be effective, and these have generally not included persons likely to be low on empathy. For example, Sentas, Malouff, Harris, and Johnson (2018) undertook an RCT of 118 university students who either received a brief online empathy enhancement intervention or who were allocated to a waiting list. The results suggested that the experimental group had increased their level of empathy compared to those who did not receive the intervention, and these differences lasted up to two months later. Also, in a meta-analysis of 18 RCTs including a total of 1,018 participants, van Berkhout and Malouff (2015) found that empathy training programmes were moderately effective at increasing empathy, but only if the participants were undergraduates or health care professionals. In the three evaluations of antisocial persons that were included in this review (Dadds et al., 2012 – children with behavioural problems; Lomis & Baker, 1985 – forensic inpatients; Pecukonis, 1990 – aggressive teenage females), only Dadds et al. (2012) had a sufficient number of participants to be considered a viable RCT. In this evaluation, empathy enhancement with a behavioural skills training component was found to be only minimally effective in increasing the empathy of children with behavioural problems six months after the intervention. Collectively, these results suggest that considerable care needs to be taken in delivering interventions that are designed to increase empathy in order to reduce offending, aggression, and bullying.

Conclusions

As this book shows, knowledge about the relation between empathy and offending, aggression, and bullying has been greatly advanced in different countries by the use of the BES. However, there is a need for a consortium of researchers in different countries to collaborate to develop and test an improved BES version 2. Ideally, this consortium should then collaborate on longitudinal research on the BES-2, using a variety of different samples, to investigate within-individual changes in empathy that are followed by within-individual changes in offending, aggression, and bullying. Longitudinal studies are also need to assess the predictive validity of between-individual differences in BES-2 scores. Ideally, researchers should also collaborate in experimental research using the BES-2, to assess the effect of interventions on offending, aggression, and bullying. This three-pronged programme of research would lead to enormous advances in knowledge about the role of empathy in antisocial behaviour, and hopefully it would also lead to decreases in offending, aggression, and bullying. That would be in everyone's interests.

Note

1 This would also be the case for those asked to complete the questionnaire in a language with which they had limited familiarity.

References

Basto-Pereira, M., & Farrington, D. P. (2021). The basic empathy scale: Psychometric properties and contributions to the understanding of antisocial behaviour. In D. Jolliffe & D. P. Farrington (Eds.), *Empathy versus offending, aggression and bullying: Advancing knowledge using the Basic Empathy Scale*. Abingdon: Routledge.

Bergstrom, H., Jolliffe, D., & Farrington, D. P. (2021). Empathy and psychopathy: How are they related in men and women? In D. Jolliffe & D. P. Farrington (Eds.), *Empathy versus offending, aggression and bullying: Advancing knowledge using the basic empathy scale*. Abingdon: Routledge.

Carré, A., Stefaniak, N., D'Ambrosio, F., Bensalah, L., & Besche-Richard, C. (2013). The basic empathy scale in adults (BES-A): Factor structure of a revised form. *Psychological Assessment, 25*(3), 679–691. doi:10.1037/a0032297

Choy, O., Raine, A., Venables, P. H., & Farrington, D. P. (2017). Explaining the gender gap in crime: The role of heart rate. *Criminology, 55*, 465–487.

Creese, B. (2016). An assessment of the English and maths skills levels of prisoners in England. *London Review of Education, 14*, 13–32.

Dadds, M. R., Cauchi, A. J., Wimalaweera, S., Hawes, D. J., & Brennan, J. (2012). Outcomes, moderators, and mediators of empathic-emotion recognition training for complex conduct problems in childhood. *Psychiatry Research, 199*, 201–207. doi:10.1016/j.psychres.2012.04.033

Defoe, I. N., Farrington, D. P., & Loeber, R. (2013). Disentangling the relationship between delinquency and hyperactivity, low achievement, depression, and low socio-economic status: Analysis of repeated longitudinal data. *Journal of Criminal Justice, 41*, 100–107.

Eisenberg, N., & Strayer, J. (1987). Critical issues in the study of empathy. In N. Eisenberg & J. Strayer (Eds.), *Empathy and its development* (pp. 3–16). Cambridge: Cambridge University Press.

Farrington, D. P. (2005). The importance of child and adolescent psychopathy. *Journal of Abnormal Child Psychology, 33*, 489–497.

Farrington, D. P. (2013). Longitudinal and experimental research in criminology. In M. Tonry (Ed.), *Crime and justice in America 1975–2025* (pp. 453–527). Chicago: University of Chicago Press.

Farrington, D. P. (2015). Cross-national comparative research on criminal careers, risk factors, crime and punishment. *European Journal of Criminology, 12*, 386–399.

Farrington, D. P. (2021a). The developmental evidence base: Prevention. In D. A. Crighton & G. J. Towl (Eds.), *Forensic psychology* (3rd ed.). Chichester: Wiley, in press.

Farrington, D. P. (2021b). The developmental evidence base: Psychosocial research. In D. A. Crighton & G. J. Towl (Eds.), *Forensic psychology* (3rd ed.). Chichester: Wiley, in press.

Farrington, D. P., & Jolliffe, D. (2021). Empathy, convictions and self-reported offending of males and females in the Cambridge study in delinquent development. In D. Jolliffe & D. P. Farrington (Eds.), *Empathy versus offending, aggression and bullying: Advancing knowledge using the basic empathy scale*. Abingdon: Routledge.

Farrington, D. P., & Loeber, R. (1999). Transatlantic replicability of risk factors in the development of delinquency. In P. Cohen, C. Slomkowski, & L. N. Robins (Eds.), *Historical and geographical influences on psychopathology* (pp. 299–329). Mahwah, NJ: Lawrence Erlbaum.

Farrington, D. P., Ttofi, M. M., Crago, R. V., & Coid, J. W. (2015). Intergenerational similarities in risk factors for offending. *Journal of Developmental and Life-Course Criminology*, *1*, 48–62.

Farrington, D. P., & Welsh, B. C. (2007). *Saving children from a life of crime*. Oxford: Oxford University Press.

Flesch, R. (1948). A new readability yardstick. *Journal of Applied Psychology*, *32*, 221–233.

Gaffney, H., Ttofi, M. M., & Farrington, D. P. (2019). Evaluating the effectiveness of school-bullying prevention programs: An updated meta-analytical review. *Aggression and Violent Behavior*, *45*, 111–133.

Grynberg, D., Luminet, O., Corneille, O., Grèzes, J., & Berthoz, S. (2010). Alexithymia in the interpersonal domain: A general deficit of empathy? *Personality and Individual Differences*, *49*, 845–850.

Hanson, R. K., & Morton-Bourgon, K. E. (2005). The characteristics of persistent sexual offenders: A meta-analysis of recidivism studies. *Journal of Consulting and Clinical Psychology*, *73*, 1154–1163.

Herrera-López, M., Gómez-Ortiz, O., Ortega-Ruiz, R., Jolliffe, D., & Romera, E. M. (2017). Suitability of a three-dimensional model to measure empathy and its relationship with social and normative adjustment in Spanish adolescents: A cross-sectional study. *BMJ Open*, *7*(9), e015347. doi:10.1136/bmjopen-2016-015347

Jolliffe, D. (2005). *Inter and intrapersonal regard: Implications for violent offending* (Unpublished dissertation). Institute of Criminology, Cambridge University, Cambridge.

Jolliffe, D., & Compton-Dickinson, S. (2021). Enhancing empathy amongst mentally disordered offenders with music therapy. In D. Jolliffe & D. P. Farrington (Eds.), *Empathy versus offending, aggression and bullying: Advancing knowledge using the basic empathy scale*. Abingdon: Routledge.

Jolliffe, D., & Farrington, D. P. (2004). Empathy and offending: A systematic review and meta-analysis. *Aggression and Violent Behavior*, *9*, 441–476.

Jolliffe, D., & Farrington, D. P. (2006a). Development and validation of the basic empathy scale. *Journal of Adolescence*, *29*, 589–611.

Jolliffe, D., & Farrington, D. P. (2006b). Examining the relationship between low empathy and bullying. *Aggressive Behavior*, *32*, 540–550.

Jolliffe, D., & Farrington, D. P. (2009). A systematic review of the relationship between childhood impulsiveness and later violence. In M. McMurran & R. Howard (Eds.), *Personality, personality disorder and violence* (pp. 40–61). Chichester: Wiley.

Jolliffe, D., & Farrington, D. P. (2011). Is low empathy related to bullying after controlling for individual and social background variables? *Journal of Adolescence*, *34*, 59–71.

Jolliffe, D., & Farrington, D. P. (2021a). Empathy versus offending, aggression and bullying: Advancing knowledge using the basic empathy scale. In D. Jolliffe & D. P. Farrington (Eds.), *Empathy versus offending, aggression and bullying: Advancing knowledge using the basic empathy scale*. Abingdon: Routledge.

Jolliffe, D., & Farrington, D. P. (2021b). Empathy and reoffending of males on probation. In D. Jolliffe & D. P. Farrington (Eds.), *Empathy versus offending, aggression and bullying: Advancing knowledge using the basic empathy scale*. Abingdon: Routledge.

Jolliffe, D., Farrington, D. P., Brunton-Smith, I., Loeber, R., Ahonen, L., & Palacios, A. P. (2019). Depression, anxiety and delinquency: Results from the Pittsburgh youth study. *Journal of Criminal Justice*, *62*, 42–49.

Jolliffe, D., & Hedderman, C. (2015). Investigating the impact of custody on reoffending using propensity score matching. *Crime and Delinquency*, *61*, 1051–1077.

Jonason, P. K., & Krause, L. (2013). The emotional deficits associated with the dark triad traits: Cognitive empathy, affective empathy, and alexithymia. *Journal of Personality and Individual Differences*, *55*, 532–537.

Koegl, C. J. (2021). The relationship between empathy, clinical problems and reoffending in a sample of Canadian male offenders. In D. Jolliffe & D. P. Farrington (Eds.), *Empathy versus offending, aggression and bullying: Advancing knowledge using the basic empathy scale*. Abingdon: Routledge.

Kraemer, H. C., Kazdin, A. E., Offord, D. R., Kessler, R. C., Jensen, P. S., & Kupfer, D. J. (1997). Coming to terms with the terms of risk. *Archives of General Psychiatry*, *54*, 337–343.

Kraemer, H. C., Lowe, K. K., & Kupfer, D. J. (2005). *To your health: How to understand what research tells us about risk*. New York: Oxford University Press.

Lomis, M. J., & Baker, L. L. (1985). Microtraining of forensic psychiatric patients for empathic counseling skills. *Journal of Counseling Psychology*, *32*, 84–93. doi:10.1037/0022-0167.32.1.84

McGee, T. R., Jolliffe, D., Eriksson, L., Bond, C. E. W., & Farrington, D. P. (2021). Low cognitive empathy and its relationship to relational, online and physical aggression in young adults in Australia. In D. Jolliffe & D. P. Farrington (Eds.), *Empathy versus offending, aggression and bullying: Advancing knowledge using the basic empathy scale*. Abingdon: Routledge.

Meade, A. W., Michels, L. C., & Lautenschlager, G. J. (2007). Are internet and paper-and-pencil personality tests truly comparable?: An experimental design measurement invariance study. *Organizational Research Methods*, *10*, 322–345.

Murray, J., Farrington, D. P., & Eisner, M. P. (2009). Drawing conclusions about causes from systematic reviews of risk factors: The Cambridge quality checklists. *Journal of Experimental Criminology*, *5*, 1–23.

Neumann, D. L., Chan, R. C. K., Boyle, G. J., Wang, Y., & Westbury, H. R. (2015). Measures of empathy: Self-report, behavioral, and neuroscientific approaches. In G. J. Boyle, D. H. Saklofske, & G. Matthews (Eds.), *Measures of personality and social psychological constructs* (pp. 257–289). London: Academic Press.

Obsuth, I., Eisner, M. P., Malti, T., & Ribeaud, D. (2015). The developmental relation between aggressive behaviour and prosocial behaviour: A 5-year longitudinal study. *BMC Psychology*, *3*, 16. Retrieved from https://link.springer.com/article/10.1186/s40359-015-0073-4

Pechorro, P., Jolliffe, D., & Nunes, C. (2021). Correlates of affective and cognitive empathy among incarcerated male and female youth offenders. In D. Jolliffe & D. P. Farrington (Eds.), *Empathy versus offending, aggression and bullying: Advancing knowledge using the basic empathy scale*. Abingdon: Routledge.

Pecukonis, E. V. (1990). A cognitive/affective empathy training program as a function of ego development in aggressive adolescent females. *Adolescence*, *25*, 59–76.

Ross, R., & Ross, R. (1995). *Thinking straight: The reasoning and rehabilitation program for delinquency prevention and offender rehabilitation*. Ottawa: Air Training and Publications.

Şahin, M. (2012). An investigation into the efficiency of an empathy training program on preventing bullying in primary schools. *Children and Youth Services Review*, *34*, 1325–1330.

Sanchez-Perez, N., & González-Salinas, C. (2021). Cognitive empathy as a moderator in the relation between negative emotionality traits and schoolchildren's aggressive behaviours. In D. Jolliffe & D. P. Farrington (Eds.), *Empathy versus offending, aggression and bullying: Advancing knowledge using the basic empathy scale*. Abingdon: Routledge.

Sassenrath, C. (2019). "Let me show you how nice I am": Impression management as bias in empathic responses. *Social Psychology and Personality Science, 11*, 752–760.

Sekol, I., Vidranski, T., & Jolliffe, D. (2021). The relationship between empathy and prison bullying in a sample of Croatian prisoners. In D. Jolliffe & D. P. Farrington (Eds.), *Empathy versus offending, aggression and bullying: Advancing knowledge using the basic empathy scale*. Abingdon: Routledge.

Sentas, E., Malouff, J. M., Harris, B., & Johnson, C. E. (2018). Effects of teaching empathy online: A randomized controlled trial. *Scholarship of Teaching and Learning in Psychology, 4*, 199–210. doi:10.1037/stl0000119

Singer, T. (2006). The neuronal basis and ontogeny of empathy and mind reading: Review of literature and implications for future research. *Neuroscience and Biobehavioral Review, 30*, 855–863.

Sorrentino, A., Baldry, A. C., Jolliffe, D., & Farrington, D. P. (2021). Risk factors for cyberbullying: The mediating role of empathy in adolescents in Italy in a one-year follow-up study. In D. Jolliffe & D. P. Farrington (Eds.), *Empathy versus offending, aggression and bullying: Advancing knowledge using the basic empathy scale*. Abingdon: Routledge.

Stavrinides, P., Georgiou, S., & Theofanous, V. (2010). Bullying and empathy: A short-term longitudinal investigation. *Educational Psychology, 30*, 793–802. doi:10.1080/01443410.2010.506004

Titchener, E. B. (1909). *Lectures of the experimental psychology of thought processes*. New York: Palgrave Macmillan.

Totten, M., & Quigley, P. (2003). *Bullying, school exclusion and literacy*. Report to the Canadian Public Health Association, Human Resource Development Canada, Hull, QC.

Uziel, L. (2010). Rethinking social desirability scales: From impression management to interpersonally oriented self-control. *Perspectives on Psychological Science, 5*, 243–262. doi:10.1177/1745691610369465

Vachon, D. D., & Lynam, D. R. (2016). Fixing the problem with empathy: Development and validation of the affective and cognitive measure of empathy. *Assessment, 23*, 135–149.

Vachon, D. D., Lynam, D. R., & Johnson, J. A. (2014). The (non)relation between empathy and aggression: Surprising results from a meta-analysis. *Psychological Bulletin, 140*, 751–773.

van Berkhout, E. T., & Malouff, J. M. (2015). The efficacy of empathy training: A meta-analysis of randomized controlled trials. *Journal of Counseling Psychology, 63*, 32–41. doi:10.1037/cou0000093

van der Stouwe, T., Asscher, J. J., Hoeve, M., van der Laan, P., & Stams, G. J. J. M. (2018). Social skills training (SST) effects on social information processing skills in justice-involved adolescents: Affective empathy as predictor or moderator. *Children and Youth Services Review, 90*, 1–7.

van Langen, M. A. M., Wissink, I. B., van Vugt, E. S., van der Stouwe, T., & Stams, G. J. J. M. (2014). The relation between empathy and offending: A meta-analysis. *Aggression and Violent Behavior, 19*, 179–189.

Vera, L. M., Boccaccini, M. T., Laxton, K., Bryson, C., Pennington, C., Ridge, B., & Murrie, D. C. (2019). How does evaluator empathy impact a forensic interview? *Law and Human Behavior, 43*, 56–68. doi:10.1037/lhb0000310

Walsh, J. A., Krienert, J. L., & McAdams, S. (2021). A retrospective examination of bullying victimization during high school: Exploring narcissism deficits and empathy.

In D. Jolliffe & D. P. Farrington (Eds.), *Empathy versus offending, aggression and bullying: Advancing knowledge using the basic empathy scale*. Abingdon: Routledge.

Zhou, Y. Q., Gan, D. Z. Q., Hoo, E. C. C., Chong, D., & Chu, C. M. (2018). Evaluating the violence prevention program: Group and individual changes in aggression, anger, self-control, and empathy. *Journal of Forensic Psychiatry and Psychology*, *29*, 265–287.

Zych, I., Farrington, D. P., Jolliffe, D., & Twardowska-Staszek, E. (2021). Empathy in Polish and Spanish children and adolescents: Validation of the basic empathy scale and its relation to bullying, cyberbullying and other antisocial behaviours. In D. Jolliffe & D. P. Farrington (Eds.), *Empathy versus offending, aggression and bullying: Advancing knowledge using the basic empathy scale*. Abingdon: Routledge.

Index

Note: Page numbers in *italics* indicate a figure and page numbers in **bold** indicate a table on the corresponding page.

For Product Safety Concerns and Information please contact our EU
representative GPSR@taylorandfrancis.com
Taylor & Francis Verlag GmbH, Kaufingerstraße 24, 80331 München, Germany

www.ingramcontent.com/pod-product-compliance
Ingram Content Group UK Ltd.
Pitfield, Milton Keynes, MK11 3LW, UK
UKHW022022180926
475701UK00005B/982
* 9 7 8 0 3 6 7 5 2 1 4 5 5 *